SPIRITUALLY ORIENTED PSYCHOTHERAPY

SPIRITUALLY ORIENTED PSYCHOTHERAPY

EDITED BY
LEN SPERRY AND EDWARD P. SHAFRANSKE

American Psychological Association • Washington, DC

Published by
American Psychological Association
750 First Street, NE
Washington, DC 20002
www.apa.org

To order
APA Order Department
P.O. Box 92984
Washington, DC 20090-2984
Tel: (800) 374-2721; Direct: (202) 336-5510
Fax: (202) 336-5502; TDD/TTY: (202) 336-6123
Online: www.apa.org/books/
E-mail: order@apa.org

In the U.K., Europe, Africa, and the Middle East, copies may be ordered from
American Psychological Association
3 Henrietta Street
Covent Garden, London
WC2E 8LU England

Typeset in Goudy by Stephen McDougal, Mechanicsville, MD

Printer: United Book Press, Inc., Baltimore, MD
Cover Designer: Mercury Publishing Services, Rockville, MD
Technical/Production Editors: Rosemary Moulton and Devon Bourexis

The opinions and statements published are the responsibility of the authors, and such opinions and statements do not necessarily represent the policies of the American Psychological Association.

Library of Congress Cataloging-in-Publication Data

Spritually oriented psychotherapy / Edited by Len Sperry and Edward P. Shafranske.
    p. cm.
  ISBN 1-59147-188-5 (alk. paper)
  1. Spirituality. 2. Psychotherapy—Religious aspects. I. Sperry, Len.
II. Shafranske, Edward P. III. Title.

RC489.S676S676 2004
616.89'14—dc22   2004017402

British Library Cataloguing-in-Publication Data
A CIP record is available from the British Library.

Printed in the United States of America
First Edition

CONTENTS

CONTRIBUTORS

David G. Benner, PhD, Distinguished Professor of Psychology and Spirituality, Psychological Studies Institute, Atlanta, GA

David E. Canter, MS, graduate student, Department of Psychology, Virginia Commonwealth University, Richmond

Lionel Corbett, MD, Professor of Depth Psychology, Pacifica Institute, Carpinteria, CA

David N. Elkins, PhD, Professor Emeritus of Psychology, Graduate School of Education and Psychology, Pepperdine University, Corona, CA

Elfie Hinterkopf, PhD, LPC, Coordinator, The Focusing Institute, Austin, TX

W. Brad Johnson, PhD, Associate Professor, Department of Leadership, Ethics, and Law, United States Naval Academy, Annapolis, MD

Francis Lu, MD, Professor of Clinical Psychiatry, University of California at San Francisco; Department of Psychiatry, San Francisco General Hospital, San Francisco

David Lukoff, PhD, Professor of Psychology, Director of the Humanistic and Transpersonal Psychology Program, Saybrook Graduate School, Petaluma, CA

Suzanne E. Mazzeo, PhD, Assistant Professor, Department of Psychology, Virginia Commonwealth University, Richmond

Lisa Miller, PhD, Assistant Professor of Psychology and Education, Teachers College, Columbia University, New York, NY

P. Scott Richards, PhD, Professor of Counseling Psychology, Brigham Young University, Provo, UT

Ana-María Rizzuto, MD, Training and Supervising Analyst, Psychoanalytic Institute of New England—East, Brookline, MA

Edward P. Shafranske, PhD, ABPP, Professor of Psychology, Graduate School of Education and Psychology, Pepperdine University, Irvine, CA

Len Sperry, MD, PhD, Professor and Director of Doctoral Program in Counseling, Florida Atlantic University, Boca Raton; Clinical Professor of Psychiatry and Behavioral Medicine, Medical College of Wisconsin, Milwaukee

Murray Stein, PhD, President of the International Association for Analytical Psychology; Training Analyst, C. G. Jung Institute of Chicago, Evanston, IL

Siang-Yang Tan, PhD, Professor of Psychology, Graduate School of Psychology, Fuller Theological Seminary, Pasadena, CA

Everett L. Worthington Jr., PhD, Professor and Chair, Department of Psychology, Virginia Commonwealth University, Richmond

ACKNOWLEDGMENTS

As editors, we know that this book could not have come to fruition without the cooperation and commitment of the contributing authors, and we want to acknowledge their stellar contribution. The task of inviting acknowledged experts to contribute to a text is a risky proposition since the more revered their reputation, the more invitations they receive to submit articles or book chapters, decreasing the likelihood that they will be available to accept your invitation. We were quite pleased that so many of the revered leaders in the field agreed that this project was important and agreed to participate. We were even more grateful that they were so gracious and willing to follow the common structure we proposed that allows for clear comparison and contrast of the ten major approaches. As one reviewer put it: getting contributors to agree to any such regimentation is akin to trying to herd cats. This disciplined effort on the part of the contributors represents their concern for the readers of this book. We very much appreciate how these authors have selflessly given of their time and expertise to this project and want to formally and publicly acknowledge their contribution.

As editors we are also mindful of those that have gone before us and pioneered the emerging field of spirituality and psychotherapy. We especially want to recognize Allen E. Bergin, E. Mark Stern, H. Newton Malony, Kenneth I. Pargament, William W. Meissner, Hendrika Vande Kemp, Roger Walsh, David Larson, Thomas Greening, William Hathaway, and Herzl Spiro. Furthermore, as editors, we wish to thank the external academic reviewers for their input and feedback on both the proposal and the completed text. Finally, as editors, we want to thank the staff at APA Books who shared our vision for this book and its potential contribution to the development of this specialty as well as to the psychotherapy profession itself. We want to recognize and thank Susan Reynolds, Gary VandenBos, Julia Frank-McNeil, Linda McCarter, and Rosemary Moulton.

SPIRITUALLY ORIENTED PSYCHOTHERAPY

INTRODUCTION

LEN SPERRY AND EDWARD P. SHAFRANSKE

Spirituality is undoubtedly one of the most misunderstood words in the English language. It conjures up images of the mystical, otherworldly, religious, or New Age, and it is associated with specific activities such as praying, meditating, attending church, and various other religious or spiritual practices. Actually, spirituality is far more basic than any of this. Distinct from religion, which is the search for significance through the sacred (Pargament, 1997), spirituality "has to do with however people think, feel, act, or interrelate in their efforts to find, conserve, and if necessary, transform the sacred in their lives" (Pargament, 1999, p. 12). Similarly, Rolheiser (1999) noted that this search reflects our deepest desire, a desire that every one of us experiences but cannot satisfy because it is always and continually stronger than any satisfaction. Ultimately, Rohlheiser contended, spirituality is what we do with that desire: "the disciplines and habits we choose to live by, will either lead to a greater integration or disintegration within our bodies, minds, and souls, and to a greater integration or disintegration in the way we are related to God, others, and the cosmic world" (Rolheiser, 1999, p. 11). Thus, spirituality is not something on the fringes of life, nor is it an option that only a few pursue or want to discuss in psychotherapy. Rather, everyone has a spirituality, and it is either life-giving or destructive, as reflected in our everyday thoughts, feelings, and actions.

3

Viewed from this perspective, spirituality and spiritual issues that clients bring to psychotherapy are not marginal to the therapeutic process nor primarily the domain of "spiritually sensitive" therapists. Rather, they are, or can be, basic therapeutic considerations and the domain of all therapists.

Not surprisingly, psychotherapists are increasingly being called on to deal with spiritual issues in psychotherapy—an unprecedented trend given psychology's seeming antagonism for the spiritual realm. Reflecting this trend has been the publication of countless books and special issues of professional journals addressing spirituality issues in psychotherapy. Although most therapists have extensive training and experience in specific therapeutic approaches (e.g., cognitive–behavioral, psychodynamic, humanistic, etc.), few have been trained to deal with spiritual issues as they arise within these specific approaches. To date, only a few books are available that emphasize a single approach to spiritually oriented psychotherapy, and there is no single text that systematically presents several approaches.

Furthermore, there are increasing indications that spiritually oriented psychotherapy is coming of age as a specialty area of psychotherapy. The marker of such a specialty area coming of age and being mainstreamed in undergraduate and graduate training programs is when survey courses on spirituality and psychology and spirituality in psychotherapy are required. Survey courses typically use texts that survey the field rather than a single approach. Although there are a few texts that emphasize a single approach to spiritually oriented psychotherapy, there is currently no single text that systematically presents several approaches, much less a book that provides a comparative analysis of these various approaches. For this specialty area to develop more fully, such textbooks will be essential. *Spiritually Oriented Psychotherapy* is the first such book that describes, illustrates, and compares 10 contemporary approaches that address the spiritual dimension in psychological treatment, including explicit spiritually oriented psychotherapy. It systematically provides the reader with an in-depth and comprehensive view of the theoretical and clinical basis for each approach and then illustrates the application of each approach with an extended case example. In addition, it provides a context for understanding and comparing these various approaches in terms of current and future issues as well as the legacies of the psychoanalytic and Jungian foundations of spiritually oriented psychotherapy.

This book will be of interest to two audiences. First, practicing therapists and clinicians with an interest or need to incorporate the spiritual dimension in their work, and, second, students at the advanced undergraduate and graduate level in survey courses in psychology and spirituality, the psychology of religious and spiritual experience, spirituality in psychotherapy, and so on. Clinicians will find theoretical and clinical information and case material that are useful and relevant to their professional lives, and perhaps even to their personal lives. Students should find that reader-friendly structure and style conducive to fostering their understanding of contemporary approaches to spiritually sensitive psychotherapy.

Our basic intention in compiling this book was to invite creators or prominent advocates of the best known and regarded spiritually oriented psychotherapeutic approaches to share both the theoretical model on which their approaches were based and compelling case material to illustrate these approaches. Our primary goal was to make this book as reader-friendly as an edited textbook can be. To this end, we charged contributors with presenting their approaches in an engaging style and follow a consistent framework to foster the reader's journey within and across chapters. To assist readers in comparing and analyzing the difference among these approaches, we believed that a separate chapter should provide a side-by-side, point-by-point comparisons of these major approaches. We also believed that it was important not only to situate the trend toward spiritually oriented psychotherapies in its historical context but also to provide the reader with some sense of the future context, that is, theoretical and clinical developments, opportunities, and challenges. The book consists of three parts that are briefly described here.

Part I, "Theoretical Foundations," introduces the reader to the basic issues involving the integration of spirituality in psychotherapeutic practice. The first chapter addresses the spiritual dimension and its implications for psychotherapy, and chapters 2 and 3 delineate the foundations of spiritually oriented psychotherapy as they evolved from psychoanalysis and Jungian-archetypal analysis.

Part II, "Contemporary Approaches," describes and illustrates 10 contemporary approaches to spiritually oriented psychotherapy: psychoanalytic, cognitive–behavioral, existential–humanistic, interpersonal, transpersonal, experiential focusing, forgiveness, theistic, soul care–spiritual direction, and integrative. The structure of each of the chapters in Part II follows a common outline. As noted earlier, a common outline structures the description and illustrative case material so that the reader can more easily follow and compare the various approaches. Each approach provides the following theoretical information: The historical and theoretical basis of the approach includes a description of both the historical circumstances and the professional(s) who created to the approach, as well as the main theoretical constructs that undergird it. The nature of the relationship between psychotherapy and spirituality is then explained and articulated with regard to its clinical implications. The therapist's skills and attributes necessary for effectively utilizing the approach are then discussed. Indicated are the professional requisites in terms of skills, training, and experience, as well as the personal attributes that a therapist should possess to utilize the approach effectively. Next, the strengths and limitations of the approach are briefly addressed, including theoretical and practical strengths and weaknesses and the appeal of the approach for certain groups of psychologists and therapists.

The indications and contraindications for the use of the approach are then addressed—specifically, which diagnostic conditions and spiritual and religious issues are most appropriate and effectively addressed by this approach, and which are less appropriate. Next, cultural and gender considerations that may affect the therapeutic process are briefly considered, particularly those that might influence therapeutic process and outcome. Finally, future developments and directions of the approach are briefly noted. These include theoretical and research developments, as well as cultural trends, that are anticipated to affect the approach in the near future. Some approaches have considerably more empirical support than others, and this is not surprising given that some approaches are relatively new. A revised edition could conceivably update both theoretical and empirical developments.

Each approach provides the following clinical information in terms of an extensive case example that illustrates its clinical application: The case begins with client demographics, history, and presenting concern. This section describes relevant client data (i.e., gender, age, religious history and upbringing, current affiliation, spiritual practices, level of devoutness and orthodoxy), relevant client history (i.e., family, social, physical health history), and presenting client problem(s) and concern(s). Next, the relationship of therapist and client is discussed. This includes the nature of the therapeutic relationship (i.e., the therapist and client as collaborators, the therapist as expert and the client as learner, the therapist as spiritual director and the client as directee, the therapist and client as fellow travelers on the spiritual journey). Because of its importance in the therapeutic process, *assessment* is then considered. The rationale for assessment are discussed (i.e., how it relates to the basic constructs of the approach, the assessment process and methods, and the type of personality and psychological, diagnostic, and religious and spiritual history and information collected). This may include a formal spiritual assessment with inquires about the client's spiritual beliefs and spiritual practices or disciplines. Next is the diagnostic and clinical case conceptualization section, which provides a summary of the diagnostic formulation, usually in terms of *DSM–IV* Axes I and II, as well as a clinical conceptualization or formulation that provides an explanation for how the presenting problem or concern relates, or may relate, to the client's religious background and spiritual factors in the client and his or her context. Then the treatment goals, process, and intervention strategies of the case are noted, indicating specific goals and objectives as well as psychological and spiritual interventions for attaining those goals. This is followed by a timeline of the course of treatment and frequency and duration of sessions. Here the typical duration of treatment for this approach and the expected frequency and duration of sessions are indicated. Next is a discussion of termination and relapse prevention, which describes indicators for termination and the process of terminating treatment. If relapse prevention is integral to a given approach, it is briefly described in this section. Finally, therapeutic outcomes: immediate and long term are discussed (i.e., the extent to which treatment goals were achieved in this particular case, as well as the client's overall level of spiritual and psychological functioning, at 6 and 12 months following termination).

The 10 approaches described in Part II are applicable to the majority of North American and European readers. We are not suggesting that these represent all possible spiritual approaches to psychotherapy, and we recognize that contributing authors have presented case examples that do not represent the full scale of diversity at this time. It would be our intent to include additional and more diverse approaches in a revised edition.

Part III, "Commentary and Critical Analysis," contains the final two chapters. The first is a comparative analysis that includes a detailed side-by-side comparison of the 10 approaches along with narrative commentary. The second addresses future directions in spiritually oriented psychotherapy and speculates on various theoretical and clinical developments as well as issues such as training, scope of practice, and related ethical and praxis issues.

REFERENCES

Pargament, K. (1997). *The psychology of religion and coping: Theory, research, practice.* New York: Guilford Press.

Pargament, K. (1999). The psychology of religion and spirituality? Yes and no. *International Journal for the Psychology of Religion, 9,* 3–16.

Rolheiser, R. (1999). *The holy longing: The search for a Christian spirituality.* New York: Doubleday.

I

THEORETICAL
FOUNDATIONS

1

ADDRESSING THE SPIRITUAL DIMENSION IN PSYCHOTHERAPY: INTRODUCTION AND OVERVIEW

EDWARD P. SHAFRANSKE AND LEN SPERRY

We are entering a renaissance in psychological healing as spirituality is being discovered anew and "the alienation that has existed between the mental health professions and religion for most of the 20th century is ending" (Richards & Bergin, 2000, p. 3; see also Richards & Bergin, 1997). A groundswell of interest in contemporary religious experience is becoming more apparent throughout the behavioral sciences as this factor, so often forgotten within the buzz of modernity, ignored by science, and marginalized in the cacophony of postmodernism, is turning out to be a robust clinical variable (George, Ellison, & Larson, 2002; Koenig, McCullough, & Larson, 2000; Larson & Larson, 2003; Larson, Swyers, & McCullough, 1997; Pargament, 2002a, 2002b; Powell, Shahabi, &Thoresen, 2003). Scholarship investigating the role of religiosity in physical and mental health and in the psychological of coping is advancing exponentially and has been addressed in every major medical, psychiatric, psychological, and behavioral medicine journal (Baumeister, 2002; Emmons, 1999; Miller & Thoresen, 2003a; Mills, 2002; Sperry, 2000). In sum, the empirical evidence suggests links between health and spiritual and religious factors, although the mechanisms by which such effects are produced are not fully understood and the evidence is sometimes exaggerated (cf. Miller & Thoresen, 2003b, p. 33). In addition to scientific inquiry, greater attention is being placed on the role of religious faith and spirituality in clinical practice, in part as an effort to humanize psychotherapy (Beck, 2003) and to bring a more comprehensive approach to intervention. Texts addressing spirituality in clinical practice now abound (Frame, 2003; G. Miller, 2003; W. Miller, 1999; Richards & Bergin, 1997, 2000, 2004; Shafranske, 1996; Sperry, 2001), whereas less than a decade ago there were but a handful (Lovinger, 1984, 1990; Stern, 1985). A further contribution to this upsurge in interest is found in the emergence of positive psychology. Positive psychology reflects a sea change in how we are beginning to approach psychological health—virtues and strengths are now being considered alongside vulnerability and psychopathology. The values that inform people's lives and the ultimate concerns in which they are invested (Emmons, 1999) are seen to be variables critical to psychological health and personal well-being. Taking seriously the contributions of religious involvement and spirituality to an individual's orienting system is in step with this paradigmatic shift. At the core of these developments is the recognition that there is "something more" to human experience than modifiable behaviors, intrapsychic conflicts, and serotonergic imbalances—we are more than the "thinking meat" of neuroscience—and with this claim we are on the threshold of the transcendent.

This position presents both an opportunity and a quandary for psychological science and the therapeutics of contemporary clinical practice. It affords the possibility of understanding more completely the broad spectrum of factors that animate and give purpose to individuals' lives. This widening of human science's aperture affords a glimpse at the spiritual and religious beliefs and experiences that have long been important to most people and that form the basis of their faith in the transcendent realities in which they experience their lives to be situated. Furthermore, it allows for a more holistic approach to psychological assessment and intervention in which the role of spirituality in psychological conflict or as a resource in psychological coping may be better understood and integrated in the therapeutic process. These developments pose challenges for psychology as a science and an applied discipline.

The quandary simply stated is this: In addressing the transcendent realities that animate spirituality, science is limited; it cannot take in all that exists. It hasn't the tools to grasp or a language to articulate what William James (1902/1982) named the "reality of the unseen" (p. 53), or in spiritual metaphor, "the cloud of unknowing." "Science itself," as Huston Smith (2001, p. 198) put it, "is meaningful throughout, but on existential and global meanings it is silent." Existential meanings are ones that personally enliven our daily existence, reflect our deepest desires, and make our lives purposeful and therefore significant. Global meanings concern the large questions, *What is the meaning of life? What is the meaning of it all?* and, more personally, *What does my life mean?* These questions present one of the elemental human problems—how to relate to the total scheme of things (Smith, 2001, p. 11). Science offers us understanding of our observable, physical world, but how do we grasp the meaning of our *being in existence?* These are essentially religious questions and ones that science, including psychological science, cannot answer. The point is that these are matters of personal faith, which involve "psychologies of commitment," rather than observable, testable realities to which science enjoys a method of inquiry. Science cannot ascertain the existence of God, for example, or verify other contents of spirituality; it can, however, examine the effects of religious beliefs and practices on health and well-being, that is, William James's (1902/1982) "fruits" of religion (see Pargament, 2002). Although in keeping with James's thesis, such an approach is inherently secular and cannot consider the real worth of spirituality, which can only be located within the religious sphere in which the commitment originated. Although science can offer no judgment or prediction regarding the veridical status or value of the destination or endpoint of spiritual striving, psychology can investigate the means by which people put into practice their religious commitments, and a spiritually oriented psychotherapy can assist in such pursuits through an understanding of spirituality.

We turn now to an examination of the nature of spirituality and its expression in contemporary culture and within the context of psychotherapy. We first consider the definitional issues faced in understanding contemporary experiences of spirituality and religiosity.

RELIGION AND SPIRITUALITY: DISTINCT, YET RELATED

Among the initial challenges faced in the development of spiritually oriented psychotherapy is defining what is meant by the term *spirituality*. For many, spirituality conveys the notion that observable, physical reality is not only located within a larger, transcendent reality but also is animated by transcendent, sacred realities. Throughout much of history, spirituality, connoting the "incorporeal" was used interchangeably with "religious"; however, it gradually came to be associated in the common vernacular "with the private realm of thought and experience while the word *religious* came to be connected with the public realm of membership in religious institutions, participation in formal rituals, and adherence to official denominational doctrines" (Fuller, 2001, p. 5). This development paralleled a centuries-long evolution in the meaning of the term religion, which resulted in a general trend toward reification: "religion became in time a fixed objective entity and each of the traditions a definable system" in contrast with its earlier more dynamic emphasis on "something that one has perceived, felt, or done oneself" (Wulff, 1997, p. 3). Increasingly, religion and spirituality, although related, appear to connote in the public's mind, institutional–public and individual–personal expressions of religious sentiments with transcendent realities. This dichotomy is in marked contrast with William James (1902/1982, p. 42), who defined religion, as "the feelings, acts, and experiences of individual men in their solitude, so far as they apprehend themselves to stand in relation to whatever they may consider the divine." Nuanced definitions of religion and spirituality abound, leading scholars struggling to clarify the "fuzziness" in the language (Zinnbauer et al., 1997). This state of definitional affairs led Bauman (1998) to conclude, " 'Religion' [and, we suggest, spirituality as well] belongs to the family of curious, and often embarrassing concepts, which one perfectly understands until one wants to define them. . . . More often then not, 'defining religion' amounts to replacing one ineffable with another—to the substitution of the incomprehensible for the unknown" (p. 55). Such may be the case in the recent introduction of *spirituality* as distinct from *religion* within popular culture. Rather than contribute another set of definitions, we present what empirical investigations suggest is meant by *spirituality* and *religion*.

Zinnbauer et al. (1997) and Scott (1997) conducted empirical studies in the attempt to cut through the semantic morass to obtain more precise understandings of the use of the terms religion and spirituality. Scott (1997) performed a content analysis of 31 definitions of religiousness and 40 definitions of spirituality and found that no single category accounted for the majority of the definitions, suggesting the lack of a comprehensive and accepted theory or theories of the constructs. Zinnbauer et al. (1997) performed a content analysis of definitions of religiousness and spirituality obtained from 305 individuals from a variety of professional and religious backgrounds. Consistent with Scott's findings, a sizable amount of variability exists in the ways in which people use these terms and, perhaps, also in the ways in which they experience religion and spirituality. Zinnbauer, Pargament, and Scott (1999) concluded that religion and spirituality have been polarized by contemporary theorists: "organized religion versus personal spirituality; substantive religion versus functional spirituality; and negative religiousness versus positive spirituality" (p. 889). Polling and interview data suggest an appreciation for the distinctiveness of the constructs as well as their interrelationship. Marler and Hadaway (2002) reported that 71% answered affirmatively to the question, "Do you think that there is any difference between being religious and being spiritual?" and, in a content analysis of interviews with marginal Protestants conducted in 1993 and 1994, found that 63% reflected that being religious or spiritual are different and interdependent concepts (p. 295). They concluded that most Americans see themselves as both (p. 297).

Pargament (1999) observed that religion is moving from a "broadband construct—one that includes both the institutional and the individual, and the good and the bad—to a narrowband institutional construct that restricts and inhibits human potential. Spirituality, on the other hand, is becoming differentiated from religion as an individual expression that speaks to the greatest of human capacities" (p. 3). Hill and Pargament (2003), consistent with Pargament (1999) and Hill et al. (2000), pointed to several dangers of this bifurcation of religion and spirituality:

> First, the polarization of religion and spirituality into institutional and individual domains ignores the fact that all forms of spiritual expression unfold in a social context and that virtually all organized faith traditions are interested in the ordering of personal affairs (Wutherow, 1998). Second, implicit in the evolving definitions is the sense that spirituality is good and religion is bad; this simplistic perspective overlooks the potentially helpful and harmful sides of both religion and spirituality (Pargament, 2002). Third, the empirical reality is that most people experience spirituality within an organized religion context and fail to see the distinction between these phenomena (Marler & Hadaway, 2002; Zinnbauer et al., 1997). Finally, the polarization of religion and spirituality may lead to needless duplication in concepts and measures. . . . Religion and spirituality appear to be related rather than independent constructs. (pp. 64–65)

The interrelationship can be found in Pargament's perspective that "religion is a search for significance in ways related to the sacred" (1997, p. 32), and spirituality is the search for the sacred that "has to do with however people think, feel, act, or interrelate in their efforts to find, conserve, and if necessary, transform the sacred in their lives" (1999, p. 12). For some scholars, these concepts are indistinguishable; for others, the nuance allows for the appreciation that for some it is possible to adopt the outward forms of religious worship and doctrine without having a strong relationship to the transcendent (John E. Fetzer Institute, 1999, p. 2) or the view of spirituality as more related to existentiality than to religion (Stifoss-Hanssen, 1999).

We find that these distinctions to be of particular value as they reflect the experiences of many clients. Often the spiritual quest, although often clothed in religion, is felt to be an utterly personal experience, not reliant on institutional affiliation and involvement. The use of religiousness and spirituality appears to go beyond semantic preference and represent a trend in the religious–spiritual landscape within the culture. Before the twentieth century, the terms were mostly interchangeable (Fuller, 2001, p. 5) and reflected the correspondence between personal religious sentiment and institutional participation (Roof, 1999). The emergence of *spirituality* as a distinctive term and the dichotomization of religiousness and spirituality point to a change in the fundamental approach many, if not most, people today take in answering existential questions of meaning and sacred purpose. Such a shift in the cultural foundation of religion is likely to reverberate throughout the four dimensions (cf. Thoresen, Harris, & Oman, 2001, p. 24) in which religiousness or spirituality is expressed: overt behaviors (practices viewed by the individual as related to the sacred); beliefs (attributions and perceptions about the sacred and one's relationship with it); motivations, values, and goals (daily strivings and purposeful living); and subjective experiences (the emotional and noetic meanings of experience).

SPIRITUALITY AND THE SELF: A CULTURAL PHENOMENON

Scholars have often observed religion to be a vital force in the lives of most Americans and have concluded the United States to be one of the most religious countries in the Western world (Fuller, 2001; Hoge, 1996; Roof, 1999). Polls indicate that 94% of Americans believe in God, 90% report praying to God on a fairly regular basis, and 9 of 10 report a religious affiliation (Roof, 1999, p. 3). Americans by and large believe in a *personal* God, who actively intervenes in the world, and almost one third report that they have had a profound spiritual experience, sudden or gradual, that has transformed their lives (Cimino & Lattin, 1998, p. 2). Of those who are religiously affiliated, 94.4% are Christians, and the remaining 5.5% are composed of Jews, Muslims, Buddhists, and persons of other religions; similar demographics are found among Canadians (Keller, 2000, p. 30). Underlying these statistics and yet obscured by the apparent similarities in beliefs is a cultural transformation, which is signaled in part by the emergence of "spirituality" in the common vernacular. A tectonic scale shift in the nature of religious life appears to be taking place in America.

The focus of spirituality may be changing from an emphasis on what is *beyond* us to what is *within* us (Gallup & Jones, 2000). Religious expression stressing the inner life of the self is emerging in which each person seeks his or her own way to significance and in relationship to the sacred. In a 1999 poll, a random sample of Americans were asked, "Do you think of spirituality more in a personal and individual sense or more in terms of organized religion and church doctrine?" Almost two thirds opted for the "personal and individual" response (Gallup, 2003b). Gallup and Johnson (2003) reported the findings of a 2002 survey using the recently developed Center for Research on Religion and Urban Civil Society/Gallup Spiritual Index, which assesses "inner" and "outer" commitments. Among the major findings were the following: most Americans yearn for spiritual growth and rely on their faith for meaning. Fifty percent of Americans described themselves as "religious," 33% said they are "spiritual and not religious," 4% described themselves as both, and 11% described themselves as neither; in a 2002 poll, 47% percent gave a "strongly agree" response to the statement, "I am a person who is spiritually committed." Sixty-nine percent of respondents said they completely or to a considerable extent feel the need to experience spiritual growth in their daily lives; 68% said that they are "spiritually committed," and 85% said that because of their faith, they have meaning and purpose in their lives. Forty-one percent of Americans, in a June 2002 survey (Gallup, 2003b), reported that the statement "I have had a profound religious experience or awakening that changed the direction of my life" completely applies to them. In sum, the opinions, captured through numerous polls, suggest that the spiritual dimension, although expressed in differing forms, is salient for most Americans (Gallup, 2003a). Increasingly the expression of religious sentiment appears to be more private, individualist, and experiential rather than public, communal, and institutional (Gallup, 2003b; Roof, 1999). Roof (1999) noted that, even among "loyalists," in a 7-year follow-up, only 46% remained active in any religious group, many switched from one group to another, and significant numbers had abandoned religious institutions altogether (p. 319).

Although the modern turn from a self situated meaningfully through its commitments to community to a protean self dislocated from its history and cultural moorings has been examined as a general phenomenon (Lifton, 1993; Reiff, 1966; Taylor, 1989), its impact is perhaps most felt in religious affiliation and involvement (Bellah, Madsen, Sullivan, Swidler, & Tipton, 1985; Roof, 1993, 1999). The increased emphasis on personal autonomy, the privileging of individual experience, the eroding of institutional authority, the exposure to a multitude of competing belief systems and diverse worldviews through patterns of immigration and the proliferation of mass media, all within the context of the postmodern critique shaking the foundations to establish any claims on truth, has led for many to a dissolution of cultural toeholds as sources of identity and value. Roof (1999) commented,

> Grand narratives as handed down through history with appeals to universal truth have lost force because of greater skepticism, relativism, and the shaping of more personal metaphysical constructions. . . . Uprooted in faiths and family traditions, many Americans are looking within themselves in hopes of finding a God not bound by the canons of literalism, moralism, and patriarchy, in hopes that their own biographies might yield personal insight about the sacred. (pp. 56–57)

Whether inside or outside of faith communities, for many people spirituality is anchored in a quest for a direct, unmediated experience of the transcendent realities in which they once more confidently believed. A shift has occurred "from a world in which beliefs held believers to one in which believers hold beliefs" (Harding, in press, cited in Roof, 1999, p. 42).

Wuthnow (1998) characterized this development as a change from "spirituality of dwelling" to "spirituality of seeking." The shift from dwelling to seeking involves a loss of a spiritual home, a *habitation* in a sacred space, which is known and trusted. "A spirituality of seeking emphasizes *negotiation*: individuals search for sacred moments that reinforce their conviction that the divine exists, but these moments are fleeting; rather than knowing

the territory, people explore new spiritual vistas, and they may have to negotiate among complex and confusing meanings of spirituality" (Wuthnow,
1998, pp. 3–4). A dialectic appears between being grounded in a place of
dwelling, such as in religious involvement, and fluidity obtained in seeking.
Such a protean character (Lifton, 1993) informs the contemporary search for
significance in ways related to the sacred. Efforts to fashion a meaningful
existence and to answer the big questions, for many may result in anomie
and existential confusion. Even for those dwelling within the sustaining structure of an organized faith tradition, doubt and disillusionment may emerge
when belief is challenged. For others, involvement in religion anchors their
ontological and historical–social identities and provides an unshakeable foundation on which to face life's inevitable challenges and disparities.

Within these postmodern times, people more than ever before are challenged to construct an individual mosaic of spirituality from "pieces" of belief, ritual, spiritual practices, and traditions obtained from a confluence of
private and public sources. The distinctions between religion and spirituality
appear to be relevant in light of data presented in this discussion and reflect
the shifting contexts in which people seek meaning and significance in ways
related to transcendent realities. For the majority of the population, religious
involvement provides a dwelling place within which faith enlivens life and
provides meaning and a foundation of purpose. For those who have experienced the collapse of a sacred canopy, however, a compulsion for a new kind
of faith may be awakened, a faith that requires inner knowledge and that
must be renewed and renegotiated with life experience (Wuthnow, 1998,
p. 169). A means or a process must be available to accomplish such an ontological undertaking. In our view, psychotherapy is often sought to address
not only psychological conflicts, narrowly defined, but also to deal with the
spiritual malaise that at times underlies symptoms of depression, anxiety, or
restless disquiet. We turn now to consideration of the clinical circumstances
in which spirituality may appear within clinical presentations.

SPIRITUALITY WITHIN PSYCHOTHERAPY

Religiosity or spirituality plays a role in the orienting systems of most
individuals and therefore requires deliberate and thoughtful assessment in
respect to its contributions to mental health and well-being. Even among
those who declare themselves to be religious or spiritual, a significant vari-
ance exists between those for whom spirituality is the centerpiece of their
lives and those for whom spirituality plays a minor role in their psychological
well-being. We assert that spirituality and religious background and involvement must be considered in each clinical case and that even in situations in
which religion appears to play a minor role, it contributes to the treatment
process and the course of therapy will influence its expression. We therefore

advocate for the practice of psychotherapy that is sensitive to spirituality. There are particular instances, however, in which spirituality is more likely to be relevant to the therapeutic process and that require not only sensitivity but the provision of *spiritually oriented psychotherapy*. We have identified three broadly defined clinical situations in which spirituality regularly appears in psychological and psychiatric consultation. These situations we refer to as (a) spirituality as a resource in psychotherapy, (b) conservation and transformation of spirituality in psychotherapy, and (c) the spiritual quest in psychotherapy. In each instance, spiritually attuned psychotherapists do not impose the incorporation of the spiritual dimension within treatment but rather recognize the potential contribution of spirituality within a holistic understanding of the patient's presenting concerns, symptoms, resources, and life narrative and history.

Spirituality as a Resource in Psychotherapy

Patients seek consultation in times of psychic pain, conflict, and suffering. A legion of conditions causes human suffering, including changes in health status, injury, personal and professional losses, conflicts in interpersonal and intimate relationships, and so on. Such situations test an individual's ability to sustain hope in the face of hardship and challenge the ability to cope and to respond adaptively. It is in such situations of maximum strain and tension that the greatest relevance of religion may be found (cf. Parsons, as cited in Fichter, 1981, p. 21), and we suggest in psychological treatment as well. Spirituality may be identified and summoned as a resource to complement psychological interventions to enhance coping and alleviate address human suffering. Pargament's body of theoretical and empirical scholarship (1996, 1997, 2002) has led the way in demonstrating the importance of religion and spirituality as a clinical variable (see also Baumeister, 2002; Koenig et al., 2001; Plante & Sherman, 2001). Religion and coping converge because religion is a *relatively available* part of an individual's orienting system and because it is a *relatively compelling* way of coping. The religious or spiritual dimension within an orienting system not only provides answers to life's explicitly religious question but also, more fundamentally, shapes perceptions, attributions, and affects in the construction of subjective experience, including experiences of human suffering (cf. Shafranske, 2001, p. 313). Pargament (2002), in a recent review of literature intended to evaluate the costs and benefits of religiousness, concluded:

> The empirical literature points to five conclusions. First, some forms of religion are more helpful than others. Well-being has been linked positively to a religion that is internalized, intrinsically motivated, and based on a secure relationship with God and negatively to a religion that is imposed, unexamined, and reflective of a tenuous relationship with God

and the world. Second, there are advantages and disadvantages to even controversial forms of religion, such as fundamentalism. Third, religion is particularly helpful to socially marginalized groups and to those who embed religion more fully in their lives. Fourth, *religious beliefs and practices appear to be especially valuable in stressful situations that push people to the limits of their resources. Finally, the efficacy of religion is tied to the degree to which it is well integrated into an individual's life.* (p. 168, emphasis added)

Spiritually orientated psychotherapists are particularly mindful of the potential of religious involvement or spirituality to have an impact on the course of treatment and the alleviation of a person's suffering. In light of the research findings, efforts may be taken to enhance the integration of healthy forms of religiousness and to bring spiritual resources into the therapeutic process. In contrast with the other general clinical situation, which we discuss later in the chapter, integrating spirituality as a resource occurs in a setting in which spirituality is not the primary focus of attention nor constitutes an area of conflict. Spirituality or religiousness has been identified to be a naturally occurring resource in the patient's orienting system. The task of the therapist is to identify and to integrate the beliefs, values, and practices involved in the patient's spirituality to enhance coping. In this clinical circumstance, spirituality is not the focus of the therapeutic discourse but is a factor in the background, one which may usefully be brought to the foreground to assist in treatment.

There are circumstances in which such an approach is contraindicated, such as when an individual's spiritual orientation is a source of negative coping and psychological distress. Attention must be paid to "red flags" that point to negative religious coping (e.g., beliefs such as "God has abandoned me") as well as to disappointment, anger and distrust of God, interpersonal strains associated with affiliation within a faith community, or problems faced in attempting to exercise the values or moral standards of religious faith (Exline, 2002; Pargament, 1997, 2002b; Pargament et al., 1998; Pargament, Smith, Koenig, & Perez, 1998). Careful clinical and ethical judgment is required when considering whether interventions should be directed at modifying religious or spiritual belief systems that appear to be leading to negative coping because such efforts pose a risk of creating iatrogenic effects and may exacerbate the patient's distress or dysphoria (Shafranske, in press; Shafranske & Falender, 2004).

Conservation and Transformation of Spirituality in Psychotherapy

Challenges to physical health or psychological well-being may also provoke crises in which spirituality must be conserved, transformed, or lost (Pargament, 1997). In these instances, the psychological symptoms of anxiety, depression, hopelessness, and despair cannot be separated from the existential and spiritual conflicts that have been activated by the present life circumstance. For example, the death of a child, a significant betrayal and violation of trust, loss of employment, or a disabling illness may bring symptoms that to a great extent emanate from the loss of coherence of meaning. The disruption of one's worldview on which significance had been established may impair the ability to use spiritual means to create significance and meaning and further exacerbate symptoms of anxiety, depression, and hopelessness (Hathaway, 2003). In such instances, consideration of the patient's faith orientation is integral to psychological well-being and spiritually oriented psychotherapy may be instrumental in conserving or transforming the patient's spirituality leading to the reestablishment of a coherence of meaning. The outcomes of such a challenge may take the form, generally stated, in terms of either conservation or transformation of the means or ends of significance (Pargament, 1997). Spiritually oriented psychotherapy may provide a context in which the patient may preserve, revaluate, reconstruct, or re-create the foundation of his or her faith perspective in the service of conserving or transforming a coherence of meaning, essential to psychological coping and return to psychological health. From our perspective, clinical situations in which the ontological bedrock of an individual has been challenged inevitably involve spirituality as a focus of the therapeutic process. One explicit treatment goal therefore includes the reestablishment or creation of the means and ends of significance, by conservation or transformation, by which existence can be meaningful and purposefully encountered. Such a process is required to support the psychological process of healing. Consideration of the meaning and spirituality, as appropriate to the faith commitments of the patient, is not extant from the psychological treatment but rather explicitly addresses dimensions that are relevant to psychological health.

The Spiritual Quest in Psychotherapy

Finding answers to the big questions concerning meaning involve a lifelong process of signification as we ponder the "wholeness" that surrounds our temporal lives. In creating a meaningful bond with the sacred, qua, religion, such wholeness may illuminate our presence on earth; without such a spiritual relationship, the vastness may cast a long shadow. For some patients, psychotherapy offers the means to initiate a spiritual quest—because psychotherapy provides a context and a process to address fundamental existential issues and matters of faith. In contrast with the previous clinical situation, the patient is not presenting a crisis of faith brought on by a psychosocial or health stressor; rather, this clinical situation reflects either a more persistent sense of ennui and meaninglessness or, in healthier individuals, a desire for a more intentional spiritual practice, complemented by advances in psychological health and increases in awareness.

The search for significance is silently initiated when as children we begin to ponder where we came from and what happens after death; we begin to form answers to the profound questions, which accompany us throughout life. For most, answers will originally come from the religious culture that is transmitted through the family. An orienting system becomes internalized and provides an initial cosmology. The sum of lived bodily experience, culturally given narratives (Shafranske, 2002) or metanarratives (Rizzuto, chap. 2, this volume), and fantasy evolve into deeply held beliefs and representations, which contribute to one's assumptive world. It is out of early developmental processes that the bedrock of personal identity is formed, including an intrinsic spirituality and notions about one's relationship within the universe. When this foundation is sustained, strengths are enhanced by virtue, a sense of coherence is formed, and the experienced joys and tribulations are meaningfully integrated.

This foundation will be tested by inevitable disappointments, setbacks, losses, and conflicts that are faced in life. In keeping with the previous discussion, people will then conserve or transform their orientation to the sacred, or they become engulfed in a vacuous state of discouragement and hopelessness or wrestle with their internal anomie. These are conditions of intense psychological and spiritual difficulty. There are clients who come to us not prompted by challenges or psychological conflicts that imperil their senses of self and well-being, but seeking psychotherapy in an attempt to find a spiritual dwelling of purpose and meaning, a home, a respite from a more chronic spiritual malaise. They include as well that portion of the population whose spirituality typifies what Wuthnow referred to as "seeking" and illustrates the nature of the protean character of religion as quest. They may seek psychotherapy to fill an existential void or to the counter the insufficiencies they find in their "empty" religion or "naked" spirituality (cf. Marler & Hadaway, 2002). Wheelis (1999) recalled a moment in his childhood when he was comforted by his mother's embrace as she drew him into her open coat, which we find captures the essence of the search for a sustaining source of meaning when a spiritual home is lost:

> The meaning of life is in that coat: it is the home to which one belonged as a child. If you're lucky, you never lose it; it simply evolves, smoothly and continuously, into that larger, more abstract home of religion, or perhaps, in a secular vein, into clan or community or ideology. Meaninglessness means homelessness. When home is lost and the nightmares begin, that's when one goes in quest of meaning. (pp. 247–248)

The search for the self and the quest for meaning are integrally associated. The search for significance, when disconnected from sustaining institutions and traditions (being "without the coat") leave many without clearly defined means for establishing a relationship with their selves and with the sacred. For many, psychotherapy serves as an avenue to explore transcendent realities in the highly experiential, personal, noninstitutional way they desire. This may particularly be the case for those who identify themselves as spiritual but not religious (Fuller, 2001) or the 40% of adults who are considered to be "unchurched." Spiritually oriented psychotherapy is particularly responsive to the nuances of the construction of meaning in which an explicit incorporation of spiritual resources and practices is considered. Such an approach involves a transformation of the self to a life orientation of meaning and purpose constructed on a relationship with the sacred or God. It some ways this might be better considered a process of transformation or conversion rather than a medical treatment. Nevertheless, the implications for psychological health are significant. The development of meaningful existence and a life oriented toward ultimate concerns appears to be a necessary yet insufficient condition for lifelong happiness—simply put, "it is impossible for long-term happiness to occur in a life devoid of meaning" (Emmons, 1999, p. 138). Furthermore, Emmons (1999), in reviewing the empirical literature, found that "what people are striving for—the content of their aims and ambitions—does matter. Not all goals are created equal, and not all goal attainment is equally healthy" (p. 49). Furthermore, Fredrickson (2002) noted that "Perhaps what is distinctly human about our emotional lives then is our ability to open our minds far enough to fathom or create a connection to God, or another Higher Power. This broadened mindset can in turn provide a wellspring of profoundly experienced emotions, many of them positive. Thus religious practices may be distinctive human ways of proactively cultivating positive emotions with their attendant adaptive benefits" (2002, p. 212; see also Snyder, Sigmon, & Feldman, 2002).

THE RELATIONSHIP BETWEEN
PSYCHOLOGY AND SPIRITUALITY

In addition to identifying situations in which spiritually oriented psychotherapy is of particular relevance, we have identified a model for considering the relationship between spirituality and psychology. The heart of the matter concerns fundamental perspectives on the nature of human existence and the intersection of psychological and spiritual realms. This discussion concerns beliefs about our basic ontological nature as beings in the world and also establishes a context on which to discern psychological development, conflict, and foci in therapy. We do not propose a definitive solution to the matter of the essence of the person; rather, we describe five possible perspectives that psychotherapists adopt in considering the relationship between spirituality and psychology (Sperry & Mansager, 2003). Although these models are discussed in greater detail in chapter 14, they are briefly noted here:

1. The psychological and spiritual dimensions of human experience and development are essentially the same with the psychological dimension having primacy.

2. The psychological and spiritual dimensions of human experience and development are essentially the same with the spiritual dimension having primacy.
3. The psychological and spiritual dimensions of human experience and development are different, although at times overlapping, with the psychological dimension having primacy.
4. The psychological and spiritual dimensions of human experience and development are different, although at times overlapping, with the spiritual dimension having primacy.
5. The psychological and spiritual dimensions of human experience and development are different, yet neither has primacy (nor is reducible to the other).

There is a temptation to ask, "Which position reflects reality?" Such a question illustrates the quandary proposed earlier—it is a question that science cannot answer. It is a metaphysical question requiring an answer born of faith. It is not a question that any psychotherapist can dodge; although, it may be a one that is not often posed. This question highlights the fact that whether or not clinicians practice spiritually oriented psychotherapy or even consider spirituality or religion to be relevant, psychologists, as O'Donohue (1989, p. 1466) contended, function as metaphysicians and explicitly or implicitly express their ontic commitments in their clinical practice of psychology or medicine. What we propose is that clinicians nevertheless use this model as a means to identify the metaphysical, spiritual assumptions that they bring to the therapeutic discourse. Furthermore, we believe that this model is useful in understanding the ontological positions on which the therapeutic approaches and practices depicted in the following chapters are established.

SPIRITUALLY ORIENTED PSYCHOTHERAPY: AN INVITATION

We introduced this chapter offering the opinion that a renaissance in psychological healing was underway through the consideration of the spiritual dimension in human experience. We stand by this claim, although we recognize the need for further explanation. Renaissance, from the French, means "to be born again" and refers to the recovery of culture, skills, learning, or knowledge that had been forgotten. In spiritually oriented psychotherapy, we aver that a particular perspective is revived—a perspective, evident in the origins of psychological healing, that places the suffering person as the focus of the process of healing (Jackson, 1999). People come to us because they suffer in meaningful ways; we do not treat symptoms, we provide care to persons. Spiritually oriented approaches place emphasis on the construction of meaning rather than on simply identifying and eliminating particular constellations of symptoms. We are not suggesting abandoning science-derived practice; rather, we are advocating for renewed application of a more holistic approach to health care that includes consideration of meaning. In the history of psychological healing, one can observe a gradual shift from attending to the whole experience of the person to eventually a myopic inspection of symptoms. Drawing on Foucault (1973), we offer that a return to listening with the intent of fully seeing and understanding the suffering of the patient is required. We suggest that spiritually oriented psychotherapy builds on what Habermas (1971) referred to as a *historical–hermeneutic* science. In contrast to the *empirical–analytical* sciences, the historical–hermeneutic approach is concerned with meanings rather than the observation of facts. This requires us to listen to the patient's experience to obtain his or her meanings. Spiritually sensitive psychotherapists offer a particular kind of listening, a listening that is receptive to the meanings of psychological difficulties within a broad and transcendent context. This volume provides an opportunity to learn how others, with varying theoretical commitments, listen for the full spectrum of meaning and address spirituality in psychotherapy as patients search for significance in ways related to the sacred.

REFERENCES

Bauman, Z. (1998). Postmodern religion? In P. Heelas (Ed.), *Religion, modernity and postmodernity* (pp. 55–78). Oxford, England: Blackwell.

Baumeister, R. F. (2002). Religion and psychology [Special issue]. *Psychological Inquiry, 13*(3).

Beck, J. R. (2003). Self and soul: Exploring the boundary between psychotherapy and spiritual formation. *Journal of Psychology and Theology, 31*(1), 24–36.

Bellah, R. N., Madsen, R., Sullivan, W. M., Swidler, A., & Tipton, S. M. (1985). *Habits of the heart: Individualism and commitment in American life.* Berkeley: University of California Press.

Cimino, R., & Lattin, D. (1998). *Shopping for faith. American religion in the new millennium.* San Francisco: Jossey-Bass.

Emmons, R. A. (1999). Religion in the psychology of personality [Special issue]. *Journal of Personality, 67*(6).

Exline, J. J. (2002). Stumbling blocks on the religious road: Fractured relationships, nagging vices, and the inner struggle to believe. *Psychological Inquiry, 13,* 182–189.

Fichter, J. H. (1981). *Religion and pain: The spiritual dimensions of health care.* New York: Crossroads.

Foucault, M. (1973). *The birth of the clinic: An archeology of medical perception* (A. M. S. Smith, Trans.). New York: Pantheon Books.

Frame, M. W. (2003). *Integrating religion and spirituality into counseling*. Pacific Grove, CA: Thomson Brooks/Cole.

Fredrickson, B. L. (2002). How does religion benefit health and well-being? Are positive emotions active ingredients? *Psychological Inquiry, 13*, 209–213.

Fuller, R. C. (2001). *Spiritual but not religious*. New York: Oxford University Press.

Gallup, G., Jr. (2003a, January 14). *Religious awakenings bolster Americans' faith*. The Gallup Organization. Retrieved February 1, 2003, from http://www.gallup.com/poll/tb/religValue/20030114b.asp

Gallup, G., Jr. (2003b, February 11). *Americans' spiritual searches turn inward*. The Gallup Organization. Retrieved March 1, 2003, from http://www.gallup.com/poll/tb/religValue/20030211b.asp

Gallup, G., Jr., & Johnson, B. R. (2003, January 28). *New index tracks "Spiritual State of the Union."* The Gallup Organization. Retrieved February 1, 2003, from http://www.gallup.com/poll/tb/religValue/20030128.asp#rm

Gallup, G., Jr., & Jones, T. (2000). *The next American spirituality: Finding God in the twenty-first century*. Colorado Springs, CO: Cook Communications.

George, L. K., Ellison, C. G., & Larson, D. B. (2002). Explaining the relationships between religious involvement and health. *Psychological Inquiry, 13*, 190–203.

Habermas, J. (1971). *Knowledge and human interests* (J. J. Shapiro, Trans.). Boston: Beacon Press. (Original work published 1968)

Hathaway, W. L. (2003). Clinically significant religious impairment. *Mental Health, Religion and Culture, 6*, 39–55.

Hill, P. C., & Pargament, K. I. (2003). Advances in the conceptualization and measurement of religion and spirituality. *American Psychologist, 58*, 64–74.

Hill, P. C., Pargament, K. I., Hood, R. W., Jr., McCullough, M. E., Swyers, J. P., Larson, D. B., et al. (2000). Conceptualizing religion and spirituality: Points of commonality, points of departure. *Journal for the Theory of Social Behavior, 30*, 51–77.

Hoge, D. R. (1996). Religion in America: The demographics of belief and affiliation. In E. P. Shafranske (Ed.), *Religion and the clinical practice of psychology* (pp. 21–41). Washington, DC: American Psychological Association.

Jackson, S. W. (1999). *Care of the psyche. A history of psychological healing*. New Haven, CT: Yale University Press.

James, W. (1982). *The varieties of religious experience*. New York: Penguin Books. (Original work published 1902)

John E. Fetzer Institute. (1999). *Multidimensional measurement of religiousness/spirituality for use in health research*. Kalamazoo, MI: Author.

Keller, R. R. (2000). Religious diversity on North America. In P. S. Richards & A. E. Bergin (Eds.), *Handbook of psychotherapy and religious diversity* (pp. 27–55). Washington, DC: American Psychological Association.

Koenig, H. G., McCullough, M. E., & Larson, D. B. (2000). *Handbook of religion and health*. New York: Oxford University Press.

Larson, D. B., & Larson, S. S. (2003). Spirituality's potential relevance to physical and emotional health: A brief review of quantitative research. *Journal of Psychology and Theology, 31,* 37–51.

Larson, D. B., Swyers, J. P., & McCullough, M. E. (Eds.). (1997). *Scientific research on spirituality and health: A consensus report.* Rockville, MD: National Institute for Healthcare Research.

Lifton, R. J. (1993). *The protean self: Human resilience in an age of fragmentation.* Chicago: University of Chicago Press.

Lovinger, R. J. (1984). *Working with religious issues in therapy.* Northvale, NJ: Jason Aronson.

Lovinger, R. J. (1990). *Religion and counseling: The psychological impact of religious belief.* New York: Continuum.

Marler, P. L., & Hadaway, C. K. (2002). "Being religious" or "being spiritual" in America: A zero-sum proposition? *Journal for the Scientific Study of Religion, 41,* 289–300.

Miller, G. (2003). *Incorporating spirituality into counseling and psychotherapy.* New York: Wiley.

Miller, W. R. (1999). *Integrating spirituality into treatment: Resources for practitioners.* Washington, DC: American Psychological Association.

Miller, W. R., & Thoresen, C. E. (2003a). Spirituality, religion, health [Special section]. *American Psychologist, 58*(1).

Miller, W. R., & Thoresen, C. E. (2003b). Spirituality, religion, health: An emerging research field. *American Psychologist, 58,* 24–35.

Mills, P. J. (2002). Spirituality, religiousness, and health [Special issue]. *Annals of Behavioral Medicine, 24*(1).

O'Donohue, W. (1989). The (even) bolder model: The clinical psychologist as metaphysician-scientist-practitioner. *American Psychologist, 44,* 1460–1468.

Pargament K. I. (1997). *The psychology of religion and coping.* New York: Guilford Press.

Pargament, K. I. (1999). The psychology of religion and spirituality? *International Journal for the Psychology of Religion, 9,* 3–16.

Pargament K. I. (2002a). The bitter and the sweet: An evaluation of the costs and benefits of religiousness. *Psychological Inquiry, 13,* 168–181.

Pargament, K. I. (2002b). Is religion nothing but . . .? Explaining religion versus explaining religion away. *Psychological Inquiry, 13,* 239–244.

Pargament, K. I., Smith, B. W., Koenig, H. G., & Perez, L. (1998). Patterns of positive and negative religious coping with major life events. *Journal for the Scientific Study of Religion, 37,* 710–724.

Pargament, K. I., Zinnbauer, B. J., Scott, A., Butter, E. M., Zerowin, J., & Stanik, P. (1998). Red flags and religious coping: Identifying some religious warning signs among people in crisis. *Journal of Clinical Psychology, 54,* 77–89.

Plante, T. G., & Sherman, A. C. (2001). *Faith and health. Psychological perspectives.* New York: Guilford Press.

Powell, L. H., Shahabi, L., & Thoresen, C. E. (2003). Religion and spirituality. Linkages to physical health. *American Psychologist, 58,* 36–52.

Reiff, P. (1966). *The triumph of the therapeutic.* Chicago: University of Chicago Press.

Richards, P. S., & Bergin, A. E. (1997). *A spiritual strategy for counseling and psychotherapy.* Washington, DC: American Psychological Association.

Richards P. S., & Bergin, A. E. (Eds.). (2000). *Handbook of psychotherapy and religious diversity.* Washington, DC: American Psychological Association.

Richards, P. S., & Bergin, A. E. (Eds.). (2004). *Religion and psychotherapy: A casebook.* Washington, DC: American Psychological Association.

Roof, W. C. (1993). *A generation of seekers: The spiritual journeys of the baby boom generation.* San Francisco: Harper.

Roof, W. C. (1999). *Spiritual marketplace.* Princeton, NJ: Princeton University Press.

Scott, A. B. (1997). *Categorizing definitions of religion and spirituality in the psychological literature: A content analysis method.* Unpublished manuscript, Department of Psychology, Bowling Green State University.

Shafranske, E. P. (Ed.). (1996). *Religion and the clinical practice of psychology.* Washington, DC: American Psychological Association.

Shafranske, E. P. (2001). The religious dimension of patient care within rehabilitation medicine. The role of religious beliefs, attitudes, and personal and professional practices. In T. G. Plante & A. C. Sherman (Eds.), *Faith and health: Psychological perspectives* (pp. 311–335). New York: Guilford Press.

Shafranske, E. P. (2002). The psychoanalytic meaning of religious experience. In M. Arieti & F. De Nardi (Eds.), *Psicoanalisi e religione* (pp. 227–257). Torino, Italy: Centro Scientifico Editore.

Shafranske, E. P. (in press). Psychology of religion in clinical and counseling psychology. In R. Paloutzian & C. Park, (Eds.), *Handbook of the psychology of religion.* New York: Guilford Press.

Shafranske, E. P., & Falender, C. A. (2004). *Addressing religious and spiritual issues in clinical supervision.* Manuscript in preparation.

Smith, H. (2001). *Why religion matters.* San Francisco: HarperSanFrancisco.

Snyder, C. R., Sigmon, D. R., & Feldman, D. B. (2002). Hope for the sacred and vice versa: Positive goal-directed thinking and religion. *Psychological Inquiry, 13,* 234–238.

Sperry, L. (2000). Spirituality and clinical practice [Special issue]. *Psychiatric Annals, 30*(8).

Sperry, L. (2001). *Spirituality in clinical practice.* Philadelphia: Brunner-Routledge.

Sperry, L., & Mansager, E. (2003). *Spirituality and psychotherapy: Five conceptual models.* Unpublished manuscript.

Stern, E. M. (Ed.). (1985). *Psychotherapy and the religiously committed patient.* New York: Haworth Press.

Stifoss-Hanssen, H. (1999). Religion and spirituality: What a European ear hears. *International Journal for the Psychology of Religion, 9,* 25–33.

Taylor, C. (1989). *Sources of the self. The making of modern identity.* Cambridge, MA: Harvard University Press.

Thoresen, C. E., Harris, A. H. S., & Oman, D. (2001). Spirituality, religion, and health: Evidence, issues, and concerns. In T. G. Plante & A. C. Sherman (Eds.), *Faith and health. Psychological perspectives* (pp. 15–52). New York: Guilford Press.

Wheelis, A. (1999). *The listener.* New York: Norton.

Wulff, D. M. (1997). *Psychology of religion* (2nd ed.). New York: Wiley.

Wuthnow, R. (1998). *After heaven: Spirituality in America since the 1950s.* Berkeley: University of California Press.

Zinnbauer, B. J., Pargament, K. I., Cole, B., Rye, M. S., Butter, E. M., Belavich, T. G., et al. (1997). Religion and spirituality: Unfuzzying the fuzzy. *Journal for the Scientific Study of Religion, 36,* 549–564.

Zinnbauer, B. J., Pargament, K. I., & Scott, A. B. (1999). The emerging meanings of religiousness and spirituality: Problems and prospects. *Journal of Personality, 67,* 889–919.

2

PSYCHOANALYTIC CONSIDERATIONS ABOUT SPIRITUALLY ORIENTED PSYCHOTHERAPY

ANA-MARÍA RIZZUTO

When psychoanalysis came into existence in 19th-century German-speaking Austria, the structure of European society was dominated by nationalism, the power of the state, and the strong presence of the Catholic and Protestant Churches regulating the life of believers. Modern science had imposed its standards and required that all knowledge conform to them. The new disciplines of archaeology, philology, and linguistics offered fascinating novel views about human life in other times and places. Socially, the nuclear family depended on the father's earning and ruling power, and women were relegated to the roles of spouse and mother under the care of the male head of household. Freud's psychoanalysis understood religion as the relationship to the monotheistic God of the culture, a Father figure. According to Freud, the child's resolution of the Oedipus complex brought about the exaltation of the paternal imago into a protective God. He deemed such a maneuver universal and saw those who clung to religious beliefs as immature individuals in need of divine protection against the uncertainty of life. Mature psychoanalysts and analyzed people were to live only on the sustenance offered by knowledge of themselves and acceptance of unavoidable frustrations. Their god was to be Logos, "human reason" and not a purported divinity in the sky.

Religion was the only word Freud had at hand. The word *spirituality* did not have useful meaning at the time and had to wait for cultural developments in the 20th century that would change its significance. Cultural circumstances favored the progressive substitution of the word *spirituality* for religion in discourse concerned with relatedness to transcendent reality, be it God, a broader sense of divinity, supernatural beings, nature, the universe, or other sacred realms beyond the human person. The replacement of the word *religion* by *spirituality* signals a shift in the psychological attitude to sacred realities. Religion, with its etymological root in linking (in Latin *religare*), points to a personal relationship with God or gods. The focus of attention is on the divinity. Religion is god-centered. Spirituality is subject and experience centered. Spirituality seeks modes of relatedness with sacred realities that suit the individual's and the community's experiences of them.

To speak about religious or spiritual experiences, one must always take into consideration the influence of culture on the psyche and the way it favors some modes of experiencing the sacred or the transcendent over others prevailing in the past. The culture subliminally and overtly encourages modes of perception of everyday and sacred realities through parenting, family and social life, political and academic institutions, and the ever-present media. All of these influences contribute to the organization of the mind as a culture-dependent structure. Language, imagery, primary process, perceptual ego dispositions and beliefs, and superego organization are colored and shaped by the subliminal presence of the cultural modes of experiencing concrete, transcendent, and sacred realities.

THE EVOLUTION OF THE TERM SPIRITUALITY

The first documented use of the term spirituality in the English language appears in 1441 (Oxford English Dictionary, 1989). It means "The body of spiritual or ecclesiastical persons." The term evolved century after century while still keeping its main referent to the ecclesiastical body. In the subsequent centuries it referred also to "attachment to or regard for things of the spirit as opposed to material or worldly interests" and to "spiritual character and function" of some reality as well as to some "incorporeal essence." The *Oxford English Dictionary* does not include the present-day meaning of spirituality as the concept encompassing broad beliefs and practices aimed at accessing experiences of relatedness with sacred or extrapersonal realities, which transcend the individual self.

The universe in which the early meaning of the word spirituality came to existence was a world in which the Church and the educated clergy prevailed over a largely illiterate laity. A sharp division was present at the time between temporal and ecclesiastical matters, offices, and also, corporeal and spiritual realms. In 1775, Dr. Samuel Johnson defined one of the meanings of spirituality as "acts independent of the body; pure acts; mental refinement" (Jones, Wainwright, & Yarnold, 1986, p. xxiv).

Jones, Wainwright, and Yarnold (1986) traced the emergence of the contemporary meaning of the term to the Spanish Quietists of the 17th century who, according to their critics, aimed at the purely immaterial. Detractors of this spiritualizing tendency in France referred to and blamed it on "la nouvelle spiritualité de Madame Guyon" (Jones et al., 1986, p. xxiv). The authors suggest that after the 18th and particularly the 19th century the term lost its accusatory meaning and became descriptive. A journal appeared in France under the name of *La Vie spirituelle*. The term described ways of prayerful piety, colored by some mystical touches. In the English-speaking world, F. P. Harton (1932) included the term in the title of his book *The Elements of the Spiritual Life*. The same year, Roman Catholic authors in France published the *Dictionnaire de la spiritualitè* focused on Catholic spirituality. The great French theologian Louis Bouyer (1960) added a dimension to the concept in his classic book *History of Christian Spirituality* by describing "his subject as the psychological or experiential counterpart of dogma" (Jones et al., 1986, p. xxv).

Protestant Christians under the influence of biblical criticism and the impact of growing skepticism in dogmatic theology favored religious practices relatively autonomous from faith-determined dogmas. "A turning-point was perhaps a conference in Durham, in August 1967, whose papers and discussions were published under the title *Spirituality for Today*" (James, 1968, p. xxv). Jones et al. (1986) continue:

> Though the word 'spirituality' bounces round these pages, there is no systematic attempt to define it, except through off-the-cuff paraphrases, not all coherent: 'the forms and structures of the life of prayer'; 'the spiritual life' (pp. 16, 19); 'some kind of wholeness'; 'spirituality means a search for meaning and significance by contemplation and reflection on the totality of human experiences in relation to the whole world which is experienced and also to the life which is lived and may mature as the search proceeds' (p. 61). (pp. xxv–xxvi)

This brief survey is the official story of the term in religious and academic institutions and publications. People, however, do not wait for academicians and high-level theologians to modify their attitudes and behaviors. Popular language was already using the term with an equally poorly defined meaning but with intense feelings of doing something different and necessary. Complex and multidetermined factors were changing the culture, the modalities of religious experiences, and the way in which people felt they wanted to participate in the realities of a world that had expanded its scope to all continents and cosmic space and, simultaneously, had become more unified, into an almost global village.

CULTURAL FACTORS CONTRIBUTING TO THE
EMERGENCE OF CONTEMPORARY SPIRITUALITIES

The development of empiricism, modern science, and philosophy of science from the 16th century onward brought about a significant change in the understanding of reality in the West. In Nasr's (1996) words, the conception of nature

> moved away from the almost universally held view of the sacredness of nature to one that sees man as alienated from nature and nature itself as no longer the progenitor of life (the very root of nature being from the Latin *nascitura*, meaning to give birth), but rather a lifeless mass, a machine to be dominated and manipulated by a purely earthly man. It also divorced, in a manner not seen in any other civilization, the laws of nature from moral laws and human ethics from the workings of the cosmos. (p. 4)

By the 19th century, modernism began to dominate the West. Modernism encompasses an approach to life that is philosophically positivistic and rationalistic and committed to the belief in a linear progress in the evolution of knowledge, nations, and history under the guidance of rational planning for an ideal social order. Technology and knowledge were standardized under the continuous impact of the industrial revolution. Politically, liberalism insisted on personal liberties and the protection of the individual. Theologically, modernism appeared as a tendency "to accommodate traditionally religious teachings to contemporary thought and especially to devalue supernatural elements" (Merriam Webster's Collegiate Dictionary, 1993).

The early 20th century encountered the emergence of communism as a political system intending liberation but imposing grave restrictions in freedom of thought and religion. By the middle of the century, the horror of the Holocaust of 6 million Jews carried out systematically and with technical perfection by Germany, a highly civilized Christian nation, raised the question about the absence of God. The postwar in Europe and Chairman Mao in China forced the atheism of the Russian state on many East European countries and on all Chinese people. The postwar era also brought about extensive migrations of people from every corner of the world to the United States, each carrying its own religious beliefs and practices. The fast-developing commercial aviation industry permitted a multitude of ordinary people to visit remote lands and to witness the lives of societies that had remained profoundly spiritual under the guidance of nonmonotheistic religions. Americans found people of such lands now living in their own backyards and practicing their devotions in their own way.

The 1960s came with radical changes. Protestant theologians Thomas J. J. Altizer and Gabriel Vahanian announced the "death of God," as Christianity had known it. They called for human beings to assume full responsibility for their lives and their relationship to the world. Vahanian hoped that a new faith in a truly transcendent God would replace the Christian faith that had become obsolete in a world dominated by science and positivistic knowledge. The movement did not spread except to a small circle of "radical theologians," but it left its mark on the culture.

Postmodernism arrived in the same decade. In reacting against modernism, it preferred heterogeneity and difference in discourse and art. It favored "Fragmentation, indeterminacy, and intense distrust of all universal and 'totalizing' discourses" (Harvey, 1990, p. 9). Harvey quoted Eagleton (1987) to illustrate the great opposition of postmodernism to vast universal conceptual narratives:

> Post-modernism signals the death of such "metanarratives" whose secretly terrorist function was to ground and legitimate the illusion of a "universal" human history. We are now in the process of wakening from the nightmare of modernity, with its manipulative reason and fetish of the totality, into the laid-back pluralism of the postmodern, that heterogeneous range of life-styles and language games which has renounced the nostalgic urge to totalize and legitimize itself. (Harvey, 1990, p. 9)

The death of "metanarratives" was bound to affect organized religions, the grand masters of encompassing narratives. Impressive dogmatic edifices were becoming shaky because they did not seem to offer to postmodern believers the experience of autonomous involvement—pragmatic and transcendent—that they needed to integrate their religion with their postmodern life. The spiritual seekers searched many sources to offer them guidance and sustenance: Indian and Oriental religions, Native American beliefs and practices, astrology, the occult, Cabalistic practices, nature religions and places loaded with transcendent energy, humanistic psychology, holistic healing, and other idiosyncratic beliefs and practices. All these groups had and have precarious organization and remain open to anyone without imposing dogmatic compliance. Some of these groups form part of the so-called New Age movement, and others remain a search for personal meaning.

To the previous considerations must be added the post-Hiroshima awakening to the fragility of the earth and the emergence of the ecological movement, colored by a certain romantic tenderness for "the planet" and "the other" as brittle beings. Ecological concerns brought about a cosmic sense of a nature brotherhood, a trembling feeling of being together in a fragile universe. This cosmos stands in stark contrast with the world created by the biblical God, who not only "saw how good it was" (Gen. 1:1–31), but who also governed it with providential care. The notion of "heaven" as the divine realm has lost all spatial credibility, even as a metaphor. The world was no longer "above" and "below." The exploration of the human genome seemed to reduce the mystery of life to the accommodation of molecules under human guidance. People *can* play God; people *have* "created" new beings. Reality has collapsed the time–space distinction into the concrete image or the writing shown on flat computer screens and television. Besides, what we see in them may be a totally human-generated virtual reality. Who can tell today what *real* reality is?

At the social level, the disappearance of the extended family and the disruption of the nuclear family by the high incidence of parental divorce and remarriage is a phenomenon of great significance for the organization of personal belief. Many children nowadays have two or three fathers or mothers, or no fathers or mothers, and an array of half-siblings with all the accompanying and contradictory emotions and factual conflicts arising from such complex family constellation. The leaders of the social institutions offer few figures for identification to enlarge the options of the new generations. States and denominational religions are no longer able to command trust and respect. There are few figures for social identification. The person is left in charge of him- or herself.

All these factors converged to create a quiet but persistent crisis in religious believers or would-be believers. The great monotheistic religions, even if their dogmas were believed, do not seem to provide a way of integrating everyday life into a postmodern world. Doubt, confusion, a sense of irrelevance and impotence, in the context of many competing religious metanarratives, confront people with the difficulty task of creating convincing personal metanarratives to sustain them in an ailing planet. In their distress, believers feel the need for personally relevant relatedness to the universe and other people, not just to a God that transcends them and who inhabits a hypothetical heaven. These, I believe, are the social and psychic antecedents to the emergence of the vaguely defined term *spirituality*.

I conclude by saying that the cultural context of the last part of the 20th-century accounts for the emergence of spirituality—not only as a term but as a series of practices aimed at offering personalized help to those in search of meaning and who find themselves alone and bewildered. These spiritualities represent a human creative response to a world that has lost its coherence and sacredness, a world that cannot, of itself, point to meaning, and finds itself, as it does, at the tail end of a civilization, the so-called Christian civilization. This moment in history leaves many of us bewildered. We are challenged to resolve in our personal beliefs the contradictions between a fragmented postmodern culture and meaningful metanarratives, capable of linking (religion) the believer to a universe or a God that transcends the individual. Spiritualities may encompass the revival of centuries-old traditions of guidance such as spiritual direction, Eastern religious masters, soul healing encounters, counseling, spiritual disciplines, pastoral counseling, and, finally, the last comer, the integration of spirituality into the practice of psychotherapy.

BELIEVING AND PSYCHIC LIFE

Children today may have difficulties connecting the official metanarratives of dogmatic religions with the postmodern experience of the world, which has structured their mode of perceiving and organizing the meaning of reality. Morally, the commandments order to love mother and father. What mother and father should a child love when there are more parents than one or none at all because the young person is the product of artificial insemination? What trustable and coherent God-representation can a child form when confronted with multiple parents? What level of worship can be evoked by saying that "God created heaven and earth" when the earth appears besieged by its own fragility? Such teachings cannot be integrated without an extraordinary creative effort, an effort that exceeds the possibilities of most people. Yet people *need* some metanarratives, some beliefs and organizing principles to give personal meaning to a confusing and fragmented reality. Believing is not an option for human beings. As I have suggested (Rizzuto, 2002a)

> *believing* is an ever-present human activity, a process in which we are always and at all times involved, whether consciously or not, which is indispensable for the normal working of the mind and foundational for psychic life. . . . Believing is a way of selecting, organizing and judging internal and external information and registering it as available conditioner of how to organize and register future information. Believing encompasses conscious and unconscious judgments about what is real or unreal, what is good or bad, what is tolerable or intolerable. Believing eventuates in a modality of expectant preparedness in orienting the organism to present-future internal and external circumstances. The believing function is essential for the functioning of the human organism in a given milieu. . . . [Beliefs] are mediating structures, akin to mental representations, susceptible of transformation through experience. (pp. 435–436)

Furthermore, cultural anthropology has demonstrated that the characteristics of a human society and the subjective experiences of its members depend on the intertwining of belief systems embedded in language, mythology, religion, and the structural organization of institutions. Those beliefs are collectively shared. Although each individual may introduce some personal variations in the manner of believing, he or she cannot escape the boundaries established by the cultural structure. We are born, develop, live, and transform ourselves in the context of that shared matrix of belief (p. 437).

Present-day cultural reality, however, is unyielding; it cannot offer personal meaning because it does not have it. All it has is dimly articulated conceptions of the reality in which we live and a multitude of conflicting and contradictory beliefs. Society today lacks a vision of the universe and of existence capable of organizing meaning for a perplexed person. Conflicting beliefs of which we are either barely aware, or explicit modern convictions confront the faithful of any of the three monotheistic religions with internal and cultural contradictions. In the face of these internal and external conflicts of belief, each individual must create personal meaning and relevance out of a fragmented smorgasbord of philosophies, theories, religions, and spiritual tools served by the culture. The task is daunting, in particular, because cultural individualism requires that each person assume responsibility for finding the way to meaning.

The psyche is the only tool we have to create relevant beliefs. All therapeutic efforts to provide mental health and spiritual help must, of necessity, pass through the person's psyche, its organization and dynamic processes of defense and integration as well as its memory and cognitive, sensory, linguistic, and fantasizing abilities. In every instance, psychic processes must mediate spiritual transformation.

The human mind is representational. It deals with reality and achieves mastery over it by representing what is external to it in the psychic realm. It could be said, beyond doubt, that what is not represented, be it consciously or nonconsciously, does not exist for the psyche. The notion of mental representation requires clarification. I am not talking about images, but about an extraordinarily complex set of neurological and dynamic processes organized around the perceptual and fantasized conceptions of certain realities, internal and external, which are arranged as memory processes. These memory processes, in turn, are under the regulatory influence of psychic defenses, whose dynamic aim is to sustain the affective equilibrium of the person (Rizzuto, 1979) by regulating the preconscious emergence of affect-laden memories. All representations have been formed and continue to be reshaped under the influence of new experiences and the defenses that make them acceptable. The nonconscious, unconscious, preconscious, and conscious representations of any object, real or imaginary, are so extraordinarily rich that no concrete instance of conscious representation can exhaust the memory sources that underline them. This assertion facilitates the understanding of the therapeutic possibility of integrating neglected aspects of existing representations and their affects with emerging experiences in treatment.

Representations of persons exist in the mind in dialectical interaction with self-representations connected with individual identity and modes of relatedness: I am a daughter because I have a father and a mother. I am a beloved or hated daughter because I *believe* that my parents love or hate me, or anything in between. Belief is always the mediatory psychic activity that organizes the affective and relational connectedness between people in reality and in imagination. I have offered the following tentative definition of believing as psychical action:

> believing is the psychic activity that cognitively and affectively interprets, at a given moment, the condition of one's being, intrapsychically and interperson-

ally, and the meaning of its human and physical context. This activity can be carried out unconsciously, preconsciously, and consciously. (Rizzuto, 2002a, p. 444)

God or transcendent realities in *locus Dei* provide the context for existential beliefs that provide meaning for existing and being in the universe. As a self we are in a dialectical relation of belief with the divine or transcendent realities: We define who we are by believing who or what they are.

The representations we form from the beginning to the end of life are not entities but process that become integrated into the very structure of the mind. The appealing aspects of the representations become the organizers of desires, primitive and mature, and their terrifying components call for ego defenses to avoid those who evoke them or could replicate with their actions the harm, real or fantasized, caused by the objects that gave rise to the earlier representation. Thus, the structures of the mind find in the representations of object and of self, in dialectical interaction, the main substance of their particular characteristics. Bodily appetites and interpersonal desires (what analysts call id derivatives), ego inclinations, dispositions, and ideals appear as forms of relationships with represented objects. Superego demands replicate demands, real or imaginary, from those objects. Preconscious or conscious representations of the self or the objects never appear in isolation but in mental scenes (Rizzuto, 2003b) of dialectical relatedness such as "God watches over me" or "She didn't like feeding me." God and objects—humanlike or symbolic—must become mentally represented to be available for religious or for spiritual beliefs and experiences. Even if the spiritual ideal is that of emptying the mind through meditation or other disciplines, the presence of desired-for self-representation and the teachings of a revered master guide the person through the process.

The North American culture is overwhelmingly monotheistic: 95% of the population believes in a single God. The question was asked for the first time in 1944 and the latest statistics remain unchanged (Hoge, 1996). This means that American adults and children have a conception of God. The representation of God is a mediatory psychic function that makes it possible to relate to a being who is not perceptible. Unable to have any sensory experience of God, children early in their lives resort to *dynamically analogical representational and affective processes* based on the experiences with their parents to form a representation of the God that religion presents as existing, feeling, desiring, and acting effectively in nonvisible reality. The elements selected to form it are not arbitrarily but dynamically chosen. If the person who is presenting God to the child or adult is kind and welcoming, it facilitates the attribution of kindness and receptivity to the God represented at that particular moment. If the person is harsh and punitive, the God-representation of the moment may also include those characteristics. Obviously, the God-representation of the adult has accumulated multitude of elements from other people and, also, from religious or spiritual practices connected to religious figures. Yet the early foundation of the God-representation in experiences with parents remains.

The representation of God is formed by the vast coordinates of multiple memory processes of bodily sensations, experienced affects or defenses against them, relational exchanges, fantasized interpretations of those exchanges, thoughts and beliefs about primary objects and objects in the present, all of which become organized by their affective and representational connection with the code word *God*. The use of the word *God*, in thought or in spoken language, brings to preconscious or conscious awareness significant aspects of the God-representation dynamically connected to the affective and existential moment in which the word was formed and also to the moment in which it is used. This concept is essential to understand the dynamic of religious or spiritual therapies.

Monotheistic religions offer very broad sources for forming representations of God and of the spiritual realm: the Hebrew Bible imagery of God as creator and as a passionate leader of his people; Gospel narratives of Jesus as a man; the Godhead as Father, Son, and Holy Spirit; liturgical celebrations presenting God as bread and wine. God frequently comes in the company of his helpers: Abraham, Moses, the prophets, angels, Mary and Joseph, and a retinue of male and female saints. This vivid array offers the developing child and the adult an abundant assortment of possible components of the representation of God to suit any possible dynamic constellation from the moment of its early formation to its later transformations and psychic use.

The relationship of the believer to God and his or her experience of God's response *must pass* through these representational processes. God, as a relational being, must submit to the relational tools available to humans and to the vicissitudes of human relations. The universal phenomenon of transference described by Freud (1912) applies in a slightly modified form to the relationship with God, because the God-representation is built on earlier patterns of relatedness subject to modification under the impact of new experiences with contemporary objects. This last assertion could be used to build an ad hoc description of religion and religious practices. We could say that religious practices (and therapies) aim at progressively differentiating the God-representation from its dynamically motivated memory sources—not to leave them behind, but to make them better integrated with both, God as an object in his own right and as a sought-after transcendent Being.

There is a paradox in the God-representation because the believer *knows* that the transcendent God of faith exceeds the representation and exists in a reality that cannot be apprehended. The distance between the God-representation and the God it portrays is not unique. It is also present in the representation of ordinary objects. We all know that people are for real and that representing them in our minds is the psychic tool we need to know them. Despite knowing the difference between actual people and our conceptions of them, we believe our representations of them and feel the affect they evoke in us when they become conscious representations. This distance opens a window of opportunity for spiritual guidance, direction, and therapy.

Many people nowadays feel uncomfortable with a personal divinity and seek to organize their relational and belief life around cosmic or nature realities that offer to them the indispensable human sense of belonging to a larger reality, a reality sacred in its own way. I believe that this phenomenon may be the combined result of a fragmented culture that cannot provide God-related metanarratives and the effect of disruptions in the relationships with parents and the nuclear families. The parental representations or the self-representations linked to them may be too conflicted or distressing to permit their transformation into emotionally tolerable God-representations. Both factors create profound difficulties for the child who must form God-representations through the mediation of *dynamic analogical processes* to the emotional and actual relations with parents. My clinical experience has convinced me that the absence of a consciously available meaningful divine being in a Western person's mind, or the avoidance of a consciously available God-representation, reflects a courageous attempt to search in other sacred realities a way to supersede conflicting psychic representations of a God that can neither offer comfortable company nor respond to the need to belong to a larger reality.

The ubiquity of religion and spiritual practices in the world points to the presence of a psychic need for metanarratives capable of encompassing in their scope the universe at large and subjective experiences of belonging to a greater reality beyond oneself, family, community, and visible realms. Developmentally, such a need appears first around the age of three when the child wants to know the "why" and "what" of all she or he sees. It becomes a moral and philosophical quest in early adolescence when the development of the ability to abstract and generalize calls for a more unified view of reality. It acquires personal meaning at the end of adolescence, when the process of differentiation and separation from parental imagos (Bloss, 1979) calls for self-discovery and new relational objects in the concrete and transcendent levels or reality. Developmentally, therefore, all individuals, in any culture, must find a personal manner of partaking in cultural beliefs about spiritual and religious narratives or create private beliefs capable of sustaining their understanding of who they are in the world. This task is psychologically unavoidable because the human psyche can only exist and subsist in the meaningful context of other psyches and its surrounding physical universe. Human beings can no more live without belief and meaning for their existence than they can live without food.

SPIRITUALLY ORIENTED PSYCHOTHERAPY

The integration of spirituality into the practice of psychotherapy as an extended and accepted practice is so new that the literature, with the exception of three or four publications belongs to the second part of the 1990s (Shafranske, 2002; Tan, 2002–2003). I fully agree that a psychological treatment cannot ignore the client's religious and spiritual dynamic organization and personal stance.

People request psychotherapy for a great variety of reasons: overt psychopathology, obvious symptoms, or feelings of dissatisfaction, emptiness, and lack of meaning in life. Other individuals want guidance from an expert in spiritual discernment to sort out religious and spiritual experiences. The latter may resort to the help of a pastor, rabbi, iman, a spiritual director, or a spiritually oriented therapist to assist them in their journey. In between these two polarities—"overt pathology and spiritual search"—are all other individuals who want help from a therapist for personal difficulties. Such people may have ego-syntonic spiritual or religious experiences or, on the contrary, may harbor spiritual longings, fears, or neurotic religious or spiritual convictions, known or unknown to them, that interfere with their life's goals and spiritual commitments. The request for the help of a therapist or a spiritual guide reflects a wish to obtain relief from suffering, orientation in moments of confusion, or the aid of a mentor during a personal journey of spiritual self-transformation. The request for help finds its motivation in anticipated desirable states of being that seem inaccessible to the individual without the help of another. The appeal for help itself reveals that the person *believes* (Rizzuto, 2002b) that the therapist or the spiritual mentor is *capable* of guiding the person during the journey to implement the desired state of being. The word *belief* is crucial because it points to a certain level of object relations that permits, at least, a minimum of *hope* (Rizzuto, 2003a) in what the work together may bring about. Such a hope requires as an antecedent the developmental experience of having been helped, at least minimally, by an adult who was, in fact, capable of being effectively helpful. During the first encounter between the helper and the helped, the patient or client will attempt to ascertain the level of professionalism and investment the helper has in committing him- or herself to assist in the achievement of the desirable transformation. In other words, the person seeking help wants to find out whether the therapist or mentor can invest him or her as a person worth helping. This description brings to light an interesting fact. Helping another person requires as a *psychodynamic condition* that the one who is in need *believes in the possibility of being helped and hopes to obtain the desired results, while the helper should be able to offer a certain degree of professional charity.* This description does not, of itself, point to a spiritual dimension but instead highlights the extraordinary significance of belief, hope, and love as dynamic conditions for seeking desirable goals with the help of another. To say it in a radical way: There is no possibility of helping another person without belief and hope on the part of the one who seeks aid and the helper's investment of the helped person as a love object in the therapeutic situation (Rizzuto, 2003b).

The engagement of two persons to work together in therapy or religious or spiritual mentorship aims at starting and achieving a process of self-transformation. The agreement to work together in a particular setting to attain such goal elicits the activation of essential psychodynamic processes. Five types of psychic processes or factors are essential for effective self-transformation:

1. The affective reevaluation and modification of self- and object-representations and their dynamic interaction. This includes representations of divine or transcendent realities.
2. The reassessment and transformation of unconscious and conscious beliefs about oneself and others and transcendent realities.
3. The objectifying of oneself for conscious self-recognition and revision.
4. The creation of an affectively engaged community of two working for the common goal of the client's self-transformation. The therapeutic community of two becomes linked to other human and transcendent realities.
5. The revision of conscious and unconscious narratives to create a personal narrative that gives meaning to the individual's stance in the world and sustains his or her beliefs in the presence of external and internal objects.

To illustrate these points, I briefly present clinical material that emerged during the analysis of Mr. T.[1] (Rizzuto, 2001). Mr. T. wanted help in relating to women. He was twice divorced and proud of his ability to seduce women, although he found most of them stupid and superficial. He was always involved in sadistic enactments. He wanted the woman to feel pain as the only way to force her to pay attention to him. He felt superior to most people and lived in a state of chronic rage because others did not sufficiently recognize his value.

Early in the analysis, he reported a dream he had long before I met him. There was a great procession of bishops advancing through the nave of a large church. He was marching along with the bishops. Suddenly, from the left upper corner of the church, above and beyond the altar, a voice from heaven addressed him saying, "Come, join us." It was God, speaking in the second person plural, inviting him to join the divinity. Mr. T. narrated this dream with great satisfaction and as though it was something he had always expected.

Mr. T. strived to demonstrate my stupidity and to show me he could outsmart me because he was superior to me. He believed he could even seduce me sexually. He soon disclosed his explicit wish to be God. He continu-

---

[1]From *L'illusione Religiosa: Rive e Derive* [Religious illusion and its variations] (pp. 25–56), by M. Alleti and G. Rossi (Eds.), 2001, Torino, Italy. Copyright 2001 by Centro Scientifico Editore. Reprinted with permission.

ously attempted to seduce me, described how he would rape me, and celebrated with sarcastic joy what he considered my errors. The analysis of these episodes led Mr. T. to acknowledge that I did not have to be "forced" to listen to him. A transferential change brought him to see that he had failed to "force" me to abandon my effort to understand him. He acknowledged that I was trying to help him. Childhood longings for maternal love emerged together with memories of desolation when he felt his mother to be an unresponsive wall. When during the analysis he felt understood, tears of painful recognition welled up in his eyes. Repeated experiences of this type brought Mr. T. to feel "fond" of me and to believe he was in love with me. Such unexpected feeling made him realize that he had never loved anybody. Mr. T. wished to understand how it happened that he had been unable to love and instead compelled to humiliate and hurt others. His childhood past unveiled a profound sexual entanglement with his mother, with afternoons spent in bed together. He enacted with his pillow the fantasy of having intercourse with her. The memories brought him to reexperience the deep hatred between mother and son frequently expressed by both in terrible insults. She hated him for his inability to perform in school while he raged at her difficulty in being emotionally involved with him. After his fifth year, the mother was immersed in the depression of having lost most of her family in the Holocaust and became unable to attend to him emotionally just at the moment he was most excited about her. She, however, remained deeply involved with Mr. T.'s father, who always declared his love for her. The father was a good man, strong and a good provider, who cared for his son but never developed a close relationship with him.

The exploration of the mother–child mutually hurtful relationship revealed Mr. T.'s intense preoedipal and oedipal frustration with her as manifested in the transference, such as a desire for fusion with me and the concomitant terror of losing himself forever. He came to see that rage against me and his mother protected him from such terror. Progressively, he relaxed his defenses and expressed his wishes for tenderness, "softness," and the mirroring his mother had not provided. He felt that I respected him and that in doing so I was helping him see that his relationship with himself was a continuation of the sadomasochistic engagement with his mother. He said, "I insulted myself. I don't hear me. . . . It is *me* that is missing. I feel love and affection for you but a "me" is missing." He reflected:

> In analysis I am getting back something that is really mine. I have to have a sense of security about myself. There is goodness in you. Myself, my "I," I have to find what is behind the "I" behind "me.". . . If I trust you, I can trust myself.

Oedipal components emerged in the second part of the analysis. Fantasies about perfect sex with his mother and with me returned in full force together with tremendous sadistic and revengeful wishes for being denied satisfaction. Soon he felt the pain of his vain struggle: "When I am revenging myself on a woman I feel like a piece of meat, completely humiliated." He concluded: "It is the soul [mine and other's] that I want to touch."

The analytic process helped him to find himself as a respectable object. This was the necessary condition for him to leave behind the frustrating maternal object, to mourn his failure to have sex with her, to accept that the mother had loved the father more than him. He reconstructed his oedipal struggle: "My mother did not belong to me. She betrayed me sexually. She betrayed me as a child because I couldn't go to her with a problem. . . . I feel the full impact of the rejection."

Mr. T. concluded: "My relationship with my mother was a lie. I was not able to be the perfect child. I chose to put myself between my parents . . . I was inferior. I felt superior."

He realized that he had to give up his wish for control and for being God, grow up, and put his parents together as a couple in his mind because he did not belong with them. This realization connected his oedipal strivings to the dream about being called to join the divinity. Now, after his reckoning with his wishes, he could renounce his oedipal wish for victory and his compelling wish to be God.

He had moments of painful self-acceptance:

> I am realizing how bad and corrupt I am. I feel ashamed. . . . I can tolerate the shame. I have tears in my eyes. The problem was that we had dishonest communication, corrupt messages with my parents . . . I never realized how arrogant I was. I needed your help.

The transference and the actual relationship with me became tender and affectionate. He said: "My love for you is in a very special place. If I trust you, then I can trust myself . . . I am changing my perception of women. There is respect here. I have respect for you." He declared solemnly: "I am opening the door for affection in me." The statement announced the oncoming termination of the analysis.

During this time, Mr. T. decided to go to Yom Kippur[2] services for the first time in years. Witnessing how people repented and asked each other for forgiveness moved him to tears. Recognizing that he had been unable to see that people were capable of humility and repentance, he wished to join in their religious celebrations and, although he did not become a pious Jew, he found in the services the occasion to feel humble with God and his fellow worshipers. This experience was the final working through of his preanalytic wishful dream to be invited to join the Godhead. Being well on the way of accepting he was not invited to join the parental marital bed, he could accept that he was the couple's child and God's creature. He was surrendering

---

[2]A Jewish holiday, meaning day of atonement, observed with fasting and prayer, following the rites described in the Hebrew Bible in Leviticus 16.

the compensatory grandiosity of making believe that he could be an equal to his parents or to God. Mr. T. no longer needed to be God because he had become a child of God.

Mr. T.'s early God-representation resembled the parental couple in erotic union as the continuation of his childhood wish to be to be placed in between his parents. His failure to obtain his mother's love convinced him that he was unlovable. Experiencing me as a female object who heard him without having to be forced by his sadistic actions, he began to feel there was something valuable, even lovable in him. Such profound change in self-representation helped him accept his oedipal failure and to shift his narcissistic balance to the point that he could remember the good side of his mother. The modification of the self-representation and parental representations brought with it a concomitant transformation of the God-representation from an envied God who excluded him to a God he could now recognize as above him and accepting of him, a God who gladly welcomed those who repent from their sins. He had moved from compensatory narcissism to object relations with the analyst, people, and God. His new self-representation as acceptable, lovable, and a person connected to and dependent on others had as a concomitant the transformation of the God-representation from an envied powerful mother and parental couple that excluded him to a God he could accept as superior to him and welcoming of him.

The process of self-transformation does not have to deal explicitly with each of the points described in this chapter and illustrated briefly in the case material. The dynamic organization of the mind as a functional unity brings about a certain transformation of each type of process when one of them is modified. The regular encounter with the therapist over a period of time will affect some aspect of preexisting self- and object-representations and beliefs and modify the sense of isolation in the community. The dialogues between them about the client's situation will modify his or her mode of self-objectification as an object (Meissner, 1996) for subjective (Meissner, 1999) knowledge about the self as a person (Meissner, 2001).

The attention of a particular therapeutic approach to some dynamic processes and its selection of the favored point of intervention privileges one aspect of the person's dynamic processes while relativizing others. Such selectivity may suppress conscious awareness of the other processes but cannot stop them from being there and undergoing their own hidden transformation or interference. Each therapeutic approach is limited in its scope in accordance with the method it selects, the aspect of psychic life it focuses on, and the results it intends to achieve. No therapeutic or spiritual approach has the capability to attend and modify all aspects of psychic life. The necessary selection imposed by our therapeutic methodologies when compared with the richness of psychic life suggests that the therapist must carry out a detailed evaluation of the client's type and levels of need before deciding on the treatment approach.

The therapist must locate the area of help that is optimal for the patient. The help each person needs must not conform to the contemporary slogan "one size fits all." The favorite approach of the therapist must not be imposed on the patient unless it fits that particular person's needs and manner or being. For this reason, I find myself in disagreement with any model that gives primacy, as a matter of principle, to either the spiritual or the psychological. What matters is what the patient needs at a concrete moment. The therapeutic intervention must attend to such need first while the therapist remains aware of the patient as a whole person and invites exploration of areas relevant to the moment, without imposing a vision of reality steaming from the therapist's personal or professional convictions.

The therapist carries out a systematic evaluation of the client's problems, history, personality, and spiritual stance at the time of the first encounters. The assessment guides the therapist to select those aspects of the patient's life that are in urgent need of professional help. Once such evaluation is completed, the therapist may decide on the optimal approach and method to accomplish the task. If the person suffers from a psychotic disturbance, the first task is to achieve the return of a more normal psychic state. If the difficulties stem from unconscious conflict interfering with life's goals, psychoanalysis is the treatment of choice; when the pathology involves personality disorders, it calls for a long-term treatment that will revisit developmental landmarks and their effects; if the disturbance manifests itself in issues of gender, sexual, or personal identity, the patient needs prolonged and respectful attention to the implications of a difficult social stance; if the problem is a mood disorder, a careful assessment of chemical metabolic imbalance may require pharmacological intervention in conjunction with the dynamic understanding of the factors triggering the depression. Finally, there are individuals whose vague malaise in life brings them to the consulting room or the spiritual counselor. In such cases, it is mandatory to carry out a well-balanced evaluation to make a differential diagnosis between subtle but persistent unconscious conflicts originating in childhood and an existential situation that may require spiritual search and healing, or the conjunction of both. Finally, there are people who have started their own spiritual pilgrimage and need assistance with their efforts to attain desirable spiritual goals. These persons frequently go to spiritual directors, pastoral counselors, or other religious helpers to guide them in their search. They also need an evaluation of their level of spiritual development (Hall & Edwards, 2002).

PSYCHOANALYSIS AND SPIRITUALITY

The factors that bring about spiritual transformation are present in all forms of psychotherapy; however, it is within psychoanalytic treatment that these dynamics are most apparent. Spirituality, to the extent that it is mediated through the mind, is subject to the same psychodynamic conditions as other phenomena because transcendent realities are also apprehended through psychic processes. Psychoanalysis views the organization of the mind as the result of the progressive structuralization of the individual's psyche as the combined result of biological, psychical, interactional, cultural, and environmental factors. The psyche is the tool the person has to satisfy desires, relate to others, connect to reality, and achieve its goals and ideals. Psychopathology results from developmental disturbances in psychic organization or from internal conflict within the self and its mind's component agencies. There are conflicts of desire, prohibitions, contradictory goals, and of ambivalence that is frequently organized in the form of unconscious fantasies or beliefs. The patient cannot achieve intended goals or understand compelling feelings emanating from fantasies and beliefs because they are not accessible to conscious awareness. To participate in a psychoanalytic treatment, the patient must be highly motivated, psychologically minded, and capable of tolerating unavoidable painful feelings and frustrations. In this sense spiritual transformation within psychoanalysis is potentially delimited by inherent psychological capacities.

Technically, psychoanalysis aims at bringing the disturbing convictions and fantasies to conscious awareness by the mediation of free association and the emergence of transferential feelings. The attentive and detailed analysis of the speech associations and the transferential experiences bring to sharp focus in the interpersonal relation between client and therapist the type of impediments that interfere with the analysand's life. The past becomes present and can be revisited and reinterpreted. Thus, self- and object-representations are reviewed, beliefs reconsidered, and the self allowed to objectify itself and to revise its stances in relation to others and to preexisting beliefs and fantasies. The core element in this process of self-transformation is the creation of a community of two based on safety, respect, empathy, attentive listening to all associations, and affective engagement of the two parties in their dialogue.

Psychoanalysis does not privilege spirituality or religion; instead, it makes them a natural part of the exploration of beliefs, fantasies, God as an object, and other dimensions of transcendent life such as purpose in life, destiny, salvation, and the relationships with others and the world of nature. Psychoanalysis understands all spiritual experiences with the double key of their developmental and dynamic meaning as well as their connection to a transcendent reality that exceeds the limits of the analytic inquiry. Spiritual development therefore occurs within the context of the totality of self-transformation, which includes beliefs, representations, fantasies, modes of relating, and so on—the sum of psychological life. The goal of analysis is not spiritual transformation per se; rather, it is to help patients to become fully honest about their lives and the beliefs they hold. When an analysis is successful, a deeper understanding of religious convictions and practices, freed from neurotic beliefs and motivations, may be obtained (Rizzuto, 2002b, p. 212). Spiritual transformation, seen in this light, cannot be separated from the inevitable changes in psychic life that are produced in an analysis.

Psychoanalysis contributes to a comprehensive understanding of spiritual transformation in its assertion that transcendent realities are apprehended through operations of the mind, which are subject to psychodynamic processes that can be observed and modified through psychotherapy. Furthermore, factors have been identified that provide an approach to the constituents of religious experience involved in personal transformation. Such a view considers spirituality to involve conscious and unconscious beliefs and representations emerging out of the seamless blend of developmental experience and fantasy and giving rise to powerful motivations and experiences relating the person with the transcendent.

REFERENCES

Bley, N. F., & King, M. V. (1981). Some thoughts about the synthetic function of the ego. *International Review of Psycho-Analysis, 8*, 333–340.

Bloss, P. (1979). *The adolescent passage: Developmental issues.* New York: International Universities Press.

Eagleton, T. (1987, February). Awakening from modernity. *London Times Literary Supplement*, p. 20.

Freud, S. (1912). The dynamics of transference. In *The standard edition of the complete psychological works of Sigmund Freud* (Vol. 12, pp. 97–108). London: Hogarth Press.

Hall, T. W., & Edwards, K. J. (2002). The spiritual assessment inventory: A theistic model and measure for assessing spiritual development. *Journal for the Scientific Study of Religion, 41*, 341–357.

Harvey, D. (1990). *The condition of postmodernity.* Cambridge, MA: Basil Blackwell.

Hoge, D. R. (1996). Religion in America: The demographics of belief and affiliation. In E. P. Shafranske (Ed.), *Religion and the clinical practice of psychology* (pp. 21–41). Washington, DC: American Psychological Association.

James, E. (Ed.). (1968). *Spirituality for today.* London: SCM.

Jones, C., Wainwright, G., & Yarnold, E. (1986). *The study of spirituality.* New York: Oxford University Press.

Meissner, W. W. (1996). The self as object in psychoanalysis. *Psychoanalysis and Contemporary Thought, 19*, 425–460.

Meissner, W. W. (1999). The self as subject in psychoanalysis: I. The nature of subjectivity. *Psychoanalysis and Contemporary Thought, 22*, 105–201.

Meissner, W. W. (2001). The self-as-person. *Psychoanalysis and Contemporary Thought, 23*, 479–523.

Merriam-Webster's collegiate dictionary (10th ed.). (1993). Springfield, MA: Merriam-Webster.

Nasr, S. H. (1996). *Religion and the order of nature*. New York: Oxford University Press.

Oxford English dictionary (2nd ed.). (1989). Oxford, England: Oxford University Press.

Rizzuto, A.-M. (1979). *The birth of the living God. A psychoanalytic study*. Chicago: University of Chicago Press.

Rizzuto, A.-M. (2001). Vicissitudes of self, object, and God representations during psychoanalysis. In M. Aletti & G. Rossi (Eds.), *L'Illusione religiosa: Rive e derive* [Religious illusion: Foundations and evolution] (pp. 25–55). Torino, Italy: Centro Scientifico Editore.

Rizzuto, A.-M. (2002a). Believing and personal and religious beliefs: Psychoanalytic considerations. *Psychoanalysis and Contemporary Thought, 25*, 433–463.

Rizzuto, A.-M. (2002b). Technical approach to religious issues in psychoanalysis. In M. Aletti & F. De Nardi (Eds.), *Psicoanalisi e religione* [Psychoanalysis and religion] (pp. 184–215). Torino, Italy: Centro Scientifico Editore.

Rizzuto, A.-M. (2003b). Psychoanalysis: The transformation of the subject by the spoken word. *Psychoanalytic Quarterly, 72*, 287–323.

Shafranske, E. P. (2002). The necessary and sufficient conditions for an applied psychology of religion. *Psychology of Religion Newsletter, 27*(4), 1–12.

Tan, S.-Y. (2002–2003). Religion in clinical practice: Integrating spiritual direction into treatment. *Psychology of Religion Newsletter, 28*(1), 1–7.

3

CONTEMPORARY JUNGIAN APPROACHES TO SPIRITUALLY ORIENTED PSYCHOTHERAPY

LIONEL CORBETT AND MURRAY STEIN

THE ARCHETYPES:
SPIRITUAL ORGANIZING PRINCIPLES OF THE PSYCHE

Jungian psychology makes the radical claim that psychotherapy is an intrinsically spiritual discipline. The rationale for this idea is that the psyche does not consist only of personal material; rather, human consciousness is seamlessly connected to a larger, transpersonal field of Consciousness, referred to as the objective psyche. The psyche, or consciousness, is permeated with, and organized by, spiritual principles that Jung referred to as *archetypes*. In antiquity, these powers and principles of the transpersonal levels of the psyche were personified and given the names of gods and goddesses. Today they are thought of as a priori fields or patterns of information that are not dependent on any learned or environmental factors. These organizing principles correspond to the traditional notion of spirit, an unseen world that radically affects human life. To the extent that we take into account the psyche's spiritual potentials, depth psychology and spirituality are two approaches to the same phenomena.

51

Contrary to popular misunderstanding, the archetypes are not stereo-types, and they are not reified essences. The archetype is the *capacity* to form an image, not the image itself; it is a potential with contents that are not given until they are filled in with lived experience. For example, all babies are archetypally predisposed to experience a mother, but the individual woman who humanizes this potential is not the archetype. The Mother archetype is a transpersonal principle found in all mythologies and religious traditions. She is given local names and coloring, but regardless of her name, there is always and everywhere a Great Mother, a Queen of Heaven, or a great God-dess who represents the feminine aspect of the divine. In the Judeo-Christian tradition, she is the Blessed Virgin Mary, Sophia or the Shechina; in Hinduism, she is Kali or Durga; in Buddhism, Quan Yin or Tara, and so on. From an archetypal viewpoint, these differences in name and form are simply a matter of local folklore and emphasis. They are all manifestations of the same underlying spiritual or archetypal principle. Similarly, the mythic traditions all have Father gods with different local names that point to an underlying Father archetype, exemplified by Yahweh or Zeus.

Just as the material world is ordered according to the laws of physics and chemistry, so the archetypes are the natural laws of the psyche. Just as we do not see the law of gravity when an object falls but we know that the law is operating, so we do not see the archetypes themselves, but rather we witness their effects or their symbolic expressions. We do not know the nature of the archetype, or spirit, any more than we know the nature of gravity. Neverthe-less, the depth psychologist can discern the operation of archetypal prin-ciples without understanding their origin, just as the physicist can do good physics without knowing the origin of the laws of physics.

For the spiritually oriented psychotherapist, the archetypes are not only important in the spiritual traditions; they act as deep structures (processes) in the psyche that govern the organization of experience and the develop-ment of personality and psychopathology. In infancy, the baby organizes its perceptual and affective life according to these innate potentials for experi-ence.[1] For example, the selfobject needs described by Kohut (1971) are ar-chetypal human needs that must be met for development to proceed nor-mally. That is to say, all children have an innate need to be mirrored, valued, and responded to in an emotionally attuned manner, just as they need an idealizing selfobject to soothe them. These archetypal potentials are filled in

---

[1]Developmental psychologists increasingly recognize the presence of innate potentials in babies, without using the term *archetype*. The idea of invariant principles in the psyche is therefore not confined to Jung. It is also found in Piaget's developmental schemas, Chomsky's linguistics, and Lévi-Strauss's structural anthropology. In ethology the archetype is called an innate release mechanism (IRM). To the ear conditioned by the unfortunate Western split between matter and spirit, an animal's IRM sounds more instinctual than spiritual. But the archetype contains both poles, which are undivided—the instincts are the spirit manifest in the body. With this sensibility, all psychological processes are a composite of spiritual and human dimensions, whether or not mainstream psychology recognizes their spiritual levels.

by myriad concrete experiences with the child's human caregivers. The memories, fantasies, and images of these interactions, and their associated emotional tone, gradually cohere to produce stable intrapsychic structures that Jung referred to as complexes. The structure of a complex thus consists of an archetypal core or potential—the Mother or Father archetype—whose contents are determined by actual interactions with human beings. The resulting intrapsychic structures radically affect the child's sense of self and his or her subsequent relationships, as described at the personal level by self–object theory and object relations theory.

Archetypal theory adds to psychoanalytic thought the presence of a spiritual principle at the core of our development and our psychopathology. Most religious traditions teach that an element of the divine lies at the center of the human personality. In the Western tradition, this element is called the *soul*. (A concept to which we return later in the chapter.) In the East, the transcendent element that is our true nature is called the *Atman*, or the transpersonal Self. Jung introduced the idea of an innate God-image into depth psychology and suggested that the Self is ultimately responsible for the organization of the empirical personality—it is the ground plan governing the development of the ego or the personal self. He considered the Self to be the totality of the psyche, so that the archetypes are aspects of the Self. Paradoxically, the Self also acts as a deep center of gravity within the psyche.

The editors of Jung's *Collected Works* chose to write this word with a lower case letter "s," to avoid the implication that Jung was writing theology. (Jung was sensitive about this charge because he felt that the experience of the Self was simply an empirical observation.) Today, however, the English-speaking world uses a capital letter "S" to distinguish the transpersonal Self from the everyday sense of the self as a person. (See Corbett & Kugler, 1989, for a comparison of Jung's concept of the Self and the psychoanalytic self.) Much of Jung's writing is an attempt to clarify the symbolic ways in which the Self appears to us. Religious traditions can be thought of as variations in the human approach to the Self, each clothing the experience of the Self with its own folklore and mythology, producing the variety of God-images that we see in the creeds. Many of these differences arose because the founders of the traditions experienced the Self in individual ways, just as we do today. We should note here that, Jung's critics to the contrary, he always insisted that we do not know to what extent the Self, the divine as we experience it, or our image of the divine, corresponds to the Unspeakable itself. The most Jung would say on this question is that there seems to be a psychological relationship between them. Accordingly, Jung resented the charge that he was doing theology disguised as empirical psychology. (See, for example, Jung, 1975b, pp. 64–71, which includes some of his typical replies to this criticism.)

The implications of these ideas for spiritually oriented psychotherapy are profound. Personality development and psychopathology cannot be seen in purely secular terms, and no longer can psychotherapy be considered a purely secular pursuit. If we have the eyes to see it, an element of the sacred is to be found at the core of our psychopathology and our character structure. The psychotherapist with this sensibility is aware of both a transpersonal and personal dimension within his or her patient's material. Consequently, we cannot separate our spirituality from our psychology. To convey this attitude, Jungians often speak of psychotherapy as "soul" work, a term that of late is in danger of becoming hackneyed through over use, although for many the idea is still a root metaphor.

The word *soul* is used in the Jungian and post-Jungian literature in various contexts, but never in its theological sense as a kind of substance. Often, *soul* is simply used as a broad synonym for psyche. Commonly, we follow the usage of Christou (1976), who suggested that body, mind, and soul are different orders of reality, each with its own perspective. The body's reality consists of sensations and emotions, whereas that of the mind consists of ideas and concepts. Our experience is more than simply a combination of these, however, so that we need to distinguish a third perspective, that of the soul. The soul is about meaning in life, what we do with our mental and physical states, what they mean to us in our deepest subjectivity. We use body and mind to live, but the soul is about *how* we live, what it is like for us to live, and about what really matters to us. It is our soul that may be troubled, innocent, lost, or noble, and the therapist works with a troubled soul. An experience is referred to as "soulful" when it is deeply significant. When in pain we search our soul, not our ego, which within this perspective is mainly useful for ordinary adaptation to society. For Jung, the soul was a necessary posit, as if we need a name for the mystery in us that makes symbols and images, for example, those in our dreams that link consciousness and the unconscious. The soul then acts as a "receiver" of spirit, the capacity to cast the experience of spirit into our awareness. This interaction produces a crucial quality of experience, that of the *numinosum*.

THE NUMINOSUM IN PSYCHOTHERAPY

The transpersonal or archetypal dimension of the psyche appears in various ways. Its most startling and obvious manifestation appears in the form of what Rudolph Otto (1917/1958) described as a "numinous" experience. Otto coined this term in his 1917 *Das Heilige*, in which he tried to capture the major quality or the essential features of religious experience.[2] The sa-

---

[2]The word *numinous* derives from the Latin *numen*, meaning a divinity, and the verb *nuere*, to nod or beckon; the etymological sense of the term is thus of divine beckoning or approval. Otto's idea that numinous experience is the essence of religion is controversial; there are other ways to think about religion. However, this approach has proved to be particularly appealing to depth psychological therapists because it fits so well with the experiences of patients seen in clinical practice.

cred texts of all traditions contain accounts of numinous encounters. In the Hebrew Bible, Moses saw a bush that was burning but not consumed by the flames (Exod. 3:2–6). God spoke to him out of the fire and gave him his mission. In the New Testament, Saul on the road to Damascus, on his way to persecute Jesus' followers, heard a voice that said, "Why do you persecute me?" (Acts 9:1–19) and was blinded by a light from heaven. The angel Gabriel appeared to Mohammed and ordered him to "recite" the material that became the Holy Koran. These are experiences of the holy, or, in Otto's words, the *mysterium tremendum et fascinans*.

A numinous experience is awesome, mysterious, powerful, and fascinating. It produces an uncanny sense of dread that somehow penetrates to our core, a dread that is different from ordinary fear. Sometimes the experience induces bliss or joy, reverence or worship, or astonishment and wonder because we are in touch with something that is obviously not a part of the human realm. We may then feel cowed, entranced, captivated, or transported, or at times unworthy, ashamed or guilty, in need of atonement or reconciliation for wrongs that we have committed. A common reaction is to realize that many of our worries are actually trivial. Sometimes it feels as if we have been addressed by an Otherness, but sometimes we may feel a profound sense of union or oneness with a larger Reality, with the world and other people, and a loss of a separate sense of self.

Jung began to use Otto's concept in the 1930s because it helped him make sense of experiences he was hearing in the consulting room that clearly could not be reduced to psychopathology. This was an important discovery, because many people were then and still are told that their numinous experiences are psychotic or hysterical. Usually, stories such as those of Moses and Saul are told of special people within the mythology of the tradition. Jung realized that many of his patients' experiences met Otto's criteria for numinous experience but did not take a Judeo-Christian form. Jung found, and subsequent experience has confirmed, that numinous experiences may happen to anyone at any time. The content of the experience may be uniquely tailored to the psychological structures of the individual concerned and is often relevant only to the subject. Numinous experiences tend to address either the subject's developmental need of the moment or his or her psychopathology. For example, the following numinous dream occurred to a Franciscan priest during an agonizing period of questioning his vocation and his loyalty to traditional Church teaching.

> I am Melchizedek. A radiant blue image of the Goddess of Willendorf looms above me. She is five times larger than I am. I hold a chalice, which contains the philosopher's stone, up to the breast of the Goddess. Milk flows from her left breast into the chalice. I am deeply aware that I am in the presence of something intensely holy. (personal communication, July 2002)

This extraordinary dream meets Otto's criteria for a numinous experience, and indeed it had a powerful effect on the dreamer. Melchizedeck was a biblical figure, a "priest of God most High" (Gen. 14:18–20) who had no known provenance but who became an important model of priesthood in the Judeo-Christian tradition. The archetypal principle of a priest "after the order of Melchizedek" (Heb. 5:7) expresses the sense that the dreamer is not simply a priest by virtue of his ordination but because of an a priori archetypal dominant in his soul. The Venus of Willendorf is one of the oldest images of the Goddess, dating back to the Paleolithic era. For many years, the dreamer had been trying to force fit his spirituality into the official container of the Church, with its predominantly male God-image, but the dream tells him that the nourishment of the feminine aspects of the divine is sacramental to him. This kind of dream carries its own authority; it was so emotionally powerful that he could not argue with its reality.[3]

Obviously, the numinosum does not appear to the dreamer in a way that accords with official Church teaching, but it is typical for numinous experience to ignore traditional norms when they are not in accord with the individual's archetypal constitution. For the Jungian approach, which relies on direct experience of the sacred rather than doctrinal or biblical accounts of the way it should appear, this dream is a manifestation of the transpersonal level of the psyche. If we accept Otto's criteria, such a dream is equivalent to those dreams reported in the Bible that are considered to emanate from the divine. Examples are Joseph's dream that Mary has conceived by the Holy Spirit (Matt. 1:20) or that the family should flee from King Herod (Matt. 2:13). The concept of *somnia a Deo missa*—dreams sent by God—is an old one, taken very seriously in this approach.

Finally, the dream says that the chalice contains the Philosophers' Stone, a reference to the alchemical tradition in which the Stone could transform base metals into gold. For Jung, the alchemical quest was a metaphor for the search for the transpersonal Self; the alchemists had unconsciously projected this search into the material operations of the laboratory.[4] As well as a communion cup, the dreamer associated the dream chalice with the legendary search for the Holy Grail. In Christian legend, this was the cup of the Last Supper or the cup in which Joseph of Arimathea caught the blood of Jesus on the cross. The legend of the search for the Grail mirrors the dreamer's lifelong quest for a spiritual center, which now appears to him in the form of the Venus of Willendorf. For this dreamer, she acts as an authentic symbol of connection to the sacred. Here we see one of the major differences be-

---

[3]Needless to say, the problem of interpretation always arises at such a moment, along with the question of the source of such an experience. The question of whether such a dream is an authentic revelation or merely a product of the personal psyche is unanswerable. One can only declare one's commitment to one position or another.

[4]Just as we project this search into the hunger for material wealth, status, and substances.

tween the experiential, or psyche-centered, approach and traditional religion; this dream provides an *individual* revelation that may not be relevant to other people. The Jungian approach does not try to codify the experience and apply it to everyone. We do not try to write a universally applicable sacred text based on any particular experience (such as the handing down of the law on Mt. Sinai), because every person experiences the numinosum in his or her own way. Nor may we assume that the dreamer is given an experience that will be forever relevant—this is what he needs now, but over time he may need a different form of sacred experience as his spirituality develops. The contrast with fixed traditional symbols, such as the cross, is obvious.

This type of experience led Edinger (1984) to suggest that we are entering a new phase of religious consciousness, a new way of understanding our experience of the sacred. Instead of divine grace being mediated by law, by faith, or by the intervention of a savior, the psychological dispensation stresses our relationship—indeed our dialogue—with transpersonal levels of Consciousness. Jungians refer to this process as the ego-Self axis, where the word *ego* refers to the empirical personality.

Needless to say, we cannot decide whether numinous experience arises from the psyche itself, or whether the psyche merely acts to transmit the experience of a transcendent divinity beyond the psyche. Jung's approach to this epistemological problem was neo-Kantian. Kant thought that the mind is not a passive recipient of impressions from the world, but rather that the mind has inherent categories or built-in structures, which determine the way the mind works. These inherent processes affect our perception of the world. The result is the world of phenomena in which we live, but because of the mind's activity we cannot be sure about the way the world is in itself, which Kant called the *noumenal realm*. Jung used the concept of the archetype rather than Kant's original categories to describe the organizing principles of the mind. Because the archetypes organize the psyche, they determine our experience of the phenomenal world in which we live. What Jung adds to Kant is the idea that our archetypal potentials are uniquely configured within every individual, so that we all view the world through different lenses—the result is what we call character structure. As Kant pointed out, the notion of a metaphysical dimension, or a transcendent Godhead beyond the psyche—Jung would say beyond the Self that we can experience—is intrinsically unprovable. Such a noumenal realm is not accessible to us. (Jung's Kantian credentials have been challenged, for example, by de Voogd, 1977.) This epistemological problem is not relevant to the practicing psychotherapist, however, whose primary task is to assist his or her patient to make sense of numinous experience and integrate it into the patient's lived experience. (For more details of this approach, see Corbett, 1996, 2000a, 2000b.)

VARIETIES OF NUMINOUS EXPERIENCE

The psyche-centered approach recognizes various types of numinous experiences beside those in dreams. A woman who had suffered an extremely abusive childhood had the following visionary experience:

> One night, when the moon was dark, and my bedroom lay in inky black-ness, I sensed a presence in the corner of the room. I was afraid. The presence grew and grew, until, pulsating, it filled the entire room, throb-bing within the confining walls. The whole room seemed to tilt, as if accommodating itself to another dimension. I lay in terror, with my eyes tightly closed. A voice, deep and gentle, said to me, "love; the whole thing is love." Slowly, the energy ebbed from the room, leaving me in paralyzed terror in the darkness.

This woman reported that there have been many occasions in her life when the memory of that experience, in her words, "calls me back to life" and to the challenge of being loving rather than giving in to an almost in-stinctive rage reaction. Such an effect of the numinosum allowed Jung (1973, p. 377) to claim that numinous experiences have a healing effect. This kind of experience also gives the therapist an important clue about the develop-ment of the individual's authentic spirituality. It is, of course, nothing new to be told that "the whole thing is love." Yet such a teaching, like many of those given by the great spiritual teachers, may have little effect when given to an individual whose developmental history does not allow the teaching to be practiced. The emotional power of a numinous experience is often great enough, however, to produce the necessary radical personality change. The therapist's task is to affirm the authenticity of the experience, based on its quality, and assist in its embodiment, helping the person to develop the nec-essary changes in attitude and behavior in the world. For this purpose, many impediments, based on other problematic aspects of the personality, may stand in the way, but the direction is clear. Such work becomes an inextri-cable mix of spiritual direction and psychotherapy—there is no need to dis-tinguish between them, just as there is no need to compartmentalize a person's psychological and spiritual lives as if they were two different things.

Numinous experiences may take a great variety of forms, depending on one's temperament and personality structure. It seems that we all have our preferred channel to the numinous. Space does not permit us to describe its many other manifestations besides dreams and visions, such as those that appear through creative work, in the body, in relationships, as sudden spon-taneous gnosis, or as synchronistic events.[5] For nature mystics, the sacred is

---

[5]Synchronicity occurs when an event in material reality, in what is conventionally thought of as the "outer" world, corresponds in a meaningful way to one's internal, psychological state, or to a dream, even though there is no causal connection between the dream and the outer event. For example, one may dream of a death or a plane crash that actually occurs at the same time as the dream. This kind of meaningful connection makes many Jungians believe that the difference between "inner" and "outer" reality exists at the level of the ego but not at the level of the Self.

mediated by the natural world. A classic example of this type is provided by Bucke (1989, p. 214), who tells of a woman who had always felt dissatisfied in the Church because she could not reconcile the biblical God-image, removed from his creation, with her profound feeling for nature. Accordingly, as a child she felt that she was a wicked skeptic, at the same time as she suffered a deep vein of sadness. She knew that there was something painfully missing from her life because she could not reach the depths of her own nature. She yearned for a larger life, for a deeper love, and constantly felt like a creature that had outgrown its shell but could not escape from it. Exhausted, at a moment when it seemed that only death would release her, she was able to let go and surrender completely. She then experienced a serene and holy Presence pervading nature, with periods of rapture such as this one, which occurred while gathering flowers:

> I looked at the large bunches we had gathered with growing amazement at their brightness. . . . A wonderful light shone out from every little petal and flower, and the whole was a blaze of splendor. I trembled with rapture—it was a "burning bush." (p. 214)

Later she reported that "deep within me a veil, or curtain, suddenly parted, and I became aware that the flowers were alive and conscious. . . . The feeling that came to me with the vision was indescribable" (p. 272). Such a person is often loath to describe her intense feeling for nature lest she be considered a "pagan," or a worshipper of nature. Yet it is surely incumbent on the psychotherapist to value any manifestation of the sacred and to encourage the development of the personality in the direction that is given. The environmental movement may look secular, but many of its members are motivated by a sensibility toward the wilderness that is spiritually important. For them, damage to the earth is a desecration of the sacred.

The numinosum does not only appear as an "outer" experience. We are also gripped by the numinosum from within the personality, because the archetypal core of our psychopathology, our painful complexes, is a numinous element that helps to account for their emotional power. In Jungian thought, the archetypes, what Jung (1975a, p. 130) called "organs (or tools) of God" in the psyche, may have either a positive or a negative emotional tone.[6] Therefore, in contrast to the doctrine that the sacred appears as only light and love, in the psyche-centered approach our emotional pain always contains a sacred dimension. For the psychotherapist, this means that work on our psychopathology is a spiritual practice that allows the possibility of a numinous encounter. This may occur in a dream such as the following, that of a physician at the beginning of her psychiatric residency:

> I enter the room of a woman patient and find her lying on the floor next to her bed in a fetal position. She is weak, emaciated, and two thirds of

---

[6]This is why, in most mythologies, there are images of the divine—gods and goddesses—that are both light and dark, benevolent and hurtful to human beings.

her body is covered with bruises where she has been beaten. I realize that she has spent all of her life in jail and has been severely abused. She also has a reputation for being dangerous, combative, and out of her head. I lift her frail body into my arms and turn her on her back so that I may listen to her heart. I lay her down gently. I can see the terror on her face and I have the sense that she is like a vicious animal and may attack me at any time. I come away with the awareness that she is very ill . . . her name is Mary, and I realize that she is in fact the Blessed Virgin Mary.

This dream illustrates the idea that the archetypal feminine, or the Goddess, may appear in the psyche of the individual in a very idiosyncratic manner that has nothing to do with her traditional iconography—the unconscious does not conform to Christian doctrine. Therapeutic work with such a patient requires the recognition that the dreamer's femininity, in both its personal and transpersonal dimensions, has been severely abused, which has made her dangerous. Redemption of this situation is both a personal and a spiritual problem for the patient and the therapist, just as it is a societal and a spiritual problem for our culture.

A SIMULTANEOUSLY SPIRITUAL AND CLINICAL APPROACH TO PSYCHOPATHOLOGY

Faced with a patient's painful material, the spiritually oriented psychotherapist may use a binocular approach. One lens sees the situation in traditional terms of psychodynamics, transference–countertransference, and so on. The other lens sees the transpersonal or archetypal background to the human level, which is at the core of the material. At times one or other level is at the foreground, but both are always present, like the warp and woof of a fabric.

With this in mind, it is not enough to suggest that the two participants are working within an intersubjective field that is constituted by the interaction of their respective psyches. For the Jungian approach, the two are also enclosed in the larger field of the transpersonal Self, a third presence in the room that is often palpable, although not acknowledged as such by schools of psychotherapy that do not focus on the transpersonal dimension of reality. Instead, within the traditional literature, the presence of the Self is referred to in terms such as "profound moments of meeting," or a "deep sense of union," or a sense of pure Presence, of the kind known to all practitioners. Seen from within this model, the patients with whom we need to work appear synchronistically, because the work will serve the soul of the practitioner as well as the patient.

The Jungian approach is a form of transpersonal psychotherapy because it takes into account material that transcends the personal. The term *transpersonal therapy*, however, is commonly used to refer to a school of practice that deliberately incorporates spiritual techniques such as meditation, shamanism, and other ways of producing altered states of consciousness, into its work. The psyche-centered approach acknowledges the value of these techniques, but we do not usually introduce them into the consulting room as primary modalities. We prefer to focus on the material that spontaneously emerges in dreams, fantasy, and whatever happens between the participants, on the grounds that the transpersonal Self (not the egos of the participants) will produce whatever is necessary. Some Jungians incorporate work with the body and expressive modalities such as art, dance, writing, and sand-tray work[7] into their practice. This work, in the tradition of spiritual practices such as prayer, meditation, or fasting, tends to activate the unconscious and may trigger numinous encounters.

The therapist interested in working with this sensibility must be well grounded in both personal psychodynamics and the manifestations of the transpersonal psyche because either level may manifest itself. Archetypal material has to be approached on its own level, without reduction. For this purpose, the therapist needs a general knowledge of symbol systems such as religions, mythology, folklore, and anthropology. It is virtually impossible to work with another person's numinous material without some personal experience of the numinosum.

This approach corrects a cultural and professional compartmentalization because it does not separate the individual's spirituality from his or her psychology. We recognize that the patient's spirituality may be highly individual, based on her or his unique archetypal endowment. Because the archetypes participate in human development—for example, by participating in the development of complexes—there is an intimate connection between the individual's character structure and his or her spirituality. Consequently, there are many ways to relate to the Self. For example, if the Great Mother archetype, or the feminine aspect of the divine, is particularly prominent in the psyche of the individual, he or she will not be attracted to a restrictively masculine God-image. As we saw in the case of man who dreamed of the Venus of Willendorf, the spirituality that results is not necessarily connected to the Judeo-Christian tradition but is an authentic expression of the soul.

Many people who enter psychotherapy have first discussed a numinous experience with a clergyman, who told the individual that his or her experience was "demonic" because it did not take a biblical form and so should be ignored. By contrast, the psyche-centered approach is concerned with the numinous quality of the experience, irrespective of its content; we assume that the sacred can appear in any form. Accordingly, we understand material to be spiritually important that the tradition would consider to be purely secular. Such material is approached using the language and hermeneutics of

---

[7]Sand-tray work is an expressive modality, similar to play therapy, in which small figures and objects are placed in a sandbox to tell a story. This symbolically represents the patient's imagery in the sand.

depth psychology rather than traditional Judeo-Christian doctrine and dogma. Sometimes a brief course of therapy begins with and centers around a numinous experience.

A LITERARY EXAMPLE OF THE EXPERIENCE OF THE SELF

The depth psychological attitude is mirrored by a short story called "The God's Script" by the Argentinean writer Jorge Luis Borges. He tells of an Aztec magician, Tzinacán, who was captured by the Spaniard Pedro de Alvarado, tortured for a confession, and finally permanently imprisoned in a deep underground dungeon. This prison is divided into two sections: on the one side lives Tzinacán; the other side is occupied by a jaguar, an animal sacred to the native peoples of the Americas. The sections are separated by a stone wall that reaches to the top of the vault, but in the wall is a window protected by bars through which Tzinacán can see the jaguar when light penetrates the space. For just a moment each day, at noon, bright sunlight enters the cell from above, as the jailer lowers the daily ration of food and water. During this brief time Tzinacán can observe the spotted jaguar, and over the years he disciplines himself to study the pacing animal and to discern the pattern of its markings. Tzinacán believes that the High God's secret code words are inscribed in the markings on the jaguar. Whoever learns and deciphers this code will become as powerful as the God Himself. If Tzinacán can only come to understand the code inscribed on the jaguar, he will understand God, and with this knowledge he will be able to free himself, avenge himself against Pedro de Alvarado, and restore his traditional religion and his tribe to greatness. Tzinacán is dedicated to this sacred mission.

For many years Tzinacán studies the spotted jaguar. He and the jailor grow old together. He loses his posture and his health, and eventually he becomes too weak even to raise himself up from the stone floor. Then one day he has a dream in which he notices a single grain of sand in his cell. He notes this, and (still within the dream) he goes to sleep again. Again he dreams, and now there are two grains of sand in his cell. A third time he goes to sleep and again he dreams of yet another grain of sand, on and on, until the grains of sand entirely fill his cell to the very top and he is suffocating and dying under their weight. He realizes the he must try to wake himself up, but as he awakens from one dream he discovers that he must awaken from yet another dream and another, on and on. To awaken fully he must reverse the entire immense sequence of dreams. The task looks hopeless. He will never be able to awaken from all of them.

Suddenly, however, the door opens high above him and sunlight floods into the cell. Tzinacán wakes up from his immense dream. Greatly relieved to be freed from this nightmare, he blesses his jailor. He even blesses this awful cell for housing him, and he blesses his old suffering body for its endurance and stamina. In this same instant he becomes radically enlightened: He sees God, and he glimpses ultimate Reality. What he actually sees is the image of a High Wheel made of fire and water that fills the whole cosmos and links everything that exists. Tzinacán suddenly realizes how small he is in the great scheme of things, that he is but one small fiber in the great fabric of life and the universe. His arch enemy Pedro de Alvarado, moreover, is also a fiber in the same fabric. As he studies this cosmic Wheel further and comes to understand its full implications, he realizes that he now can read the script written on the coat of the jaguar. The code has suddenly become intelligible to him. It is a formula of 14 random words that, if spoken aloud, will give him all the power he needs to accomplish everything he has been longing for during this long exile in misery. At last he holds in his hand the power to abolish his prison, to renew his body, to destroy his enemy, to restore his people and their religion, and to rule as Montezuma once ruled over all of Mexico.

> Forty syllables, fourteen words, and I, Tzinacán, would rule. . . . But I know I shall never say those words, because I no longer remember Tzinacán. . . . Whoever has seen the universe, whoever has beheld the fiery designs of the universe, cannot think in terms of one man, of that man's trivial fortunes or misfortunes, though he be that very man. That man *has been he* and now no more matters to him. (p. 173)

Like Job, who also fell silent when he saw the awesome majesty of God, Tzinacán seals his lips and accepts his infinitely small place in the High Wheel of ultimate reality. He does not utter the "God words" because his ego has directly experienced the Master Object (the Self) of which it is but a tiny sliver.

Is analysis not also, in some sense, a quest to perceive the script encoded on the jaguar that we name the unconscious? Is it not an attempt to answer the riddle of our personal existence, to free us from our shackles and prisons, and to discover the master object (the Self) that contains our ego in a much larger network of associated psychic process and content? The search for psychic pattern and the attempt to decipher its code have been central to psychoanalysis since Freud published *The Interpretation of Dreams* 100 years ago. This search takes place within the sealed *temenos*, the sacred space, of the analytic structure.

Despite his determination to keep psychoanalysis "high and dry" above the murky regions of "occultism," magic, and mystical experience, Freud accidentally opened the door to the world of spirit when he suspended directed thinking in favor of free association and dream images. The "flood of occultism" against which he warned Jung (1989, p. 150) could not be kept completely at bay. From the beginning of the psychoanalytic movement, artists, poets, theologians, philosophers, and other nonscientific and nonmedically trained (or biased) people have taken part in its practice and theorizing.

They have been drawn to it not primarily because of its mechanistic and scientific claims (and, one may add, pretensions), but because it delves into the mysterious sources of creativity, imagination, and the irrational creation of order. Psychoanalysis studies the jaguar that occupies the other cell of the mind, the unconscious.[8]

FREUD, JUNG, AND THE SPIRITUAL

It must also be noted that only a generation or two separated the founding figures Freud and Jung from age-old religious traditions. Freud's grandfather was an orthodox rabbi, and Jung's father and maternal grandfather were Swiss Protestant clergymen. What the forefathers learned, and perhaps also experienced, in their traditions, the sons and grandsons found again in their inner psychic worlds. The images and symbols of the unconscious, discovered and studied in psychoanalysis, created echoes of lost religious worlds. These echoes in turn were actually represented in the founders' psychoanalytic working spaces. In Freud's case, this is somewhat disguised but present nevertheless in his famous antiquities collection. Rizzuto (1998) commented on these numerous "sacred objects" in Freud's consulting rooms: "They offered him what God offers to the believer: the assurance of a constant presence and the joy of sublimated emotional contact with the enticing father . . . they were always there as a needed presence serving the same function that God's presence has for the believer" (p. 259). Jung's bow to religious tradition is more transparent. He installed stained glass windows from a medieval church in his study and hung a copy of the shroud of Turin across from his writing desk. Jung's psychological theory itself can be read as a version of biblical theology. The "doctrine" of synchronicity, for example, is Jung's restatement of the familiar Protestant doctrine of Divine Providence (cf. Stein, 1995).

Both psychoanalytic pioneers reminded themselves of spiritual realities that they as modern men no longer "believed in" but nevertheless found surprisingly meaningful and important to them. In a way, these old religious objects and images continued to be living symbols for these modern men.

It is ironic that Freud, who so severely repudiated the spiritual and theological (if not the cultural) aspects of his Jewish tradition, inadvertently opened the way to a modern form of spirituality. Jung became acutely aware of this dimension of psychoanalysis and reflected on it extensively in his later writings. The "oceanic feeling" discussed by Freud in *Civilization and Its Discontents* is an experience common to poets, mystics, dreamers, and occa-

---

[8]Often, too, there is a power motive at the outset of analysis. "If I can only get control of the unconscious," the analysand may think, "I will have great powers to transform my life and the world around me." One hopes that this power quest will end with the realization of the ego's relative place within the larger universe of the psyche.

sionally also to analysands and analysts within the *temenos* of analysis. It is the precondition for Tzinacán's vision of the High Wheel and the realization of his place in it. It is also the common ground of much later psychoanalytic work and theory, as described by Milner (1987), Eigen (1998), Ogden (1999), Bollas (1999), and many others.

A CLINICAL ILLUSTRATION

We believe that the term *spirituality* must be understood somewhat differently from its usual meaning within traditional religious discourse or even New Age renditions. A new patient brings a first dream to analysis. A particular detail in the dream catches my[9] attention. He is having breakfast in a resort hotel room, and the window is wide open. Outside he sees the ocean. A moderately strong sea breeze billows a white curtain into the room. I ask him to describe this detail more carefully.

"It's a mild breeze," he says, "very fresh. Sometimes there is a gust of wind and the curtain, you know, billows," he adds, gesturing widely with his arms. "It's a clear sunny day and the breeze is fairly strong, but not threatening. It's a good day for the beach, or for sailing."

As he tells me this, he enters into a mild state of reverie, and I follow him there. For a moment it seems as if we have entered the dream together, and I can almost feel the breeze and taste the salty air. (It's a sort of "oceanic feeling" we are mutually entering into here.) I muse to myself: The window is open, there is access to the unconscious, the timing is propitious. (As I write this, I think also of the sky door opening above Tzinacán's cell, when for a moment he can see the world beyond his own cell and study the jaguar in the adjoining space.)

Several weeks later, he brings in a second dream. He is standing on the bank of a large river. Around him and in the water he sees many women and children playing, bathing, and generally relaxing. As he enters the water and begins swimming, he notes how clear and clean this river is. He can see the bottom, and he enjoys the refreshing cool feeling of the clean water on his skin. He swims out quite a long distance and is about to round a bend when suddenly he spots the form of a great white shark lying quietly on the bottom of the river some 20 or 30 feet beneath the surface. Stunned, he quickly turns back and gets out of the water. He wonders why the women and children do not seem to care and go on swimming and playing around in the water. Don't they see the shark? Or do they know it is not dangerous? Or has he hallucinated the shark and it's not real? He does not know.

The dream is disquieting but not terribly frightening. The shark is quiet right now, but what does its presence mean? We both instantly associate the

---

[9]The therapist referred to in this section is Stein.

shark to a psychotic break the patient had during a drug trip some 30 years earlier. This was a major experience in his life. His life was completely changed, and it took him years to recover ego integrity. "I was frozen in the eye of God," he says. "I could see my sin. God was pointing his finger of accusation right at me. I *knew* [said with strong emphasis] that I was utterly corrupt and rotten. Everything I did was bad. I was the greatest sinner in the world. Only there was nobody else around: I was all God was looking at, and His judgment was absolute and final."

The great white shark had once upon a time attacked and devastated his ego. For him this was a spiritual experience of the first order, but also it was distorted, paranoid, and pathological. He had felt unconsciously guilty for the death of his father who had died of leukemia when the patient was 6 years old. Just before the drug experience, moreover, he had been reading, on the recommendation of a born-again cousin who was a former drug addict, the Book of Revelation, a powerful and gory tale of God's judgment and punishment for sin.

"That's why I got out of the river of life," he said. "My life stopped at that moment. I longed to go back to the person I was before the attack, but I couldn't. I was trapped by this knowledge that God had me in his vision and that I was totally bad. And I couldn't figure out why other people weren't equally devastated by this knowledge."

"The shark is quiet right now," I ventured.

"Oh yes, but he can attack at any moment. Those sharks can move like lightning, and when they do it's all over."

"The women and children seem OK," I pointed out.

"Yeah, that's strange. I don't get it."

In Borges's story, Tzinacán is protected from the jaguar by a thick stone wall and a barred glass window. In my patient's dream, nothing but clean water separates the swimmer from the shark. This is an important difference, indicating different structures and psychic defenses against the terror of a primitive master object. Jung (1958/1969, p. 451) wrote in *Answer to Job*,

> God has a terrible double aspect: a sea of grace is met by a seething lake
> of fire, and the light of love glows with a fierce dark heat of which it is
> said *"ardet non lucet"*—it burns but gives no light. That is the eternal, as
> distinct from the temporal, gospel: *one can love God but must fear him.*

Jung was not referring here to a theological or metaphysical God such as is found in the writings of theologians and philosophers, but rather to the psychological God of primary religious experience. This God can easily take the symbolic form of a great white fish or a jaguar. The God of psychological experience is theriomorphic, animal-like. It is a force of nature.

The window of analysis opens to the paradoxical nature of the master object. Spirituality in the context of psychoanalysis is a high-risk venture into the unknown, into the waters of the unconscious and to the other side of our walled-off psychic prisons. The pioneers—Freud and Jung—knew well the fear of confronting the unconscious and venturing into these uncharted areas of the mind. Freud facing the sphinx, Jung confronting the archetypes of the collective unconscious—these are the images the founders of psycho-analysis have bequeathed us as emblems of the enterprise. Is psychoanalysis not a quest to discern the central mysteries of human existence and to con-sider its major riddles, if not answer them? This is the kind of spirituality psychoanalysis entails.

POSITIVE AND NEGATIVE LIBERTY WITHIN
SPIRITUALITY AND PSYCHOTHERAPY

To define further what we mean by spirituality in psychotherapy, we may follow Isaiah Berlin's famous distinction between two types of liberty (Ignatieff, 2000). Berlin drew a line between positive liberty and negative liberty. Positive liberty, he said, entails the use of freedom to instruct, shape, form, and reform society. It is the freedom of parents to shape and influence their children, of kings and queens and governors to "improve the common folk." Berlin was skeptical about positive liberty when applied to society and culture. Those who favor it tend to take it upon themselves to instruct others how to live the "good life" based on their own (actually limited) certainties about what constitutes self-actualization, growth, and enhanced living. These heirs of Rousseau and the Romantics turn out to have been some of the worst tyrants, dictators, and fascists of modern times. All were intent on improving society, or even the human race, but their certainties and their strong exer-cise of power turned ugly and lethal for people who did not fit their para-digms. Negative liberty, on the other hand, is the state of freedom from ex-ternal compulsion, from authoritarian (even if well intended) thought and behavior police. It is the condition of being able to do what you want to do, when and how you want to do it. Berlin recognized the dangers of this kind of liberty, but he favored it because on the whole, he assumed, people can figure out for themselves what is best for them and muddle through.

Applied to spirituality, the positive variety is taught and preached by people grounded in the certainties of religious dogma and practice. The nega-tive form of spirituality, on the contrary, is empty of content and relies on an attitude of openness to the unknown. It is based on an attitude that the Chinese have called *wu-wei*, that is, letting things happen and unfold on their own (Hinton, 1999). Freud's method of free association and his recom-mendation to analysts to cultivate evenly hovering attention toward their patients' psychic material move in this direction of negative spirituality, as does Jung's practice of active imagination. In psychoanalysis one studies the markings on the jaguar; one does not try to rearrange them.

There are forms of psychotherapy today that use positive spirituality in their methodologies. Practitioners who combine spirituality with cognitive behavioral therapies will tend to favor this approach. These therapies are programmatic rather than exploratory, convinced of the correctness of their objectives rather than open to surprise and individual difference, more pro-active than reflective. Psychoanalysis tends much more strongly to take the side of negative spirituality, recognizing that the spirit bloweth where it listeth and that humans cannot foresee its directions or control its ways. The spirit of the unconscious must reveal itself ever anew, ever fresh.

A patient told me (Stein) about a dream that totally surprised him. It is, in my view, an example of the unconscious spirit's freedom and genius for novelty and invention. The context for the dream was extraordinary. The dream occurred while sitting on a bench at the hospital waiting for his daughter to have her third baby. The patient and his wife were desperately unhappy that their daughter was having this child—she was not married and had no means to support herself and her other two children, let alone another. She had refused to undergo an abortion and had insisted on carrying the child to term. So here he was at 2 a.m., waiting with his daughter until she would be taken into the delivery room. He fell asleep on a bench and dreamed that he found himself in his daughter's room. Some women are hovering around, tending to things. Suddenly he has a vision (in the dream), in which he sees some 20 people standing around his daughter's bed waiting for the birth. They are here to celebrate this joyful event. He realizes that each of these people is someone he knows from the past. He searches their faces—there is his childhood chum, his friend from college, his former mentor, on and on. He knows them all. In the dream vision, they are the ages they were when he knew them. He becomes ecstatic and filled with joy because he realizes that this is a vision and that some of these people are actually now dead. But here they are: They have returned and have come here for him, to be with him at the birth of his new grandchild, and he is overwhelmed with gratitude that they are here. He weeps for joy to be with his friends again. At this moment his daughter wakes him up and says it is time to go in and give birth.

This dream/vision of a network of relationships, of links between past, present, and future, is akin to Tzinacán's vision of the interconnectedness of all things and beings on the High Wheel. In such moments we are privileged to transcend our limited ego views and preferences. There are larger realities, temporal and atemporal. The ego's position is relativized. Tzinacán forgot himself; my patient put aside his distress and objection to this birth. A greater perspective takes hold.

The type of spirituality that arises in analysis is spontaneous, surprising, and almost always contrary to the ego's limited attitudes and expectations. It may enter a session in the form of a slip. A patient was very carefully telling me about his wonderful new relationship with a nearly perfect woman, but in which now, after 3 or 4 weeks, a few minor conflicts and disharmonies were

beginning to appear. His girlfriend had just a few little mannerisms and behavioral quirks that bothered him, but only ever so slightly, he wanted to say.
"In *no* way do I want to say that these things are *not* important," he emphasized. Then he halted, realizing the double negative had said the opposite of
what he was consciously intending to say. He is himself a psychologist and
understands the meaning of slips. When he heard himself, he began to laugh
sheepishly.

"You *will* tell the truth whether you want to or not," I said, chuckling
with him.

The spirit of psychoanalysis is truth telling, is it not? This guides our
work, whether or not the ego finds itself in a cooperative mood.

Transference is another entry point into the greater vision and is at
least as royal a road to the unconscious and to the master object as is the
dream. Jung (1953/1966) tells of a case of a young woman who idealized him
to the high heavens and dreamed of him as a Father God carrying her in his
arms through a wheat field as the wind swept the grain into waves.[10] The sea
wind—*pneuma*, or spirit—also blew gently through the open window in my
patient's initial dream. I neglected to mention that I, the analyst, was also a
figure in that dream. I was watching the dreamer enjoy a hearty breakfast of
eggs, toast, and orange juice. I seemed impatient with him, and he wondered
if I would end up respecting or rejecting him. This reminded him of his father
and stepfather. In the transference, a spirit is born that connects the past to
the present and leads (we hope) to a new future. As Freud told us, the bond
that develops in analysis is profound and resembles the earliest ties we know,
the child–parent relationship. To fathom, study, and fully experience this
bond is a central work of analysis, and perhaps the heart of the spiritual exercise that psychoanalysis becomes as it deepens in complexity and gathers its
full strength. What Jung called *transformation* in analysis has its central energies in the fertile context of the transference–countertransference relationship (Stein, 1998, chap. 3).

Finally there are moments of synchronicity, when we are shown the
surprising connectedness of things, often in the context of a close human
relationship. The patient who slipped and told the truth in spite of himself
related, in the same session, an unusual happening. He is not at all given to
mystical thinking and strives to be a rational, skeptical, modern man in all
ways. So he was nonplused by an incident that took place the day before our
session. His daughter had called from another country and told him about a
near fatal accident she had been in while driving over a narrow mountain
road. A tire blew out on her vehicle and nearly caused her to tumble to her
death in the deep ravine below. She was shaken but not hurt. He was re-

---

[10]This case was first presented in 1916. It is an early clinical vignette of what today we would call an
idealizing transference. At the time, Jung recognized this transference as the result of the patient's
search for a divinity. This kind of material led Jung to describe "a transpersonal control-point" in the
psyche, an idea that evolved into the concept of the Self.

counting this fearful event to his son as they were driving into the city to see a play. Just at the moment of telling him about the daughter's blowout, one of the tires on his own car blew out with a terrific noise and with such force that the rim of the wheel was instantly grinding on the pavement. He was speechless. The hidden network of object relations, which includes the psychological and physical domains of our lives, shows its presence in astonishing ways. If we could see the full extent of it, we would see what Tzinacán saw in the High Wheel. We are each threads in a great fabric whose extent and intimate design are beyond our comprehension, and we touch each other in strange ways and surprising places.

Psychoanalysis, as a method of investigation, discovery, and healing, studies the patterns on the jaguar's back when the light shines into the *temenos* that is our analytic cell. It is a practice of negative spirituality, observing the irrational, the surprising, the hidden linkages that infiltrate our lives and connect us to all that exists. It is a sustained reflection on the divine script, which becomes manifest as we attend deeply to our subjectivity. The realization of the message inscribed in our souls heals our one-sidedness and neurotic sicknesses. The end is awe, and our lips are sealed in silence.

THE APPLICATION OF A JUNGIAN APPROACH TO SPIRITUALLY ORIENTED PSYCHOTHERAPY

Here a caveat is in order. The Jungian approach is difficult or impossible to apply in the case of people who are developmentally presymbolic because they tend to concretize symbolic material and may not be able to appreciate its metaphorical nature. Thus, although many borderline personalities are attracted to such work, they find its affective intensity overwhelming. Without a firm sense of self and the capacity to tolerate intense affect, numinous experience may trigger psychotic episodes. Clinical acumen and tact are required in such situations. Other people have the necessary personality strength to work with transpersonal material, but their worldview (or resistance to the experience of the numinosum) will not allow it to be discussed in the consulting room, where it is likely to be dismissed as "God-talk." Needless to say, this approach is of limited value to therapists who are fully committed to a particular tradition. For example, many fundamentalist Christian therapists do not accept the basic premise of the Jungian approach, which is that revelation is ongoing and may take novel forms. (Fundamentalists believe that revelation ended with the conclusion of the New Testament. Many deny the value of any psychotherapeutic approach, e.g., Bobgan & Bobgan, 1987.) The approach is of no interest to therapists with a materialistic orientation, who, when their patients present them with numinous material, tend to dismiss it as defensive, hysterical, psychotic, or the result of an overheated imagination. Because of the danger that numinous experience will be dismissed or reduced, many people are wary of discussing it. Perhaps the *Diagnostic and Statistical Manual of Mental Disorders* needs a category of "normal numinous experience."

With these reservations, the approach is useful for people who wish to approach their emotional distress in a way that does not separate its psychological and spiritual dimensions. This approach is open to any manifestation of the sacred and is useful when traditional pastoral advice has not been helpful or when the transpersonal psyche appears in unusual ways. Some people who abhor organized religion nevertheless describe themselves as "spiritual" in the sense that they are concerned with a relationship to a hidden dimension of being and transcendent values. The Jungian approach suits this group because it is not burdened with traditional religious language. When a person is committed to an existing religious tradition, this approach can be helpful in deepening the person's commitment, if his or her material allows it to be cast in terms of the tradition. For this reason, the Jungian approach is popular among liberal Christians and Jews. Buddhists have also found the approach useful when it deals with material that is not be helped by the application of meditation techniques or other traditional teachings. The approach is contraindicated in psychotic and pre-psychotic people whose self-structures are too fragile to allow exploration of the unconscious.

CONCLUSION: A JUNGIAN COMMENTARY ON SPIRITUALITY WITHIN PSYCHOTHERAPY

A further apologia is in order here. Part of the difficulty faced by comparative studies in psychotherapy is that, from the point of view of any one theory, all the other approaches to psychotherapy seem to be incomplete. Accordingly, one may only write from a particular perspective—we all work in the service of our own myth. From the Jungian point of view, it does not matter if the practitioner's theoretical orientation pays little or no attention to the unconscious and its archetypal dimensions. Consciously felt or not, the transpersonal Self is in the room and will influence the outcome of the work, although its presence may be disguised, as we saw for example in the form of an idealizing transference when the Self, or the search for a divinity, is projected onto the therapist. It matters not if the overt undertaking is formal spiritual direction, cognitive behavioral therapy, psychoanalysis, or any modality in between. The Self influences the relational field within which the participants work and spontaneously prompts the participants by means of the unconscious. Even the fact that a patient is drawn to a particular therapist is often synchronistically important. The psyches of both participants become engaged in concerns of mutual importance—not simply because of induction, but because of the field effect of the Self that grips both participants. (See, for example, Spiegelman & Mansfield, 1996). The unconscious does not simply appear in the form of dreams, symptoms, and the transference; in the outer world, we experience the unconscious in the form of people and events with which we engage. This is so because we are not really separate from each other; we feel separate at the levels of the ego, the body, and the personality, but at the level of the transpersonal psyche consciousness is undivided—the Self is the same in all of us. We enter psychotherapy with a set of difficulties, but the direction taken by the work, in whatever mode, is often surprising, apparently because the Self has its own agenda and goal for the personality. It is well to become consciousness of this calling, because otherwise, Jung believed, we would be dragged to this goal. Thus it is that, within the Jungian perspective, the removal of symptoms as a final goal of therapy is an incomplete approach. The symptom is a wakeup call from the Self to greater consciousness. The process by which we become conscious of, and then embody, more and more of the potentials of the Self is actually an incarnation. The therapist's task is to facilitate this process for the patient, but the practitioner should not imagine that he or she is immune from the effects of the therapeutic relationship. Jung (1959/1975, p. 71) likened the interaction of therapist and patient to a chemical reaction, in which, if anything is to happen, both participants must be radically changed.

REFERENCES

Bobgan, M., & Bobgan, D. (1987). *Psychoheresy: The psychological seduction of Christianity*. Santa Barbara, CA: Eastgate.

Bollas, C. (1999). *The mystery of things*. New York: Routledge.

Borges, J. L. (1964). The God's script. In *Labyrinths*. New York: New Directions.

Bucke, R. M. (1989). *Cosmic consciousness*. Secausus, NJ: Citadel Press.

Christou, E. (1976). *The logos of the soul*. Zurich, Switzerland: Spring.

Corbett, L. (1996). *The religious function of the psyche*. New York: Routledge.

Corbett, L. (2000a). A depth psychological approach to the sacred. In D. P. Slattery & L. Corbett (Eds.), *Depth psychology, meditations in the field*. Eisiedeln, Switzerland: Daimon Verlag.

Corbett, L. (2000b). Jung's approach to the phenomenology of religious experience. In R. Brooke (Ed.), *Pathways into the Jungian world*. NY: Routledge.

Corbett, L., & Kugler, P. (1989). The self in Jung and Kohut. In *Dimensions of self experience: Progress in self psychology* (Vol. 5). Hillsdale, NJ: Analytic Press.

de Voogd, S. (1977). *C. G. Jung: Psychologist of the future, philosopher of the past* (pp. 175–182). Dallas, TX: Spring.

Edinger, E. (1984). *The creation of consciousness*. Toronto, Canada: Inner City Books.

Eigen, M. (1998). *The psychoanalytic mystic*. London: Free Association Press.

Hinton, D. (1999). *The selected poems of Po Chü-I*. New York: New Directions.

Ignatieff, M. (2000). *A life of Isaiah Berlin*. London: Random House.

Jung, C. G. (1966). *Collected works of C. G. Jung: Volume 7. Two essays in analytical psychology*. Princeton, NJ: Princeton University Press. (Original work published 1953)

Jung, C. G. (1969). Answer to Job. In *Collected works of C. G. Jung, Volume 11. Psychology and religion*. Princeton, NJ: Princeton University Press. (Original work published 1958)

Jung, C. G. (1973). *Letters* (Vol. 1; G. Adler & A. Jaffe, Eds., R. F. C. Hull, Trans). Princeton, NJ: Princeton University Press.

Jung, C. G. (1975a). *Letters* (Vol. 2; G. Adler & A. Jaffe, Eds., R. F. C. Hull, Trans). Princeton, NJ: Princeton University Press.

Jung, C. G. (1975b). Problems of modern psychotherapy. In *Collected works of C. G. Jung, Volume 16. The practice of psychotherapy*. Princeton, NJ: Princeton University Press. (Original work published 1959)

Jung, C. G. (1989). *Memories, dreams, reflections*. New York: Vintage Books. (Original work published 1963)

Kohut, H. (1971). *The analysis of the self*. New York: International Universities Press.

Milner, M. (1987). *Eternity's sunrise*. London: Virago.

Ogden, T. (1999). *Reverie and interpretation*. London: Karnac Books.

Otto, R. (1958). *Das Heilige* [The idea of the holy, 2nd ed.]. (J. W. Harvey, Trans.). London: Oxford University Press. (Original work published 1917)

Rizzuto, A.-M. (1998). *Why did Freud reject God?* New Haven, CT: Yale University Press.

Spiegelman, J. M., & Mansfield, V. (1996). On the physics and psychology of the transference as an interactive field. In J. M. Spiegelman (Ed.), *Psychotherapy as a mutual process*. Tempe, AZ: New Falcon Press.

Stein, M. (1995). Synchronicity and divine providence. In J. M. Spiegelman (Ed.), *Protestantism and Jungian psychology*. Tempe, AZ: New Falcon Press.

Stein, M. (1998). *Transformation: Emergence of the self*. College Station: Texas A&M University Press.

II

CONTEMPORARY APPROACHES

4

SPIRITUALLY ORIENTED COGNITIVE–BEHAVIORAL THERAPY

SIANG-YANG TAN AND W. BRAD JOHNSON

DESCRIPTION OF THE APPROACH

Although the concept of spirituality is often employed to describe a number of human experiences, we see *spirituality* as emphasizing personal experiences related to transcendence and the search for the sacred (Pargament, 1997). For example, among Christians, spirituality relates more specifically to the experience of communion or connection to God, Jesus, or the Holy Spirit. We see the psychological and spiritual dimensions of human experience as different, although at times overlapping. Neither the psychological nor spiritual dimension is fully reducible to the other, but we do view the spiritual dimension as ultimately having primacy. In our view, however, the effective spiritually oriented cognitive–behavioral psychotherapist will move comfortably between psychological interventions and spiritual counseling, depending on the specific client's presenting concerns and preferences. At times, a religious client may be strictly interested in symptom relief. At other times, a religious client may introduce concerns related to transcendence broadly or religious concerns more specifically. The ethical and competent spiritually oriented psychotherapist discerns these differences and responds accordingly.

Historical and Theoretical Basis

Cognitive–behavioral therapy (CBT) evolved from traditional behavior therapy during the 1960s. A number of factors contributed to the evolution of CBT as a major school of psychotherapy (Dobson & Block, 1988; also see Dobson & Dozois, 2001) including (a) dissatisfaction with strict stimulus–response (S-R; nonmediational) models of behavior, (b) rejection of the alternative to behaviorism—psychodynamic models, (c) development of information processing models of cognition that helped to explain certain clinical constructs such as anxiety and, ultimately, the emergence of a number of theorists and therapists who identified themselves as cognitive–behavioral in orientation (Beck, 1976; Ellis, 1962; Mahoney, 1974; Meichenbaum, 1977). The pioneers of CBT, Albert Ellis and Aaron Beck, were both trained psychoanalytically and both developed a theoretical perspective that assumed the existence of internal or covert cognitive events called thinking or cognition. They also held that these cognitive events mediate emotion and behavior and that such underlying cognitions are appropriate targets of intervention (Beck, 1976; Beck, Rush, Shaw, & Emery, 1979; Dobson & Block, 1988; Jones & Butman, 1991). A number of others influenced the development and elaboration of CBT (Bandura, 1977; Mahoney, 1974; Meichenbaum, 1977).

Today, CBT is a broad term incorporating a wide array of discrete and overlapping approaches that share three fundamental propositions: (a) cognitive activity affects behavior, (b) cognitive activity may be monitored and altered to produce relief from negative psychological symptoms, and (c) desired behavior change may be affected through shifting or modifying core dysfunctional schemas or assumptions (Dobson & Block, 1988; Propst, 1996). CBT therapies typically share several additional assumptions and practices (Craighead, Craighead, Kazdin, & Mahoney, 1994; Dobson & Block, 1988; Ellis, 2000b; Hollon & Beck, 1994). These common constructs include the following: (a) CBT is time limited and CBT therapists attempt to effect change rapidly, (b) CBT usually limits the target of change, (c) CBT is explicitly educative in nature, (d) CBT typically employs a range of both cognitive and behavioral principles and techniques, (e) clients are seen as the architects of their own misfortune—they largely cause their own disturbance, (f) although clients often attribute their disturbance to events, their own cognitive distortions and irrational beliefs actually cause disturbance, and (g) to experience relief and prevent future dysfunction, clients must learn to work at correcting distortions and disputing faulty beliefs.

Although all CBT approaches hold that thinking plays a causal role in the etiology and maintenance of most emotional disturbance, and although most CBT interventions attempt to produce change by influencing thinking (Hollon & Beck, 1994; Mahoney, 1977), there are notable differences among the primary schools of thought within CBT. The original CBT approaches, rational emotive therapy (RET) now called rational emotive behavior therapy (REBT; Ellis, 1962), and cognitive therapy (CT; Beck, 1976) serve as a good case in point. REBT postulates that emotional or behavioral upset is nearly always the result of core irrational beliefs or schemas (e.g., "I *must* be loved and approved of by everyone who is important to me"), and associated irrational demands and evaluations ("If people do not love me, it is catastrophic, and just shows that I am worthless"). REBT consistently targets these irrational beliefs as the primary focus of intervention (Ellis, 2000b; Ellis & Dryden, 1997). Cognitive Therapy, on the other hand, holds that humans often get themselves into emotional trouble because of misperceptions, misinterpretations, or dysfunctional idiosyncratic interpretation of situations (Beck & Weishaar, 2000). Cognitive therapists challenge clients to use empirical tests of the accuracy of their perceptions about events: "The patient's maladaptive conclusions [about self, others, and the world] are treated as testable hypotheses. Behavioral experiments and verbal procedures are used to examine alternative interpretations and to generate contradictory evidence that supports more adaptive beliefs and leads to therapeutic change" (Beck & Weishaar, 2000, p. 241). Whereas Ellis strives for philosophical conversion based on reason and logic ("let's assume she does hate your guts, why does that have to be catastrophic?"), Beck encourages a reliance on scientific empiricism to change misperceptions about events themselves ("How do you know she hates your guts? I'm not sure that conclusion is warranted. How can you test that thought more carefully?").

How can CBT techniques be differentiated from other psychotherapies (e.g., psychodynamic and interpersonal therapies)? A recent review of comparative psychotherapy process literature identified six distinctive activities of CBT therapists (Blagys & Hilsenroth, 2002) and they include (a) use of homework and outside-of-session activities, (b) active direction of session agenda and activities, (c) teaching skills (CBT therapists often espouse a highly psychoeducational approach, (d) emphasis on preparing for more effective future functioning, (e) provision of explicit information about CBT treatment so that clients have detailed information about their disorder and the rationale for treatment interventions, and (f) a cognitive intrapersonal focus (illogical or irrational beliefs are directly related to psychiatric symptoms and maladaptive behaviors).

The rapid ascension of CBT as a theory of change and a major approach to treatment has been facilitated by increasing demands for shorter and more cost-effective treatments as well as by the marked flexibility and adaptability of the model itself (Craighead et al., 1994). Additionally, CBT is among the most thoroughly researched and empirically supported forms of psychotherapy in existence today (Chambless & Ollendick, 2001; also see Tan, 2001). For all of these reasons, CBT has emerged as the predominant therapeutic orientation among psychotherapists during the last decade (Norcross, Karg, & Prochaska, 1997).

Spiritually Oriented CBT (SO-CBT)

The rise of CBT as a major treatment orientation has been paralleled by increasing interest in accommodating CBT to the worldview and spiritual experience of religious clients (Ellis, 2002a; Nielsen, Johnson, & Ellis, 2001; Propst, 1980, 1996; Tan, 1987). Jones and Butman (1991), for example, in reflecting on the tremendous compatibility between CBT and Christianity, noted, "Perhaps no other therapy approach so closely mirrors a biblical balance of cognition and action orientation as cognitive–behavioral therapy" (p. 218). These authors highlighted biblical support for the underlying CBT assumption that belief has tremendous implication for personal well-being (e.g., Phil. 4:8–9: "Whatever is true, whatever is noble, whatever is right, whatever is pure, whatever is lovely . . . think about such things . . . and the God of peace will be with you"). CBT is also congruent with the doctrine and writings of many other religions (Nielsen et al., 2001). Consider the following scriptures from Judaism (Prov. 23: "As a man thinketh in his heart, so is he") and Buddhism (Dhammapad 1.1: "All that we are is the result of what we have thought").

There are several reasons CBT is a particularly helpful, or as Albert Ellis has stated, an "elegant" approach to treating religious clients or clients with problems of a religious or spiritual nature (Ellis, 2000a; Johnson, 2001; Nielsen, Johnson, & Ridley, 2000; Propst, 1996). First, CBT is highly belief oriented and focuses on clients' foundational or core beliefs and assumptions. Clients from most religious traditions are familiar and comfortable with belief-oriented language and share the assumption that what one believes is an essential component of feeling and behavior. Second, the CBT emphasis on teaching and education is familiar to many religious clients who often respond well to homework assignments involving scripture reading or religiously integrated activities (e.g., imagery, relaxation, prayer). Finally, the CBT emphasis on modifying and transforming cognitions and beliefs and the hard work required to achieve growth and change are often highly appealing to religious people. Many of the doctrines, stories, and traditions of major religions emphasize changing mind, heart, or behavior. Prayer, fasting, memorization of scripture, and confessional rituals exemplify religious approaches to personal transformation (Nielsen et al., 2001).

Several authors have developed CBT approaches that accommodate or integrate secular techniques to the unique views and practices of religiously committed clients (Azhar & Varma, 1995a, 1995b; Azhar, Varma, & Dharap, 1994; Backus, 1985; Craigie & Tan, 1989; Hawkins, Tan, & Turk, 1999; Johnson, DeVries, Ridley, Pettorini, & Peterson, 1994; McMinn, 1991; Nielsen et al., 2001; Pecheur, & Edwards, 1984; Propst, 1980, 1988; Propst, Ostrom, Watkins, Dean, & Mashburn, 1992; Razali, Aminah, & Khan, 2002; Tan, 1987, 1996a, 1996b, 1999; Tan & Ortberg, 1995, 2004; Wright, 1986; also see McCullough, 1999; Worthington & Sandage, 2001). We call these spiritually oriented CBT (SO-CBT) approaches and each of them works to blend client religious belief with CBT assessment and intervention. When practicing from a SO-CBT perspective, practitioners adopt what Bergin (1980) termed *theistic realism*—they honor the client's views about God, the relationship of humans to God, and the possibility that spiritual forces influence behavior.

Those practicing from a spiritually oriented CBT perspective have utilized a number of specific interventions with religious clients. These include cognitive disputation using scriptural or other religious evidence to combat or argue against irrational and self-defeating beliefs (beliefs that are nearly always counter to the tenets of one's own faith), use of religious imagery to decrease anxiety or heighten comfort, and use of scripture reading or prayer in session or as adjuncts to other cognitive homework.

When it comes to cognitive disputation of problem beliefs, those practicing SO-CBT may address irrational thinking at either a general or specialized level (Johnson, 2001). In general disputation, a client's evaluative–demanding beliefs are challenged without challenging the client's unique religious views. For example, a client struggling with low frustration tolerance regarding God's apparent failure to answer a prayer may be asked, "Where is there any good evidence that you can't stand not having an answer from God?" In specialized disputation, a therapist with greater knowledge and expertise relative to the client's faith may dispute those religious beliefs or practices that are both dysfunctional and idiosyncratic or incongruent with the client's own identified religious culture or faith. For example, a specialized disputation with a Christian client with low frustration tolerance might be, "God says that "In this world, you will have tribulation" (suffering) [John 16:33]. So where exactly is it written that *you* will not?" DiGiuseppe, Robin, and Dryden (1990) pointed out that religious clients sometimes make incomplete or inaccurate interpretations of scripture, or *selective abstractions*. Thus, clients are not disturbed by religiousness per se, but by selectively abstracting certain elements of their religion to the exclusion of attending to others. Johnson (2001) offered an example of a cognitive disputation for this tendency in a self-damning (human-worth rating) client who believes he or she is going to hell: "Well, I understand that you believe this kind of transgression is especially damnable and that you are somehow worse than others as a result, but the Bible says that all have sinned and fall short of the glory of God [Rom. 3:23]. It seems that God doesn't think any of us are that special just because of the 'way' we sin" (p. 46).

Such disputations can be equally useful with clients from other religions. For example, a Buddhist client with poor frustration tolerance may be prone to self-statements such as "self-denial is unbearable," or "it is intolerable that I have such bad karma." This client might be reminded that Buddha himself struggled to learn to accept intense boredom, discomfort, and the agony of long-term reflection. But hard work and discomfort are inevitable features of the journey toward enlightenment. The therapist might inquire, "where is it written the Buddha says this should be easy for you?"

The Nature of the Relationship Between Psychology and Spirituality

Tan (1996b) has described two major models for integrating religion or spirituality and psychological therapy: implicit integration (a more covert model) and explicit integration (a more overt model) as two ends of a continuum:

> *Implicit integration* . . . refers to a more covert approach that does not initiate the discussion of religious or spiritual issues and does not openly, directly, or systematically use spiritual resources . . . *Explicit integration* . . . refers to a more overt approach that directly and systematically deals with spiritual or religious issues in therapy, and uses spiritual resources like prayer, Scripture or sacred texts, referrals to church or other religious groups or lay counselors, and other religious practices. (p. 368)

The crucial factor in integrating religion or spirituality in clinical practice is *intentional integration*, with the therapist using implicit or explicit integration or both, moving appropriately along the continuum, depending on the client, and his or her problems and needs. Such integration is conducted in a professionally competent, ethically responsible, and clinically sensitive way, always with the clear informed consent of the client, and for the growth and benefit of the client. The therapist therefore does not force his or her beliefs or spiritual practices on the client. Tan (1996b) has pointed out that explicit integration may be more easily adopted by cognitive–behavior therapists and humanistic–existential therapists than by psychodynamic or psychoanalytically oriented therapists, because CBT especially is already a more structured, directive, and explicit approach.

Of the two common models of the relationship between psychology and spirituality, our approach is closer to the model that states "spirituality parallels psychological growth but it does not depend on it" rather than the model that states "spiritual growth builds on and follows psychological growth." In the section that follows, we offer an example of integrating CBT with a Christian spiritual approach. We do so because the majority of writing on integrative CBT has been done in the Christian tradition and we are most familiar with this approach. There are several other examples of the integration of CBT with the religious and spiritual concerns and traditions of Muslim, Hindu, Jewish, and other clients (e.g., see Lovinger, 1984; Nielsen et al., 2001; Razali et al., 2002; Richards, & Bergin, 2000).

A more specific biblical or Christian approach to CBT (see Tan, 1999) will include the following as described by Tan (1987):

1. Emphasize the primacy of agape love (1 Cor. 13) and the need to develop a warm, empathic, and genuine relationship with the client.

2. Deal more adequately with the past, especially unresolved developmental issues or childhood traumas, and will use inner healing or healing of memories judiciously and appropriately (see Tan, 1996a, for a seven-step model for inner healing prayer, pp. 371–374).

3. Pay special attention to the meaning of spiritual, experiential, and even mystical aspects of life and faith, according to God's wisdom as revealed in scripture and by the Holy Spirit's teaching ministry (John 14:26), and will not overemphasize the rational, thinking dimension, although biblical, propositional truth will still be given its rightful place of importance.

4. Focus on how problems in thought and behavior may often (not always, because of other factors, e.g., organic, or biblical) underlie problem feelings (Prov. 23:7; Rom. 12:1–2; Phil. 4:8; Eph. 4:22–24) and will use biblical truth (John 8:32), not relativistic values, to conduct cognitive restructuring and behavioral change interventions.

5. Emphasize the Holy Spirit's ministry in bringing about inner healing as well as cognitive, behavioral, and emotional change. It will use prayer and affirmation of God's Word (or scriptures, see Kruis, 2000; Miller, 2002) in facilitating dependence on the Lord to produce deep and lasting personality change and will be cautious not to encourage sinful self-sufficiency inadvertently (cf. Phil 4:13).

6. Pay more attention to larger contextual factors such as familial, societal, religious, and cultural influences and hence will utilize appropriate community resources in therapeutic interventions, including the church as a body of believers and fellow "priests" to one another (1 Cor. 12; I Peter 2:5, 9).

7. Use only those techniques that are consistent with biblical truth and will not simplistically use whatever techniques work. It will reaffirm scriptural perspectives on suffering, including the possibility of the "blessings of mental anguish," with the ultimate goal of counseling being holiness or Christ-likeness (Rom. 8:29), not necessarily temporal happiness. Such a goal will include, however, being more open to receiving God's love and grace and thereby growing to be more Christ-like, and overcoming mental anguish due to unbiblical, erroneous beliefs (i.e., misbeliefs).

8. Utilize rigorous outcome research methodology before making definitive statements about the superiority of CBT. (pp. 108–109)

Other spiritual approaches to CBT will likewise emphasize similar spiritual or religious perspectives. For example, a Muslim approach to CBT would emphasize the authority of the Quran (or Koran, the Holy Scriptures for Muslims), the importance of prayer for relaxation, and discussion of religious issues relevant to the Muslim patient (see Worthington & Sandage, 2001).

Therapist's Skills and Attributes

To achieve success, CBT therapists must do three tasks well: (a) establish a collaborative therapeutic relationship, (b) have a sound case conceptualization, and (c) select and apply appropriate techniques (Dobson & Shaw, 1993). In terms of therapist skills and attributes, Dobson and Shaw (1993) recommended that CBT practitioners in training be selected on the basis of interpersonal warmth, lack of personal psychopathology, motivation to learn CBT techniques, ability to tolerate negative client affective states, and abstract conceptual abilities. To these criteria, we would add respect for client religious beliefs, traditions, and spiritual experience; an assumption of theistic realism (Bergin, 1980); and both interest and skill in the accommodation of established CBT approaches to the unique religious surround of theistically or spiritually inclined clients.

CBT is characterized by a more active and directive stance on the part of the therapist. Although CBT therapists have occasionally been criticized for being superficial or mechanical, reviews of empirical studies reveal that CBT therapists employ relationship skills (Rogerian empathy, positive regard, nonpossessive warmth, and genuineness) at least as much as therapists from other orientations (Keijsers, Schaap, & Hoogduin, 2000).

To be effective at SO-CBT, CBT therapists are additionally willing to accommodate and explicitly integrate religious practices, beliefs, and scriptural material into traditional cognitive–behavioral techniques when such integration appears likely to help religious clients and when these clients have given informed consent for spiritually oriented interventions. During their training, effective therapists will be well trained in CBT theory and practice and will develop supervised expertise in the timing and application of specific CBT interventions. They will also demonstrate competence with regard to using client religious and spiritual beliefs and practices (e.g., inner healing prayer or healing of memories and use of scripture) to enhance health and reduce distress. The personal faith perspective of the therapist may influence the effectiveness of SO-CBT. Although Propst et al. (1992) found that the nonreligious therapists were the most effective in delivering the protocol, it may be preferable for the therapist and the client to be of the same faith—particularly when the client holds strong beliefs about the necessity of working with a same-faith professional (Bergin, 1980; Ellis, 2000a). Further empirical investigation is required to assess the importance of spiritual values similarity in the therapeutic relationship.

A final dimension of therapist skill relates to ethical sensitivity bearing on client religious and spiritual views and practices (Johnson, 2001). SO-

CBT therapists must be sensitive to avoid two primary ethical problems with religious clients. First, they must not ignore or trivialize client religious beliefs—no matter how unfamiliar or objectionable. Second, ethical therapists guard against overt or covert efforts to undermine or dispute the clients' fundamental religious commitments. Although SO-CBT practitioners may address the negative effects of idiosyncratic religious views or the incongruence of such beliefs with the doctrine or scripture of the client's own religious community, disputing fundamental faith commitments raises ethical concern.

Strengths and Limitations

A particular strength of the CBT approach in general is the empirical evidence standing in support of the fact that cognitive appraisals of events can effect responses to those events and that there is clinical value in modifying the content of these appraisals (Beck et al., 1979; Dobson & Block, 1988; Lazarus & Folkman, 1984; Mahoney, 1974; Meichenbaum, 1977). Currently, there is almost no disorder, type of emotional distress, or type of client for which CBT interventions are considered inappropriate (Craighead et al., 1994). CBT therapies have been shown to be efficacious in the treatment of clinical depression, generalized anxiety disorder, obsessive–compulsive disorder, panic disorder, phobias, posttraumatic stress disorder, eating disorders, addictive behaviors, marital and sexual dysfunction, behavioral and disruptive disorders of childhood, and in various applications within behavioral medicine such as preparation for noxious medical procedures and coping with chronic pain (Craighead et al., 1994; Hollon & Beck, 1994; Persons, Davidson, & Tompkins, 2001). More than any other approach to psychotherapy, CBT has been evaluated in randomized controlled trials (Persons et al., 2001; also see Chambless & Ollendick, 2001). With specific reference to the treatment of depression, CBT has been shown to be as effective as antidepressant medication and interpersonal therapy or behavior therapy, as well as superior to antidepressant medication alone, in preventing relapse in depressed patients. It is also cost-effective (Persons et al., 2001).

Spiritually oriented or religiously accommodated CBT in particular has also been shown to be effective in outcome research with depressed religious clients. In fact, CBT is the only approach to therapy that has been empirically supported with religious populations (Worthington, Kurusu, McCullough, & Sandage, 1996). In three studies using religiously accommodated versions of Beck's Cognitive Therapy for depression (Beck et al., 1979), Christian clients made significant clinical gains when cognitive therapy included religious imagery and religiously-oriented challenges to cognitive distortions (Pecheur & Edwards, 1984; Propst, 1980, Propst et al., 1992). Similarly, Christian clients receiving a Christian version of Ellis's REBT showed significant decreases in depression during two brief treatment outcome studies (Johnson & Ridley, 1992; Johnson et al., 1994).

Overall, however, these five studies of individual psychotherapy found that religiously accommodated CBT was equal to (and only occasionally superior to) secular CBT with religious, Christian clients in reducing depression, but generally superior to secular CBT in increasing spiritual well-being (see Worthington & Sandage, 2001). More recently, a Christian-accommodative study using both individual and group therapy with Christian adult inpatients with clinical depression found that patients who chose the Christian CBT program ($n = 18$) did as well as those who chose the standard or secular Beckian CBT program ($n = 11$) in significantly reducing depression, but the Christian CBT group had greater improvement in spiritual well-being compared with the standard CBT group. Unfortunately, the two groups or treatments were not comparable because the Christian CBT group had an average of 7.5 days of inpatient treatment versus the 5.4 days for the standard CBT group. Also, the patients in the two groups selected their own treatments and therefore were not randomly assigned to their treatments (Hawkins et al., 1999).

Worthington and Sandage (2001) also recently summarized the findings of three Muslim-accommodative individual psychotherapy studies that compared a Muslim approach to CBT with a standard treatment consisting of supportive psychotherapy plus medication. The Muslim CBT approach added religious, Muslim CBT (e.g., reading verses from the Holy Quran, encouraging prayers of relaxation, and discussing religious issues relevant to the patient) to the standard treatment. The three studies respectively involved Muslim patients with generalized anxiety disorder (Azhar et al., 1994), dysthymic disorder (Azhar & Varma, 1995b), and major depression that included grieving the loss of a loved one (Azhar & Varma, 1995a). The results in all three studies showed that supplementary Muslim CBT led to symptom reduction (whether anxiety or depression) beyond that produced by the standard treatment of supportive psychotherapy plus medication, although there were some methodological problems with these studies.

In addition to these six studies of Christian CBT and three studies of Muslim CBT (see Worthington & Sandage, 2001), another more recent outcome study showed that Muslim CBT that incorporated readings from the Holy Quran produced more rapid improvement in Muslim patients with generalized anxiety disorder (Razali et al., 2002). There are therefore now 10 studies (6 Christian and 4 Muslim) that provide some empirical support for the efficacy of SO-CBT with religious clients, especially those with clinical depression and, to some extent, those with generalized anxiety disorder.

Beyond established efficacy, SO-CBT approaches are also brief, problem-focused, and highly collaborative approaches to treatment. They therefore are appealing to many professional therapists and lay counselors, as well as to clients who appreciate effective, efficient, and ethical ways of helping people. Managed care and health maintenance organizations that provide reimbursements for psychotherapy services also prefer efficient forms of therapy and now demand greater accountability and empirical support for therapeutic interventions used by therapists. Long-term, insight- or psychoanalytically oriented therapists may not find CBT or SO-CBT as appealing. Clients are encouraged and even required to be actively engaged in their own treatment, and many clients find this emphasis on therapeutic work both reassuring and empowering. The psychoeducational emphasis of CBT is designed to equip clients with enduring skills for self-application and therefore prevention of subsequent disturbance. As discussed earlier, CBT relies on a body of empirical research to substantiate its claims and to establish effective clinical procedures. Present limitations concern the paucity or small number of controlled empirical studies demonstrating the efficacy of distinctively spiritually oriented CBT and opportunities for training and supervision in many graduate programs.

Indications and Contraindications

As already pointed out, SO-CBT has been found to be effective in the treatment of depression and, to a certain extent, anxiety with religious clients (i.e., Christians and Muslims). Spiritually oriented CBT approaches may also be appropriate or indicated for the treatment of many other disorders for which secular or standard CBT has already been found to be efficacious. As is true of most other therapeutic approaches, CBT may be less effective in the treatment of psychotic problems and personality disorders.

Tan (1996a) also noted the following cautions and contraindications regarding the use of spiritual interventions in psychotherapy, which are relevant to SO-CBT in particular:

> With more severely disturbed or psychotic clients . . . after better control of psychotic symptoms is achieved with medications or other treatments, some of the spiritual disciplines may then be helpful. Prayer with a patient with schizophrenia that is relatively well controlled with appropriate antipsychotic medications, can still be a very helpful and comforting experience for such a patient, who may also have a deep commitment to and love for God.
>
> While the use of spiritual disciplines seems widely applicable in psychotherapeutic practice and mental health settings (e.g., in inpatient treatment groups), the spiritual disciplines can also have negative or harmful effects if applied indiscriminately to all clients with all kinds of problems. For example, clients from very harsh and legalistic Christian backgrounds where they were forced to practice certain spiritual disciplines such as prayer and Scripture reading daily, may not benefit as much from such disciplines until they have been helped to see and experience God and his loving grace more deeply. They may even be in active rebellion against God and such spiritual disciplines at the moment. Another example is when inner healing prayer involving images of God as Father

or Jesus hugging the client is used insensitively or inappropriately with clients who have been sexually abused by their human fathers. They may have very negative reactions initially to such images. Careful history taking, diagnosis, assessment, and discernment are still crucial for the effective and ethical application . . . of the spiritual disciplines to mental health settings and the practice of psychotherapy. (p. 24)

Cultural and Gender Considerations

Certain ethnically diverse populations, such as Asian Americans, may prefer a more directive, situationally oriented, structured, and problem-solving approach to therapy, such as CBT (see Tan & Dong, 2000). Asian American clients who are religious, especially if they are Christian, usually will prefer a biblical, Christian approach to CBT. It is essential, however, when practicing SO-CBT with religious clients to avoid asking them to engage in behaviors that would violate important religious beliefs, norms, or commitments (Abramowitz, 2001). It should be noted, as Hall (2001) has pointed out, that the efficacy of empirically supported treatments (ESTs), many of which are CBT interventions, has not received adequate empirical support specifically with ethnic minority populations. More research is needed.

The recent emphasis on using ESTs has also been critiqued on other grounds (see Tan, 2001, 2002), with Beutler (2000) specifically proposing going beyond empirically supported treatments to empirically informed principles of treatment selection. More recently, Norcross (2002) underscored the need for greater attention to be paid to empirically supported therapeutic relationships (ESRs) or psychotherapy relationships that work (see Tan, 2003a).

Sue and Sue (2003) described other cultural and gender considerations relevant to effective counseling with a culturally diverse clientele. For example, with regard to counseling women, they provided several helpful guidelines for clinical practice, including the following:

> Recognize that most counseling theories are male-centered and require modification when working with women. For example, cognitive approaches can focus on societal messages; employ skills that may be particularly appropriate for the needs of women, such as assertiveness training, gender role analysis, and consciousness raising groups. As with any approach in which traditional perspectives are challenged, clients need to understand the consequences of making changes; and help clients realize the impact of gender expectations and societal definitions of attractiveness on the mental health of women so that they do not engage in self-blame. (p. 420)

In SO-CBT with Christian clients in particular, it may be necessary at times to clarify what the scripture actually teaches about women and their significant role in ministry so that traditional gender biases against women can be dealt with. This must be done gently and sensitively, however, especially with religious clients from fundamentalist backgrounds, for example, by using appropriate wording that focuses more on the significance of women's ministries rather than on women's ordination per se.

Expected Future Developments and Directions

A great deal more research is required to evaluate the efficacy of SO-CBT with specific clinical disorders and specific religious groups. To date, six studies have been conducted with Christian clients and four with Muslim clients. Furthermore, it is unclear which of the varied spiritual CBT interventions (e.g., cognitive disputation, religious imagery, prayer) are most useful, and under which circumstances. It will be particularly important to expand the literature bearing on the application of SO-CBT with Jewish, Hindu, Buddhist, and other religious clients, in addition to the Christian and Muslim clients already studied. Because SO-CBT often helps clients to tie therapeutic gain to religious and spiritual practice and belief, it is also expected that research will show these approaches to be more enduring than a cognitive–behavioral approach that neglects salient spiritual dimensions of the client's life. The more specific integration of *spiritual direction* into psychotherapy, including SO-CBT, will continue to receive greater attention, within appropriate ethical guidelines, which include obtaining informed consent from the client and making sure that a particular spiritual intervention, such as spiritual direction, is relevant to the treatment of the clinical disorder or problem presented by the client (see Tan, 2003b). Finally, more work will continue to be done in developing both CBT (e.g., see White, 2001) and SO-CBT (e.g., see Tan & Dong, 2001) interventions for chronic medical or health problems.

CASE EXAMPLE OF THE APPROACH

Client Demographics, Relevant History, and Presenting Concern

Grace was a 23-year-old single White female and first-year seminary student. A recent university graduate (with highest honors), she hailed from the Midwest and from a very close-knit Presbyterian family. An only child, Grace described herself as a "high achiever" from an early age. Active in sports, various clubs, and church activities, Grace was reasonably popular with her peers and beloved by teachers who saw her as a serious student and perpetual hard worker. Grace was elected student-body vice president her senior year and landed a scholarship at a top Midwest university. She was also active in church youth activities and had been confirmed in the Presbyterian Church at the customary ninth-grade juncture.

Grace was traditional but not particularly evangelical in her Christian beliefs and practices. She felt strongly connected to her family's long-standing Presbyterian traditions and doctrinal beliefs and was most comfortable with the more staid approach to worship and practice characteristic of this denomination. Most of her good friends had been church members, and during college, she had been very active in a local Presbyterian church. Grace woke early each day for scripture reading, meditation, and prayer. She was punctilious in church attendance, tithing, and service in several church-sponsored ministries (Habitat for Humanity and services to the homeless). During her junior year in college, she had decided to attend seminary and pursue a divinity degree with the purpose of eventual ordination as a pastor. She had been accepted to each of the five seminaries to which she had applied and was aware that her parents, extended family, and members of her home church were both delighted and quite proud of her accomplishments and pastoral aspirations.

In the spring of her first year at seminary, Grace responded to an advertisement for brief counseling posted by the seminary's counseling clinic. The ad specifically mentioned assistance for depression and anxiety. On her intake forms, Grace mentioned both social anxiety of 6 months' duration and depression of 3 months' duration. During October of her first semester in the Master's of Divinity Program, Grace had been startled to find herself feeling extremely anxious before presentations in class. On several occasions, this anxiety had fueled unpleasant speaking experiences that she later described as "meltdowns," meaning that she experienced near-panic while speaking and felt that others saw her as excessively anxious and "weird" as a result. Her symptoms were most intense in a communication class (a prelude to formal preaching courses) and she began to experience extreme anxiety more than a week before each presentation. Toward the end of the semester, Grace began to experience extreme anxiety in any class or church situation in which she would become the focus of attention as a speaker or performer (she also played piano in church). Over the Christmas break, she had become increasingly depressed about her anxiety and had begun to question whether she was "cut out" for the ministry after all. Her depression worsened when the spring semester commenced and her anxiety continued and even increased. By the time she sought counseling, Grace had dropped a class that required oral presentations and began to feel increasingly "disabled" and unlikely to succeed in her chosen vocation.

Relationship of Therapist and Client

I (WBJ) treated Grace for anxiety and depression in the seminary's psychological services center. Grace understood that I was a clinical psychologist, a Christian, and a professional who specialized in brief interventions. Because she had responded to an ad for time-limited REBT, Grace understood that our work together would run for a maximum of eight sessions with one follow-up session scheduled 3 months after treatment termination. She also understood that treatment could be continued with another clinic practitioner in the event that additional treatment was indicated or desired. Although many seminary and Christian college students have been especially careful to inquire about my religious faith at the outset of therapy, Grace did not address this issue, nor did she request that we pray together in the session—something other Christian clients occasionally do. Although she had responded to an ad for "Christian"-oriented CBT, it was clear in the initial session that Grace was emotionally distressed and primarily concerned with finding a way to lower her anxiety.

Assessment: Rationale and Type of Data Collected

REBT, like most CBT approaches to therapy, views assessment as an active–directive process and as something that is ongoing throughout treatment. Not only are CBT practitioners interested in accurate assessment of general pathology and specific symptom distress, they are uniquely interested in identification of a client's specific pattern of (a) activating event, (b) irrational belief or cognitive distortion, and (c) subsequent emotional disturbance. Before her first session, Grace completed a detailed client history and biographical form (including a sentence-completion questionnaire), and three formal psychological measures. These included (a) the SCL-90-R (Derogatis, 1977), a multidimensional 90-item self-report symptom inventory designed to reflect the psychological symptom patterns of psychiatric patients; (b) the Beck Depression Inventory (BDI; Beck, Ward, Mendelson, Mock, & Erbaugh, 1961), a 21-item self-report scale constructed to measure clinical depression; and (c) the Automatic Thoughts Questionnaire (ATQ-30; Hollon & Kendall, 1980). She also completed the Spiritual Well-Being Scale (SWB; Ellison, 1983), which measures both religious and existential well-being as two major components of spiritual well-being, with an overall score for spiritual well-being.

Grace's background questionnaire revealed much of what is reported at the outset of this case study. Additionally, Grace denied any history of previous psychological disturbance and denied any previous mental health treatment. She did acknowledge a history of "perfectionism" and rather stringent self-expectations for high performance. There was no apparent family diathesis for psychiatric disturbance, and Grace reported good physical health, strong Christian commitment, and an interest in blending faith and treatment. Her score on the SCL-90-R revealed clinically elevated scores on the obsessive–compulsive, interpersonal sensitivity, depression, and anxiety scales. Her scores suggested moderate feelings of depression and anxiety as well as acute self-consciousness and a tendency toward obsessive rumination. The Global Severity Index of this measure (a general index of symptom distress) indicated moderate clinical distress when compared with other psychiatric outpatients. Grace received a BDI score of 21 suggesting mild to moderate clinical depression, and an ATQ-30 score of 77, indicating a moderate tendency to engage in depressotypic cognitive rumination (e.g., "I hate myself" or "I'm a failure"). Several of Grace's responses to the sentence completion questionnaire had some assessment value (e.g., to me the future looks "gray unless I get over this," my greatest weakness "is my inability to trust God completely and give up this panic," I know its silly but I'm afraid of "letting everyone down"). Her overall score on the SWB was 82 at the beginning of treatment.

During the initial session, an REBT assessment revealed that a specific activating event (A) generally preceded episodes of extreme (paniclike) anxiety (C). The common A was speaking or otherwise performing (e.g., playing the piano) in front of others. She reported that the first episode occurred in her communication class and took her completely by surprise (she had never experienced more than minor nervousness, or "butterflies" as she described it, prior to speaking or performing). Symptoms during recent episodes of anxiety included sweating, trembling, difficulty concentrating, racing heart, profound social embarrassment, and a strong drive to escape the situation.

CBT clinicians assume that, contrary to the client's assumption, A does not directly cause C, but rather, one or more irrational and dysfunctional beliefs (Ibs) enter in and cause emotional disturbance. These Ibs are typically demands (stated as dogmatic "musts," "shoulds," "ought to's," and "have to's"), or evaluations evidenced in global ratings of self or others, "awfulizing," and low frustration tolerance. Like many REBT clients, Grace initially had difficulty articulating her primary Ibs, instead focusing on the qualities of the speaking task or context (A) that were most threatening to her. To this I responded, "Yes, but if we agree that one or two people in your class do not experience any anxiety when speaking, and several others experience only minor nervousness, then it must not be just the demand to speak, but something more. What are you telling yourself *about* speaking in front of others to get yourself anxious?" Grace acknowledged that there were several irrational thoughts at play in this situation (e.g., "I *must* not get nervous," "it will be *awful* if they see me tremble or stutter," "*I can't stand* feeling anxious like this"). Furthermore, two of her primary Ibs were religious in nature (e.g., "I *must* model God's peace for others," and "if I can't just 'let go and let God,' it shows I am spiritually cut off").

As is often the case, Grace had developed a secondary emotional problem (C^2) as a result of the first. Specifically, her bouts of anxiety (C^1) had become the activating event (A) for mild to moderate clinical depression (C^2). Thus, because she had not been able to reduce her social anxiety, she had become depressed about her anxiety. She had attempted to use calming prayer and recitation of scripture during these episodes but her anxiety had not diminished. Thus, in part, her depression was linked to a belief that she was failing spiritually as well as psychologically when unable to speak calmly in public. Grace was able to articulate specific depression-causing beliefs and cognitive self-statements. These included (a) "I *must* not be so anxious and feel so out-of-control," (b) if I am disabled by this anxiety, it just shows I am *worthless*, (c) with God's help, I *should* be able to conquer this!"

Grace presented as spiritually mature, flexible yet devoutly committed to her Christian faith, and open to exploring areas of belief that may be selectively abstracted or based on an incomplete or skewed rendering of scripture. She was able to describe the months preceding therapy as a time of great spiritual challenge and admitted fleeting questions about why God appeared to ignore her fervent prayers for equanimity in the face of anxiety-provoking social situations. She demonstrated insight regarding her tendency to perceive anxiety as an indication of spiritual weakness or failing.

Diagnostic and Clinical Conceptualization

Following a review of the assessment materials and data gathered during the extended intake session, the following *DSM–IV* diagnosis was developed to conceptualize Grace's presentation in formal diagnostic terms:

Axis I 300.23 Social Phobia
    309.0 Adjustment Disorder with Depressed Mood
Axis II Obsessive–Compulsive Personality Traits
Axis III No Diagnosis
Axis IV Recent difficulties with social performance, fear of failing in seminary
Axis V GAF = 65 (current), 90 (last year)

Grace presented as a socially anxious and dysphoric first-year seminary student who had experienced her first episode of extreme social anxiety during a class oral presentation. Grace presented as very intelligent, quite high in need for achievement, and obsessive–compulsive in her undergirding personality structure. Grace was driven, self-motivated, and used to exerting control over all facets of her life. As an only child, she additionally carried a self-imposed burden for pleasing her parents and, to a large extent, God. During the 2 months preceding therapy, she had grown increasingly depressed about her inability to "get over" her anxiety. She began to question her own spiritual maturity and wondered whether her emotional problems were an indication that she had either displeased or grown distant from God. At my request, Grace scheduled a thorough physical examination to rule out any physiological etiology for her anxiety. This was completed during the second week of treatment and all results were negative.

Treatment Goals, Process, and Intervention Strategies

As noted earlier in this chapter, REBT focuses on the mediating effects of belief on emotions and behavior. In the case of dysfunctional emotional states, REBT posits that the client's tendency toward extreme and irrational evaluations and demands (irrational philosophies) tend to fuel disturbance. Spiritually oriented REBT is sensitive to the way in which religious or spiritual belief and practice may shape or influence dysfunctional emotions and works to incorporate faith-congruent, and faith-enhancing scriptures and practices as tools for therapeutic change.

In Grace's case, we quickly agreed to begin therapy with her primary emotional problem (anxiety) because her secondary problem (depression about her anxiety) was not particularly acute, because she did not believe her depressed mood would inhibit her work on the anxiety problem, and because she was extremely motivated to reduce her anxiety. In other cases, a client's secondary emotional problem may inhibit work on the initial difficulty. In religious clients, the secondary problem frequently has some connection to shame or guilt ("I must be a disappointment to God," and "If only I were stronger in my faith, this wouldn't be happening").

During the initial intake session, Grace was introduced to the REBT approach and demonstrated an affinity for the idea that her own beliefs largely dictated her emotional reactions to situations. This may have appealed to her strong needs for control and self-efficacy. After identifying the primary A (speaking in front of others), the notable C (extreme anxiety), and several specific demanding and evaluative beliefs (Ibs) related to A, several general disputations were used to show Grace the process of disputing irrational beliefs, and to reinforce the connection between belief and emotional consequence (known as the "B-C connection"). Examples of religion-neutral disputations for Grace's Ibs included the following: (a) empirical, "where is it written that you, Grace, cannot or must not be anxious?" (b) logical, " if you are anxious, how does it make sense for you to demand that you not be?" (c) pragmatic, "help me understand how your belief or demand that you not be as you are is helping you to get what you want (including lower anxiety)." Although REBT therapists may use a number of disputation styles, Grace responded especially well to Socratic questioning (e.g., "help me understand," or "I'm not clear why . . ."). In addition to this Socratic style, I also offered some didactic disputations (e.g., "physiological evidence indicates that almost nobody dies giving speeches, even people who get themselves very anxious"), and humorous disputations (e.g., "I know you believe your anxiety before a speech is *awful*, or worse than 100% bad, but isn't it true that it would be even worse if you had convulsions and seizures and projectile vomiting up in front of everyone? So, isn't it fair to say your current anxiety is actually less than 100% bad, and certainly less than awful?"). After the initial two sessions, Grace showed some initial relief and stated an enhanced sense of hope that "things would get better." She also showed good understanding and acceptance of the REBT therapy model.

Because Grace was devoutly committed to a Christian view of the world and demonstrated an abiding personal faith in God and Christ, I began to incorporate elements of Christian doctrine and scripture into cognitive disputations of Grace's primary irrational beliefs. In such general accommodation of technique to faith (Johnson, 2001), the spiritually oriented therapist works to blend faith and treatment. In SO-CBT, the client must be helped to ask the question, "how is it that my *style* of thinking about God, self, and faith (*evaluative* and *demanding*) is getting me distressed?" Grace acknowledged a strong preference for using her faith in therapy.

For her awfulizing about anxiety, Grace found several disputations helpful (e.g., "remind me how it is that rating your situation as catastrophic is helping you to keep your focus on God and serve Him more effectively? Job lost his wife, his children, and his property. He had painful boils covering his body. If his situation was 100% bad, where would your classroom anxiety fall on the scale?"). For her demanding that she "get better" and "stop fretting," Grace found several disputations useful (e.g., "God saw the good which would come from His son's death and Job's suffering. God sees things about our unpreferred circumstances that we cannot. Instead of stubbornly demanding that things be different than they are, what might God want to hear from you instead?").

Although Grace found these cognitive disputations useful, it became clear that the most pressing irrational belief was the view that she could not tolerate being so anxious in front of peers and church members and that the humiliation she routinely suffered during bouts of social anxiety was simply unbearable. Therefore, much of our time together was spent disputing her low frustration tolerance. Some of the disputations focused on modifying her poor frustration tolerance included the following: (a) "If God created you, understands your capacities, and has allowed you to end up in this situation, He must believe that you *can* stand it!" (b) "The apostle Paul begged God to remove his 'thorn in the flesh [2 Cor.]. He suffered and yet chose to tolerate his discomfort to keep serving God." and (c) "Imagine that God appeared to you and explained that He needed you to tolerate feeling anxious for an important reason. Could you stand it then?"

In the third through the sixth sessions, Grace began to see that she in fact could stand far more distress and suffering than would ever be caused by social anxiety. She further developed insight and acceptance regarding the idea that demanding the anxiety dissipate instantly, and catastrophizing the experience of being anxious were both counterproductive and largely counter to her own religious beliefs. As Grace learned the REBT process, we tried alternative cognitive interventions such as role-plays in which Grace would take the rational–biblical perspective and I would take the role of her irrational side. I would then make irrational demands and statements likely to generate social anxiety while she was encouraged to dispute these claims *vigorously* with her favorite rational alternative statements. Because of her capacity for humor, Grace also found humorous exaggeration helpful in disputation. For example, on one occasion, I role-played God and asked her to dispute this claim: "Because Grace is feeling anxious at times, she is entirely worthless to me and a deep source of disappointment. In fact, I God, can't stand thinking of Grace getting anxious, it upsets me too much!" This of course struck Grace as utterly absurd and quite counter to the entire New Testament witness to God's unconditional love.

In addition to social anxiety, Grace also struggled with shame and depression about her anxiety and her perceived failure to perform adequately in performance situations. Because these secondary symptoms were driven largely by irrational self-rating (self-damning) beliefs, faith-integrative disputations for self-rating were helpful disputations for Grace during our final sessions together. Some of these disputations were theological ("If you are God's creation, how does it make sense for you to call yourself worthless or disappointing to God?"), some were based on religious evidence ("What did Jesus say about the worth of sinners? The lost sheep? The lost coins? The prodigal son? What do these parables [all in Luke 15] say about your worth even when you get yourself so anxious you can't speak the way you'd prefer?"), some focused on the dysfunctional nature of her self-rating ("When you call yourself an 'idiot' or 'pathetic' for feeling nervous before a speech or performance, is it actually helping you to feel calmer and focus more on the calming presence of God?"), and, finally, some self-rating disputations were designed to offer religiously congruent alternative beliefs ("It seems to me that when you get anxious and feel distressed, God is giving you an opportunity to experience His comfort and grace, Grace! You have always excelled and performed with unusual competence in every area. I wonder if God needed to get your attention and remind you that you need Him?").

In addition to these cognitive interventions, Grace also agreed to work at several shame-attacking exercises (Ellis & Dryden, 1997). Similar to the behavioral technique of flooding, this REBT intervention emphasizes frustration tolerance and in vivo exposure to feared situations (typically situations prone to eliciting anxiety and shame). Shame attacking is especially useful for clients such as Grace who present with unrealistically exaggerated negative reactions to social situations. The exercise involves asking the client to deliberately act "shamefully" in public to work at self-acceptance and toleration of discomfort. Initially, Grace agreed to matter-of-factly tell her parents, peers, and even her professors that she was petrified about speaking in public. Although this was very difficult for her and although she did not tell all of her professors, she experienced some relief at diluting the secrecy and seriousness of her experience. In the sixth session, Grace agreed (with some reluctance) to stand up in the one class in which she was required to speak occasionally and give a short impromptu speech about the nature of performance anxiety, how it had diminished her interaction, and how she was working against her tendency to avoid speaking. Although she felt quite anxious during this experience, she was able to practice some covert disputing of her Ibs both before and following the speech. To her surprise, she also received a short ovation from the class (led by the professor) and subsequently reported feeling far less threatened about speaking in front of a group that understood her anxiety.

Finally, Grace found imagery to be a useful tool. Most CBT approaches to anxiety incorporate imagery techniques. In rational emotive imagery, the client is asked to imagine a feared situation, to generate the negative emotions typically accompanying this situation, and then to modify the image and the emotions using cognitive disputation of self-talk and belief. Grace found that the most calming and helpful approach to imagery involved imaging Jesus sitting with his hand on her back before speaking, then rising with her as she stood to speak, and smiling reassuringly at her as she spoke. In her image, it was obvious that nothing about her performance would possibly affect Jesus' love and the entire image was deeply reassuring. She also included praying to Jesus and thanking him. After practicing this technique of religious imagery and prayer several times in session, Grace was asked to practice it several times each day at home, as well as just before and during her shame-attacking behavioral assignments.

Course of Treatment and Frequency and Duration of Sessions

Although SO-CBT may vary markedly based on variables such as therapist preference, clinical problem, and client factors (e.g., personality pathology or strong religious resistance to treatment), for the most part, SO-CBT will be shorter in duration than most other approaches to treatment covered in this volume. CBT approaches often span 6 to 20 sessions. For social anxiety like Grace experienced, 6 to 10 sessions is common when practicing from an REBT orientation. Although sessions are usually 50 minutes long, shorter sessions are common as treatment nears completion, as are brief "booster" sessions (e.g., at 2 weeks, 1 month, and 3 months posttreatment). In addition, SO-CBT therapists are often willing to accompany clients to in vivo exposure experiences (e.g., speeches for a client with social phobia or trips to a shopping mall for one with agoraphobia) or may schedule longer "marathon" sessions for intensive imagery experiences.

Termination and Relapse Prevention

Because CBT theory hinges on the construct of collaborative empiricism—the therapist and client collaborate in all phases of treatment from goal setting to evaluating treatment outcomes—indicators of termination (typically clearly measurable reductions in distress or increases in desired behaviors) are often clearly evident to both parties. In the case of Grace, client and therapist agreed in the first session that Grace would move from a "9" on her own 1-to-10 scale of anxiety to "3" when anticipating some social performance. CBT is unique in its focus on alleviation of symptom distress. That is, rather than assume the client may not fully understand what sort of change might indicate treatment success, the therapist assumes that the client's primary complaint is indeed the focus of therapy and that the client is the best judge of appropriate treatment goals and accompanying indicators of treatment completion. Relapse prevention is a significant part of nearly all CBT approaches. To this end, treatment is always somewhat psychoeducational; clients are taught focal skills to be practiced and self-applied between sessions as homework and posttreatment as methods of preventing recurrence of the problem. For instance, Grace was encouraged to practice disputation of Ibs, Christian rational emotive imagery, and shame attacking between sessions and after termination.

Therapeutic Outcomes: Immediate and Long Term

Grace completed the brief outcome measures again during the eighth and final session. Her BDI score was 7 (nonclinical range), and she reported very little depression after the fourth session. Her ATQ-30 score of 42 indicated a significant decrease in automatic negative thoughts but showed that she continued to engage in mild depressogenic thinking at times. Her overall SWB score was 98 at the end of treatment, reflecting greater spiritual well-being compared with her initial overall score of 82. Perhaps most important, Grace had decided to stay in seminary and disagreed vehemently with the statement, "It is awful and I don't belong here if I sometimes feel anxious speaking" (this was one of the irrational statements she disputed during role-play disputation practice). On her own experiential anxiety scale (ranging from 1 to 10), her modal score when preparing to speak in class had decreased from 9 to 5. She found this to be a significant improvement and also found that she was able to endure this level of anxiety. She reported believing that no speaking or performing situation would feel unbearable (as she had regarding most such situations before treatment), and she found her anxiety becoming less consuming each time she did speak or play the piano in public. Grace was able to laugh at her own human tendency toward strong unbiblical thinking—particularly her proclivity toward poor frustration tolerance and her nearly automatic habit of self-damning when she perceived herself to have a weakness or failing. Because she maintained strong commitments to morning devotions and prayer, it was relatively easy to get her to weave cognitive disputation exercises and rational emotive imagery (particularly imagery bearing on Jesus, grace, and calming) into her existing daily routine, thus ensuring frequent practice of CBT skills. During a brief 30-minute, 3-month follow-up session, Grace had largely maintained her practice regimen and continued to report diminished social anxiety. Her BDI score at this final contact was 6. She agreed that no further treatment was needed but knew that she could contact me again in the future if necessary.

Although this case offers a window into how I (WBJ) might practice spiritually oriented REBT with a religious (in this case, explicitly Christian) client, keep in mind that other spiritually oriented CBT practitioners might employ other techniques. For example, I (SYT) might employ prayer for inner healing if the client so desired. Still others might place greater emphasis on behavioral strategies (e.g., reinforcement and punishment) or focus more intensively on the client's distorted perceptions of the activating event (A). Finally, although Grace was responsive to spiritually oriented CBT, other clients may be less so.

CONCLUSION

CBT approaches emphasize the propositions that cognitive activity affects behavior and that modification of cognitive activity can produce relief from negative emotional and behavioral consequences. Spiritually oriented CBT uses a CBT framework to help explicitly religious clients or clients who present with spiritual or religious concerns. SO-CBT enjoys preliminary empirical support with both Christian and Muslim clients. SO-CBT begins with an assumption of theistic realism and assumes both competence with CBT theory and technique and sensitivity (if not competence) with the client's unique spiritual and religious surround. Because it is belief oriented, educative, directive, and pragmatic, CBT is often particularly appealing to religious clients. The case study offered in this chapter highlights the SO-CBT emphasis on ongoing assessment, disputation of irrational beliefs and philosophies, active collaboration between therapist and client, and willingness of the therapist to use both general CBT techniques and SO-CBT techniques designed to challenge incomplete or selectively abstracted elements of the client's own faith. Although some approaches to SO-CBT have been empirically evaluated, a significant amount of research is still needed to determine the efficacy of SO-CBT with Jewish, Hindu, Buddhist, and other types of religious clients. Furthermore, the field will be bolstered by comparative research that examines the relative efficacy of alternative SO-CBT approaches in treating focal psychological or religious problems.

REFERENCES

Abramowitz, J. S. (2001). Treatment of scrupulous obsessions and compulsions using exposure and response prevention: A case report. *Cognitive and Behavioral Practice, 8*, 79–85.

Azhar, M. Z., & Varma, S. L. (1995a). Religious psychotherapy as management of bereavement. *Acta Psychiatrica Scandinavia, 91*, 223–235.

Azhar, M. Z., & Varma, S. L. (1995b). Religious psychotherapy in depressive patients. *Psychotherapy and Psychosomatics, 63*, 165–173.

Azhar, M. Z., Varma, S. L., & Dharap, A. S. (1994). Religious psychotherapy in anxiety disorder patients. *Acta Psychiatrica Scandinavia, 90*, 1–3.

Backus, W. (1985). *Telling the truth to troubled people.* Minneapolis, MN: Bethany House.

Bandura, A. (1977). *Social learning theory.* Englewood Cliffs, NJ: Prentice Hall.

Beck, A. T. (1976). *Cognitive therapy and the emotional disorders.* New York: International Universities Press.

Beck, A. T., Rush, A. J., Shaw, B. F., & Emery, G. (1979). *Cognitive therapy of depression.* New York: Guilford Press.

Beck, A. T., Ward, C. H., Mendelson, M., Mock, J., & Erbaugh, J. (1961). An inventory for measuring depression. *Archives of General Psychiatry, 4*, 561–571.

Beck, A. T., & Weishaar, M. (2000). Cognitive therapy. In R. J. Corsini & D. Wedding (Eds.), *Current psychotherapies* (6th ed., pp. 241–272). Itasca, IL: Peacock.

Bergin, A. E. (1980). Psychotherapy and religious values. *Journal of Consulting and Clinical Psychology, 48*, 95–105.

Beutler, L. E. (2000). David and Goliath: When empirical and clinical standards of practice meet. *American Psychologist, 55*, 997–1007.

Blagys, M. D., & Hilsenroth, M. J. (2002). Distinctive activities of cognitive–behavioral therapy: A review of the comparative psychotherapy process literature. *Clinical Psychology Review, 22*, 671–706.

Chambless, D. L., & Ollendick, T. H. (2001). Empirically supported psychological interventions: Controversies and evidence. *Annual Review of Psychology, 52*, 685–716.

Craighead, L. W., Craighead, W. E., Kazdin, A. E., & Mahoney, M. J. (1994). *Cognitive and behavioral interventions: An empirical approach to mental health problems.* Boston: Allyn & Bacon.

Craigie, F. C., & Tan, S. Y. (1989). Changing resistant assumptions in Christian cognitive–behavioral therapy. *Journal of Psychology and Theology, 17*, 93–100.

Derogatis, L. R. (1977). *SCL-90-R: Administration, scoring, and procedure manual.* Baltimore: Johns Hopkins University Press.

DiGiuseppe, R. A., Robin, M. W., & Dryden, W. (1990). On the compatibility of rational–emotive therapy and Judeo-Christian philosophy: A focus on clinical strategies. *Journal of Cognitive Psychotherapy: An International Quarterly, 4*, 355–368.

Dobson, K. S., & Block, L. (1988). Historical and philosophical bases of the cognitive–behavioral therapies. In K. S. Dobson (Ed.), *Handbook of cognitive–behavioral therapies* (pp. 3–38). New York: Guilford Press.

Dobson, K. S., & Dozois, D. J. A. (2001). Historical and philosophical bases of the cognitive–behavioral therapies. In K. S. Dobson (Ed.), *Handbook of cognitive–behavioral therapies* (2nd ed., pp. 3–39). New York: Guilford Press.

Dobson, K. S., & Shaw, B. F. (1993). The training of cognitive therapists: What have we learned from treatment manuals? *Psychotherapy, 30*, 573–576.

Ellis, A. (1962). *Reason and emotion in psychotherapy*. New York: Lyle Stuart.

Ellis, A. (2000a). Can rational emotive behavior therapy (REBT) be effectively used with people who have devout beliefs in God and religion? *Professional Psychology: Research and Practice, 31*, 29–33.

Ellis, A. (2000b). Rational emotive behavior therapy. In R. J. Corsini & D. Wedding (Eds.), *Current psychotherapies* (6th ed., pp. 168–204). Itasca, IL: Peacock.

Ellis, A., & Dryden, W. (1997). *The practice of rational emotive therapy* (2nd ed.). New York: Springer.

Ellison, C. W. (1983). Spiritual well-being: Conceptualization and measurement. *Journal of Psychology and Theology, 11*, 330–340.

Hall, G. C. N. (2001). Psychotherapy research with ethnic minorities: Empirical, ethical, and conceptual issues. *Journal of Consulting and Clinical Psychology, 69*, 502–510.

Hawkins, R. S., Tan, S. Y., & Turk, A. A. (1999). Secular versus Christian inpatient cognitive–behavioral therapy programs: Impact on depression and spiritual well-being. *Journal of Psychology and Theology, 27*, 309–318.

Hollon, S. D., & Beck, A. T. (1994). Cognitive and cognitive–behavioral therapies. In A. E. Bergin & S. L. Garfield (Eds.), *Handbook of psychotherapy and behavior change* (pp. 428–466). New York: Wiley.

Hollon, S. D., & Kendall, P. C. (1980). Cognitive self-statements in depression: Development of an automatic thoughts questionnaire. *Cognitive Therapy and Research, 4*, 383–395.

Johnson, W. B. (2001). To dispute or not to dispute: Ethical REBT with religious clients. *Cognitive and Behavioral Practice, 8*, 39–47.

Johnson, W. B., DeVries, R., Ridley, C. R., Pettorini, D., & Peterson, D. R. (1994). The comparative efficacy of Christian and secular rational–emotive therapy with Christian clients. *Journal of Psychology and Theology, 22*, 130–140.

Johnson, W. B., & Ridley, C. R. (1992). Brief Christian and non-Christian rational–emotive therapy with depressed Christian clients: An exploratory study. *Counseling and Values, 36*, 220–229.

Jones, S. L., & Butman, R. E. (1991). *Modern psychotherapies: A comprehensive Christian perspective*. Downers Grove, IL: InterVarsity Press.

Keijsers, G. P. J., Schaap, C. P. D. R., & Hoogduin, C. A. L. (2000). The impact of interpersonal patient and therapist behavior on outcome in cognitive–behavior therapy. *Behavior Modification, 24*, 264–298.

Kruis, J. G. (2000). *Quick scripture reference for counseling* (3rd ed.). Grand Rapids, MI: Baker.

Lazarus, R. S., & Folkman, C. (1984). *Stress, appraisal, and coping*. New York: Springer.

Lovinger, R. J. (1984). *Working with religious issues in therapy*. New York: Jason Aronson.

Mahoney, M. J. (1974). *Cognition and behavior modification*. Cambridge, MA: Ballinger.

Mahoney, M. J. (1977). Reflections on the cognitive learning trend in psychotherapy. *American Psychologist, 32,* 5–13.

McCullough, M. E. (1999). Research on religion-accomodative counseling: Review and meta-analysis. *Journal of Counseling Psychology, 46,* 92–98.

McMinn, M. (1991). *Cognitive therapy techniques in Christian counseling.* Dallas, TX: Word.

Meichenbaum, D. (1977). *Cognitive–behavior modification: An integrative approach.* New York: Plenum.

Miller, P. A. (2002). *Quick scripture reference for counseling women.* Grand Rapids, MI: Baker.

Nielsen, S. L., Johnson, W. B., & Ellis, A. (2001). *Counseling and psychotherapy with religious persons: A rational emotive behavior therapy approach.* Mahwah, NJ: Erlbaum.

Nielsen, S. L., Johnson, W. B., & Ridley, C. R. (2000). Religiously sensitive rational emotive behavior therapy: Theory, techniques, and brief excerpts from a case. *Professional Psychology: Research and Practice, 31,* 21–28.

Norcross, J. C. (Ed.). (2002). *Psychotherapy relationships that work.* New York: Oxford University Press.

Norcross, J. C., Karg, R. S., & Prochaska, J. O. (1997). Clinical psychologists in the 1990's: Part I. *The Clinical Psychologist, 50,* 4–9.

Pargament, K. I. (1997). *The psychology of religion and coping: Theory, research, practice.* New York: Guilford Press.

Pecheur, D. R., & Edwards, K. J. (1984). A comparison of secular and religious versions of cognitive therapy with depressed Christian college students. *Journal of Psychology and Theology, 12,* 45–54.

Persons, J. B., Davidson, J., & Tompkins, M. A. (2001). *Essential components of cognitive–behavior therapy for depression.* Washington, DC: American Psychological Association.

Propst, L. R. (1980). The comparative efficacy of religious and nonreligious imagery for the treatment of mild depression in religious individuals. *Cognitive Therapy and Research, 4,* 167–178.

Propst, L. R. (1988). *Psychotherapy in a religious framework: Spirituality in the emotional healing process.* New York: Human Sciences Press.

Propst, L. R. (1996). Cognitive–behavioral therapy and the religious person. In E. P. Shafranske (Ed.), *Religion and the clinical practice of psychology* (pp. 391–407). Washington, DC: American Psychological Association.

Propst, L. R., Ostrom, R., Watkins, P., Dean, T., & Mashburn, D. (1992). Comparative efficacy of religious and nonreligious cognitive–behavioral therapy for the treatment of clinical depression in religious individuals. *Journal of Consulting and Clinical Psychology, 60,* 94–103.

Razali, S. M., Aminah, K., & Khan, U. A. (2002). Religious–cultural psychotherapy in the management of anxiety patients. *Transcultural Psychiatry, 39,* 130–136.

Richards, P. S., & Bergin, A. E. (2000). *Handbook of psychotherapy and religious diversity.* Washington, DC: American Psychological Association.

Sue, D. W., & Sue, D. (2003). *Counseling the culturally diverse: Theory and practice* (4th ed.). New York: Wiley.

Tan, S.-Y. (1987). Cognitive–behavior therapy: A biblical approach and critique. *Journal of Psychology and Theology, 15,* 103–112.

Tan, S.-Y. (1996a). Practicing the presence of God: The work of Richard J. Foster and its applications to psychotherapeutic practice. *Journal of Psychology and Christianity, 15,* 17–28.

Tan, S.-Y. (1996b). Religion in clinical practice: Implicit and explicit integration. In E. P. Shafranske (Ed.), *Religion and the clinical practice of psychology* (pp. 365–387). Washington, DC: American Psychological Association.

Tan, S.-Y. (1999). Cognitive–behavior therapy. In D. G. Benner & P. C. Hill (Eds.), *Baker encyclopedia of psychology and counseling* (2nd ed., pp. 215–218). Grand Rapids, MI: Baker.

Tan, S.-Y. (2001). Empirically supported treatments. *Journal of Psychology and Christianity, 20,* 282–286.

Tan, S.-Y. (2002). Empirically informed principles of treatment selection: Beyond empirically supported treatments. *Journal of Psychology and Christianity, 21,* 54–56.

Tan, S.-Y. (2003a). Empirically supported therapy relationships: Psychotherapy relationships that work: *Journal of Psychology and Christianity, 22,* 64–67.

Tan, S.-Y. (2003b). Integrating spiritual direction into psychotherapy: Ethical issues and guidelines. *Journal of Psychology and Theology, 31,* 14–23.

Tan, S.-Y., & Dong, N. J. (2000). Psychotherapy with members of Asian American churches and spiritual traditions. In P. S. Richards & A. E. Bergin (Eds.), *Handbook of psychotherapy and religious diversity* (pp. 421–444). Washington, DC: American Psychological Association.

Tan, S.-Y., & Dong, N. J. (2001). Spiritual interventions in healing and wholeness. In T. G. Plante & A. C. Sherman (Eds.), *Faith and health: Psychological perspectives* (pp. 291–310). New York: Guilford Press.

Tan, S.-Y., & Ortberg, J., Jr. (1995). *Understanding depression.* Grand Rapids, MI: Baker.

Tan, S.-Y., & Ortberg, J., Jr. (2004). *Coping with depression* (2nd ed.). Grand Rapids, MI: Baker.

White, C. A. (2001). *Cognitive behavior therapy for chronic medical problems.* Chichester, England: Wiley.

Worthington, E. L., Jr., Kurusu, T. A., McCullough, M. E., & Sandage, S. J. (1996). Empirical research on religion and psychotherapeutic processes and outcomes: A 10-year review and research prospectus. *Psychological Bulletin, 119,* 448–487.

Worthington, E. L., Jr., & Sandage, S. J. (2001). Religion and spirituality. *Psychotherapy, 38,* 473–478.

Wright, H. N. (1986). *Self-talk, imagery and prayer in counseling.* Waco, TX: Word.

5

A PSYCHOANALYTIC APPROACH TO SPIRITUALLY ORIENTED PSYCHOTHERAPY

EDWARD P. SHAFRANSKE

DESCRIPTION OF THE APPROACH

Psychoanalysis has long considered religious experience to be an essential aspect of culture, which informs individual psychology. Although Freud personally rejected religious faith (Gay, 1987; Rizzuto, 1998), he observed religious ideas to be prized possessions of civilization (Freud, 1961/1923, p. 20) and within his opus sought to identify their real worth (1961/1907, 1961/1913, 1961/1927, 1961/1930, 1961/1939). Contemporary psychoanalysis, drawing on the accretion of theoretical and clinical knowledge, has taken up this challenge and offers multiple perspectives through which an understanding of the psychodynamics of religious faith and spirituality can be obtained. Although Freud declared an incompatibility between religious dogma and the scientific mind, postmodern thinkers embrace a hermeneutic approach in which religious experience may be approached as psychological phenomena while allowing other signification to be held. Psychological and spiritual dimensions of human experience are seen to be different in light of the meanings they inspire and, although religious experiences can be reduced to psychoanalytic categories, a privileged stance to reality is not asserted. Thus the potential iconoclasm of psychoanalysis is denuded by acknowledgment of a "double possibility" of faith and nonfaith, in which the veridical status of the religious content cannot be determined within clinical investigation (Ricoeur, 1970, p. 230).

A spiritually oriented psychoanalytic approach examines the psychological and developmental underpinnings of faith while remaining open to realities outside of its epistemic reach. Such a posture allows for consideration of parallel psychological and spiritual trajectories, which, although related and at times intertwined, are fundamentally distinctive. In practice, such a perspective is in keeping with a nonpositivistic, hermeneutic stance to psychic realities, which a priori includes an admixture of fact and fantasy in the construction of meaning (Arlow, 1996). Such an approach listens to religious experiences with an empathic ear, mindful of potential misunderstanding when singular and reductionistic readings of psychological and spiritual experiences are posited as statements of truth.

Historical and Theoretical Basis

Contemporary psychoanalytic treatment builds on Freud's seminal understanding of the role of unconscious conflict in the creation of neurotic symptoms and in their amelioration by means of insight and remembering. Today psychoanalysis has expanded to include what Wallerstein (1988) considered to be a pluralism of theory, including ego psychological, object relational, self-psychological, Kleinian, Bionian, and Lacanian, and so on, perspectives. Rangell (1997) countered in proposing a unitary view, in which the succession of clinical discoveries finds a home within a total composite theory (2000). In addition to such theoretical advances, clinical practice now includes a range of applications, including psychoanalysis, psychodynamic psychotherapy, and brief psychodynamic psychotherapy, and spans the continuum between expressive and supportive forms of treatment (Gabbard, 2000; Messer & Warren, 1995).

Intrapsychic conflict, initially considered within ego psychology, results when wishes are incompatible with unconscious moral proscripts, prescripts, and ideals. Reflecting processes of internalization, such intersystemic conflicts arouse unconscious anxiety and lead to the maladaptive employment of defenses, ineffective compromise formation, and ultimately to symptoms and to neurosis. Freud, followed by the contributions of Anna Freud (1936) and others, provided a theoretical and clinical foundation on which the study of unconscious psychodynamics could be undertaken incorporating dynamic, genetic, structural, and adaptive viewpoints. Ongoing clinical investigation has led to an appreciation of pathological internalized object relations, internal working models, and threats to the cohesiveness of the self in conflict, drawn from object relations, attachment theory, and self-psychological theories, respectively. In addition to the conflict model, psychoanalysis has identified deficits in ego functioning or self structure to be elemental in the development of personality disorders. Such deficits result from a multifactorial etiology, including constitutional features, conditions of neglect, and exposure to varying degrees of trauma and pathological interpersonal experiences, which compromise psychological development. In such circumstances, characterological rather than situational uses of defense impair interpersonal relating, interfere with healthy expression and sublimation of drives, and establish self-reinforcing, maladaptive patterns.

Psychoanalytic treatment, whether conducted as formal analysis or psychodynamic psychotherapy, achieves its transformative effects by facilitating a process in which the patient *articulates through speech* psychic experience (Rizzuto, 2003, p. 288). Through vicarious introspection (Kohut, 1959) the psychotherapist becomes empathically attuned to the patient's inner life and facilitates a process of discovery, understanding, as well as constructs meaning. The underlying sources of the patient's difficulties are encountered, reexperienced, and reenacted in the therapeutic relationship involving remembering, catharsis, insight, and eventual retranscription, in which the past as memory is altered, namely, Freud's concept of *Nachtraglichkeit* (Modell, 1990). The ways in which the patient has habitually perceived and related in the world, under the shadow of past early object relations, are brought to light through close attention to all forms of unconscious expression, particularly in the form of transference.

Through reliving the past within the analytic situation, the unconscious repetitive organization of the past changes and novel solutions are forged within the present experience and relationship with the psychoanalyst (Loewald, 1980). In addition to insight, therefore, the provision of a corrective emotional experience within the context of a new relationship, sustained by empathy, is seen to contribute to changes in psychological structure and functioning. Gradually the patient's capacity to know, feel, express, and contain is expanded and a greater sense of control and mastery is obtained.

History of the Psychoanalytic Approach to Religion

Psychoanalysis provides a clinical approach, research procedure, and theory to examine the developmental and intrapsychic dynamic processes that contribute to the formation of a person's faith. It provides a means to further explain how religion "establishes powerful, persuasive, and long-lasting moods and motivations" that give form, purpose, and meaning to life (Geertz, 1966/1973, p. 90). The relationship is best put as psychoanalysis *of* religion to emphasize that the fundamental stance to spirituality is as an object of study rather than to imply a more reciprocal or even dialectical relationship between the fields as equivalent informants of the nature of reality. A historical review finds an antagonism in Freud's posture as he voiced that "religion alone is the serious enemy" (1961/1933, p. 160) of his rationalist, scientific agenda. We turn first to a précis of Freud's critique of religion (for more extended discussion see De Luca, 1977; Gay, 1987; Kung, 1979; Meissner, 1987; Rieff, 1961; Rizzuto, 1979, 1998; Shafranske, 1995; Van Herik, 1982).

Freud's Critique of Religion

For Freud, religious experience was a regressive phenomenon, and his argument stood on a series of interrelated postulates based on clinical material and substantively drawn from speculative perspectives concerning phylogeny and ontogeny. His central thesis was that religious sentiments were illusions born of archaic unconscious sources and reflecting both wishes and the primordial origins of the Oedipus complex. Freud conjectured that religious ideas were wish fulfillments derived originally in response to conditions of helplessness. In commenting on his friend Romain Rolland's sensation of eternity, unbounded as if it were "oceanic," Freud (1961/1930) remarked that it was the "source of the religious energy" (p. 64) and concluded that it was an expression of a strong need derived from infantile helplessness (p. 72). The creation of God fulfilled the longing for the father and complemented Feuerbach's thesis (1841) that God was merely the projection of the essence of man. Freud extended his argument beyond individual ontogeny to universal forces of phylogeny suggesting that religious ideas not only contained projections derived from regressive needs but also were repetitive phenomena, which represented the history of the origins of civilization. Freud (1961/1923) posited, "the ideational image belonging in childhood is preserved and becomes merged with the inherited memory-traces of the primal father [during the time of the primal horde and in which the murder of the father was the bedrock of the Oedipus complex] to form the individual's idea of God" (p. 85). Religion, drawn from multiple sources, is an illusion, which stems from the individual's wish for protection and favor and out of fear of destruction and injury. Religious beliefs were motivated by wish fulfillment and thus were made from the fabric of illusion and bore the imprint of memories of a distant, primal past. Freud extended his thesis in proposing that for both the adult believer and a culture built on religious illusion, renunciation of instincts occurred out of deference and supplication to the internalized father–God within the psychological structure of the superego with the resolution of the Oedipus complex. As such, renunciation was not based on rational processes but rather was the outcome of unconscious oedipal dynamics, much in the same way as the neurotics he treated. He acknowledged, "Religion has clearly performed great services for human civilization. It has contributed to the taming of asocial instincts" (Freud, 1961/1927, p. 47), but at what cost? For Freud, the cost was exacted in forestalling the progress of civilization (see Van Herik, 1982). Smith (1990) summarized,

Since Freud took religion to be primarily motivated by fear of retribution that went hand in hand with infantile, preemptory needs for love, care, and protection, it followed that he saw religion not only as an unreliable basis for ethics but also a generally pacifying and therefore inhibiting factor in the development of the individual and the race. For Freud it was fear and needy love that motivated religion, with little allowance for the role of non-peremptory, freely given love. (p. 35)

The sine qua non of Freud's argument is that God is a human creation, a projection, whether derived from ancestral memory traces or needs. The God-imago built on internalizations of the father and necessarily delimited by that human interaction under the pressure of instinctual renunciation within the setting of the Oedipus complex. Religious experience in this view is tethered to human history and is temporal in contrast with a spiritual orientation, which reaches to the transhistorical and transcendent—God is this view can only be the product of human psychology. In this understanding, spirituality is reduced to psychological processes anchored in wish fulfillment. Religious and mystical experiences represent regressive phenomena related to the oceanic experiences of early merger and wish fulfillment.

Post-Freudian Considerations

A substantive body of literature has developed both expanding on and dissenting from Freud's original commentary. Contributions from the perspectives of ego psychology, object relations theory, self psychology, feminist theory, relational psychoanalysis, Lacan, and so on have broadened and refined the psychoanalytic approach to religious experience. Of particular importance is the reconceptualization of the dynamic processes involved in the creation of God-imagos.

In contrast to Freud's static conception of God modeled after the father, Rizzuto (1979) countered that God-representation

is more than the cornerstone upon which it was built. It is a *new* original representation which, because it is new, may have the varied components that serve to soothe and comfort, provide inspiration and courage —or terror and dread—far beyond that inspired by actual parents. (p. 46)

God-representations, culled from myriad sources, are neither illusions nor objective realities; they are mental contents owing their vitality to functioning within the transitional realm, which as described by Winnicott is the wellspring of religion. Within this intermediate area an interweave of subjectivity and objective observation conjoins and serves as the ground on which the anthropomorphic, personalistic representation of the sacred takes form. Such representations are not simply "ideas" but rather in this transitional realm are psychological objects in which the relationship to the transcendent is experienced as manifestly human in quality—capable of empathy, concern, love, cruelty, and so on—the full range of emotion and intention. These representations bear the impressions that living within a world of human objects has created and yet are not fully bounded by these temporal experiences. Indeed, an emerging literature is establishing empirically the relationship between the level of object relations attained and the God-representations that are formed. This research demonstrates a correspondence between psychological features derived from relations with parents and the qualities that appear to be available to form God-representations (Brokaw & Edwards, 1994; Hall, Brokaw, Edwards, & Pike, 1998) as well as between quality of attachment and attachment to God, religious beliefs, and religious affiliation (Granqvist & Hagekull, 1999, 2001; Kirkpatrick, 1992, 1997, 1998, 1999; Rowatt & Kirkpatrick, 2002).

A spiritually oriented perspective appreciates the nature of projection in the formation of God-representations while holding open to meanings that are not reduced to earth-bound, psychological processes. Such a psychoanalyst does not fall prey to the "reification of mischief" of Feuerbach in which the premise is made that there is only a religious object out there if one could find it (cf. Smith, 1962, p. 47, cited in McDargh, 1983, p. 14). Spero (1992), in his critique of what he considered to be an exclusive anthropocentric view of God-representations, proposed the inclusion into theory of a deocentric dimension in which an existing God–object is afforded the status of reality within an assumed positivistic framework. This proposal is relevant when considering the assumptions held in theistic-oriented psychotherapy (Richards, chap. 11, this volume; Richards & Bergin, 1997); however, the positivist demand such a statement makes cannot be empirically tested. In my view, this muddies the epistemological waters; it is more clinically useful to consider a patient's experience of God as similar with their experiences of other significant psychological objects—no demand is issued to ascertain the veridical status of the patient's psychic experience. The hard distinctions between reality and psychic reality collapse when we take into consideration that all psychological experience is constructed within the setting of ever-present psychodynamics and under the pressure of unconscious motivations and conflicts (Arlow, 1985, 1996). Observable "reality" pales next to the association-laden, subjective experience, which actually constitutes our knowledge of and relationship with others.

Psychoanalytic theory has broadened to include a more sophisticated appreciation for the relational dimension in psychological life. We are not isolated minds but social beings whose selves exist within a relational, self-sustaining matrix of other selves. From this perspective when we speak of spirituality, we are talking about our relationship with God, with the transcendent, with the sacred, rather than about an internalized mental representation or conscious idea in our minds. This viewpoint does not negate the contributions, which have come before, but rather casts particular light on what *animates* religious experience. It is not simply that there is a transcendent dimension or a sacred canopy—what is important to us is that we have a relationship *with* the transcendent and that we *live under* a sacred canopy. Self psychology offers a perspective in which the cohesiveness and vitality of the self relies on selfobjects within the surround to respond joyfully, to be available as sources of idealized strength and calmness, and to be silently present but to share in essence commonality of experience (cf. Kohut, 1984, p. 52). Religion meets the deepest needs of the self within these three realms of mirroring, idealizing, and twinship (Strozier, 1997, p. 172). For example, religion provides a concept of the Absolute that the self requires to mirror and to focus its integrative processes (Jones, 1996, p. 42) or twinship as a congregation, despite diversity of members, joins together in moments of authentic spiritual reverie. A relational perspective takes seriously Guntrip's (1968) early view:

> Since religion is preeminently an experience of personal relationship, which extends the personal to the *n*th degree, to embrace both man and his universe in one meaningful whole, the integrating nature of fully developed personal relationship experience, is our most solid clue to the nature of religious experience. (p. 324)

Such a perspective allows for consideration of the desire for an intimate relationship between the self and God as progressive rather than regressive and is more in keeping with the lived experiences of patients for whom "the most salient figures organizing their felt relationship to the ultimate conditions of their existence are their object relations of 'God' " (McDargh, 1993, pp. 182–183). This echoes Erikson (1958), who rhetorically asked, "But must we call it regression if man thus seeks again the earliest encounters of his trustful past in efforts to reach a hoped for and eternal future?" (p. 264). Furthermore, a relational perspective allows for a psychoanalytic consideration of our relationship to transcendental reality, or our lack of it, which may reflect the relational patterns throughout our life (cf. Jones, 1996, p. 45).

A psychoanalytic perspective also considers that religious narrative may reflect not only the nature of a patient's spirituality or relationship with God but also may serve to represent and give expression to ineffable, emotional states of mind. Religion offers culturally accepted leitmotifs, infused with *significations* of the most profound human experiences—suffering, rebirth, resurrection, and so on—which provides a means for experience to be evocatively represented (cf. Shafranske, 2002). In this view, spirituality may provide a language that contributes to the mentalization and integration of psychic experience.

Psychoanalysis may also shed light on the dynamics involved in certain ascetical practices and contemplative disciplines that are situated within approaches to spiritual development and in mysticism. Deliberative alterations in psychological state, through fasting, self-sacrifice, and "dying of the self" can be understood as adaptive regressions in service of the ego (Fauteux,

1994; see also Kakar, 1991). Such experiences, however, require careful clinical assessment, because ego regressions are perilous for vulnerable patients; for others, such practices support the aim of purgation and ultimately spiritual illumination. Although beyond the reach of this chapter, important convergences have also been identified between psychoanalysis, Eastern thought, and meditative practices in which states and operations of the mind are the primary focus and in which unique states of psychological mindedness occur (Engler, 1983; Epstein, 1988; Finn, 1992; Suler, 1993).

The Nature of the Relationship Between Psychoanalysis and Spirituality

In my view, psychoanalysis provides a dynamic heuristic to grasp many of the psychological, developmental, and cultural contributions to an individual's experience of and relationship with transcendent realities. Such understanding acknowledges the inherent limitations in reducing any phenomenon, including spirituality, to psychological categories. A tension therefore exists between the desire to know and the limitations of knowing, between understanding and mystery. This tension is respected as it reflects the nature of both psychic and spiritual life. My own view is in keeping with that expressed by De Mellow Franco (1998):

> If analysis is an adventure in the sense of a process directed towards the unknown, it also contains within itself an infinite range of possibilities of assigning new meaning to the personal and universal, immanent and transcendental experience of contact with a God whom we simultaneously create and discover. (p. 128)

Therapist's Skills and Attributes

Beyond clinical proficiency, established through requisite training that includes postgraduate education, personal analysis, and supervised control cases, skills in empathy, affect attunement, psychological mindedness, self-awareness, open-mindedness, appreciation for complexity, patience, respect, and integrity are necessary professional attributes. Although holding a faith perspective consonant with that of the patient is not required to conduct a psychoanalytic treatment sensitive to a patient's spirituality (Sorenson, 1994, 1997), it may be more readily accomplished in therapists for whom spirituality is a meaningful dimension. Bartoli (2001) found that religious identification often had little influence on psychoanalysts' outlooks or how they chose to address religious material clinically. She reported, however, that analysts who appear to treat religious material in complex and sensitive ways perhaps have "a sense about there being something not merely psychological about religious involvement . . . those who treat religion in more reductionistic ways seem not to separate the spiritual side of religious involvement from the psychological one" (pp. 173–174). This finding lends support to the notion that analysts who personally experience spirituality to be distinctive may be better prepared to engage with the interrelated yet separate discourses of psychoanalysis and spirituality.

Strengths and Limitations

Psychoanalytic treatment offers an approach that aims to address symptoms at the point of their origin within the dynamic context of the totality of personality functioning. Therapeutic efforts are targeted to structural change, and "psychoanalytic efficacy is measured by enhancement of psychological functioning and symptom amelioration" (Galatzer-Levy, Bachrach, Skolnikoff, & Waldron, 2000, p. 19). Its limitations are in part a consequence of its ambitious objectives. Psychoanalysis, in particular, requires a significant commitment of resources, including time and finances, and requires personal investment and strong motivation. Today, many forms of treatment are available, including brief psychodynamic psychotherapy, that offer the benefits of a psychoanalytic perspective. Although the scientific study of the psychoanalytic process and its clinical effectiveness is intrinsically difficult, psychoanalysis is limited by insufficient attention to establishing empirical support for its claims.

Indications and Contraindications

Psychoanalytic treatment is indicated for a wide range of clinical conditions and is perhaps best suited to patients possessing a sufficiency of psychological-mindedness, motivation to address acute symptoms in terms of more pervasive underlying intrapsychic conflicts and relational difficulties, and sufficient ego strength to engage meaningfully in a psychoanalytic process. Patients seeking only symptom relief or those without the requisite cognitive abilities to profit from an insight-oriented approach are contraindicated. Patients with psychopathic character structures or those assessed with severe borderline personality organizations are generally contraindicated for psychoanalysis or outpatient insight-oriented psychodynamic psychotherapy.

Cultural and Gender Considerations

Limited empirical research has been conducted on the impact of culture on the psychoanalytic process. Emphasis on individual psychodynamics and dyadic and triadic developmental influences has resulted in a relative lack of appreciation of the role of culture separate from its transmission within familial dynamics. Theoretical advances in feminist and gender theory and incorporation of constructivist and postmodern contributions has heightened awareness of gender as an important factor in the psychoanalytic process. Increased appreciation of the relational model of human nature has brought attention to the role of one's relationship to the sacred and the cultural forms in which such a relationship takes shape (Jones, 1991, 1996; Sorenson, 2004).

Expected Future Developments and Direction

Further developments will likely be advanced through quantitative and qualitative research on the psychoanalytic process; continuing contributions derived from academic developmental psychology, particularly as focused on attachment and object relations models; and through integrative theoretical and empirical investigation within neuroscience and psychoanalysis. The development of psychometrically sophisticated measures of spirituality, particularly in respect to God-representational processes and the role of attachment, will herald a new epoch in the psychoanalytic study of religious experience.

CASE EXAMPLE

Client Demographics, Relevant History, and Presenting Concern

Joan, a 33-year-old, married Caucasian woman, presented as a youthful, engaging person who was highly verbal and generally thoughtful in the initial assessment interviews. Her outward manner conveyed an air of confidence, befitting her professional training as a corporate attorney. Married 3 years to Mark, aged 39, an investment banker, she reported that she loved her husband, and although they were generally well suited, she found herself becoming increasingly anxious in his presence, which resulted in feelings of unease and dysphoria. She reported that this was not necessarily caused by his behavior but rather had to do with an inner disquiet and foreboding sense of impending doom. Her present experience was in marked contrast to the excitement she felt before they married. She tearfully remarked toward the end of the session that her feelings might have something to do with their discussions about starting a family.

In subsequent sessions, I learned that beneath the veneer of self-assurance, Joan experienced trepidation in many relationships, particularly those involving men she perceived to be powerful. She worried over presentations she gave to senior management in her job and became nervous and self-critical of any missteps in her public demeanor. She offered that she knew that these reactions were overblown and irrational; when actually confronted either personally or professionally, she could hold her own. Her present fears reminded her of an earlier time in her life when she felt intimidated or embarrassed. Recently, she found herself avoiding sexual relations even though she experienced desire and she had always enjoyed an active and satisfying sex life. Considered together, these symptoms suggested escalating distress and conflict affecting every dimension of her life.

Joan was the eldest of five children of an intact, lower middle-class, family. Her father was a grocer, and her mother was a homemaker whose life was centered on her family and activities associated in the neighborhood Catholic parish. She described her family as chaotic; her parents rarely communicated to each other in a civil manner and conflicts between the siblings often devolved into physical assaults. She described her mother as a loving but ineffectual woman who sought companionship from her daughters and relied heavily on her own mother for advice and comfort. She considered her mother to be "scatterbrained" and believed that she never completely "grew up." She recalled that her mother would often be forgetful, failing to pick up her children at school at the prescribed hour or appearing to be confused. Her posture of helplessness would extend to asking her children repeatedly to show her how to use household gadgets or to make simple decisions. Although Joan took pleasure in the fact that her mother sought her out, she felt awkward hearing about intimate details of her mother's dissatisfaction in her marriage, vulnerability, and the sense of responsibility she felt for her welfare. Although her mother relied on her eldest daughter for support, she would often report what Joan had said in confidence, which left Joan feeling betrayed and angry. She reported that her father was a mostly gruff, unhappy man, who complained of the pressures of supporting his large family. She approached him warily, fearing that he would explode in anger. His central role appeared to be as the breadwinner for the family and reported their relationship to be distant. Her siblings affected her deeply, particularly, when they would tease her mercilessly until she would leave the dinner table in tears. She experienced an intense rivalry with her brother, 3 years her junior. She appeared to have been the victor when they were young; however, he could win out by bringing her to tears with taunts in which he narrowed in on her personal vulnerabilities. The picture she portrayed of her childhood was one of anxiety in which she felt vulnerable and developed a stance of control and vigilance.

She reported school to be a place of marked contrast, where she felt safe and accepted. She was a good student, became involved in student government and clubs, maintained a job throughout high school, and had a number of friends. She reported a long-standing interest in boys and dated throughout late childhood and adolescence. She always had a boyfriend and by her own admission was both controlling and fickle, rarely making a clear commitment to a relationship. She reported that she enjoyed an active sexual life commencing early in high school and particularly enjoyed introducing elements of "danger" into her sexual experiences, such as having intercourse in public places. She continued this pattern in college, dating a number of men and at times enjoying being somewhat promiscuous. Her only serious interest was in her academic studies in which she achieved success. She went on to study at a first-tier law school and graduated in the top quarter of her class. She took a position in a major law firm and after 6 years left to join the legal department of a major corporation. She met Mark through a mutual friend, and they married following a 6-month whirlwind romance. She commented that when she met Mark, who was attractive, fun to be with, and successful, she "surrendered" to the idea of marriage. She recalled that she never really thought much about marriage; she just assumed that eventually when the time was right she would marry and have a family. She reported that the first 2 years of their marriage was enjoyable; she and Mark got along well, developed a wide circle of friends, traveled, and bought a new home. It was a busy and exciting time. Feelings of anxiety and then depression appeared following their move to the suburbs, particularly when Mark broached the issue of starting a family. This idea began to plague her, and she noticed feeling "out of sorts," became angry at him more readily, and felt increasingly guarded and self-critical.

An inquiry into Joan's religious history revealed ambivalence. She reported that Catholicism had played a central role in her family, primarily due to her mother's influence. Every Sunday the family would attend church although this was often fraught with grief, as the demands of getting all of the children to early Mass and on their best behavior stretched everyone's resources and patience. Nevertheless, she had positive memories of attending novenas with her mother, singing in the choir, and religious retreats. She dreamed of being crowned the May Queen during her years of parochial school and went through periods of intense religious fervor. She moved away from religious participation during and subsequent to college. Her ambivalence concerned what she saw as the patriarchy in the Church and her beliefs that the Church was not in step with the demands of modernity, including moral positions on abortion and sexual ethics. She commented however that when times get rough, she could always rely on her faith and that "no one can ever really stop being a Catholic." In the course of the treatment we would discover that spirituality played a larger role in her orienting system than she initially realized.

Relationship of Therapist and Client

The relationship was conceptualized within the social–constructivist paradigm (Hoffman, 1983, 1991, 1992; Stern, 1991), which considers the therapeutic discourse to be shaped and interpreted through a process of reciprocal, interpersonal influence and best viewed to be egalitarian (Gill, 1994; see also Ogden, 1994). The therapist does not direct behavioral change or offer advice but rather attempts to facilitate an analytic process in which the patient brings into awareness the unconscious invariant organizing principles that shape perception and behavior, defenses that are enacted to address situations of perceived danger, as well as uncovering past events and relationships that constitute the prologue for present experience. A position of neutrality was offered, reflecting respect for the client's "essential otherness," individuality in beliefs, worldview, and self-agency (Poland, 1984) while striving to be open and receptive to the nuances of the patient's verbal and nonverbal communications. Technical neutrality was not considered an absolute as the "irreducibility of the analyst's subjectivity" (Renik, 1993) is always at play. Particular emphasis was placed on transference as expressed in the "here and now" interactions between the client and clinician with an understanding of the intersubjective nature of the clinical interaction.

Assessment: Rationale and Type of Data Collected

The psychoanalytic approach to assessment extends beyond a descriptive diagnosis and includes a dynamic formulation, considering the characteristics of the ego, quality of object relations, cohesiveness of the self, and level of personality organization (Gabbard, 2000; McWilliams, 1994). Unlike medical interviewing, the dynamic perspective views assessment to be an integral and ongoing aspect of psychoanalysis. Diagnostic inquiry is conducted mindful of initiating rather than interfering with the development of an analytic process.

In addition to eliciting descriptive information and history, Joan was encouraged to explore the dynamic meanings of her symptoms. Through the use of direct and open-ended questions, clarifications, opportunities for free association, close attention to shifts in affective states of mind, and employment of defenses, as well as to the clinician's feelings and countertransference responses, an assessment of symptoms and structural analysis was obtained.

Symptoms were considered the results of intrapsychic conflict and were located within the context of the patient's life history and present experience within a developmental sociocultural framework. The client's ability to profit from psychoanalytic treatment was assessed in light of her level of personality organization, intelligence, psychological-mindedness, and motivation to understand beyond symptom relief. Although not required in this case, psychological testing is often helpful in further assessing ego functions and level of personality organization when determining the appropriate treatment in respect to a patient's available psychological resources and motivation.

The role of spirituality was assessed through inquiry into her present and past religious involvement, education, participation in normative religious milestones, e.g., confirmation, etc., and more importantly through asking her to describe experiences of conflict and difficulty. Although a formal, comprehensive interview of religious experience can be conducted (Chirban,

2001), in my view, the salience of spirituality is best identified as it appears spontaneously in the client's narrative when recalling times of loss, conflict, or hopelessness: Do religious faith and spiritual practices appear to contribute to psychological distress or to be resources in its resolution? Understanding a patient's unconscious God-representations and beliefs is gradually obtained through associations, dreams, transference, and memories during the course of treatment. The degree to which spirituality and God-representations become a focus in analysis varies in respect to their contributions to the patient's orienting system and reflects the unique psychodynamics of a specific period in the life of the person.

Diagnostic and Clinical Conceptualization

The preliminary assessment suggested that Joan was suffering from a mixed anxiety–depressive disorder in which features of anxiety were predominant. An initial formulation considered these symptoms to be the result of conflicts related to the anticipated change in status and role in becoming a mother and to adjustments in her marital relationship. Although changes in role are often accompanied by anxiety; for Joan, her symptoms were clinically significant, appeared to be eroding her self-confidence, and were negatively affecting many dimensions of her life, including her sexual life. The distress appeared to be focal to specific interpersonal settings and originated from unconscious sources rather than as a result of increased external demands, trauma, or to be symptomatic of chronic generalized anxiety. These symptoms were differentiated from an adjustment disorder as her history suggested long-standing anxiety in situations in which she perceived a disparity in power and control, particularly with men. The current descriptive nomenclature (DSM–IV) would yield the following diagnosis:

Axis I   300.00 Anxiety Disorder NOS [not otherwise specified]
           302.79 Sexual Aversion Disorder (Acquired, Generalized Type Due to Psychological Factors)
Axis II   799.9 Diagnosis deferred on Axis II
Axis III   No diagnosis
Axis IV   Problems with primary support group involving anticipation of pregnancy
           Occupational problems involving heightened sensitivity to self-evaluation of job performance
Axis V   GAF = 70 (current)
           GAF = 95 (highest level past year).

A psychoanalytic diagnosis provides an assessment of personality organization, defenses and a tentative formulation of the intrapsychic conflict underlying the patient's symptoms. Joan's level of personality organization was identified to be in the neurotic-level in which object constancy had been attained and mature defenses (repression, isolation of affect, sublimation, intellectualization) were utilized in a situation-specific manner. Her symptoms suggested an anxiety neurosis, which was exacerbated by consideration of her becoming pregnant, starting a family, and assuming the role of a mother. The idea of assuming such a role conjured a fixed identification with her mother and appeared to represent a loss of autonomy and competence. She noted that the recent episodes of anxiety and increasing vigilance about how she was perceived by others paralleled her thinking about commitments made in her marriage and her recent discussion with Mark and her friends about the possibility of becoming a mother. The idea of depending more on her husband and forming a more intimate and trusting relationship ushered Joan into states of mind reminiscent of her childhood in which she often felt criticized, embarrassed, and "not good enough." She reported nightmares in which she lost her purse, couldn't find her car, or had her hair cut, which left her feeling desperate and anxious. The air of confidence, independence, and even her sexual behaviors were evaporating and appeared to have been compensatory in nature. She had gained the ability to interact in the world but not to relate intimately or to experience a sustaining sense of security. The assessment indicated, however, that she possessed the psychological resources and motivation to benefit from an insight-oriented explorative psychoanalytic approach. She appeared to be motivated to resolve what she accurately perceived as deep-seated conflicts rather than simply to obtain symptom relief.

Initial inquiry into her history indicated that Catholicism played a major role throughout her childhood and into adolescence. Although she had stopped going to church when she went away to college, her spiritual perspective figured prominently as a resource when she was under periods of stress. She believed that God had a plan for every person and that life was purposeful. Her religiosity was assessed to be intrinsic in orientation, and her essential spiritual beliefs were unquestioned. She gave a hint at some anxiety regarding her relationship with God in confessing that she hadn't always been a good or devout person but that she believed that ultimately she would be saved. She hoped for a sign from God that everything would be all right if she had a child or that somehow she could put off the idea of having a child. This underscored the importance of listening carefully for the dynamic contribution of her spirituality and unconscious God-representations to her psychology. That being said, it is important to consider that even in cases in which spirituality plays a central role, we can only know, as Rizzuto (2001) aptly stated,

> a cross section of a life, a moment in a long developmental course that will continue as long as the individual lives. Not even the great attention to detail characteristic of the analytic process can do more than see glimpses of those God representations that have preceded the moment

of treatment nor can it predict with certainty its later transformations or the relevance that the God representations at the time of the treatment's termination may have in the future. (pp. 26–28)

Treatment Goals, Process, and Intervention Strategies

The aim of treatment was the elucidation and working through of intrapsychic conflict in which modifications in psychological structure would be accomplished and through which the presenting symptoms would abate. From an ego psychological perspective, this would involve the "uncovering and reordering of the psychic realities to bring them into a logical ego-syntonic order within themselves and with other realities" (Rangell, 1995, p. 17). Joan's unconscious construction of motherhood, formed through processes of identification, reflected beliefs, fixed in past experience, that produced irrational anxiety and constricted her psychic and behavioral freedom. Psychoanalytic treatment would provide a means to bring into conscious awareness the origins of these beliefs as well as an opportunity to modify these cognitions and unconscious identifications by working through the experiences out of which such thoughts and anxiety emanated. The modification in modes of defense, namely, ego and superego functioning, and her ability to express desires more directly were objectives in the treatment. Modifications in her internal representational world (Sandler & Sandler, 1998) and schemas in respect to mothering (Chodorow, 1978; Stern, 1995) were anticipated to be outcomes of the therapeutic process in which internalizations of the therapist and the experiences of new modes of relating would contribute.

The analytic process is established through conditions of empathy and the development of a therapeutic relationship. No analytic work can be achieved outside of the development of a relationship that minimally offers the conditions of concern, safety, respect, and empathy. Free association is the cornerstone of psychoanalytic technique in which the patient attempts to say whatever comes to mind. This leads to the exploration of associations, memories, dreams, and fantasies, which come into consciousness within the context of the intersubjective field and under conditions of resistance. The analyst facilitates the process through faithful attention to the therapeutic alliance and to transference and countertransference and by offering clarifications, confrontations, and interpretations (Gabbard, 2001; Greenson, 1967). Interpretations may be seen as interventions primarily offered to aid the continuation of the patient's speech, in part through an empathic reading of his or her experience as disclosed in the present (cf. Vergote, 2002, p. 16).

The psychoanalytic situation provides a unique psychological space through which religious associations, spiritual experiences, and God-representations may be elicited and through which the origins and psychodynamic functions of personal religious ideas may be disclosed. The provision of certain technical features, such as free association, the analytic frame, and safeguarding transitional modes of experience, allow for the elaboration of psychoanalytically drawn meanings of spirituality. Because religious associations share the common thread of purpose as other associations, the same rules of interpretation apply. Such associations are not a privileged class of psychological phenomena, nor should they be seen as isolated or tangential to the psychoanalytic discourse but as equally essential to the analytic work. Such a stance emphasizes the psychic utility in which unique spiritual experiences and leitmotifs derived from normative religious culture are enlisted to express individual psychological experience (Shafranske, 2002). Finally, the clinical approach is guided by openness to the meanings of spirituality held by the client and to the transformations that may result. Discussion of the clinical process will be delimited to consideration of the spiritual dimension in treatment, specifically to God-representational processes.

It is useful at the beginning of this discussion of this case to comment that every analytic relationship and analysis is absolutely unique and, as Freud (1961/1913) posited, "the wealth of determining factors oppose any mechanization of technique" (p. 123). Analysts, although similarly attending to unconscious processes, do differ in their conduct of analysis. My own approach, perhaps different from some contemporary analysts, places emphasis on facilitating the development of a transitional space for the transference to evolve by being quiet and allowing a place for the patient's flow of associations. Others might have offered a more interactive, interpersonal stance with a greater degree of self-disclosure. Also, in keeping with total composite theory, I drew from a number of theoretical models in couching interpretations. Lastly, my own faith perspective and experience of the sacred, I conjecture, contributed in unknown ways to the process, a process that was intersubjective and co-constructed by definition. I was affectively moved during many moments of the analysis and experienced a range of associations, reflecting not only my care for Joan but also a reverential awe for the transcendent quality of the work—that we are called to deep, abiding relationships within the sacredness of existence. Analyses are not just about the past but are also about developing our capacity in the moment to experience more completely the world in which we live, including the transcendent realities at which we can only glimpse, our historicity is located, or which are "juxtaposed with an ahistorical, a timeless dimension in human life" (Loewald, 1980, p. 76; see also Shafranske, 1991).

The early phase of treatment focused on the development of an analytic process in which free association was the primary activity. Despite feeling awkward and concerned about my responses to her associations, Joan attempted to follow the basic rule of saying what came to mind. She found it alarming that she could not find cues in my behavior to orient her self-presentation. Her associations gradually evolved from her everyday life situations to an elaboration of themes involving past events, present conflicts, and the therapeutic relationship. This led to a further transition from psychodynamic psychotherapy to her commitment to commence formal psychoanalysis.

As trust developed and the work deepened, she disclosed that when she thought of being a mother, all she could feel was a paralyzing sense of inadequacy and fear. She had worked hard throughout her life to not be in the situation of *her* mother. She questioned her ability "to do analysis right" and reported a series of memories in which demands were placed on her by her parents to look, act, and think properly. She felt at times a nameless anxiety and guilt that she actually was a fraud and that her academic and professional achievements were lacking. She described a silent anxiety, which accompanied her throughout much of her childhood—fears that she might say the wrong thing or "look funny"—and how she overcame these feelings when she discovered she could gain boys' interest. This phase of the analysis involved a strong consolidation of the working alliance as well as anxiety about the psychic territory that she was reentering. She reported being quite moved by her sense that I actually understood, and she would often cry while driving home from the sessions.

It was during this period that her first associations relevant to spirituality occurred. These were memories of reading the lives of the saints as a little girl, of hearing sermons about Christ's suffering and death, and of her fervent attempts at prayer. She recalled how close she felt to her mother when they attended novenas together or when they would stop by the church to recite a prayer. She had a strong sense of spiritual presence in which she felt loved by God but also believed that he exacted strict obedience. Her preparation for first confession was marked with anxiety, exacerbated by her mother's insistence that she must recount all of her sins to be forgiven. Her mother now insisted that she was at the age of reason, which was an idea that she did not fully understand, yet felt that this meant she had to be "good." She recalled that she had a sense that everything was changing inside and that she had to become a better person. Accompanying these memories was an increase in anxiety as she attempted to follow the rule of free association. She was becoming concerned about the feelings that she was developing toward me as well as fear that she was revealing so much to me. She felt herself in a double bind: She felt compelled to follow the rule and yet to do so would mean to express feelings, impulses, and fantasies that she had learned to suppress. This created a circumstance of intersystemic conflict and anxiety.

In one session, following discussion of sadness and allowing herself to cry, she fell silent. Her next stream of associations concerned vivid images of people being shot and a number of corpses lying on a bridge. I commented that she experienced danger in sharing what was coming to mind. Joan sobbed deeply and described how hard it was to know who she was and what she believed and felt. In a subsequent session, she described a dream in which she was lying on an examining table and her dress began to shrink almost to the point of uncovering her genitals. Her associations led to her anxiety that she was revealing too much. I interpreted that the shrinking of her dress might suggest a subtle change in her defenses and, in a later session, that she might be anxious about my observing her sexual impulses or fantasies. She associated that she had been having more dreams in which I appeared but had been nervous to tell me. She recalled then a scene from television in which a man was publicly beaten. She was confused by the emergence of this association as it "had come out of the blue." I offered that she might be feeling anxious about her fantasies, desires, and feelings being made public to me and that unconsciously she believed she should be punished, or "beaten." This led to an outpouring of affect and to a memory of sitting next to her father's chair and wanting to hold onto his leg, at which he point he kicked her away. I commented that she was lying on a couch next to my chair. This led to a painful set of associations about her feelings toward her father and a protective stance that would never allow her to get that close to Mark or to be in that situation again. She reported having dreams of judgment day and recalled lying awake as a child at night imagining the "fires of hell" and praying to be saved. She believed that she was "bad" and that God would punish her. It seemed that her God-representations involved not only a loving God but also a wrathful father–God who not only perceived her actions but also peered into her every thought. She seemed to incorporate religious ideas with the dangers she felt at home about being embarrassed and taunted.

This analytic exploration illuminated the functions of a harsh, punitive superego, and her memories suggested the origins of her internalizations. It appears that her childhood experiences provided conflicted images of a perfect, controlled way of being and shaming and condemnation for breaches of appropriate behavior. She recalled observing her father's tirades at her mother for forgetting her responsibilities as well as his demanding sex from her, which her mother would recount in confidence. Her religious training reinforced a view that there were no distinctions between fantasy and action and that all experience was under the scrutiny of an all-powerful, yet distant father–God. The sense of loving awe, which she experienced as a young child, had turned primarily to fear. Her superego prohibitions were pronounced and inferred to be the source of her anxiety when other drives and psychological motivations would impinge.

We came to understand that her "wild sexual life" had been mostly defensive, not so much an expression of intrapsychic freedom as the need to introduce "danger" and heightened levels of excitement that served to enact the unconscious situation of danger and to minimize feelings of intimacy with her partner. As she considered having a child, her dreams and conscious fears revealed an identification with mother that suggested powerlessness and physical abuse associated with sexuality and subjugation that resulted from having children. In one dream, she pictured being strung by a line over a cliff to be shot at and wounded by men; her father stood observing this scene, declaring with sinister pleasure that this was her feminine fate and must be accepted. She vividly remembers hearing her father's demands for sexual relations with her mother as they would fight late at night. She pictured her father's body as a huge weight crushing her mother and felt anxious and nauseated by these associations. She reported a series of dreams in which her purse or car were lost or stolen. These symbols appeared to represent her sexuality and sense of self or identity, respectively, that would be taken from her or simply lost. The examination of this material brought a number of vivid memories and her affective experience to the surface. She identified that sexuality was the one means she had to have power and that she at times used to mask her anxiety and control interpersonal relationships. It became clear that her conflicts about the Church in part reflected aspects of her unconscious beliefs and conflicts that God allowed women, that is, mothers, to be in positions of subjugation and powerlessness.

Although beyond this discussion, let it suffice that over time she worked through this material and became able to develop a more emotionally engaged relationship with me and with herself in the analysis. She gradually allowed her relationship with her husband to become more authentically intimate, which changed the subjective experience and behaviors within their sexual life. The lengthy middle stage of the treatment, which involved working through of past experience primarily through the vehicle of transference, gradually led to modifications in her representational world and defenses, and her symptoms diminished. She was able to better view her present experience with an appreciation *for the past* rather than solely from the perspective *of the past*.

Late in the analysis, references to her image of God and spirituality again came into awareness as she dealt with the death of a close friend. She spoke of a renewed interest in spirituality and was struck that her friend's passing had brought a deeper appreciation for life rather than fear. She was struck that she could fully feel her experience of loss and sadness rather than feel anxious as she had in the past, when she would attempt to avoid affective experience. She reported feeling in ever-increasing moments that life was a wonderful opportunity and that she was cared for in some everlasting way. She reported that her sense of the presence of God was different in some essential way—God wasn't really the "gods" of her childhood any longer, and she felt no anxiety or awe but rather that whoever the divine was, she was accepted. Although she no longer believed that God directly intervened in one's life, God was nevertheless with her. With her decision to have a child, she began searching for a faith community that would sustain her family. This search would lead her to further clarify her religious and spiritual beliefs. The analytic space provided her a place to explore her beliefs and the psychological factors influencing her spiritual perspective. Joan continued in analysis through her pregnancy and terminated treatment shortly after the birth of her daughter. In her view, analysis had provided a space to talk about her experiences in ways she had never before and that she had grown to trust and feel safe with me, which she was then able to do more readily with others. Without the burden of anxiety, she was more spontaneous and able to express her own desires and experiences, which included developing a meaningful spiritual life.

Course of Treatment and Frequency and Duration of Sessions

The course of treatment was initiated in psychotherapy with a frequency of two sessions per week and within the first year transitioned to formal psychoanalysis at a frequency of four times per week. The treatment lasted a little less than 4 years.

Termination and Relapse Prevention

Indicators for termination included the absence of symptoms and her ability to engage in self-analysis to understand her ongoing psychological experience, to engage intimately with her husband, and to be effective in her interpersonal and professional relations. She was better able to make decisions and to carry forth in living her life in accordance with her needs and values, tempered with a healthy, reality-based appreciation for the inevitable challenges and disappointments. We agreed that we would have a follow-up consultation 6 months after termination and that should she wish further consultation in the future, that could be arranged.

Therapeutic Outcomes: Immediate and Long Term

The immediate and long-term outcomes from a psychoanalytic perspective involved structural change in which an increased capacity for psychological experience was obtained. This resulted in a diminution of unconscious anxiety, lessened the need for defensive responding, and increased her ability to experience her thoughts, feelings, and needs. Although analyses do not eliminate areas of conflict and psychological vulnerability, Joan was better able to recognize the origins of conflict and to respond in the present. In terms of spirituality, there was a gradual transformation or expansion in her conscious and unconscious representations of the sacred, and in a fashion her spirituality was no longer exclusively tethered to more archaic representational processes. Her increased psychological capacity and psychic freedom presented the opportunity for greater depth of experience, including the experience of the sacred and transcendent realities. Psychoanalysis did not intend to change her spiritual stance. Nonetheless, the transformation of the four factors that Rizzuto (chap. 2, this volume) has identified—self- and object-representations, exploration of unconscious beliefs, objectification of the self, affective participation in a meaningful community of two within the analysis—brought her to accomplish the last factor: "to create a new personal narrative, human and divine: she is in the company of her God who won't subjugate her because she has become a mother. She can return safely to the house of God, a faith community" (A.-M. Rizzuto, personal communication, May 20, 2003).

CONCLUSION

Psychoanalysis provides a unique context for the illumination and transformation of deeply held religious beliefs and God-representations. Through the psychoanalytic process, one arrives at and comes to know the place where spirituality took its first breath. Although psychoanalysis is not a spiritual discipline nor does it intend to contribute directly to spiritual growth, it does enable the self to approach and experience more fully the vast horizon of human existence, which touches the heavens.

REFERENCES

Arlow, J. A. (1985). The concept of psychic reality and related problems. *Journal of the American Psychoanalytic Association, 33,* 521–536.

Arlow, J. A. (1996). The concept of *psychic reality*—how useful? *International Journal of Psycho-Analysis, 77,* 659–666.

Bartoli, E. (2001). Psychoanalytic practice and the religious patient: The politics of agency and responsibility (Doctoral dissertation, University of Chicago). *Dissertation Abstracts International, 62*(10), 4772. (UMI No. AAT 3029474)

Brokaw, B. F., & Edwards, K. J. (1994). The relationship of God image to level of object relations development. *Journal of Psychology & Theology, 22*(4), 352–371.

Chirban, J. T. (2001). Assessing religious and spiritual concerns in psychotherapy. In T. G. Plante & A. C. Sherman (Eds.), *Faith and health: Psychological perspectives* (pp. 265–290). New York: Guilford Press.

Chodorow, N. (1978). *The reproduction of mothering.* Berkeley: University of California Press.

De Luca, A. J. (1977). *Freud and future religious experience.* Totowa, NJ: Littlefield, Adams.

De Mello Franco, O. (1998). Religious experience and psychoanalysis: From man-as-God to man-with-God. *International Journal of Psycho-Analysis, 79,* 113–131.

Engler, J. H. (1983). Vicissitudes of the self according to psychoanalysis and Buddhism: A spectrum model of object relations development. *Psychoanalysis and Contemporary Thought, 6,* 29–72.

Epstein, M. D. (1988). The deconstruction of the self: Ego and "egolessness" in Buddhist insight meditation. *Journal of Transpersonal Psychology, 20,* 61–69.

Erikson, E. (1958). *Young man Luther: A study in psychoanalysis and history*. New York: Norton.

Fauteux, K. (1994). *The recovery of the self. Regression and redemption in religious experience*. Mahwah, NJ: Paulist Press.

Feuerbach, L. (1841/1957). *The essence of Christianity* (E. G. Waring & F. W. Strothmann, Eds.). New York: Ungar.

Finn, M. (1992). Transitional space and Tibetan Buddhism: The object relations of meditation. In J. Gartner & M. Finn (Eds.), *Object relations theory and religion* (pp. 109–118). Westport, CT: Praeger.

Freud, A. (1936). *Ego and the mechanisms of defense*. New York: International Universities Press.

Freud, S. (1961). A seventeenth century demonological neurosis (and the undeveloped part). In J. Strachey (Ed. & Trans.), *The standard edition of the complete psychological works of Sigmund Freud* (Vol. 9, pp. 72–105). London: Hogarth Press. (Original work published in 1923)

Freud, S. (1961). Obsessive actions and religious practices. In J. Strachey (Ed. & Trans.), *The standard edition of the complete psychological works of Sigmund Freud* (Vol. 9, pp. 115–127). London: Hogarth Press. (Original work published 1907)

Freud, S. (1961). On beginning the treatment. In J. Strachey (Ed. & Trans.), *The standard edition of the complete psychological works of Sigmund Freud* (Vol. 12, pp. 121–144). London: Hogarth Press. (Original work published 1913)

Freud, S. (1961). Totem and taboo. In J. Strachey (Ed. & Trans.), *The standard edition of the complete psychological works of Sigmund Freud* (Vol. 13, pp. 1–162). London: Hogarth Press. (Original work published 1913)

Freud, S. (1961). The future of an illusion. In J. Strachey (Ed. & Trans.), *The standard edition of the complete psychological works of Sigmund Freud* (Vol. 21, pp. 5–56). London: Hogarth Press. (Original work published 1927)

Freud, S. (1961). Civilization and its discontents. In J. Strachey (Ed. & Trans.), *The standard edition of the complete psychological works of Sigmund Freud* (Vol. 21, pp. 167–172). London: Hogarth Press. (Original work published 1930)

Freud, S. (1961). The question of a weltanschauung. New introductory lectures, Lecture XXXV. In J. Strachey (Ed. & Trans.), *The standard edition of the complete psychological works of Sigmund Freud* (Vol. 22, pp. 158–182). London: Hogarth Press. (Original work published 1933)

Freud, S. (1961). Moses and monotheism. In J. Strachey (Ed. & Trans.), *The standard edition of the complete psychological works of Sigmund Freud* (Vol. 23, pp. 3–139). London: Hogarth Press. (Original work published 1939)

Gabbard, G. O. (2000). *Psychodynamic psychiatry in clinical practice* (3rd ed.). Washington, DC: American Psychiatric Press.

Galatzer-Levy, R. M., Bachrach, H., Skolnikoff, A., & Waldron, W., Jr. (2000). *Does psychoanalysis work?* New Haven, CT: Yale University Press.

Gay, P. (1987). *A Godless Jew: Freud, atheism and the making of psychoanalysis*. New Haven, CT: Yale University Press.

Geertz, C. (1973). Religion as a cultural system. In C. Geertz (Ed.), *The interpretation of cultures* (pp. 87–125). New York: Basic Books. (Reprinted from *Anthropological approaches to the study of religion*, pp. 1–46, by M. Banton, Ed., 1966, London: Tavistock.)

Gill, M. (1994). Comments on "Neutrality, Interpretation, and Therapeutic Intent." *Journal of the American Psychoanalytic Association, 42,* 681–684.

Granqvist, P., & Hagekull, B. (1999). Religiousness and perceived childhood attachment: Profiling socialized correspondence and emotional compensation. *Journal for the Scientific Study of Religion, 38,* 254–273.

Granqvist, P., & Hagekull, B. (2001). Seeking security in the new age: On attachment and emotional compensation. *Journal for the Scientific Study of Religion, 40*(3), 527–545.

Greenson, R. R. (1967). *The technique and practice of psychoanalysis* (Vol. 1). New York: International Universities Press.

Guntrip, H. (1968). Religion in relation to personal integration. *British Journal of Medical Psychology, 42,* 323–333.

Hall, T. W., Brokaw, B. F., Edwards, K. J., & Pike, P. L. (1998). An empirical exploration of psychoanalysis and religion: Spiritual maturity and object relations development. *Journal for the Scientific Study of Religion, 37*(2), 303–313.

Hoffman, I. (1983). The patient as interpreter of the analyst's experience. *Contemporary Psychoanalysis, 19,* 389–422

Hoffman, I. (1991). Discussion: Toward a social–constructivist view of the psychoanalytic situation. *Psychoanalytic Dialogues, 1,* 74–105.

Hoffman, I. (1992). Some practical implications of a social–constructivist view of the psychoanalytic situation. *Psychoanalytic Dialogues, 2,* 287–304.

Jones, J. W. (1991). *Contemporary psychoanalysis and religion: Transference and transcendence.* New Haven: CT: Yale University Press.

Jones, J. W. (1996). *Religion and psychology. Psychoanalysis, feminism, and theology.* New Haven, CT: Yale University Press.

Jones, J. W. (2002). *Terror and transformation.* East Sussex, England: Brunner-Routledge.

Kakar, S. (1991). *The analyst and the mystic.* Chicago: University of Chicago Press.

Kirkpatrick, L. A. (1992). An attachment-theory approach to the psychology of religion. *The International Journal for the Psychology of Religion, 2,* 3–28.

Kirkpatrick, L. A. (1997). A longitudinal study of changes in religious belief and behavior as a function of individual differences in adult attachment style. *Journal for the Scientific Study of Religion, 36,* 207–217.

Kirkpatrick, L. A. (1998). God as a substitute attachment figure: A longitudinal study of adult attachment style and religious change in college students. *Personality & Social Psychology Bulletin, 24,* 961–973.

Kirkpatrick, L. A. (1999). Toward an evolutionary psychology of religion and personality. *Journal of Personality, 67,* 921–952.

Kohut, H. (1959). Introspection, empathy, and psychoanalysis. *Journal of the American Psychoanalytic Association, 7,* 459–483.

Kohut, H. (1984). *How does analysis cure?* Chicago: University of Chicago Press.

Kung, H. (1979). *Freud and the problem of God* (E. Quinn, Trans.) New Haven, CT: Yale University Press.

Loewald, H. W. (1980). On the therapeutic action of psychoanalysis. In *Papers on psychoanalysis* (pp. 221–256). New Haven, CT: Yale University Press.

McDargh, J. (1983). *Psychoanalytic object relations theory and the study of religion.* Washington, DC: University Press of America.

McWilliams, N. (1994). *Psychoanalytic diagnosis. Understanding personality structure in the clinical process.* New York: Guilford Press.

Meissner, W. W. (1987). *Psychoanalysis and religion.* New Haven, CT: Yale University Press.

Messer, S. B., & Warren, C. S. (1995). *Models of brief psychodynamic psychotherapy.* New York: Guilford Press.

Modell, A. H. (1990). *Other times, other realities.* Cambridge, MA: Harvard University Press.

Ogden, T. H. (1994). The analytic third: Working with intersubjective clinical facts. *International Journal of Psycho-Analysis, 75,* 3–20.

Poland, W. (1984) On the analyst's neutrality. *Journal of the American Psychoanalytic Association, 32,* 283–299.

Rangell, L. (1995). Psychoanalytic realities and the analytic goal. *International Journal of Psycho-Analysis, 76,* 15–18.

Rangell, L. (1997). At century's end: A unitary theory of psychoanalysis. The unitary theory of Leo Rangell. *Journal of Clinical Psychoanalysis, 6,* 465–484.

Rangell, L. (2000). Psychoanalysis at the millennium: A unitary theory. *Psychoanalytic Psychology, 17,* 451–466.

Reiff, P. (1961). *Freud: Mind of the moralist.* New York: Doubleday.

Renik, O. (1993). Analytic interaction: Conceptualizing technique in light of the analyst's irreducible subjectivity. *Psychoanalytic Quarterly, 62,* 553–571.

Richards, P. S., & Bergin, A. E. (1997). *A spiritual strategy for counseling and psychotherapy.* Washington, DC: American Psychological Association.

Ricoeur, P. (1970). *Freud and philosophy: An essay on interpretation* (D. Savage, Trans.). New Haven, CT: Yale University Press.

Rizzuto, A.-M. (1979). *The birth of the living God.* Chicago: University of Chicago Press.

Rizzuto, A.-M. (1998). *Why did Freud reject God?* New Haven, CT: Yale University Press.

Rizzuto, A.-M. (2001). Vicissitudes of self, object, and God representations during psychoanalysis. In M. Aletti & G. Rossi (Eds.), *L'Illusione religiosa: Rive e derive* [Religious Illusion] (pp. 26–55). Torino, Italy: Centro Scientifico Edtore.

Rizzuto, A.-M. (2003). Psychoanalysis: The transformation of the subject by the spoken word. *Psychoanalytic Quarterly, 72,* 287–323.

Rowatt, W. C., & Kirkpatrick, L. A. (2002). Two dimensions of attachment to God and their relation to affect, religiosity, and personality constructs. *Journal for the Scientific Study of Religion, 41,* 637–651.

Sandler, J., & Sandler, M. (1998). *Internal objects revisited*. New York: International Universities Press.

Shafranske, E. P. (1991). Subjective historicity and teleology. In H. N. Malony (Ed.), *Psychology of religion: Personalities, problems, possibilities* (pp. 563–570). Grand Rapids, MI: Baker.

Shafranske, E. P. (1995). Freudian theory and religious experience. In R. W. Hood Jr. (Ed.), *Handbook of religious experience* (pp. 200–230). Birmingham, AL: Religious Education Press.

Shafranske, E. P. (2002). The psychoanalytic meaning of religious experience. In M. Arieti & F. De Nardi (Eds.), *Psychoanalisi e religione* (pp. 227–257). Torino, Italy: Centro Scientifico Editore.

Smith, J. H. (1990). On psychoanalysis and the question of nondefensive religion. In J. H. Smith & S. A. Handelman (Eds.), *Psychoanalysis and religion*. Baltimore: The Johns Hopkins University Press.

Sorenson, R. L. (1994). Therapists' (and their therapists') God representations in clinical practice. *Journal of Psychology & Theology, 22*, 325–344.

Sorenson, R. L. (1997). Transcendence and intersubjectivity: The patient's experience of the analyst's spirituality. In C. Spezzano & G. J. Gargiulo (Eds.), *Soul on the couch: Spirituality, religion, and morality in contemporary psychoanalysis* (pp. 163–199). Hillsdale, NJ: Analytic Press.

Sorenson, R. L. (2004). *Minding spirituality*. Hillsdale, NJ: Analytic Press.

Spero, M. H. (1992). *Religious objects as psychological structures*. Chicago: University of Chicago Press.

Stern, D. (1991). A philosophy for the embedded analyst—Gadamer's hermeneutics and the social paradigm of psychoanalysis. *Contemporary Psychoanalysis, 27*, 51–80.

Stern, D. N. (1995). *The motherhood constellation*. New York: Basic Books.

Strozier, C. B. (1997). Heinz Kohut's struggles with religion, ethnicity, and God. In J. L. Jacobs & D. Capps (Eds.), *Religion, society, and psychoanalysis* (pp. 165–180). Boulder, CO: Westview Press.

Suler, J. R. (1993). *Contemporary psychoanalysis and Eastern thought*. Albany: State University of New York Press.

Van Herik, J. (1982). *Freud on femininity and faith*. Berkeley: University of California Press.

Vergote, A. (2002). At the crossroads of the personal word. In M. Arieti & F. De Nardi (Eds.), *Psychoanalisi e religione* (pp. 4–34). Torino, Italy: Centro Scientifico Editore.

Wallerstein, R. S. (1988). One psychoanalysis or many? *International Journal of Psycho-Analysis, 69*, 5–22.

6

A HUMANISTIC APPROACH TO SPIRITUALLY ORIENTED PSYCHOTHERAPY

DAVID N. ELKINS

DESCRIPTION OF THE APPROACH

My approach to spirituality, presented in this chapter, has been influenced strongly by William James (1902), whom I regard as one of the major forerunners of humanistic psychology. Following James, I would characterize the approach as follows: The human personality, at its further limits, opens into the spiritual realm. Speaking metaphorically, one might say that the human personality is a river that, if navigated to its end, opens into the ocean of the mystical realm. Any psychotherapy that explores the deeper regions of the human psyche will eventually come to the brink of this spiritual realm, whether the client and therapist recognize the place or not. It is my opinion that human personality and spirituality exist on the same continuum and that a more complete psychology would encompass that entire continuum in terms of theory, research, training, and practice.

Historical and Theoretical Basis

This section provides a historical overview of humanistic psychology along with a summary of the author's own spiritually oriented approach which is based on humanistic principles.

The author wishes to thank Thomas Greening, L. James Hedstrom, Larry M. Leitner, Kirk J. Schneider, and E. Mark Stern for reading the manuscript while this chapter was in preparation and making helpful suggestions.

Historical Overview of Humanistic Psychology

As Schneider, Bugental, and Fraser Pierson (2001) pointed out, the historical roots of humanistic psychology are found in four major periods in which humanism flourished in Western culture: (a) the classical period of ancient Greece in the 5th century B.C.E. when philosophers such as Socrates and Plato turned their attention from the gods to that which concerns the human being; (b) the European Renaissance when scholars, returning to the classics of ancient Greece, focused on the *studia humanitatis* in contrast to the *studia divinitatis*; (c) the Enlightenment of the 17th and 18th centuries when rationalists and romanticists—both participants in the movement—debated whether cognition or emotions distinguish the human being; and (d) the turn of the 20th century when humanism arose once again and in psychology took the form of a reaction again the determinism of Freudianism and the mechanistic assumptions of Watsonian behaviorism. William James (1902), Carl Jung (1933), Otto Rank (1958), and Ludwig Binswanger (1963) were among the early proponents of a less deterministic and mechanistic psychology.

Although humanistic psychology as we know it today draws on all these historical periods, it is more immediately associated with the 1950s and 1960s when Abraham Maslow, Carl Rogers, Rollo May, James Bugental, Gordon Allport, Henry Murray, George Kelly, and others began to raise concerns about mainstream American psychology, which was dominated at the time by psychoanalysis in clinical training and behaviorism in academia (Elkins, 2000; Taylor, 1999). Maslow and the other founders of what would become humanistic psychology wanted to create a psychology focused less on pathology and the prediction and control of human behavior and more on the positive potentials and distinctive attributes of the human being. The seeds of the new psychology were planted in various writings and meetings in the 1940s and 1950s, and the movement blossomed and flourished in the 1960s. The *Journal of Humanistic Psychology* was launched in 1961, and a year later the American Association for Humanistic Psychology (AAHP), later renamed the Association for Humanistic Psychology (AHP), was formed. In 1964, AAHP held its "First Invitational Conference on Humanistic Psychology" at Old Saybrook, Connecticut. Henry Murray gave the keynote address, and Rogers, Maslow, and May were among those who presented papers. The Old Saybrook conference helped clarify the vision and set the future course of humanistic psychology in the United States. Within a few years, humanistic psychology would become a major "third force" in American psychology. It would attract thousands of psychology students, spawn numerous humanistic organizations, provide a penetrating critique of reductionistic science, articulate new methodologies and more qualitative "ways of knowing" in research, emphasize the healing power of the relationship and the intersubjective "between" in psychotherapy, and generate an array of new approaches to psychotherapy and counseling that focused less on pathology and more on the actualizing possibilities of the human being.

As Taylor and Martin (2001) pointed out, humanistic psychology was strengthened by the inclusion of European existentialism and phenomenology. In 1958, Rollo May, along with Angel and Ellenberger, edited *Existence: A New Dimension in Psychiatry and Psychology* (1958), a book that brought the psychological fruits of European existentialists and phenomenologists to the attention of American psychology and under the umbrella of humanistic psychology. Also, Viktor Frankl (1963), a Viennese psychiatrist and holocaust survivor whose book *Man's Search for Meaning* was a best-seller after World War II, contributed to the new movement through his logotherapy, an existential therapeutic approach based on what Frankl called the "will to meaning." The *Journal of Humanistic Psychology*, housed at Brandeis University where Maslow was chair of the psychology department, became the primary organ of the new movement. The avant-garde thinking in its pages was taken seriously in academia and other scholarly circles, and its editorial board included some of the most respected and influential figures in psychology and related disciplines of that period. Humanistic psychology's focus on the self-actualizing possibilities of the human personality, its emphasis on authentic and emotionally mature relationships, and its nonreductionistic approach to values, love, meaning, art, culture, religion, and spirituality had a strong impact on American psychology. Highly generative in nature, the new psychology opened up vistas of human personality and experience that more reductionistic approaches had attempted to explain away or had left unexplored. This more inclusive perspective that focused on the strengths and potentials of the human being was, for many academicians and clinicians, a breath of fresh air after 50 years of Freudian psychology and animal experiments in academic laboratories.

The humanistic movement did not, however, ultimately live up to its early promise. Eugene Taylor (1999, 2000), a William James scholar at Harvard and professional historian of the movement, has pointed out that humanistic psychology thrived as a respected alternative perspective in academia from 1941 to 1969, but at that time the scholarly focus of the movement was overshadowed by the political and social ferment of the times. Humanistic ideals, which fit the revolutionary milieu of the day, were preempted by the American counterculture. Humanism, which had a distinguished history stretching back to ancient Greece and serving as the main force behind the European Renaissance, was trivialized by extremes within the counterculture so that humanistic ideals were used as an excuse for any unusual personal or group experiment that members of the counterculture decided to try. This is not to condemn the counterculture of the 1960s, which addressed major political and social issues and helped change our nation in positive directions, but it is to point out that when humanistic psychology was used to support the anti-intellectualism and almost exclusive focus on the body and emotions that characterized certain parts of the counterculture, it had a chilling effect on the field's respectability in academic and other scholarly circles where serious intellectual thought was the sine qua non. Even today, scholars and other thoughtful proponents of humanistic psychology continue to pay a price in terms of credibility because of the 1960s stereotypes that still hover about the movement. As Taylor and Martin (2001) put it, "Mainstream psychologists, if they have any name recognition at all when asked about the movement, think of humanistic psychology as unscientific, guilty of promoting the cult of narcissism, and a thing of the past" (p. 25).

The truth is, the stereotypes of the 1960s have little to do with the scholarly segment of the humanistic movement. In fact, some of the avant-garde thinking in psychology today focuses on topics that humanistic and existential thinkers have been discussing for many years, including Seligman's positive psychology (1990, 1993; Seligman & Csikszentmihalyi, 2000), Stolorow's intersubjective field (Stolorow, Atwood, & Brandchaft, 1994), and Kohut's self psychology (1971, 1977, 1984). For example, Kohut's theory of the self is widely known and respected, but Carl Rogers's developmental theory relative to the self structure is seldom discussed, even though it is arguably as detailed and clinically relevant as Kohut's. Also, the nature, dynamics, and quality of the therapeutic relationship have been the central focus of humanistic psychotherapy, and Martin Buber (1965, 1970, 1988), who influenced Carl Rogers and other humanistic psychologists, wrote extensively about the therapeutic power of the intersubjective "between" long before Stolorow and others made the topic famous. My intent here is not to pit one theorist against another or to argue for the superiority of one perspective over another. Rather, I am trying to show that humanistic psychology has always had a strong scholarly component and that it has made important, even groundbreaking, contributions to the field.

In terms of contemporary scholarly activity, a major "re-visioning" of humanistic psychology is currently underway that involves dozens of scholars and researchers, numerous humanistic organizations, and hundreds of humanistically oriented professionals from the United States and around the world (Elkins, 2000). Also, Schneider et al. (2001) recently published *The Handbook of Humanistic Psychology*, a tome of 700 pages that contains contributions from more than 60 contemporary scholars associated with the humanistic movement. In addition, articles focused on humanistic research and theory are regularly published in journals such as *The Humanistic Psychologist*, *Journal of Humanistic Psychology*, *The Psychotherapy Patient*, *Journal of Phenomenological Psychology*, *Review of Existential Psychology and Psychiatry*, *The Journal of Constructivist Psychology*, and others. Humanistic scholars— which include humanists, existentialists, phenomenologists, constructivists, and transpersonalists—have much to contribute to the intellectual discourse now taking place in psychology and related fields. Those of us associated with humanistic psychology would encourage colleagues and psychology students to disregard the stereotypes and explore for themselves the philosophical, theoretical, and research contributions of the humanistic movement.

Spirituality in Humanistic Psychology

Humanistic psychology has always considered spirituality to be an integral part of the human personality. Abraham Maslow, the main theoretical architect of the humanistic movement, included spirituality as a major component of the humanistic vision. Instead of pathologizing religious needs, Maslow (1962) said, "The human being needs a framework of values, a philosophy of life, a religion or religion surrogate to live by and understand by, in about the same sense he needs sunlight, calcium, or love" (p. 206). In contrast to Freud's view that religion was a sign of neurosis, Maslow (1976) said, "Humanistic psychologists would probably consider a person sick or abnormal in an existential way if he were not concerned with these 'religious questions' " (p. 18).

Maslow was among the first to insist that spirituality should be brought under the umbrella of psychology and become the focus of psychological research. In *Religions, Values, and Peak Experiences* (1976), he wrote,

> I want to demonstrate that spiritual values have naturalistic meaning, that they are not the exclusive possession of organized churches, that they do not need supernatural concepts to validate them, that they are well within the jurisdiction of a suitably enlarged science, and that, therefore, they are the general responsibility of all mankind. (p. 33)

Although Maslow believed that spirituality was a universal human phenomenon that was not the exclusive possession of any religion, he was not opposed to organized religion per se, nor did he believe a nontheistic view was the only viable philosophical or theological perspective. In fact, Maslow (1976) said that "the essential core-religious experience may be embedded in either a theistic, supernatural context or a nontheistic context" (p. 28).

Maslow's interest in spirituality eventually led him to launch another movement in American psychology devoted specifically to its exploration. As Taylor (1999) said, Maslow believed that mystical states—what he called peak experiences—represented a new frontier for psychology. In 1967, at the peak of humanistic psychology's influence and popularity, Maslow announced the emergence of transpersonal psychology, a "fourth force" in American psychology. In 1969, the *Journal of Transpersonal Psychology* was launched and in 1971, the American Association of Transpersonal Psychology, later renamed the Association for Transpersonal Psychology (ATP), was formed. For the past 30 years, transpersonal psychology has continued to grow, attracting scholars such as Charles Tart (1975a, 1975b, 1989), Ken Wilber (1977, 1980, 1981, 1995), Frances Vaughan (1979, 1986), Roger Walsh (1993, 1995, 1999), and others.

As Hastings (1999) pointed out, one of the ongoing debates in humanistic and transpersonal circles is whether transpersonal psychology is truly an independent "fourth force" or should be included under the umbrella of humanistic psychology. My own view is that transpersonal psychology, which originally sprouted and grew in humanistic soil, has gone on to develop its own theories and perspectives. Whereas some humanistic psychologists have embraced transpersonal theories to describe their own spiritual outlook, others do not necessarily view transpersonal psychology as representing their own spiritual perspective. It does seem, however, that humanistic psychologists have allowed transpersonalists do most of the "spirituality work" for both movements and have not developed and articulated a specifically humanistic vision of spirituality.

A recent survey conducted by Elkins, Lipari, and Kozora (1999) confirmed that contemporary humanistic psychologists remain interested in spirituality. A 71-item questionnaire, which included a section of items on spirituality, was mailed to all 615 members of Division 32 (Humanistic Psychology) of the American Psychological Association. Of the 230 (37%) who completed and returned the questionnaire, 77% said that they considered spirituality "important" or "very important" in their lives. When asked how important organized religion is in their lives, 22% said it is "important" or "very important." Another 26% said it is "somewhat important," and 49% said it is "not important at all," When asked to select the statement that best represents their spiritual orientation, 55% chose "I am spiritual but not religious," 32% chose "I am both religious and spiritual," and only 6% chose "I am neither religious nor spiritual." Finally, 75% affirmed belief in some type of higher power or transcendent force, and 43% professed faith in a personal god. These findings suggest that the great majority of humanistic psychologists view spirituality as an important dimension of their lives. Even more interesting is the fact that 43% profess faith in a personal God, a finding that challenges the myth that humanistic psychologists are nontheistic (for example, see Richards & Bergin, 1997).

A Humanistic Model of Spirituality: Theory, Constructs, and Clinical Application

In my own work as a humanistic psychologist, I have attempted to develop a model of spirituality that is accessible, clinically useful, and based on humanistic principles. I respect the contributions of transpersonal writers, but my own approach is based more on the writings of scholars such as William James (1902), Carl Jung (1933, 1964), Rudolph Otto (1923), Paul Tillich (1948, 1952, 1957), Mircea Eliade (1959), Martin Buber (1970), Gordon Allport (1961), Viktor Frankl (1963), Erich Fromm (1950), James Hillman (1975), and Abraham Maslow (1954, 1962, 1971, 1976).

I was originally trained as a minister in a conservative church, but in the late 1960s, because I could no longer support some of its fundamentalist teachings, I was fired and excommunicated for being too liberal in my theological views. Nevertheless, my interest in spirituality continued, and in the 1970s, when I was a doctoral student in psychology, I entered psychotherapy with a Jungian analyst who taught me about the care and feeding of the human soul. My spiritually oriented therapy with this analyst, along with my own studies of spirituality as a professor and clinical psychologist, led me eventually to develop my own approach to spirituality. A summary is presented in the following paragraphs. For a fuller discussion of this approach, readers are referred to my book, *Beyond Religion* (Elkins, 1998).

Major Constructs

The Soul. The word *soul* comes from Old English and Anglo-Saxon roots meaning "breath" or "life force." Soul is not easy to define, especially in a discipline that insists on operational definitions. In his lectures at Yale University, Jungian scholar James Hillman (1975) pointed to the difficulty: "The soul is immeasurably deep and can only be illumined by insights, flashes in a great cavern of incomprehension" (p. xvi). Soul is not a tangible entity but a construct that points to the spiritual dimension of the human being. As Thomas Moore (1992) put it, " 'Soul' is not a thing but a quality or a dimension of experiencing life and ourselves. It has to do with depth, value, relatedness, heart, and personal substance" (p. 5).

Ironically, the very fact that soul is so difficult to define provides an important clue to its nature. The soul does not fit our Western need for abstract definitions. Soul reminds us that there is a deeper, more primordial world than our logical processes. We know the soul when we are stirred by a poem, moved by a piece of music, touched by a painting. Soul is the deep resonance that vibrates within us at such moments. Thus, the soul can be touched, felt, and known but never defined. Soul will slip through the bars of every conceptual system and defy all attempts to capture her in abstract terms. The soul is found in poetry, music, art, literature, ceremonies, symbols, rituals, intimate relationships, and other events and experiences sympathetic to her imaginal nature. In Western culture we tend to believe that thinking can open every door, unlock every secret. Thus, we know little about the world of the soul where cognition is dethroned and imaginal processes are more important. As a result, we often mistake the menu for the meal and delude ourselves that we understand once we have an abstract definition in place. Yet unless our knowledge of the soul is rooted in personal experience, our abstract definitions simply hang in space, devoid of meaning and rooted in nothing.

How then can we arrive at a common understanding of the soul? Common understandings emerge from an epistemology that acknowledges the importance of personal and experiential knowing. Without such an epistemology, the soul cannot be known and scholars will be forever discussing the menu instead of the meal. Yet among those who do their own spiritual work and become familiar with the spiritual domain, it becomes increasingly possible to speak of these matters with a common vocabulary.

The Sacred. When the sociologist Emile Durkheim studied native cultures, he noticed that when members of the tribe went away to commune with the *sacred*, they returned to the village with a renewed power that they called *mana*. This led Durkheim (1915, p. 416) to write, "The believer who has communicated with his god is . . . stronger. He feels within him more force, either to endure the trials of existence, or to conquer them."

Mircea Eliade, who for many years was chair of the Department of the History of Religions at the University of Chicago, believed that humans have always had encounters with the sacred. In his classic work, *The Sacred and the Profane*, Eliade (1959) defined the sacred and described the mysterious power that Durkheim had observed. He wrote,

> The sacred is equivalent to a *power*, and, in the last analysis, to *reality*. The sacred is saturated with *being*. Sacred power means reality and at the same time enduringness and efficacity. The polarity sacred–profane is often expressed as an opposition between *real* and *unreal* or pseudo-real. . . . Thus, it is easy to understand that religious man deeply desires *to be*, to particulate in *reality*, to be saturated with power. (pp. 12–13)

Although this language may sound strange to Western ears, Eliade was talking about something that is central to spirituality. Along with Durkheim, he was suggesting that sacred experiences have a powerful and fortifying effect. Rudolph Otto (1923), the theologian who wrote *The Idea of the Holy*, did a phenomenological analysis of sacred encounters and concluded that these experiences contain several elements including a sense of being overwhelmed, a feeling of fascination, a sense of mystical awe, and an experience of intense energy. The "intense energy" that Otto mentions is similar to Durkheim's *mana* and Eliade's *power* and *being*.

What does this have to do with psychotherapy? I would suggest that there is a certain ontological power associated with spirituality that can help heal and fortify our clients' lives. This power can help them—in Durkheim's words—"to endure the trials of existence, or to conquer them." Some may ascribe the power to God or some other transcendent force, and others may view it as simply the untapped spiritual resources of the human personality. Regardless of how one explains it, these scholars suggest that there is a special power associated with spirituality that can give grounding and strength to human beings. One goal of spiritually oriented psychotherapy is to help clients access this sacred power.

Spirituality. The word *spirituality* comes from the Latin root *spiritus*, which means "breath" and refers to the animating principle of life. Spirituality is based on the assumption that we live in two worlds—a material world we know through the five senses and a nonmaterial world that is known through intuition, inner reflection, and imagination. Spirituality has to do with the nonmaterial world, the world that mystics, poets, artists, shamans, prophets, and philosophers have told us about for thousands of years. This world is vitally important to our existence as human beings, and in it we find our deepest values and most profound meanings.

In *Beyond Religion* (Elkins, 1998), I presented my own view of spirituality in the following words:

> First: Spirituality is universal. By this, I mean that spirituality is available to every human being. It is not limited to one religion, one culture, or one group of people. In every part of the world, one finds those who have cultivated their souls and developed their spiritual lives.
>
> Second: Spirituality is a human phenomenon. This does not mean that it has no divine component, but it does mean that spirituality is an inborn, natural potential of the human being. It also means that authentic spirituality is grounded in our humanity; it is not imposed from above or from without.
>
> Third: The common core of spirituality is found at the inner phenomenological level. Spirituality manifests in countless outer forms—from the rain dances of Native Americans to the prayer services of Southern Baptists, from the whirling dervishes of Islam to the meditating monks of Zen Buddhism, from the ecstatic worship services of charismatic churches to the solemn silent meeting of the Quakers. But underneath these outward forms, there is a common longing for the sacred, a universal desire to touch and celebrate the mystery of life. It is in the depths of the soul that one discovers the essential and universal dimensions of spirituality.
>
> Fourth: Spirituality has to do with our capacity to respond to the numinous. The essential character of spirituality is mystical, a fact easily overlooked in a scientific and material age. Spirituality is rooted in the soul and cultivated by experiences of the sacred; it feeds on poignancy, wonder, and awe. Its very nature is an expression of the mystery of life and the unfathomable depths of our own being.
>
> Fifth: There is a certain mysterious energy associated with spirituality. Every culture has recognized a life force that moves through all creation. Mystics, poets, artists, shamans, and others are familiar with this force and have described it through the centuries. The soul comes alive when it is nurtured by this sacred energy, and one's existence becomes infused with passion, power, and depth.
>
> Sixth: The aim of spirituality is compassion. The word *compassion* literally means "to suffer with." Spiritual life springs from the tenderness of the heart, and authentic spirituality expresses itself through loving action toward others. Compassion has always been the hallmark of authentic spirituality and the highest teaching of religion. Loveless spirituality is an oxymoron and an ontological impossibility. (pp. 32–33)

Statement of the Theory

I have described three major constructs—the soul, the sacred, and spirituality. These three constructs and their dynamic relationship to one another are the building blocks of my approach to spirituality. Simply stated, the theory is this: When the soul is nourished through regular contact with the sacred dimension, the result is spiritual growth or spirituality. All human beings have a soul. All human beings have access to the sacred. Thus, all human beings, whether traditionally religious or not, can learn to access the sacred, nourish their souls, and develop their spiritual lives.

Clinical Application

The clinical application of this theory is based on two assumptions: the first is that the client is suffering at the level of the soul and the second is that psychotherapy is the process by which the client's soul is nurtured and healed. Because this kind of language sounds strange in a profession dominated by medical and mechanistic models, I will provide a context for this approach before describing its clinical applications.

The word *psychology* comes from the Greek words *psyche* and *logos* and literally means "the study of the soul." The word *therapist* originally meant "servant" or "attendant." Thus, etymologically, a psychotherapist is a "servant or attendant of the soul." This is why Jungian scholar James Hillman (1975) defined psychotherapy as "soul-making" and views the therapist as a servant of the soul-making process. Even the word *psychopathology* points to the soul. It comes from the Greek words *psyche* and *pathos* and literally means "the suffering of the soul."

Throughout the history of psychology, there have been respected psychologists and psychiatrists who recognized that pathology is sometimes the result of spiritual conflicts and deprivations. This distinguished list includes Carl Jung, William James, Viktor Frankl, Gordon Allport, Abraham Maslow, Irvin Yalom, and others. So the idea that psychopathology is sometimes rooted in the spiritual domain is not a new idea.

Spiritually oriented psychotherapy is the process by which we attempt to assuage a client's suffering by nurturing and healing the soul. But how does one do this in practical terms? First, the therapist's relationship with the client is crucial if one wishes to heal at the spiritual level. For many years, we have known that the quality of the therapeutic relationship is an important factor in psychotherapy. As Yalom (1980) pointed out, there are hundreds of research studies demonstrating that the quality of the therapist–client relationship is significantly related to therapeutic outcome. Yalom went on to say that the most important lesson the psychotherapist must learn is that it is the relationship that heals. But what does it mean that the relationship heals? From a spiritual perspective, I believe this is another way of saying that the therapist nurtures the client's soul, and through this nurturing the client is healed. Love is the most powerful healer of the suffering soul, and in the therapeutic relationship love takes the form of empathy, respect, honesty, caring, and acceptance. These factors make soul-to-soul contact possible and have a profound effect on the client's inner life.

Second, although a caring and spiritually sensitive therapist can nurture a client's soul, it is important for clients to realize that psychotherapy is not simply a place where people come to have their souls nurtured by someone else but that it is also a training ground where they learn how to care for their own souls. The client should be shown that there are many activities and experiences that can nourish the soul. Almost anything that touches, stirs, or speaks to the client's depths has this capacity, including music, literature, poetry, plays, movies, paintings, religion, nature, and countless other possibilities. Like a shaman carefully choosing roots and herbs, the therapist must help each client discover the activities and experiences that nurture his or her unique soul. Some clients are nourished by listening to music or going to art galleries and poetry readings. Others prefer going on camping trips or hiking in the mountains. What is important is that each client is helped to identify what best nurtures his or her own spiritual life.

Third, the client should be encouraged to begin a regular program of soul nurturing. For one client this may mean taking daily walks on the beach or along the river; for another it may mean setting aside time to read poetry or listen to music; for still others it may mean planning regular retreats to a mountain cabin. Clients should choose several activities that nourish their souls and engage in these on a regular basis. The case example presented later in this chapter will demonstrate how this can be implemented in psychotherapy.

The Nature of the Relationship Between Psychology and Spirituality

I believe psychology and spirituality are intimately related. Historically, there was a rift between psychology and religion, but, as I stated in the introduction to this chapter, a broader, more inclusive psychology can and should encompass the spiritual dimension of the human being.

Psychology often describes the human being in terms of four major dimensions: body, mind, emotions, and behavior. Unfortunately, the soul, or the spiritual dimension, is almost always left out. The soul is an important construct because it points to a dimension not covered by these other constructs. Such a construct gives us a way to discuss a client's spiritual capacity and to focus on its development in psychotherapy. Of course, once the soul, or the spiritual dimension by any other name, is brought under the umbrella of psychology, this has implications for psychological research, training, and practice. An immediate implication would be that psychologists and graduate students would have to be trained in spiritual issues of clients in the same way they are currently trained in regard to the mind, body, emotions, and behavior of clients.

Therapist's Skills and Attributes

In his book *I and Thou*, Martin Buber (1970) said that there are two basic ways of relating, which he called I-It and I-Thou. In the I-It mode, the other is an object or a means to an end. In the I-Thou encounter, the other ceases to be an object and we are drawn into a deeper kind of relationship. Buber went on to say that when we relate to another as an It, we are also affected because the I that goes forth to meet an It is very different from the I that goes forth to meet a Thou.

Buber's thinking is subtle but powerful. To translate this into terms relevant to this discussion, one might say that psychotherapists can only heal at the level of the soul when they are in contact with their own souls. We can touch our clients only as deeply as the place from which we come within ourselves. If we are intimately familiar with our own souls and can access the spiritual dimension of our own being, we will be able to make contact with our clients at a deeper, more profound level and create a relationship in which *cura animarum*, "cure of the soul," becomes possible. This is not to say that therapists who are have not developed their own spirituality cannot address religious and spiritual issues in psychotherapy and provide some help to the client suffering at the soul level, but it is to say that such therapists may be forced to deal with the client on an I-It basis and may have difficulty relating to the client's spiritual struggle on a more personal and profound level. When dealing with a client's spiritual life, the deeper we have gone in our own spiritual journey, the greater our chances of engaging the client on a soul-to-soul basis and being of help to the client. As existential theologian Paul Tillich put it, "Depth speaks to depth" (Elkins, 1998, p. 177).

Strengths and Limitations

Perhaps the major strength of this approach is that it is based on the assumption that spirituality is a universal human phenomenon that does not belong exclusively to any religion or spiritual system. Although psychologists who hold orthodox views about the importance of a particular religion may find this assumption unattractive, psychologists who are searching for a nonsectarian and more universal approach to spirituality will find the approach congruent with those values. Also, all clients—whether religious or nonreligious—can use this approach to nourish their souls and develop their spiritual lives.

The major limitation of the approach has to do with the difficulty of defining such constructs as *spirituality*, *soul*, and *sacred*. Such "phenomenological realities" do not easily lend themselves to operational definitions and scientific investigation using the traditional methods of psychological science. Thus, it is difficult to move these ideas out of the realm of theory into the realm of scientifically verified facts. Most psychotherapies are "construct-laden," however, and researchers who are willing to define science in broader, less traditional "scientistic" terms can find ways to verify and articulate knowledge in these areas. A broader view of science—one that values subjectivity and phenomenological realities—is needed along with research methods that can more appropriately handle such subtle but important phenomena (Elkins, 1998; Giorgi, 1970).

Indications and Contraindications

This approach to spirituality is most useful to clients who have a well-developed capacity for self-reflection and who are already familiar with that dimension of their inner lives that the theory refers to as the soul or the spiritual dimension. Although these clients are the ones most likely to benefit from the approach, other clients may also find it useful. For example, many clients who do not think of themselves as spiritually inclined are nevertheless able to recall songs, movies, plays, concerts, poems, works of art, ceremonies, rituals, places in nature, relationships, and other experiences that touched them profoundly. Such experiences provide an opening in psychotherapy, a place to begin to help clients become more aware of their spiritual dimension and more adept at nurturing that part of their inner lives.

Clients who would not be appropriate for this approach include (a) those who do not have the mental capacity for self-reflection and inner work, (b) those recovering from a psychotic episode or who may be especially vulnerable to psychosis, (c) those whose defenses are tenuous and who need supportive therapy before moving to more inner-directed work, and (d) those who simply prefer not to make spirituality part of their psychotherapy.

Other clients who *might not be* appropriate for this approach (and thus should be evaluated carefully) include (a) those who have been deeply wounded by religious or spiritual systems or by authorities associated with such systems and (b) those who are so committed to fundamentalist or conservative religious beliefs that their psychological equilibrium might be seriously disturbed by alternative, more relativistic views of spirituality. A clinical interview that includes a detailed exploration of the client's psychological and religious history, along with traditional psychological testing, may be useful in making these determinations.

Cultural and Gender Considerations

Although this approach is based on a universal view of spirituality that recognizes the importance of spirituality in all cultures, it grew from the roots of a Western historical tradition, that is, humanism, and has inherent and unavoidable cultural biases that may not fit the cultural background of some clients, particularly those from non-Western cultures.

For example, Western spirituality, including this approach, tends to focus on the spiritual growth of the individual, whereas many other cultures think in terms of the communal group. Nevertheless, because this approach is based on a deep respect for all forms of spirituality, the therapist who is willing to listen and learn about the unique cultural values of clients may be able to make adjustments in the theory and adapt parts of the approach to clients with non-Western cultural value systems.

With regard to gender considerations, I am unaware of any major concerns relative to the applicability of the theory. My own observations indicate that men and women sometimes differ in terms of the kinds of experiences that nourish their souls, but the theory has enough built-in flexibility to adapt to both individual and gender differences. Because the starting point of the applied theory is to discover what nourishes this particular client's unique soul, the theory is highly adaptable to both men and women.

Expected Future Developments and Directions

It is unclear what the future holds relative to spirituality in the humanistic movement and what new developments will take place in time. Venturing a guess, I would say that humanistic psychologists will continue to place a high value on spirituality in both their personal lives and in their clinical work; they will continue to view spirituality as a universal human phenomenon that is distinct from organized religion; they will continue to explore the topic in an effort to find new and better ways of making spirituality part of psychotherapy; and they will incorporate more ideas from Eastern religions and other spiritual systems—without sacrificing the positive contributions of Western humanism—in an effort to create a spiritual approach that is increasingly sensitive to people from non-Western cultures. Finally, I predict that organized religion with its rituals and ceremonies will always remain important to many humanistic psychologists but that they will tend to relativize all spiritual systems, including their own, as expressions of a more fundamental need of all human beings to look up in wonder and awe.

CASE EXAMPLE

Client Demographics, Relevant Histories, and Presenting Concern

The following case is a composite constructed to demonstrate my approach. Sheila, a 37-year-old divorced Caucasian woman, came to therapy because she was feeling depressed. During the intake interview, when I asked about her religious background, Sheila told me that she had grown up in a conservative Protestant family in the Midwest and that as a child and teenager she had attended church on a regular basis. When she left home to attend college, she began to have doubts about religion and eventually stopped going to church. She said that she still believed in God but no longer prayed or engaged in any kind of religious activities.

Sheila was physically healthy, had no history of psychological difficulties, and had experienced no unusual illnesses or trauma during her childhood. She had grown up in a small town where her father ran the local grocery store. Her mother had stayed home most of the time to take care of Sheila and her younger brother. Sheila said that she had always felt loved and supported by her parents and that she continued to have a good relationship with them and also with her brother. Sheila's parents and brother all still lived in the same town where Sheila had grown up, and she went home for visits about twice per year.

After completing a bachelor's degree at a university in Ohio, Sheila and a female friend moved to Southern California, where she found a job as an accounting clerk in a technology company. When she was 24, she fell in love with a man, and a year later they were married. After 6 years of marriage, however, they both came to the conclusion that the marriage was not working. In her words, they were both "good people but not good marriage partners." A divorce ensued and was finalized when Sheila was 31. When Sheila came to therapy, she had not dated anyone on a serious basis since her divorce 6 years earlier. She said that her job required a lot of time and she wasn't that interested in dating. Sheila was competent and well liked at work, where she had been promoted to accounting supervisor. She also had several friends outside of work whom she saw on a regular basis.

Finding nothing unusual in Sheila's history or current situation, I asked her more specifically about her depressive feelings. She said that she had felt "blue" off and on for years but that in recent months the feelings had become more intense. "I don't think I'm depressed," she told me. "I have a good life but sometimes I look around and say, 'Is this all there is?' I'm unhappy and it feels like something's missing." Further discussion revealed that Sheila had first begun to have these depressive feelings during college, a few months after she had quit going to church. As she thought about this more deeply, she said that as a child she had always gone to church and just assumed that God was watching over her. But when she stopped attending church during college, she had begun to feel cut off from God and, in her words, "very alone in the world." Her marriage had kept these feelings at bay, but they had returned with considerable force after the divorce. When I asked Sheila if she had considered returning to church, she told me that she no longer believed many of the things Christianity taught and had no desire to return to church. She was still interested in spirituality, however, and had even attended a few workshops on Buddhist spirituality.

Assessment and Clinical Case Formulation

Typically, I do a traditional clinical interview in the first session. I make it a practice, as part of this interview, to ask about the client's religious and spiritual life. If I had not specifically asked Sheila about this, I might not have discovered this important information. At the same time, if Sheila had not made the connection between her depressive feelings and her sense of being cut off from God and alone in the world, I probably would not have pursued this further but would have explored other possible reasons for the troubling emotions she was experiencing. Obviously, other explanations could have included the fact that she was in California, away from her original family; that she had no husband or significant other in her life; that she was under stress at work; and so forth. In fact, I am sure that all these factors did contribute to her depressive feelings at times, but the core problem seemed to be spiritual—a perspective with which she agreed when we explored the issue. My hypothesis was that the rituals and ceremonies associated with her church had nourished her soul, at least to some degree, but when she stopped attending church, she also stopped nourishing her spiritual life. After discussing this with Sheila, I told her that I thought she was feeling depressed because her soul needed to be nourished. Once I explained that this did not mean that she had to return to church but that we would look for other ways to nourish her spiritual life, she became intrigued and was ready to proceed in that direction. We agreed that this would be the focus of her therapy for a few weeks to see if this perspective proved helpful.

Treatment Goals, Therapeutic Relationship Process, Intervention Strategies, and Course of Treatment

My primary goal was to help alleviate Sheila's depressive symptoms by showing her how to nourish her soul. My first task, however, was to establish a positive, supportive relationship by listening carefully with a type of "active empathy" or what Tillich called "listening love".[1] Next, I determined the kind of activities and experiences that nourished her soul. I gave Sheila a homework assignment that involved three exercises designed to help her answer this question. One involved simply setting aside time to reflect on activities and experiences that had nourished her soul in the past. The instructions were as follows:

> Think back over your life and ask yourself the following question: What experiences have touched me most deeply? Think of the most poignant moments you have experienced, events that touched and stirred your soul. You may have felt awe, reverence, wonder, humility, or gratitude. Tears may have come to your eyes. These experiences may have occurred when you were listening to music, making love, talking with a friend, reading a poem, attending a play. Make a list of all these experiences and bring them to therapy so we can discover common themes and get a

---

[1] Humanistic psychology views the quality of the therapist–client relationship as a central component of therapeutic healing. Carl Rogers' ideas about the importance of empathy, positive regard, and congruence have shaped my therapeutic style. While not denying the reality of transference, humanistic psychology emphasizes that when the focus is on modeling and developing a relationship characterized by empathy, acceptance, and therapist authenticity, most clients will respond to this interpersonal milieu by gradually recognizing and discussing their own interpersonal limitations and moving toward a more authentic way of being in both the therapy and in their lives outside the therapy.

clearer picture of the kinds of activities and experiences that nourish your particular soul.

The second exercise had the same goal but was more structured. I gave Sheila a worksheet that had a list of categories of activities that many people find spiritually nourishing. The categories included movies, music, poems, nature, religion, theater, art, literature, places, food and dining, family, romantic experiences, sexual experiences, and friendships. I asked Sheila to reflect on her life and write down all the soul-nourishing experiences she could recall in each category. I asked her to bring these results to therapy so that we could examine her answers to help determine the kinds of activities that nourished her soul.

The third exercise focused on her immediate spiritual needs. It involved another homework assignment that instructed her to relax and allow her imagination to come up with the kinds of activities or experiences that her soul needed at the present time. The instructions, too extensive to include here, involved sitting in a comfortable chair, closing her eyes, relaxing, and then imagining that she was in a beautiful, soul-nourishing place of her own choosing. She was then to allow a fantasy to unfold in which she received what she most deeply needed at the spiritual level. She was cautioned not to force the fantasy but to let it occur as though she were watching a video. When the fantasy came to a natural conclusion, she was to stop that part of the exercise, write down the fantasy in detail using the present tense, and then examine the fantasy to see if it contained clues as to what her soul needed at the present time.

Based on the rather extensive information these homework assignments provided, Sheila and I were able to determine numerous activities and experiences that nourished her soul. Using this information, we collaboratively designed a 3-month program that involved three "little" soul-nourishing activities each week and one "big" soul-nourishing experience each month. For her weekly "little" activities she chose (a) to set aside time to listen to classical music for at least 1 hour per week, (b) to take a walk along the beach at sunset 1 day per week, and (c) read and meditate on poetry for 1 hour per week. Her once-per-month "big" activities were (a) to spend a weekend with an old friend in San Diego, (b) to attend the play *Phantom of the Opera*, which was in Los Angeles at the time, and (c) to spend a weekend in Taos, New Mexico, a place that nourished her soul.

As part of her program, I also asked Sheila to begin what I call a "Soul Journal" in which she would record her spiritual experiences related to the soul-nourishing activities as well as daily reflections about her spiritual life. I asked Sheila to find a quiet place where she could go each day to reflect on her spiritual life for at least 20 minutes and then enter her thoughts and feelings in her journal. (I do not typically ask clients to engage in formal meditation because of the inherent risks, for some clients, of doing this without a guide. If clients already practices meditation, they are free to substitute meditation for the 20-minute reflection period provided they also record their experiences in the journal.)

Sheila followed her 3-month program conscientiously. She had considerable capacity for inner reflection and benefited significantly. It was quite common for her to use the first part of her therapy sessions describing the various poignant moments she had experienced as she followed the program. The therapeutic interaction often focused on the emotions Sheila experienced during her soul-nourishing activities. Primarily, I attempted to listen carefully and help her to explore and clarify what she was experiencing. At times I brought in poems and readings myself that I thought would illumine our explorations or speak to Sheila's situation. By the end of the first month, we both noted that her depressive symptoms were beginning to lift, and at the end of the 3 months, she was experiencing new energy and was excited about a number of things in her life.

Termination, Relapse Prevention, and Therapeutic Outcomes

After collaboratively designing another 3-month program of soul-nourishing activities, we mutually decided that the therapy should end, on the condition that if she experienced a relapse, she would return for additional therapy. I asked her to contact me once in a while to let me know how she was doing. She contacted me about twice a year for almost 4 years and each time reported that she was still doing well. As time went on, she incorporated various activities into her life in a more natural, less programmed way, so that nourishing her soul became a regular part of her life.

Final Comment

Obviously, not every client is as well suited for this spiritual approach as Sheila. In addition, to emphasize the spiritual dimensions of her therapy, I have not included the various discussions we had that focused on other parts of her life, including her job, her family, and various conflicts that arose in her daily life during the 3 months she was in therapy. I do not believe that my distinctly spiritual approach to Sheila should be viewed as a model for how to treat all depressive feelings or other forms of emotional suffering. I am quite traditional in terms of psychological interventions and believe that spiritual interventions should be used only when there is clear reason to believe that they will address the problems with which the client is struggling. In my opinion, those of us who use spiritual approaches must be vigilant for alternative explanations of the client's psychological difficulties and always open to discussing whatever the client needs to address, while at the same time continuing to focus on spiritual issues as long as this is relevant to the client's concerns and continues to generate therapeutic progress.

CONCLUSION

For more than 40 years, humanistic psychology has provided open arenas for discussions about spirituality, refusing to institutionalize any particular point of view. My own approach should be viewed as simply one perspective in this ongoing discussion of spirituality in the humanistic movement. In this chapter, I have presented a vision of spirituality as a universal human phenomenon that is not the exclusive possession of traditional religions. Furthermore, I have presented a practical theory of spirituality based on three major constructs and their dynamic relationship to one another. The soul is the deepest core of our spiritual life; the sacred is a power that can nourish our souls; and spirituality is the result of having our souls nourished by poignant experiences of the sacred. Finally, I have presented a case to demonstrate how this approach can be used with clients to nourish the soul and relieve emotional suffering. I hope this chapter proves useful to clinicians who are searching for ways to integrate spirituality into their therapeutic practices.

REFERENCES

Allport, G. W. (1961). *The individual and his religion*. New York: Macmillan.

Binswanger, L. (1963). *Being-in-the-world: Selected papers of Ludwig Binswanger*. New York: Basic Books.

Buber, M. (1965). *The knowledge of man* (M. Friedman, Ed.). New York: Harper & Row.

Buber, M. (1970). *I and thou* (W. Kaufmann, Trans.). New York: Scribner.

Buber, M. (1988). *Between man and man* (R. G. Smith, Trans.). New York: Macmillan.

Durkheim, E. (1915). *The elementary forms of religious life*. London: Allen & Unwin.

Eliade, M. (1959). *The sacred and the profane*. New York: Harper & Row.

Elkins, D. N. (1998). *Beyond religion: A personal program for building a spiritual life outside the walls of traditional religion*. Wheaton, IL: Quest Books

Elkins, D. N. (2000). Old Saybrook I and II: The visioning and re-visioning of humanistic psychology. *Journal of Humanistic Psychology, 40*(2), 119–131.

Elkins, D. N., Lipari, J., & Kozora, C. J. (1999). Attitudes and values of humanistic psychologists: Division 32 survey results. *The Humanistic Psychologist, 27*, 329–342.

Frankl, V. E. (1963). *Man's search for meaning*. Boston: Beacon.

Fromm, E. (1950). *Psychoanalysis and religion*. New Haven, CT: Yale University Press.

Giorgi, A. (1970). *Psychology as a human science*. New York: Harper & Row.

Hastings, A. (1999). Transpersonal psychology: The fourth force. In D. Moss (Ed.), *Humanistic and transpersonal psychology: A historical and biographical sourcebook* (pp. 192–298). Westport, CT: Greenwood.

Hillman, J. (1975). *Re-visioning psychology.* New York: Harper & Row.

James, W. (1902). *The varieties of religious experience.* New York: Longmans, Green.

Jung, C. G. (1933). *Modern man in search of a soul.* New York: Harcourt Brace & World.

Jung, C. G. (1964). *Man and his symbols.* Garden City, NY: Doubleday.

Kohut, H. (1971). *The analysis of the self.* New York: International Universities Press.

Kohut, H. (1977). *The restoration of the self.* New York: International Universities Press.

Kohut, H. (1984). *How does analysis cure?* Chicago: University of Chicago Press.

Maslow, A. H. (1954). *Motivation and personality.* New York: Harper & Row.

Maslow, A. H. (1962). *Toward a psychology of being.* New York: Van Nostrand Reinhold.

Maslow, A. H. (1971). *The farther reaches of human nature.* New York: Viking.

Maslow, A. H. (1976). *Religions, values, and peak experiences.* New York: Penguin.

May, R., Angel, E., & Ellenberger, H. (Eds.). (1958). *Existence: A new dimension in psychiatry and psychology.* New York: Basic Books.

Moore, T. (1992). *Care of the soul.* New York: HarperCollins.

Otto, R. (1923). *The idea of the holy.* London: Oxford University Press.

Richards, P. S., & Bergin, A. E. (1997). *A spiritual strategy for counseling and psychotherapy.* Washington, DC: American Psychological Association.

Rank, O. (1958). *Beyond psychology.* New York: Dover.

Schneider, K. J., Bugental, J. T., & Fraser Pierson, J. (2001). Introduction. In K. J. Schneider, J. T. Bugental, & J. Fraser Pierson (Eds.), *The handbook of humanistic psychology* (pp. xix–xxv). Thousand Oaks, CA: Sage.

Seligman, M. (1990). *Learned optimism.* New York: Knopf.

Seligman, M. (1993). *What you can change and what you can't: The complete guide to successful self-improvement.* New York: Knopf.

Seligman, M. E. P., & Csikszentmihalyi, M. (2000). Positive psychology: An introduction. *American Psychologist, 55,* 5–14.

Stolorow, R. D., Atwood, G. E., & Brandchaft, B. (1994). *The intersubjective context of intrapsychic experience: The intersubjective perspective.* Northvale, NJ: Jason Aronson.

Tart, C. T. (1975a). *States of consciousness.* New York: Dutton.

Tart, C. T. (1975b). *Transpersonal psychologies.* New York: Harper & Row.

Tart, C. T. (1989). *Open mind, discriminating mind.* New York: Harper & Row.

Taylor, E. (1999). *Shadow culture: Psychology and spirituality in America.* Washington, DC: Counterpoint.

Taylor, E. I., (2000). What is man, psychologist, that thou are so unminded of him? Henry A. Murray on the historical relation between classical personality theory and humanistic psychology. *Journal of Humanistic Psychology, 40*(3), 29–42.

Taylor, E. I., & Martin, F. (2001). Humanistic psychology at the crossroads. In K. J. Schneider, J. T. Bugental, & J. Fraser Pierson (Eds.), *The handbook of humanistic psychology* (pp. 21–27). Thousand Oaks, CA: Sage.

Tillich, P. (1948). *The shaking of the foundations*. New York: Scribner.

Tillich, P. (1952). *The courage to be*. New Haven, CT: Yale University Press.

Tillich, P. (1957). *Dynamics of faith*. New York: Harper & Row.

Vaughan, F. (1979). *Awakening intuition*. New York: Doubleday.

Vaughan, F. (1986). *The inward arc: Healing in psychotherapy and spirituality*. Boston: Shambhala.

Walsh, R. (1993). The transpersonal movement: A history and state of the art. *Journal of Transpersonal Psychology, 25*, 123–140.

Walsh, R. (1995). The problem of suffering: Existential and transpersonal perspectives. *The Humanistic Psychologist, 23*, 345–356.

Walsh, R. (1999). *Essential spirituality*. New York: Wiley.

Wilber, K. (1977). *The spectrum of consciousness*. Wheaton, IL: Quest Books.

Wilber, K. (1980). *The atman project*. Wheaton, IL: Quest Books.

Wilber, K. (1981). *No boundary*. Boston: Shambhala.

Wilber, K. (1995). *The eye of the spirit*. Boston: Shambhala.

Yalom, I. D. (1980). *Existential psychotherapy*. New York: Basic Books.

7

INTERPERSONAL PSYCHOTHERAPY FROM A SPIRITUAL PERSPECTIVE

LISA MILLER

DESCRIPTION OF THE APPROACH

Interpersonal psychotherapy conducted from a spiritual perspective (IPT-S) holds that psychological events serve as a barometer for a more fundamental spiritual reality. Our psyche detects spiritual truth. Suffering and elation index the extent to which we are living in a way consistent with the great force of creation. IPT-S works to ameliorate suffering and improve spiritual clarity through understanding and renegotiating our relationships. Our psychological experience tells us how we are doing in our relationships. Relationships are viewed as divine gifts, quite purposefully brought into our lives by the Creator, to offer us opportunity for spiritual growth.

Historical and Theoretical Basis

IPT is a short-term, structured treatment for depression that was initially formulated by Klerman, Weissman, Rounsaville, and Chevron (1984) for use with moderate and severe depression. IPT has been validated as an efficacious psychotherapy for depression in more than 12 National Institute of Mental Health (NIMH)-funded clinical trials (see also Klerman & Weissman, 1993; Weissman, Markowitz, & Klerman, 2000). Conceptually, IPT is predicated on the assertion that we are inherently social beings whose need for relationships is central to mental and physical health and as such might be viewed as emanating from the interpersonal perspective of Sullivan or the attachment work of Bowlby and, later, Ainsworth.

Over the past 20 years, IPT has become a widely used treatment for depression in the context of academic psychology departments, outpatient clinics, and medical centers. IPT has been researched extensively in NIMH clinical trials and shown to be an effective treatment for depression, commensurate in magnitude of curative effects with cognitive–behavioral therapy. Some evidence suggests that IPT is particularly effective with women (Weissman et al., 2000).

The immediate goal of IPT is the amelioration of depressive symptoms and improvement in social functioning. IPT does not comment on long-term psychological reorganization or alterations in personality. In its initial formulation, IPT is fashioned around Axis I disorders (*DSM–IV*), which is to say, episodic disorders rather than personality disorders. IPT addresses the well-researched fact that interpersonal problems serve to perpetuate and exacerbate depression. The primary mechanism of treatment holds that depression, irrespective of its initial etiology, occurs in a social context. Learning to renegotiate the social context lifts symptoms of depression and protects against the onset of future episodes.

Four Interpersonal Problem Areas

Central to the work of IPT is the understanding of current social stressors from within a specific interpersonal formulation, which consists of locating the current stressors within one or more of four fundamental "problem areas": interpersonal disputes, interpersonal transitions, grief, or interpersonal deficits.

An interpersonal dispute concerns any ongoing conflict in which two or more people hold disparate expectations that have been aggravated by an event or series of related events. A dispute can be represented in an all-out boisterous argument, or it might be expressed through a smoldering ongoing impasse. Resolution of a dispute involves first the identification of the expectations of all people involved, followed by the acknowledgment among all people involved of every other person's expectations, and finally the development of a new system of behavior on which all people involved can compromise. A common example of an interpersonal dispute at the level of an impasse is seen in a wife who wants her husband to spend more time with the family, repeatedly asks him, stops asking, and then carries an angry grudge while the spouse becomes more distant.

An interpersonal transition concerns a shift in life events that radically changes a person's role with respect to the most significant people in his or her life. Life events that precipitate interpersonal role transitions include a child leaving home for college, a new job or retirement, divorce, illness, and a relocating to a new part of the country. Such life events and interpersonal transitions occur constantly. Distress arises, however, when we have effectively been unemployed from our old role, have de facto assumed a new role, but have yet to accept this change and adjust our lives to function within the new role. For instance, a parent whose youngest child leaves home for college might miss being involved in the daily events of the child's life, may feel loss of community from the child's school, and may experience a vast emptiness in the house.

Grief is the complicated morning process surrounding a death. In classic IPT, the problem area of grief refers only to death. All other losses are understood as interpersonal transitions. Grief work functions much like transitional work. The person is mourned, as are his or her strengths and weaknesses and the positive and negative experiences of the relationship. Feelings of missing the person are expressed, and the absence of the person in a palpable daily sense is explored. IPT holds a classic view of grief, namely, that through an honest evaluation of the relationship, a natural healing process will start to occur such that the client may be in mourning but is no longer depressed.

Interpersonal deficits in IPT are generally viewed as the most intractable of problem areas to treat because they concern lack of social skill or an innate dearth of social acumen. Basic skills training in how to meet other people, initiate a conversation, or build a relationship is taught in a psychoeducational and social–behavioral sense. Development of social expectations commensurate with skills often accompanies skill building.

IPT Occurs Over Three Phases

The initial phase of IPT helps the client link current depressive symptoms and overall suffering to specific current interpersonal struggles. The four problem areas are introduced, and the current difficulty is understood to fall primarily with in a chief problem area. The therapist and client build an understanding of the frame of treatment, that is, a collaborative stance that focuses on helping the client to become his or her own therapist. IPT is an "open-book" therapy in which the techniques and methods of analysis are overtly shared with the client.

The middle phase of treatment focuses on developing methods to renegotiate the most immediate problem area. The technique involves review in fine detail of the events of the past week, particularly the interpersonal exchanges that precipitated depression. The client is encouraged to consider alternative ways to handle the social exchange and to practice with the therapist in session. The new skills are practiced over the course of the week and then reviewed in the subsequent session. Here the client and therapist collaboratively refine the methods of renegotiation.

In the final phase, the therapist recaps treatment gains and helps the client to see how he or she is prepared to be his or her "own therapist" when confronting similar interpersonal problems in the future.

Interpersonal Psychotherapy and Spirituality

IPT as originally formulated does not encourage, discourage, or hold as taboo the discussion of spiritual issues. Traditional IPT is simply silent on matters of spirituality. In none of the research or theoretical articles on IPT to date is the client's experience of a spiritual reality discussed.

From both a technical and theoretical perspective, classic IPT does promulgate a tight focus around the interpersonal events of the previous week for many spiritual and religious persons. Therefore, with little extrapolation, it might soundly be inferred that it is within the bounds of IPT to examine germane daily relationships as carrying spiritual significance. For a spiritual client, interpersonal relationships function in accordance with spiritual laws. Interpersonal events are spiritual events. In addition, for many religious persons, relationship with the sacred or divine is experienced as a unique interpersonal relationship and is subject to the vicissitudes of human conflict as well as support and intimacy.

Therapist Use of IPT With Spiritually Oriented Clients

I came to practice IPT from within a spiritual perspective because it was the only true way to work with many of my clients. Upon entering treatment, almost all of my IPT clients were clearly spiritually oriented. This is not surprising because the research literature shows that most people in the United States do claim a spiritual or religious orientation (Gallup & Bezilla, 1992; Larson & Larson, 1994). I felt to be on somewhat new territory in conducting IPT from a spiritual perspective, because it was not normative to consider spirituality in the clinical trails and hospitals outpatient clinics in which I practiced. To be honest to the work, helpful to the client, and, most significantly, reverent to the Truth (by which I mean the ultimate reality expressed through every client's personal spiritual awareness or faith perspective), I have tried to do IPT in a way that embraces these clients' spiritual realities.

Demographically, my IPT clients have ranged economically from middle class to very poor and in education from college educated to having not finished high school; most were raised within some form of Christianity; ethnically, all have been African American, European American, or of Latin descent. Most of my IPT clients have been women. Not every client with whom spiritually oriented IPT has seemed appropriate would call him- or herself "spiritual," and fewer would consider themselves to be "religious." When I speak of the spiritual reality of the client underlying perception of relationship, I specifically refer to a set of assumptions and understandings that the client holds; generally the women I have treated believe that we live under a loving and guiding Creator. The daily events of our lives, most saliently within our relationships, are reflections of this loving and guiding Creator.

Despite working in a context in which discussion of spiritual issues is somewhat uncommon, once clients understand that it is permissible to speak on a spiritual plane, they generally do. I have found that discussions rarely drift into the theoretical. Rather, spiritual reality is brought up when it is central to understanding the immediate pressing relationships being understood through IPT.

IPT as I have conducted it from a spiritual perspective does not represent a set of techniques or a theoretical formulation that I architected a priori. The IPT approach I share arose on its own through my being (or trying to be) present to the client. As IPT conducted from a spiritual perspective took on a life of its own, I started to notice remarkable commonality across treatments with different clients. I share this spiritual approach to IPT (IPT-S) as a matter of reflection.

Relationships as Spiritual Reality

Because this is the first explication of a theory of spiritually oriented IPT, I necessarily draw primarily from my own direct experiences and from the experiences of my clients. The work of integration, although based on traditional IPT, emanates from clinical experiences that point to the spiritual dimensions accessible through IPT. Therefore, I begin with the experiences of three clients for whom profound interpersonal pain was ultimately resolved through a spiritual understanding.

Young Claire. A 13-year-old from a family that had recently become very poor, Claire lost her father when he was murdered behind the checkout counter of his deli. This young adolescent girl had brought herself to treatment, without parental assistance, to ameliorate her severe grief. She felt she was painfully alone in the world, a child without love or comfort. Her substance-abusing mother and rigid and punitive grandmother offered her little sustenance compared with her overwhelming admiration and love for her deceased father.

As we worked on her grief over her father's death, this early pubertal girl, gradually over the course of treatment, tentatively started to explore her burgeoning interest in boys. Claire brought in large posters she had made from magazine clippings of young male rock stars. She needed a safe distance from boys, as she spoke guardedly of her male classmates who threatened her sense of correctness and safety. She seemed to feel unsure around young men without a father to protect and love her.

Treatment progressed steadily (as it always does given the innate resilience of a 13-year-old), but only truly soared following a pivotal interpersonal event that the girl strongly understood from a spiritual perspective. One spring day, she came skipping into my office. "You will never believe this. OK, guess what happened? I met a boy. He was so nice. So responsible.

Not like the others in my class. I feel totally safe with him. And then guess what his name is . . . Elvis, just like my father. (Then, in the most matter-of-fact, excited tone.) My father sent him. He is looking out over me." For Claire, the continued guardianship and loving presence of her father, despite his physical passing, gave her the certainty to take an interest in young men. She felt safe and protected under the directive of her father's spirit. Claire's certainty of her father's presence was resolute and personal, yet her view of the afterlife emanated from her family's religion. In keeping with their beliefs, once a month following her father's death, and the every 6 months thereafter, Claire joined her extended family in religious ceremony designed to help her father in his journey through the afterlife. At these ceremonies, the family experienced her father's spirit.

A *Distressed Mother*. Grace, a mother in her mid-30s, had been profoundly depressed for 3 years, since learning that her son had cystic fibrosis (CF). At the time of treatment, she had just purchased a custom-made new stroller for her 4-year-old son because he still could not walk. Her pain over his limitations and her strangling enmeshment with him became the topic of treatment. She felt despair to the point of depression in watching him function suboptimally compared with peers. She did not understand why this had happened, explaining that she had observed good prenatal care, taken all precautions, and now felt depressed that life had been "unfair." Grace now doubted the very virtue and gift of motherhood. She refused her husband's desire to have another child, despite assurance from a genetic counselor of a very low risk for conceiving a second child who also suffered from CF.

From an IPT perspective, her sorrow was understood as falling within an interpersonal role transition (recall that grief is reserved for death). She had wanted to be the mother of a healthy son; she was de facto the mother of a sick son. Her enmeshment, which held her captive of the illness, was formulated from within IPT as emerging from an interpersonal dispute. She grasped to maintain sole control as caretaker, at times to the detriment of her son's care and psychological well-being. Grace needed to trust, to relinquish full control and make space for others. Her burden and isolation could have been lifted substantially if she learned to make a team with doctors, nurses, counselors, and her spouse. Gaining faith in the good intentions and capable care of other people was for Grace a spiritual journey toward developing trust. Although Grace did not use spiritual language at this juncture in therapy, her lack of trust extended beyond the nurses and doctors to the very universe that gave her a sick son. Repeatedly Grace would mourn the illness of her son, saying, "its not fair, I did everything right."

As Grace came to realize she could relinquish some control and gain more trust in the caretakers surrounding her son, she felt far less divided from adult company and was less apt to isolate her son. In turn, she started to shift out of depression. She felt more like a whole woman who was a mother with a sick son, rather than a full-time aid whose identity was that of a defective woman who had borne a sick child.

Once she gained greater interpersonal trust, Grace started speaking in spiritual terms. She saw the universe as generous, rather than unfair, and her son as a blessing, to her and potentially to a sibling. Now she reconsidered carrying a second child. "If the second child is healthy, then just think how having an older brother with an illness like CF will make that child sensitive and kind. And, if I do have another child with CF, [pause] then I guess it's my purpose of earth to take care of sick children." The ultimate resolution of her interpersonal problems hinged on awakening to the gift of motherhood and her spiritual calling as a mother.

Out-of-the-Blue Treatment. We recently did a clinical trial in which we called depressed mothers with young children on the telephone, out of the blue, to offer them a 12-week IPT treatment (Miller & Weissman, 2002). In the midst of going about her busy life, each woman got a cold call to receive a validated treatment (although never before done systematically on the telephone) for depression. The women we called (in their late 20s and early 30s) had suffered on average more than 200 weeks with depression in their young adults lives Yet most had sought and received less than couple months of treatment.

About half of the women we called said that they would very much like to do IPT over the telephone. Most striking to me, was that nearly all who accepted treatment said, "I was just thinking I would like to get therapy, there must be a reason (or purpose) that you called now." The clients felt certain that it was not a random accident that I called just then, nor that just then they had been thinking that they wanted some help. It is in these moments that clients may experience deeply held spiritual sentiments. The offer of assistance for some clients reflects a beneficent spirit operating in their lives and purposefulness. Certainly in a treatment that starts from a spiritual understanding of the meeting of client and therapist, the interpersonal events discussed in treatment might readily be viewed as holding spiritual significance.

All of these clients, somewhere in the course of treatment, see relationships as expressions of a spiritual reality. Remarkable commonality in understanding emerges between the spiritual visions of these clients. I have tried to sum up this shared spiritual view of relationships with some core concepts.

Formulation and Implications of a Spiritual View of Relationships

The spiritual view of relationships is founded on three interrelated postulates.

1. Relationships are divine. We are expressions of the Creator. We come together in relationship, a gift of the Creator. This gift is one given in love and is a guided process. Just as we are

created by the divine, so, too, our meeting through relationship is expression of the Creator.

2. Relationships are vehicles for spiritual evolution. Our work in relationships is work that helps us to evolve spiritually. We learn love, compassion, forgiveness, justice, and many spiritual truths through loving each other in relationship. Relationships are sacred opportunities for the revelation of spiritual truth and spiritual growth. In relationships, we have a chance to better know the Creator and to grow closer to the divine. Relationships are as central to our spiritual growth as other forms or spiritual work, such as individual or private contemplation.

3. Relationships are architected for spiritual growth. The people who come into our lives are just right to help us grow, and we are just right to help them grow. This does not mean that it will be easy to get along. Such experiences can be replete with challenges. Nobody we pass on the street, wed, debate at work, or love, no one with whom we argue, may cross our path without transforming us, nor do they appear accidentally. The right people come at the right time. All relationships transform us.

We clearly have choices in how we handle the opportunity of a relationship, but its occurrence is perfectly purposeful. Feeling a premonition before meeting a significant person, or once meeting feeling immediately "at home" is a phrase many clients share in speaking of the most important people in their lives. The tone and energetic quality to this description usually strikes me as revealing something stronger than a match of interpersonal style. It feels more like a power greater than ourselves delivering us to each other. This appreciation for many clients led into a more explicit consideration of spirituality and in keeping with IPT involved addressing their relationships with the divine.

Core Interpersonal Formulation and Depression

Classic IPT holds that depression can be cured through renegotiating our interpersonal context. In IPT-S, relationships comprise the theatre of our spiritual evolution, brilliantly cast by the Creator to usher us through our development. Given the purpose and exquisite design of relationships, the ones that drive us to treatment are particular opportunities in our spiritual path. We can be particularly grateful for our difficult relationships from a spiritual perspective. We even can appreciate our depression. Depression hales attention toward just that area where we need to grow. Depression is a spiritual growing pain without which we might miss precious opportunity.

Renegotiation in IPT From a Spiritual Perspective

A unique concern when conducting IPT from a spiritual perspective is that all interpersonal resolutions that yield short-term relief from depression are not equal. Classic IPT was not explicitly posited from a secular materialist perspective. Based on the cosmology of the individual psychotherapist, however, it has at times been practiced from a position of hedonics: If the client would be relieved by divorce or might feel better by reversing a social or professional commitment, then it is an acceptable resolution of the interpersonal problem.

Spiritual IPT embraces a form of absolutism that upholds commonsense axioms of right living. There is often little confusion about what works to help us thrive in life and what causes decay and suffering. Strangely, however, in our morally relativistic culture, psychologists do not often accept this. Yet increasingly the notion of universal axioms of right living has entered into the psychotherapy discourse. Richards and Bergin (1997) proposed a nondenominational notion of the "Spirit of Truth," the existence of a body of laws of living that, if followed, derive a thriving life. If the Spirit of Truth is defied, life devolves. Among the axioms delineated by Richards and Bergin within the Spirit of Truth are kinship and commitment. Application of these laws is self-evident. If I uphold commitments to my family, my life thrives; if I break my promises and breach commitments, I ultimately suffer. These basic guidelines, when taken from the Spirit of Truth or one's own religious denomination, help to guide us through interpersonal problems, conflict, and transitions that seem uncharted in our experience. IPT from a spiritual perspective would hold that depression as a spiritual growing pain might often be alleviated through more closely integrating the Spirit of Truth into our actions. The route of right action, that path which follows the Spirit of Truth, is guided by the life passage that we face. A child has different lessons to master from those of a mother or elder. The Spirit of Truth, therefore, finds expression through our life-cycle transitions and related struggles.

Four Interpersonal Problems Areas in IPT-S

Within IPT-S the four interpersonal problem are viewed as spiritual opportunity for evolution.

Interpersonal Transitions. From a spiritual perspective, life-cycle transitions are inherently part of the human journey and carry specific spiritual opportunities for growth. A universal vehicle of spiritual growth is change throughout the life cycle; we all age, have the opportunity to make lifelong commitments, must garner sustenance, and carry and raise children or mentor young people. Ignoring the necessary transitions in the life course or breaking from the inherent challenges of the life course causes suffering. For instance, in IPT-S coming of age for an adolescent necessarily involves accounting for the desire for quest, integration of fertility into psyche and awareness of heightened power and efficacy in a way that joins the adolescent with the Creator and with a positive community. The absolute calling of distinct life transitions suggests that the Spirit of Truth might be revealed in different ways at different times across the life span.

Transitional work is inherently necessary from a bio-psycho-social-spiritual perspective. Struggle with an interpersonal transition emanates from ignoring or failing to embrace necessary development or failing to appreciate its absolute meaning and value. Most traditional cultures and religious denominations address transitions as carrying absolute value. There is value in becoming a parent, in aging, and in dying. Where this is not done in our culture, we still seek this process, sometimes turning to therapy. We must actualize as adolescents, as parents, and as elderly facing death. These are all life-course events that we cannot control, and yet our participation in these events radically shapes our faith and spiritual growth, much as described by Pargament's (1997) model of religious coping.

Interpersonal Disputes. From a spiritual perspective, disputes represent human error, our blind spots, the ways in which we have yet to achieve understanding, empathy, and compassion. Renegotiating conflict allows us to develop awareness of the other person's perspective. Each new person's perspective draws us asymptotically towards ultimate truth. We become distanced from erroneous and often entrenched habits. Stepping away from error allows us to experience a more full reality, a more ultimate reality. Experiencing an ultimate reality necessarily fosters greater compassion.

Grief. Beliefs about the afterlife or awareness of the presence of the deceased are naturally included in discussion of bereavement. A client's experience of an active relationship with the deceased is viewed as feasible and embraced. The relationship with the deceased is understood as carrying meaning and purpose with respect to spiritual growth for both members of the relationship.

Interpersonal Deficits. In IPT-S, an interpersonal deficit might be addressed behaviorally and still embraced as part of the balance that makes up our individuality. The place of deficits or "suboptimal" functioning is viewed from a broader perspective than simply functionality. Our deficits carry uniqueness of experience and are complemented with the development of other strengths. It is not necessarily a tragedy if we are less capable than other people. Our interpersonal deficits may teach us spiritual lessons, as well as be instructive to those who share our lives. For instance, at the level of the family, the mother with a 4-year-old son with CF came to realize that her boy would sensitize and humanize a young sibling. CF was a loss from her former aspirations for her son, but it was part of the actual gift of her son and carried its own spiritual lesson.

The Nature of the Relationship Between Psychology and Spirituality

The core spiritual tenet underlying IPT-S is that there exists an absolute spiritual meaning in the human life cycle. Spiritual growth is the most fundamental human path and purpose. All other forms of development—cognitive, psychological, and social—serve spiritual growth.

Spiritual growth accordingly underlies psychological health. Interpersonal relationships provide an opportunity for spiritual growth. Suffering in the context of relationships indicates a call for spiritual evolution. The spiritual reality is most fundamental; psychological reality is a way of detecting and participating in spiritual reality. In that we have incarnated as separate people, our interpersonal relations present a great opportunity through which to learn spiritual lessons. When we suffer in relationships, there is a spiritual reason. We can spiritually evolve to better know the unity of the universe through the love that transpires in relationships. We can use our psychological experience as guide; it is the barometer of our relationship to the absolute Laws of Creation. Spiritual Laws are readily understood, just like common sense, by all clients and course through all religious denominations.

Therapist's Skills and Attributes

From a technical perspective, IPT-S maintains the major conceptualization and techniques of IPT while orienting around a central spiritual belief about relationships. Overriding therapeutic techniques are the same as in any IPT treatment. The therapist listens for the elevated area of social upheaval, that area most directly related to current depression, and then assists the client in understanding how better to negotiate the current interpersonal crisis. Any good therapist most likely would be good at IPT.

The most powerful thrust of IPT-S, however, is that this process occurs within the context of beliefs in the primacy of spiritual growth and the spiritual significance of all interpersonal relationships. The flow of the session carries a life of its own once these core beliefs are operative. It is the deep conviction that suffering is not in vain but serves the process of spiritual growth that allows IPT-S to advance.

The perception of a random or pointless universe in which we "make meaning" is not compatible with the work because it would not advance the process of discovery of absolute laws of living, nor allow for the current interpersonal situation to be viewed as merely fodder for a greater purpose. As such, it would be difficult to imagine the conduct of IPT-S by a therapist who did not happen to hold the related beliefs. I doubt it would be enough to appreciate the client's beliefs, given that relinquishing control of the session to these beliefs seem to propel the healing process, not the therapists' techniques. I therefore would be inclined to suggest that being spiritually oriented, or at least extremely open to the presence and momentum of spiritual revelation through relationship, is required in conducting this form of IPT-S.

Strengths and Limitations

As a spiritually informed psychotherapy, a primary strength of IPD-S is that it interweaves insight with action. IPT-S builds upon insight to mandate spiritually informed action within our relationships. Spiritually informed action, in some religious traditions termed Right Action, can be directly transforming.

The suitability of IPT-S to the client and to the therapist hinges on an a priori buy-in to the view of a purposeful loving universe, which guides us through relationships. Herein, of course, lies the chief practical limitation of the IPT-S—namely, it may not immediately appeal to everybody. IPT-S may not be particularly useful for clients strongly committed to a nontheistic or agnostic stance on the universe.

Another limitation, both theoretical and practical, is that when suffering occurs, its ultimate purpose is not always clear. Sometimes the purpose of events is revealed over much time or we do not perceive it accurately, and potentially never will. Clearly understanding strife or suffering endemic to interpersonal relationships from a spiritual perspective necessitates a great humility around the limitations of our insight. The reasons that relationships enter into our realm, transforms our lives, or cause a form of pain that yields growth is not always evident in the beginning of a treatment, or at the end, for that matter. The therapist and client must refrain from a stance of interpretative finality or all-knowingness. Often there is a sense of peace in allowing the meaning to unfold over time into the future with a sense of faith. The immediate work of treatment must focus on an attempt to right a relationship, not only by achieving harmony, but also by bringing the relationship in line with spiritual laws of living.

Indications and Contraindications

Rich and varied spiritual traditions, across cultures, support a spiritual language and a set of principles around absolute Laws of Creation. The notion that a common set of universal spiritual laws sustains humanity, expressed through unique timing and developmental mandates within the individual, may be reconciled with religious diversity through the Eastern notion of darma. Namely, as we journey our spiritual path, we may find teaching and truth from numerous cultural and religious traditions. For instance, we can absorb and prosper from tenets of Catholicism, Hinduism, and Judaism. All teachings, at the right time in the right moment, are compatible and necessary information for our spiritual growth.

There are moments in which IPT-S suggests an ongoing mindfulness of the balance between our human contribution to our growth and divine guidance through life events. For instance, the pull of fatalism might emerge and need to be countered with awareness of the impact of our decisions in contributing toward our spiritual growth. A relentless slide toward fatalism in the client, therefore, might contraindicate use of IPT-S.

A similar contraindication, or at least a strong note of caution, might proceed from a client who speaks a great deal of spiritual reality but for whom there appears little integration with psychological or interpersonal life. Such a "flight" into the spiritual, while lacking insight into the impact of our decisions on our emotions and those of others, at very least, would suggest that the initial steps of IPT-S focus on interpersonal and psychological awareness. We need to have an honest appreciation of our interpersonal wake before we may understand our relationships as paths toward spiritual revelation.

Expected Future Developments and Directions

Most people in the United States view their lives as carrying spiritual significance. A large number of those Americans seek spiritual counsel or guidance around interpersonal strife from people who may offer spiritual insight but who may not help the client integrate spiritual understanding with daily functioning. IPT-S has a useful quality of working in the concrete here-and-now to digest and act on great truths. It is a psychotherapy that hinges on spiritual reality, allowing for integration of spiritual revelation into concrete social functioning.

IPT-S helps people by integrating spiritual meaning and practice into social functioning. It is through the details of our relationships that we come to know compassion, love, and the transcendental greatness of the Creator. We hear the voice of the Creator as coming through the people we know so well. Once the spiritual meaning in the germane relationships becomes clear, it is equally through right negotiation with our spouse, or junior or senior colleague, or young child, that we practice spirituality.

From the perspective of the clinical and academic community, it would seem reasonable that structured psychotherapies adjust to meet the spiritual reality of our clients. It may be that psychotherapists working in short-term models already have adapted treatments to embrace the spiritual reality but that this has been little discussed in academic, clinical, or medical circles. I suppose that a clinical trial could be conducted in which IPT-S was tested against IPT conducted from a secular–materialist perspective. For me, however, this poses a series of serious ethical dilemmas. I would be more inclined to make the study an effectiveness study in which people get that treatment that they request. After all, IPT-S seems appropriate for people who operate a priori from within a spiritual perspective and people who currently do not might opt to undergo treatment from a different worldview. As well, a person who might readily be served through a spiritual perspective is perhaps granted an injustice by deliberate silence on spiritual issues within psychotherapy.

Although IPT has been shown in clinical research to be an effective treatment for depression, IPT-S to date has been tested in a single open clinical trial that tested its feasibility, acceptability, and helpfulness (Miller, Gur, & Shanok, 2004). The results of this study may now serve to justify more extensive clinical research testing the efficacy or effectiveness of the treatment in a controlled trial.

CASE EXAMPLE

I choose the case of a group of young pregnant girls in Harlem to share the processes of IPT-S. When asked if they considered themselves to be spiritual, the group of girls responded along a bell curve. Every girl in the group, however, felt convinced about keeping the gestating fetus because she believed it was a sacred life. The spiritual beliefs underlying IPT-S were implicit spiritual assumptions on which all of the girls seemed to live.

Client Demographics, Relevant History, and Presenting Problem

This case study focuses on a group treatment using IPT-S as prevention against depression in pregnant adolescents. In collaboration with a public high school in Harlem, every enrolled pregnant girl received IPT-S as a prevention intervention during the period of the day regularly committed to health class. In the group reported here, girls ranged in age from 13 to 15 years, with 14 years being the mean age. The girls were either African American or Hispanic and were in at least the fourth month of pregnancy at the start of the group. Most of the girls reported being raised in a Christian denomination, although a few reported being raised in a family without a religious affiliation. Within this context, it is of note that all of the girls reported feeling that abortion was "wrong," none reported being strongly upset upon learning that they were pregnant, and all at the point of contact with treatment reported currently being excited about having their babies.

All of the girls lived in severe poverty; for instance, most of the girls could not afford the subway fare to come to school, none had maternity clothes, and few could afford to eat what they wanted when they wanted to meet the needs of pregnancy. The majority of girls lived with their mothers, a few girls lived with their grandmothers, and two girls lived in foster care. As the colloquial term implies, most of the girls believed that the "baby's father" would be an interested and committed father, although not a loyal boyfriend over the next several years. Boyfriends generally were older by 5 to 15 years, most were not monogamous, and a few were in prison. Very few of the girls anticipated relying on the baby's father for financial support of the baby. Hence, most were faced with the challenge of building an appropriate "nest," materially and socially, for their child. Although some degree of financial assistance was available to the girls through social services, many avoided contact with government agencies.

Within the IPT model, clients are traditionally selected into treatment based on their level of depressive symptoms. Although this was the first prevention intervention of IPT, related prevention interventions using structured psychotherapies often are conceived of as secondary prevention and therefore target clients whose symptoms appear at a subclinical threshold level. As a step forward in prevention interventions, we targeted girls who were at risk for depression based on depressogenic mechanism within the IPT model, namely, an unprocessed interpersonal transition. All of the girls in the study were becoming mothers with little emotional assistance.

Presenting problems surrounding the transition to young motherhood were shared by nearly all the girls. Upon learning of the pregnancy, most of the girls faced severe lack of support from their own mothers, many of whom had also once been pregnant adolescents. Although few lived with a father, those who had contact with their father or who had uncle figures were generally scolded or criticized. Many of the girls felt urged by school counselors to have an abortion. Although it is illegal to require a girl to transfer school due to pregnancy, several of the girls felt very strongly pushed to leave their school on the grounds that they were setting a "bad example" in the hallways.

Despite high rates of adolescent pregnancy in the community, the girls felt that their pregnancy was met with gossip and ongoing commentary from peers, and they often felt ridiculed by passing strangers. For instance, girls felt scrutinized on the public bus and noticed critical expressions from older women. The most frequent message to be conveyed to the girls from their parents was that "now they would not amount to anything." This statement implied that young motherhood precluded the opportunity for finishing school and starting work. Pregnant or not, adolescents are sensitive to the commentary from their community, making these messages particularly hurtful and destructive.

For some of the girls, the lack of acceptance from their mothers carried consequences. For instance, a 13-year-old girl was looking for a job at 1 month postdelivery because her mother refused to purchase diapers for the baby; several of the girls' mothers placed Christmas gifts under the tree only for the gestating baby, not for their daughters. Some of the mothers, however, gradually became very excited and far more supportive of the girl.

Relationship of the Therapist and Client

The presence of the Creator through motherhood was alive in the treatment. A great spiritual process of becoming a mother was underway and needed to be respected and midwifed. My goal was to let motherhood run its course.

To midwife the girl's spiritual growth and support this most magnificent process was my goal. I wanted to help the girls embrace and integrate that which was spiritually alive, namely, the vital desire to be a good mother and the overwhelming love they felt for their child.

We met for the intervention 12 times, weekly for 50 minutes. Most of the girls spoke and seemed to feel comfortable sharing intense experiences. Over the course of treatment, it became clear that the girls had much to share and overtly stated that they would like us to continue beyond 12 sessions.

Diagnostic and Case Conceptualization

Sixty percent of the girls were at least moderately depressed. Some had been depressed before becoming pregnant; others became depressed around the pregnancy or as the pregnancy evolved. IPT holds that despite its etiology, depression occurs within a social context, which if renegotiated will help to alleviate the symptoms. IPT-S adds spiritual meaning and opportunity for spiritual evolution to the work of identifying the problem area and then renegotiation.

For the pregnant girls in this school, the chief interpersonal problem area from a classic IPT perspective was an unprocessed and unsupported interpersonal transition. The girls clearly were becoming mothers, perhaps the greatest transformation in a woman's life, without a whisper of interest or support. Rather, the powerful transformative process was being muted, degraded, disrupted, and ridiculed by institutional and community voices. It seemed reasonable that the girls might be less depressed if this powerful transition were supported.

From within an IPT-S perspective, I considered the profound spiritual reality, power, and meaning to becoming a mother. I had only to listen to the girls describe their own transformation. Before becoming pregnant, most had been hanging out with drug dealers, had been exposed to violence, and were doing drugs; some had prostituted and begged to survive, and all were alienated from the maternal forces in their lives, such as mothers and grandmothers. Many lived in an untrustworthy, abusive, and dangerous world not only because of poverty but also because of adolescent risk taking and an unprocessed right of passage. Once choosing to become pregnant (more than 90% of the girls reported some degree of choice in pregnancy) and then becoming pregnant, the girls had changed radically. Not a single girl I met claimed to be doing drugs or drinking. Girls were upset now about their boyfriends' violent friends and the implications for such company on the safety of the child. Several girls asked their boyfriends to stop doing drugs, to work more, to visit the baby only with her, when alone, or with their own mothers. Girls moved back home with their mothers, rather than staying with their boyfriends, siblings, or friends or boyfriends. They were establishing matriarchy by rebuilding relationships with their mothers. Everything was different now. Several girls stated that they would likely be dead had they not become pregnant. Many of the girls actively started to consider how they would support the baby; how they might find sufficient material sustenance for their child in their current social arrangement—now and in the longer term.

Motherhood now had supremely changed the girl. The power of the Creator moved her to change her life. Yet motherhood was not being integrated with her full psyche, her interpersonal functioning, or her social and material world. To the degree that the girl still needed to build a "nest," and saw little forthcoming help in its construction, she became depressed.

Treatment Goals, Process, and Intervention Strategies

Within IPT-S, the girls were seen as having an unsupported interpersonal, material, and spiritual transition to motherhood. My goals were first to support the inherent spiritual transformation of motherhood and then to help the girls integrate this great transformation into a concrete reality. The powerful transforming effects of motherhood had a life of its own. My job as therapist was to usher, or midwife, the birth of these young mothers. The force of emerging motherhood in the girls propelled the group forward; I primarily set a tone of acceptance and made occasional comments that acknowledged the collective process of spiritual awakening.

To highlight more precisely within the psychotherapeutic process the tenets of IPT-S, the interpersonal transition to adolescent motherhood was understood as a purposeful divine intervention in which human relationships were the material stage for spiritual evolution. In other words, from a spiritual perspective, the group sought insight into why each girl was pregnant now with her specific baby. Spontaneously and often without my direct inquiry, the girls explored this question along the three fundamental tenets of IPT-S, namely, the girls assumed that relationships are divine, are vehicles for spiritual growth, and are architected for spiritual growth. Every girl in the group seemed to believe that the formation of the child was a decision of the Creator, a purposeful gift of relationship from the Creator through which they would now grow. The mother–infant relationship, in keeping with this view, was exquisitely architected for the spiritual growth. Tanya (age 14 years and 8 months pregnant), shared that she had spent the past few years flagrantly disrespecting the authority of her mother, who Tanya, realized in retrospect, had been strict and limited her freedom to protect her against violence and the pattern of attacks against women in her neighborhood. Tanya now felt that she had often been rude and unappreciative of her mother's love. Knowing that her baby was to be a girl, Tanya felt strongly that this was an opportunity to understand the challenges her mother had faced. The baby's sex was not an accident, but a divine plan designed to complete Tanya's appreciation of mothering a girl from both sides of the dyad, mother and daughter.

Angela (age 15 years and 7 months pregnant) had been living on the streets begging, stripping, and selling drugs for money to eat. She had feared going home (where she was repeatedly sexually molested by her mother's boyfriend) or returning to the government group home (where she felt physically unsafe), preferring to have some self-determination, which she viewed as her dignity. Eventually Angela met a man, 12 years her senior, with whom she now lived (so that he could pay her bills). The man had fathered her current pregnancy, as well as that pregnancy carried by another woman with a due date within 6 weeks of Angela's.

Angela explained, "I was doing all sorts of drugs and taking big chances. A lot can happen out there. If I had not become pregnant with this baby, right now I would probably be dead." The baby, to Angela, was viewed as a form of savior. I sensed that Angela might even have conceived for this reason; she anticipated that motherhood might necessarily change her and inspire her life away from the streets. The divine gift of her relationship to the new infant was a relationship through which she could reform herself and her life. Her long-term goal was to be an operator at the telephone company, a job that she had researched and found to pay sufficiently to support her child so that she might leave her current boyfriend.

Ramala (a young 14 years of age in her 6th month of pregnancy) explained to the group that she had become a much better person after becoming pregnant. "I used to get into fights all the time, if you crossed me, boy, I smacked you. But now it just doesn't matter. The baby is much more important. I am a mother. When you're pregnant, you're already a mother. When people give me a hard time on the street, someone will say, 'Hey, she's going to be a mother,' and then they back off. A mother is higher." Ramala explicitly stated for the group, "that's why G-d[1] made me pregnant." Toward the completion of the group's meetings, Ramala decided to approach the social worker at her school and avail herself of helpful services that included child care, a residence, and tuition at a community college.

As expressed by these three girls, most members of the group had found that pregnancy brought teaching, wisdom, and salvation, gifts from the Creator. At the level of process, these comments usually occurred organically, without my inquiring. Often when I did prompt the discussion, the question I asked would be psychotherapeutically standard, such as, How did you become pregnant? How has your life changed lately? Are you different now that you are becoming a mother? In doing IPT-S, however, I almost always encouraged and joined with discussions entailing a spiritual calling within the pregnancy. Had I not, I sense that these discussion may not have continued. Such discussions are infrequent in mainstream social services, and these girls knew social services quite well. As the group progressed and more material emerged, I initiated spiritual discussion by asking the girls if they saw a

---

[1]The author does not write in full the name of God.

"purpose or plan" to the conception or a life circumstance surrounding the pregnancy. By this point in the group, I hardly felt I was bringing a foreign perspective to their experience, but was rather fueling discussion along terms that they shared and had owned.

IPT-S, as mapped out in this chapter, holds an absolute view of the purpose of interpersonal transitions. Motherhood, as a clear interpersonal transition, in this viewed by IPT-S as a supreme inherently spiritually transforming experience. For the group of pregnant girls, the power of this truth was obvious. The many degrading messages from our society surrounding adolescent pregnancy had, however, nearly invalidated the spiritual calling of motherhood. Our work was to let the new voice of motherhood speak, applaud her, and ultimately support the burgeoning of a new life style around motherhood. Letting motherhood speak meant listening carefully to the inherent responsibilities and emergent powers of a mother.

Jemala (16 years in her 6th month of pregnancy) faced a Faustian challenge. The father of her baby held a senior position in a gang, which offered Jemala the opportunity for a baby shower if she allowed her infant to be sworn into a gang. Deep inside, this felt wrong to Jemala, yet she had no other social support for the baby—in the form of a baby shower or even in the form of celebration for the new life. Over the course of a several sessions, Jemala shared with the group her decision-making process, which appeared to be influenced by the climate of the group. Early in the course of the group, she shared her rage over the words of a recent visiting school speaker who had said that 50% of African American boys die or go to jail. "What kind of thing is that to say to mothers? We have a choice in how our boys grow up." As the therapist, I responded to her outrage and fear by highlighting the extraordinary power a mother has in the eyes of her young child. I said, "You are the sun and the moon and the stars to your child. The mother has a special moral authority. Your child believes what you say." This authority, I asserted, extends to the child's care from all members of the family. As she continued to struggle with her decision midway through the group, Jamala emphatically burst out that she did not want her son to look to her in 10 years and know that she had encouraged him to be in a gang. Toward the end of the group, Jemala told the group that she had decided against the swearing into the gang and would forsake a baby stroller, crib, and new clothes for the child. "What kind of mother sets up her son to be in a gang? He would know that I had done this. It would be my responsibility that he was now in a gang." Jamala had started to come into her power of righteousness as a mother. She never used spiritual language, but it would seem reasonable to consider as spiritual the preservation of life and moral authority of motherhood against poverty and deficit of regard for life. Jemala shared with the group toward the end of treatment that she hoped to become a judge in the long term, a journey which she intended to start through her enrollment in community college.

Anna Maria (14 years old) felt profoundly depressed by the very same world that had in the recent past been thrilling, adventurous, and exciting to her. Her boyfriend, a drug dealer, smoked marijuana several times a day and constantly threw parties with his friends. She had not cared that he used drugs before she became pregnant, but now she was very concerned that her boyfriend continued to do so and would soon be exposing their child to drugs. Anna Maria also feared the company her boyfriend kept would at the very least distract him from responsible parenting, potentially even directly harm their child. I heard her shift in perspective and her related severe depression as the voice of motherhood. The inherent responsibility and care for the child was being obstructed by the adolescent culture of risk that once seemed so exciting. A source of clarity, power, and strength beyond the current interpersonal strife, it seemed, was to empower the growing mother. As in the case of Jemala, I encouraged the group to explore the moral authority and ultimate responsibility of motherhood by asking, "Who ultimately will protect the child?" and eventually by overtly stating, "There is only one mother—you alone." Once she felt more certain of her moral authority, the group also assisted Anna Maria in developing a voice through which to share her ultimatum with her boyfriend. She decided to explain that his drug use made her feel that he "did not care about their child," appealing to his very real love as a young father, an approach which appeared helpful in initiating a process of transforming her boyfriend more fully into fatherhood.

By embracing the inherent spiritual awakening of motherhood, both Jemala and Anna Maria started to inspire their boyfriends, and immediate social network, to honor the infant as sacred and to protect, nurture, and refine themselves to better love the baby. By contrast, for Consuela, who had no boyfriend, discovering motherhood was expressed through a heightened understanding of her own mother. Consuela (age 15 years and 5 months pregnant) shared the following: "Your friends all say, 'I got your back, I got your back.' But when I got pregnant where were they? They're gone. Its your mother whose there for you always. All you have is your mother." Also echoing a renewed appreciation for motherhood, as expressed in their own mother, Emela (the oldest of the girls at 18 years) moved out of her boyfriend's apartment and home to her mother once the baby was born. "The refrigerator worked better at my mother's house. And also, she knows things about how to raise a baby. She and I have gotten along much better since I became a mother."

Clearly the adolescent girls did not need to be taught about motherhood. The girls needed to validate the voice of motherhood as it came through their experience. Overall, in keeping the IPT-S formulation of inherent spiritual calling for growth in transitions, I supported overtly the absolute value of motherhood. In an early session, I brought pictures of ancient cave paintings and figures celebrating the sacredness birth and the spiritual aliveness of pregnant women. I shared the information that the ancient cave drawings on record to Western culture was not a depiction of a hunt or war, it represented a birth. I showed the pregnant girls images of the Venus of Willendorf, the oldest representation of human figure, with her extraordinary fertile build. The room of girls fell silent, and you could have heard a pin drop. The girls clearly felt that motherhood was being affirmed.

Once motherhood as a spiritual path is supported, these girls experienced a flood of concerns over the obstacles to this transition. Being young, having no money, lacking paternal commitment at this point in treatment were discussed as obstructing the process of building the maternal "nest" and realizing the call of motherhood, *not* as invalidating the call to motherhood. The destruction that surrounded the girls was understood as such. Community and institutional ridicule was viewed as not sustaining spirituality. Depression and anger were linked with lack of support for this most momentous interpersonal and spiritual transition.

Broadly speaking, during the middle phase of IPT-S, the renegotiation phase, we explored how to build a social and material world that supported each girl's new status as a mother and protector of her child. As a mother, the girl had heightened power, authority, and responsibility to protect her baby. We explored her inherent moral authority as the mother, both in the eyes of her child and strikingly in the eyes of her community if rightly embraced. Her moral authority included her right to insist on how the child is treated and her obligation to create the circumstance for care. Her evolution as a mother also inspired taking responsibility through work or engagement with social services. As a growing mother, she also explored how she might seek interpersonal emotional supports to help her foster her motherhood. Who were the women who could mentor her in motherhood, how could she embrace these women as teachers? Who were the men who supported or protected her? Although the boyfriends were usually unreliable, many of the girls had fiercely loyal brothers whose conviction the new mother might direct.

Termination involved the girls expressing how relieving and helpful it felt to discuss these issues. Whereas they had felt alone and confused before the program, they now discussed these issues on their own. I was particularly struck that the girls seemed to take enormous pride in their new status and viewed themselves as empowered to help themselves and their children through their elevated status as mothers.

Termination, Relapse Prevention, and Therapeutic Outcomes

Whereas 60% of the girls were depressed at the beginning of the intervention and previous research would predict that more girls would become depressed over the subsequent 3 months, with treatment more than 90% were no longer depressed at termination. These findings suggest to me that depression for these girls emanated from the obstruction of the natural momentum of motherhood, as spiritual calling, and the invalidation of their journey toward spiritual growth through the divine orchestrated plan of their pregnancy. More broadly, depression might be viewed as the obstruction of spiritual growth.

Beyond prevention and treatment of depression, from the perspective of psyche, these girls owned and integrated the most precious spiritual gift given to women—the opportunity to be a mother and to mother. The work of the IPT-S group made this inherent process explicit and validated and supported the thrust of maternal transformation so that the girls could participate in their own evolution. While this was understood within IPT-S as a spiritual process, it did not necessitate spiritual language. Sometimes the girls explicitly used spiritual or religious language, such as "G-d gave me this baby," "G-d saved me by giving me this child." or "I am not killing my child, this child has a soul." Other times however, the language of spirituality felt foreign to the girls. Spirituality was defined by their actions, as they honored creation beyond the norms of their adolescent social world and their immediate personal welfare. I have no data on how the girls did a year or so into motherhood. It is my hope that the view of their new motherhood role as a regal and spiritual calling will endure.

CONCLUSION

For the pregnant girls in the IPT-S group, the relationship with the new baby, the father of their baby, and their own mother emerged as primary opportunities for spiritual growth. Becoming a mother, in the view of IPT-S, is an interpersonal transition that carries an absolute charge to evolve in specific ways: to protect, to claim and uphold moral authority, to love without limits, and to appreciate one's own mother. The girls came to IPT-S with a sense of its major tenets: Relationships are divine vehicles for spiritual growth, purposefully architected. The pregnant girls took to IPT-S, used it toward their own spiritual growth, and were measurably less depressed by the end of 12 weeks of treatment. The girls simply understood that the people who enter our lives are there for us, and we are there for them, to join in a process of spiritual growth. Recall, however, that not all of the girls considered themselves to be spiritual nor used spiritual language.

IPT-S may be one way of engaging the suffering that arises in interpersonal relationship toward spiritual growth. The psychological experience that comes through our relationships marks spiritual growth. Love in this sense is more than a palatable emotion; it reveals that we are in consort with the laws of the Creator. Anger, rage, and depression show us the door to spiritual growth. Many religious denominations comfortably link psychological emotion and spiritual reality. Given this apparently universal understanding, it might benefit our clients to see emotion as revelation of the more fundamental spiritual Truth.

REFERENCES

Gallup, G. H., & Bezilla, R. (1992). *The religious life of young Americans*. Princeton, NJ: George J. Gallup International Institute.

Klerman, G., & Weissman, M. M. (1993). *New applications in interpersonal psychotherapy*. Washington, DC: American Psychiatric Press.

Klerman, G., Weissman, M. M., Rounsaville, B., & Chevron, E. (1984). *Interpersonal psychotherapy of depression*. New York: Basic Books.

Larson, D., & Larson, S. (1994). *The forgotten factor: Review of research on religion and health*. Rockville, MD: National Institute of Health Research.

Miller, L., Gur, M., & Shanok, A. (2004). *Interpersonal psychotherapy with poor pregnant girls, depression and anxiety*. Manuscript submitted for publication.

Miller, L., & Weissman, M. M. (2002). Interpersonal psychotherapy delivered over the telephone to recurrent depressives. A pilot study. *Depression and Anxiety*, 16, 114–117.

Pargament K. I. (1997). *The psychology of religion and coping*. New York: Guilford Press.

Richards, P. S., & Bergin, A. E. (1997). *A spiritual strategy for counseling and psychotherapy*. Washington, DC: American Psychological Association.

Weissman, M., Markowitz, J., & Klerman, G. (2000). *Comprehensive guide to interpersonal psychotherapy*. New York: Basic Books.

READINGS THAT INFORMED THE AUTHOR'S FORMULATION OF SPIRITUAL INTERPERSONAL PSYCHOTHERAPY

Charlton, H. (1989). *Saints alive. Golden Quest Series Volume III*. New York: Golden Quest.

Dass, R. (1974). *The only dance there is: Talks given at the Menninger Foundation, Topeka, Kansas, 1970, and at the Spring Grove Hospital, Spring Grove, Maryland, 1972*. Garden City, NY: Archor.

Lundstrom, M., & Belitz, C. (1998). *The power of flow: Practical ways to transform your life with meaningful coincidence*. New York: Three Rivers Press.

8

A TRANSPERSONAL–INTEGRATIVE APPROACH TO SPIRITUALLY ORIENTED PSYCHOTHERAPY

DAVID LUKOFF AND FRANCIS LU

DESCRIPTION OF THE APPROACH

Transpersonal psychotherapy draws on both psychology and spiritual traditions to create a bold new vision of a psychologically informed spirituality and a spiritually based psychology. Perhaps the core assumption of transpersonal psychology is that individuals are essentially spiritual beings rather than simply a self or a psychological ego (Sperry, 2001). The psychological and spiritual dimensions of human experience are seen as different, although at times overlapping, with the spiritual as foundational (Cortright, 1997). The core qualities associated with spirituality are considered not only appropriate as a focus in psychotherapy, but as goals of transpersonal psychotherapy:

> Spirituality presupposes certain qualities of mind, including compassion, gratitude, awareness of a transcendent dimension, and an appreciation for life, which brings meaning and purpose to existence. Whereas spirituality is essentially a subjective experience of the sacred, religion in-

177

volves subscribing to a set of beliefs or doctrines that are institutionalized. (Vaughan, 1991, p. 105)

Historical and Theoretical Basis

The Association for Transpersonal Psychology (ATP) was founded in 1971 by many of the original founders of the Association for Humanistic Psychology, including Abraham Maslow, Anthony Sutich, Miles Vich, Stanislav Grof, Michael Murphy, and James Fadiman. Sutich and Maslow are generally regarded as the midwives for the articulation of the transpersonal view within humanistic psychology (Valle, 1989). They saw the need for a psychology that was willing to study and explore experiences, particularly spiritual experiences, in which the sense of identity extends beyond the individual or personal (*transpersonal*) to encompass wider aspects of humankind, the natural world, and the cosmos. Behaviorist theory ("first force"), psychoanalytic theory ("second force"), and humanistic psychology ("third force") lack a systematic place to study spirituality and consciousness.

> The emerging transpersonal psychology ("fourth force") is concerned specifically with the empirical, scientific study and responsible implementation of the findings relevant to becoming, individual and species-wide meta-needs, ultimate values, peak experiences, B-values, ecstasy, mystical experiences, awe, being, self-actualization, essence, bliss, wonder, ultimate meaning, transcendence of the self, spirit, oneness . . . and related concepts, experiences, and activities. (Sutich, 1969, p. 16)

Such states are notoriously difficult to study, as William James pointed out in *Exceptional Mental States* (E. Taylor, 1983). James's philosophy of radical empiricism argued that a true science must be based on the study of all human experiences, not just those that can be manipulated in a laboratory. The discipline of transpersonal psychology attempts to study scientifically the reports of transpersonal experiences and behaviors (Krippner, 1990). Consciousness and spirituality continue to be the keynotes in transpersonal psychology and practice.

One can, however, trace back larger historical forces leading to the founding of transpersonal psychology. The Greek Eleusinian Mysteries used an LSD-like ergot in rituals to induce transpersonal states (Wasson, Hofmann, & Ruck, 1978). E. Taylor (1990) attributed the origins of transpersonal psychology to the unique cultural context provided by the United States, which began as a spiritual democracy that was home to many mystical religious groups (e.g., Quakers, Shakers). The Quakers, for example, maintained that one could be moved by the inner light, thus obviating the need for priests, books, buildings, or other parts of religious organizational bureaucracies. Transcendentalism, spiritualism, and Swedenborgianism took hold on American soil in the 1800s and can also be seen as predecessors of transpersonal psychology. The Boston School of Psychotherapy, which flourished from 1880 to 1920, was a direct forerunner of transpersonal psychotherapy in its use of diverse religious iconography and practices in therapy and led to the founding of pastoral counseling and Alcoholics Anonymous. This school was supplanted in mainstream academic and clinical psychology by the Freudian psychoanalytic and behavioral approaches, but the counterculture movement in 1964 provided a return to the focus on inner and communal religious experience. Several transpersonal psychology graduate schools were founded in the 1960s and 1970s, including the Institute of Transpersonal Psychology, Saybrook Graduate School, the California Institute of Asian Studies (now California Institute of Integral Studies), JFK University, and Naropa, which train students in transpersonally oriented psychotherapy.

Transpersonal psychotherapy evolved concurrently with transpersonal psychology. Sutich (1973) wrote an article on this topic shortly after the founding of the ATP in which he described it "as therapy directly or indirectly concerned with the recognition, acceptance, and realization of ultimate states. As such, it is not new; rather it is perhaps the oldest of all the therapeutic approaches" (p. 10). The focus on "ultimate states" in the early days of transpersonal psychology has expanded over the past 30 years to address the whole person, not just one's transpersonal experiences. Initially it was important to bring attention to these areas that had been pathologized and ignored in other models of psychology. More recently in transpersonal psychology, attention has shifted to examining the way the spiritual is expressed in everyday life. A similar shift occurred in transpersonal psychotherapy, which now addresses the whole person, including ordinary consciousness, suffering, pain, abuse, mental disorders including psychosis, and relationship conflicts. As Vaughan (1993) expressed this shift, "Transpersonal psychotherapy is a healing endeavor that aims at the integration of physical, emotional, mental, and spiritual aspects of well-being. Its goals include the classic ones of normal healthy functioning" (p. 160).

Main Theoretical Constructs

Jung was an important precursor to transpersonal psychology. He personally translated his term *überpersonlich* as transpersonal, but most translations use the term *collective unconscious*. He explored the psychological value of many spiritual traditions, writing the introductions to the first translations of the *I Ching* and *Tibetan Book of the Dead*. Assagioli (2000) developed a theory of psychosynthesis that drew on spiritual teachings. He introduced the concept of the soul into psychological theory, along with distinguishing between "higher" and "lower" levels of the unconscious, a point that has continued to be elaborated in the transpersonal field.

Grof's theoretical approach is perhaps the most comprehensive in that it incorporates, and provides explicit accounts of a wide range and diversity of transpersonal experiences. The origins of Grof's theory lie in his extensive investigations of the therapeutic potential of LSD and later of holotropic breathwork. Grof found that the types of extraordinary experiences reported were remarkably similar and included sensory alterations, emotional reliving of past events and traumas, death and rebirth episodes, as well as a variety of psychic, archetypal and mystical experiences. Grof defines the transpersonal as follows:

> To understand the transpersonal realm we must begin thinking of con-
> sciousness in an entirely new way . . . as something that exists outside
> and independent of us, something that in its essence is not bound by
> matter. . . . Transpersonal consciousness is infinite, rather than finite,
> stretching beyond the limits of time and space. (S. Grof, 1993)

Wilber is another leading transpersonal theoretician who developed a comprehensive model of consciousness, spirituality, psychology, and therapy that is popular among transpersonal psychologists, along with a following in diverse academic and professional fields. He posited evolutionary changes in consciousness, beginning with the mystical participation in nature experienced by the earliest humans, through a series of "eras" involving magical, mythical, and mental–egoic consciousness, to our present-day capacity for existential authenticity and transpersonal identity. All psychological and spiritual systems contain partial and complementary truths, and different psychotherapies address specific levels. Whereas most psychotherapies are directed toward the lower levels of the consciousness spectrum, transpersonal approaches focus on the upper levels (Wilber, 2000). Wilber's (2000) integral psychology model provides a spiritual framework for psychotherapy that addresses diverse spiritual experiences, developmental levels, and issues. He has proposed which types of spiritual practices should be employed or avoided at each stage and which types of psychopathology are related to specific developmental stages.

The Relationship Between Psychology and Spirituality

Although the roots of transpersonal thinking and practices are ancient, transpersonal psychology has adapted ideas and practices from many religions, cultures, and epochs to a Western, modern and postmodern psychological language as well as to practical applications in therapy. Transpersonal psychology rigorously inquires into the multiplicity of spiritual techniques, disciplines, and methods to distill their essence and commonalities (Walsh, 1999). Transpersonal psychology has been greatly influenced by Huxley's (1944/1990) perennial philosophy, which posits universal themes shared by all religions.

By incorporating a spiritual dimension, transpersonal psychology stands in marked contrast to earlier schools. Transpersonal psychology considers spirituality in its own right, distinct from Freud's reduction of religion as wishful illusions, Ellis's irrational thinking, or Skinner's manifest disregard.

A transpersonal therapist is not merely accepting of spirituality, however, but actively helps clients achieve or strengthen their spirituality. All transpersonal therapists address spirituality in therapy; some even fill the role of spiritual guide for their clients (Vaughan, 1991). Other transpersonal therapists see the therapist–client relationship as "two fellow spiritual sojourners becoming intuitive to inner promptings and intimately involved in spiritual quests" (Lines, 2002, p. 109). Kornfield (1993) discussed how the boundaries between the two provinces are not at all clear, and, in practice, there is significant overlap.

Vaughan (1993), however, pointed out that whereas psychotherapy supports spiritual work, it is not the same. Two principal differences between psychotherapy and spiritual work are the following:

1. Therapists let the clients lead and determine the content of the sessions.
2. Teachers provide the content to be learned or the practice to be followed by their students. In keeping with standard therapeutic tradition, most transpersonal therapists would not teach a client a specific spiritual philosophy.

When transpersonal therapists incorporate spiritual practices such as meditation in psychotherapy, they point the client to the original practice for continued exploration outside of therapy and use the therapy to explore the psychological meaning and value to the client of their spiritual experiences, beliefs, and practices (Hutton, 1994). Non-transpersonal therapists, however, may use spiritual practices such as meditation based solely on their clear health benefits without adopting a transpersonal perspective (Benson, 1975).

Spiritual Context

Context refers to the attitude and orientation of the therapy, its basic assumptions and attitude toward suffering, healing, and human potential. Vaughan (1979) maintained that holding a transpersonal context for therapy, rather than specific techniques, is what defines a transpersonal approach. Transpersonal therapists utilize techniques from psychodynamic, behavioral, family, and other therapies as well as from spiritual disciplines (Hutton, 1994). Similarly, for Boorstein (2000),

> Foremost is the spiritual context within which I hold all of my patients. I have no doubt that this helps me stay in a caring mode—especially with difficult patients. To convey to a patient that you see him or her as being a piece of the Divine is incredibly powerful to begin to counter a life-long view of worthlessness. It can only be done when appropriate for the given patient, and it will not be effective if the therapist does not

actually believe it in his/her mind and experience it in his/her heart. (p. 413)

The context is not always explicitly articulated to the client, as exemplified in the case of Bryan presented later in this chapter.

Spirituality and Psychopathology

Some people attempt to avoid dealing with their emotional and behavioral problems by turning to spiritual practices instead. Welwood (2000) called this "spiritual bypassing." Several kinds of spiritual bypass have been identified: fear of intimacy leading to monastic lifestyle, joining a cult to deal with a fragile ego, accessing nonordinary states of consciousness to avoid feelings of depression, "surrendering" to a higher power to avoid confronting one's problems. Some people engaged in spiritual practice suffer from psychological wounds including self-hatred, aggression, narcissistic egocentricity, and depression, for which a course of egoic-level psychotherapy could support and further their movement toward spiritual development.

Mindfulness Practices

Transpersonal psychotherapy has adapted and incorporated mindfulness practices beginning with meditation in the early 1970s. Benson (1975) established the value of meditation for treating medical diseases such as high blood pressure in the 1960s. The importance and application of meditation in mental health was first discussed in talks by Ram Dass (1970) that were published in the *Journal of Transpersonal Psychology* along with several other articles on meditation in psychotherapy (Goleman, 1971; Van Nuys, 1971). Ram Dass had been a coinvestigator in LSD studies with Timothy Leary, then traveled to India in 1967 and met a spiritual teacher. Despite a recent stroke, he continues to influence transpersonal psychology, sharing his explorations with a variety of spiritual practices, including yoga, chanting, and Sufism from his wheelchair. Alan Watts contributed to the meditation–psychotherapy dialogue in articles in the *Journal of Transpersonal Psychology* and several popular books (Watts, 1957, 1974).

Buddhism has had a large influence on transpersonal therapy because Buddhist mindfulness practices involve training in the qualities of attention and presence required to do effective therapy. In addition, meditation trains self-observation skills, which can also be beneficial to the therapist: "Becoming aware of one's primary interrupting factors can be diagnostically and therapeutically significant because one can clearly see unhealthy, habitual mental processes" (Deatherage, 1996, p. 209). Buddhism also includes techniques for addressing anger, anxiety, forgiveness, and other psychotherapeutic issues. It can help patients go beyond merely recognizing their problems to healing them by complementing therapy and leading to new dimensions of wisdom and wholeness (Epstein, 1998). Meditation has expanded as a psychotherapeutic modality into a whole field of mindfulness practices used in the treatment of both somatic and psychological problems (Kabit-Zinn, 1990).

Other Asian spiritual practices have also influenced transpersonal psychology. Aikido is a Japanese spiritually oriented martial art that emphasizes working with a partner, not fighting against an opponent as in competitive tournaments. The essence of the practice is the blending of movement and breathing, which physically creates harmony in a conflict situation.

Aikido has influenced the practice of transpersonal psychotherapy through the graduate program at the Institute of Transpersonal Psychology (ITP), founded in 1975 by Robert Frager. Frager, who studied aikido with its creator, Master Ueshiba, has taught aikido four times a week as part of a required mind–body healing course at ITP. Charles Tart (1992) incorporated concepts from aikido in his influential theoretical work in transpersonal psychology. Aikido as an adjunct to therapy has been described in individual psychotherapy (Fagianelli, 1995), adolescent treatment (Heckler, 1985), and family therapy (Saposnek, 1980).

Yoga (Scotton & Hiatt, 1996), Sufism (Deikman, 1996), qigong (Mayer, 1999), and many other Asian practices have been adapted as modalities for transpersonal psychotherapy (see Boorstein, 1996, for case examples).

Nonordinary States of Consciousness in Transpersonal Psychotherapy

William James first explored how nonordinary states of consciousness can be induced and the value that they have for providing access to special knowledge that cannot be gained through ordinary consciousness. Many schools of psychology "adhere to an unnecessarily restricted view of the psyche [and refuse to] work therapeutically with spiritual experience and experiences of nonordinary reality" (Scotton, 1996, p. 3). In transpersonal psychotherapy, induction of nonordinary states of consciousness has a respected place. Transpersonal psychotherapists have explored the healing potential of many states of consciousness, including those associated with meditation, bodywork, movement, dreamwork, guided imagery, prayer, drumming, chanting, sweat lodges, fasting, shamanic journeying, and psychedelic drugs (Cortright, 1997). Anthropologist Michael Harner (1990) and Native American psychologist Leslie Gray (2002) have developed shamanic counseling approaches based on shamanic practices that induce nonordinary states (particularly drumming).

New techniques to induce nonordinary states have also been developed such as holotropic breathwork, an experiential procedure developed by Stanislav and Christina Grof involving several-hour sessions of music, energy work, and hyperventilation to simulate psychedelic drug experience (K. Taylor, 2003).

Therapist's Skills and Attributes

Scotton (1985) and Wittine (1989) have both posited requirements essential for those practicing transpersonal psychotherapy. These include the following:

1. Openness to the transpersonal dimension, including the belief that contact with the transpersonal realm may be transformative and healing
2. The ability to assess the presence and value of transpersonal experiences that occur in spiritual practices, dreams, visions, synchronous events or interactions with a spiritual teacher
3. Knowledge of a variety of spiritual paths
4. Ability to facilitate spiritual and nonordinary state experiences, both inside and outside of therapy, to promote transformation and healing
5. Active pursuit of his or her own spiritual development
6. Grounding in other psychotherapy approaches and psychological theory

The transpersonal therapist's own consciousness and presence "provide the guiding light for the therapeutic journey" (Cortright, 1997, p. 238). Therefore, transpersonal therapists are expected to continue to work on their own development and develop qualities of attention, clarity, compassion, and nonattachment. They should also have firsthand experience of transpersonal states to work effectively with those who seek guidance in dealing with them. Firsthand experience is often interpreted to mean having a discipline that provides grounding in spirituality (Walsh & Vaughan, 1996).

Transpersonal psychotherapists must also be able to address the unique ethical issues associated with nonordinary states, such as ecstatic blissful states associated with mystical experiences and detachment associated with meditative states. "Adequate training to induce nonordinary states of consciousness requires many personal therapeutic experiences *as the client* in nonordinary consciousness" (K. Taylor, 1995, p. 49). Because clients in nonordinary states may also be more suggestible and vulnerable, transference, and countertransference issues can be heightened. An informed consent form should include comprehensive information about the kinds of experiences that may occur, agreements about touch, duration of sessions, availability of the therapist in case of distress, and therapeutic procedures, in addition to fees, confidentiality, and the other informed consent requirements.

Strengths and Limitations

Strengths

Transpersonal psychotherapy provides a basis of theory and practice that allows for cross-cultural communication and for genuine dialogue with traditional healers, such as shamans and Native American medicine healers. Edwards (1995), a South African professor of psychology, has noted that

Transpersonal psychology has a number of features of its research and practice that make it particularly relevant to the South African context. It is a multistate discipline, which recognizes the importance of a variety of states of consciousness. Many counseling models adopt a unistate perspective. . . . This position has made meaningful contact between African Traditional Healers almost impossible. Transpersonal psychology, with a perspective which is much less Eurocentric than many other approaches in psychology, provides a basis of theory and practice which allow for genuine dialogue with African Traditional Healers. (n.p.)

Weaknesses

Transpersonal psychology has not achieved theoretical agreement among practitioners, such as cognitive–behaviorists and psychoanalysts largely have. There are certain commonalities to the major transpersonal theories of Abraham Maslow, C. G. Jung, Roberto Assagioli, Stanislav Grof, and Ken Wilber. All view transpersonal experiences as ones that go beyond both egoic and existential identity. All concur on the importance of spiritual experience. There is also basic agreement about what constitutes basic spiritual qualities: compassionate, loving, wise, receptive, intuitive, spontaneous, creative, inspired, peaceful, awake, and connected (Vaughan, 1991).

But "Where the theories fail to agree is in their *conceptual understanding* of the transpersonal self, and in their *developmental psychology* or explanations of how transpersonal identity may be achieved" (Daniels, 2002, p. 5). The result is that transpersonal psychology has at times been splintered by contentious internal debates about the validity of competing theories. In addition, this lack of generally agreed-on theory has provided an opportunity for critics of the field to question its validity. When transpersonal psychologists petitioned the American Psychological Association (APA) for the formation of a formal transpersonal psychology division in 1990, the proposal was denied due to some concerns about the "unscientific" nature of transpersonal psychology. The second proposal, submitted shortly afterward, was also denied, this time due in part to criticism from prominent humanistic psychologists such as Rollo May who disparaged transpersonal psychology for trying to "leap across" the dark side of human nature, focusing on transcendent states and ignoring suffering, guilt, and jealousy. Albert Ellis attacked transpersonal psychology for an irrational belief in divine beings, a tendency toward dogmatism, and opposition to science. May and Ellis seem to have focused on New Age popularizations of transpersonal approaches, however, "a common confusion between transpersonal psychologists and 'transpersonalists'" (Chinen, 1996, p. 13). Currently there is no division within APA focused on transpersonal psychology, although Division 32 (Humanistic Psychology) does include transpersonal psychologists on its board and transpersonal presentations in its programs at APA annual meetings.

Indications and Contraindications

Because transpersonal psychotherapeutic approaches pay attention to and accept the importance of nonordinary states, they have been successfully used in the treatment of spiritual crises and psychotic disorders (both acute and chronic; Lukoff, 1996). Psychotic states of consciousness hold a special place in transpersonal theory. In Wilber's (1980) spectrum model of consciousness, psychosis is neither *prepersonal* (infantile and regressive) nor *transpersonal* (transcendent and Absolute), but is *depersonal*—an admixture of both higher and lower elements. Wilber (1980) wrote, "[Psychosis] carries with it cascading fragments of higher structures that have ruinously disintegrated" (p. 64). Thus, he continues, psychotic persons "often channel profound spiritual insights" (p. 108). Transpersonal psychologists do not view psychosis as a higher state, however, but as one that is problematic for both the individual and society. Some individuals have been able to benefit from such experiences, but the potential for a tragic outcomes and lifelong impairment suggests that alternative paths to such breakthroughs through therapy and spiritual practices are safer and more reliable.

The two case studies in this chapter concern patients who had psychotic episodes and were able to integrate their experiences through transpersonal approaches. Although long-term follow-up studies documenting the effectiveness of transpersonal approaches and which kinds of patients are more likely to benefit from them have not been conducted, case studies such as the ones included here have included long-term follow-ups with successful outcomes. Some criteria have been proposed to make differential diagnoses between serious psychotic disorders that may require hospitalization and medication, and spiritual emergencies (Lukoff, 1985). Even with mental disorders, acknowledging the powerful and often positive transpersonal experiences that occur in psychosis can be helpful to develop a therapeutic alliance necessary for ensuring medication compliance (Jamison, Gerner, Hammen, & Padesky, 1980).

Transpersonal approaches have also been used in addiction disorders, which have been viewed as a misguided "spiritual thirst" for connection with a higher power (C. Grof, 1993; Miller, 1990). The nonordinary states involved in many drug addictions have been addressed through the use of transpersonal interventions to induce alternative nonordinary states (Peteet, 1993).

Transpersonal psychotherapy has also been applied to death and grief by incorporating the insights from spiritual traditions which address these issues (see *Journal of Transpersonal Psychology* articles: Garfield, 1975; Leslie, 1976; Lieff, 1982; Richards, Grof, Goodman, & Kurland, 1972; Waldman, 1990). This is another area that has been heavily influenced by Buddhism, including books such as the *Tibetan Book of Living and Dying* (Sogyal Rinpoche, 1994).

Cultural and Gender Considerations

Some religious and spiritual beliefs and practices include values and images that are patriarchal (Campbell, 1972) that, if adopted in their original form, can be repressive toward women. The transpersonal perspective, however, is generally very accepting of feminine values and feminine religious iconography (e.g., the article in *Journal of Transpersonal Psychology* titled "The Feminine Principle in Tibetan Vajrayana Buddhism: Reflection of a Buddhist Feminist"; Asante, 1984). ATP conferences have included many presentations on feminine spirituality by Jean Bolen, June Singer, and others.

Studies have consistently shown that patients would very much like their health care professionals to talk with them about spiritual needs related to their health problems, and only a small percentage (5%–10%) of the U.S. population is not comfortable with explicit religious or spiritual concepts, language, and practices (Koenig, McCullough, & Larson, 2001). Thus, transpersonal therapists, by explicitly acknowledging the importance of spirituality, are more aligned with the majority of the population who want to have sensitive and informed discussions about spirituality with their health care providers.

Expected Future Developments and Directions

Many of the major political conflicts in the world are drawn along religious lines. Transpersonal psychology can contribute to interreligious dialogue in an increasingly global context that could aid in the resolution of contemporary conflicts (Rothberg, 1990).

In the future, transpersonal clinical approaches will greatly expand and evolve, often without using transpersonal psychology constructs. Forgiveness practices based on diverse world religions are becoming widely used to address group conflicts and in individual psychotherapy (Luskin, 2001). Another example is the positive psychology movement spearheaded by Martin Seligman former president of the American Psychological Association. In a study, he reported that one of the major statistical buffers against depression is serious religious commitment (Sethi & Seligman, 1993), and he has declared that spirituality and religion have a major role to play in addressing the epidemic of depression sweeping across the United States and other countries (Seligman, 2001). Another example is mindfulness interventions, originally the province of transpersonal psychology but now widely incorporated in the burgeoning field of complementary and alternative medicine. Spiritual healing and shamanism, also foci in transpersonal psychotherapy, are being investigated as spiritual interventions in complementary and alternative medicine (http://nccam.nih.gov).

CASE EXAMPLES

Transpersonal therapy can enable persons to realize the transformative aspects of their psychotic episodes. It is based on an alternative perspective of psychosis as potentially "breakthrough rather than breakdown" as Laing (1972) described it. Transpersonal therapy involves delving into the contents of a patient's hallucinations and delusions to find personal insights and spiritual dimensions. It can be conducted both during the acute stage and the postpsychotic integration phase but is approached differently in the two situations. Therapy with acutely psychotic individuals is oriented toward getting them safely through their inner journey. In the postpsychotic integration phase, on which these two case studies focus, the major work involves helping clients construct a new narrative of their psychotic episode, one that functions as a positive guide to a more passionate and meaningful life.

The proposal for the *DSM–IV* category Religious or Spiritual Problem (V62.89) had its roots in the concerns of transpersonal psychologists about the misdiagnosis and treatment of spiritual emergencies that present with psychotic symptoms. Such spiritual emergencies were the subject of several presentations at ATP conferences and *Journal of Transpersonal Psychology* articles (Lukoff, Lu, & Turner, 1998). The diagnostic category was initially conceived of as "psychospiritual crisis," and the proposal was later expanded to include religious problems (Lukoff, Lu, & Turner, 1992). This diagnostic category is not a mental disorder but is listed in the section, "Other Conditions That May Be the Focus of Clinical Attention." Thus, it is not considered a form of psychopathology, but rather a problem that is associated with religious and spiritual experiences. In this sense, it is similar to the *DSM–IV* category of Bereavement, which can include depressive symptoms but is not a mental disorder because it is considered a normal reaction to loss (Lukoff, 2003). Furthermore, all diagnoses in this section can occur concurrently with a related or unrelated mental disorder in the *DSM–IV*.

HOWARD

Client Demographics, Relevant History, and Presenting Concern

In 1981, Howard (a 28-year-old man) telephoned me at my (DL) office at the UCLA Neuropsychiatric Institute where I was on the faculty. He had seen an announcement for a workshop I was giving titled "Psychosis: Mysticism, Shamanism, or Pathology?" He was unable to attend the workshop but told me that he was sure I'd be interested in the story of his "Mental Odyssey." We arranged to meet for lunch, where he began to tell me about the experiences surrounding his 6-week hospitalization 9 years earlier. I invited him to present at my UCLA seminar for psychiatry residents, psychology interns, and nursing staff. Several other ex-patients had already come and discussed their psychotic episodes, their treatment by the mental health system, and the difficulties they had encountered in readjusting to consensual reality and societal norms. Howard responded eagerly to my invitation to present because he said he never before had an opportunity to tell the complete story of his Mental Odyssey. His talk was spellbinding, and I was particularly intrigued with the profuse symbolic imagery that permeated the account of his psychotic experience. I asked him if he would be willing to work with me on a case study documenting the occurrence of a positively transformative psychotic episode that fit the transpersonal model of a spiritual emergency. I recorded his presentation and had it transcribed and this led to a series of 15 meetings over 2 years to prepare a case study titled "The Myths in Mental Illness" (Lukoff & Everest, 1985).

At the time of his hospitalization, Howard had just returned to his parents' house in central California after spending 8 months hitchhiking around the United States and Mexico following graduation from high school. He told how, after staying up all night composing and retyping a poem,

> By daybreak, I was in a state of rapture. That morning I greeted my parents with the announcement, "I have been reborn. My father is the sun; my mother is the moon; and I am a child of the universe. . . . My experiment is a success!"

Howard became preoccupied with symbolic images and themes from ancient myths. For example, he recounted a simple afternoon hike up a mountain as being a journey to heaven during which he encountered magical paths of entry, power spots, sacred mountains, guiding spirits, and powerful enemies. Afterward he told his family that he had returned from hell, been reborn, and had taken up his rightful place in the Kingdom of Heaven. "I am the albatross; you are the dove," he announced. Howard also drew elaborate mandalas—he called them "keys." They included many well-known symbols and cultural motifs: the Islamic crescent and star, the yin and yang symbol, the infinity sign, along with pierced hands, eyes, and circles (see Figure 8.1).

On the fourth day after he returned home, his father, a general practitioner physician, asked him to go to the hospital.

> "We'd like to run some tests on you," he said. I agreed, thinking about the potential value for science and humanity. "The medical community should look at the experience I'm having and learn something from it," I told him. "Medical experts could scientifically monitor it, chronicle it, and the world would benefit. I am definitely benefiting and it needs to be shared with everyone." At the psychiatric unit, I signed a paper thinking I was giving my consent for tests. Then my father left me with an attendant. I suggested we start the tests since I had to leave to finish my experiment. "Take it easy," he said. "Settle in. You'll be here for a while."

While his medical records had been destroyed after 7 years, I was able to obtain a copy of his admission note, according to which Howard was diagnosed as having an Acute Schizophrenic Reaction.

Figure 8.1. Howard's pencil drawing of his "key" on the day he was first hospitalized. From "The Myths in Mental Illness," by D. Lukoff and C. Everest, 1985, *Journal of Transpersonal Psychology, 17*, p. 136. Copyright 2000 by the Association for Transpersonal Psychology. Reprinted with permission.

Assessment

I administered a 1-hour retrospective mental status exam (Wing, Cooper, & Sartorius, 1974) to Howard to determine what types of psychotic symptoms were present in his Mental Odyssey. Several delusions were elicited:

- *Delusions of Thought Insertion:* "It seemed as though these words were entering from an outside source . . . not forged out of my own cognitive processes."
- *Delusions of Reference:* "Mexican guy was here for a specific purpose—to test me, my will. Janitor knew more than he seemed to know, had another function."
- *Grandiose Abilities:* "I was the Pied Piper—calling people to the experience to show it could be done, to open the door so others could come through." "Events were preparing me for Enlightenment and mastery over eternity, time and space."
- *Religious Delusions:* "I would be one of the first of a series of people to enter the Kingdom of Heaven."

Hallucinations and Bizarre Behavior were also rated:

- *Visual Hallucinations:* "I saw the face of Death laughing. In my hospital room, saw three yellow birds. Sky was brilliant orange."
- *Tactile Hallucinations:* When rays were projected at my (Howard's) stomach, " I felt a dull stabbing in my solar plexus . . . poked or pressed by a blunt object."
- *Bizarre Behavior:* Ritualized behavior, including walking in figure eights, turning in different directions, and whistling and yelling incomprehensible words.

He was rated for elevated mood leading to hospitalization (Criterion A) and for five symptoms listed in *DSM–IV* as characteristic of a manic episode (Criteria B):

- *Elevated/Expansive Mood:* Reported feeling "ecstatic" for the 4 days before hospitalization and throughout his 6-week hospitalization.
- *Manic Symptoms:* decreased need for sleep, talkativeness, flight of ideas, inflated self-esteem, and distractibility.

Diagnostic and Clinical Conceptualization

At the time of his hospitalization, Howard's psychotic symptoms led to his being assigned the *DSM–I* (American Psychiatric Association, 1952) diagnosis of Acute Schizophrenic Reaction. (Actually, because the *DSM–II* [American Psychiatric Association, 1968] was in effect at the time, his proper diagnosis should have been Acute Schizophrenic Episode, 295.4.) He was diagnosed, medicated, and treated as a person with schizophrenia.

In the latest edition, *DSM–IV–TR* (American Psychiatric Association, 2000), this episode meets the criteria for bipolar disorder, manic with mood-incongruent psychotic features (296.44). Brief reactive psychosis would be ruled out because the symptoms persisted for more than 1 month. He would also meet the diagnostic criteria for religious or spiritual problem, however, because there were components of his experience that had spiritual dimensions (described later).

Transpersonal Diagnosis

Howard is a good illustration of a patient with a "spiritual emergency." Beginning in the 1960s, interest in Asian spiritual practices such as meditation, yoga, and tai chi, as well as experimentation with psychedelic drugs, triggered many mystical and visionary experiences, some of which were problematic for their practitioners. Christina Grof and Stanislav Grof coined the term *spiritual emergency* and founded the Spiritual Emergency Network at Esalen Institute in 1980 to assist people experiencing psychological difficulties associated with spiritual practices and spontaneous spiritual experiences.

Grof and Grof (1989) described spiritual emergencies as spontaneous nonordinary states that lead to

> crises when the process of growth and change becomes chaotic and overwhelming. Individuals experiencing such episodes may feel that their sense of identity is breaking down, that their old values no longer hold true, and that the very ground beneath their personal realities is radically shifting. In many cases, new realms of mystical and spiritual experience enter their lives suddenly and dramatically, resulting in fear and confusion. They may feel tremendous anxiety, have difficulty coping with their daily lives, jobs, and relationships, and may even fear for their own sanity. (back cover)

Although spiritual emergencies are often seen and treated as psychotic disorders, they should be treated as spiritual problems that are potentially conducive to healing and transformation.

In Howard's Mental Odyssey, there is considerable overlap with mystical experiences. It has often been noted that ecstatic mood is characteristic of both manic and mystical states (Podvoll, 1990). Mystics also share the sense of gnosis or "newly gained knowledge" that preoccupied Howard (James, 1902/1958).

Howard exhibited many positive prognostic features such as good preepisode functioning, acute onset of symptoms, and a positive attitude toward the experience. He did not show conceptual disorganization, which is characteristic of schizophrenia (Buckley, 1981). The phenomenological overlap with mystical experiences and good prognostic features indicate that Howard fits the spiritual emergency type of client (Lukoff & Everest, 1985).

In the 1970s, Jungian analyst John Perry established Diabasis, a residential facility in San Francisco, which serves as a model therapeutic environment for persons in an acute psychotic renewal process. Diabasis created a homelike atmosphere where diagnostic labels were not used and staff members were selected for their ability to be comfortable with intensive inner processes. Perry reported that

> Under such conditions, to our surprise, we found that our clients got into a clear space very quickly!. . . The acute hallucinatory phase . . . usually lasts about six weeks. This, by the way, corresponds to the classical description of visionary experiences in various religious texts. (Perry, 1992, n.p.)

Howard would probably have done well at Diabasis, where he would have been encouraged to explore his "Great Experiment" in a safe environment. He could have spent 6 weeks drawing mandalas, enacting rituals, and creating power objects while on his inner Mental Odyssey instead of 6 weeks in a psychiatric unit where his condition was seen only as psychopathological. Recognizing such episodes as spiritual problems would legitimize transpersonal therapeutic approaches that could circumvent costly hospitalizations and lead to more cost-effective treatments.

Treatment Goals, Process, and Intervention Strategies

During the 2 years of our meetings, I conducted 15 interviews, administered some assessment instruments, asked Howard to write about his symbol system, and obtained some of his hospitalization records and other material from that period. In these sessions, Howard recounted further details, brought in drawings and other artifacts from this experience, and reviewed drafts of the case history. I soon realized that preparing the case study was helping him to integrate his psychotic experience. Howard had informed me at our initial lunch meeting that he had never told anyone the full story of his Mental Odyssey. In one interview, he stated that

> Periodically I tried to share my new-found knowledge with friends and family, but it was not well-received. I could see I was still considered "crazy." I have learned not to talk about these matters with others. When we discuss other subjects, my relationships with those who witnessed my experiences have been fine.

Howard received no acknowledgment from others about the possible value in his experience during his hospitalization nor afterward. The role of the transpersonal psychologist is to help psychotic patients see the "message" contained in their experiences. James Hillman (1992) argued that recovery means recovering the divine from within the disorder, seeing that its contents are authentically religious.

In several of my meetings with Howard, he mentioned that the symbols in his "key" (see Figure 8.1) still held great importance for him. So I asked him to write a commentary regarding its meaning and to redraw his "key." The 18 pages of interpretation that Howard wrote included extensive references to diverse religious and spiritual sources including alchemical and esoteric texts, Native American beliefs, and Jungian concepts, as in this excerpt:

> The parallels to Native American belief in the centrality of the Four Directions and to Jung's squaring of the personality into the four types are apparent. I see the albatross as representing intuition; the owl, sensation; the eagle, thinking; and the dove, feeling. I termed these birds "mythic vehicles" and understood them to be very personal expressions of a universal truth.

The Buddhist psychiatrist Podvoll (1990) observed that in manic psychosis, "religious truths are realized, *the* religious truths, the ones of the desert fathers and the great mystics" (p. 118). Howard's account, written 10 years after his episode, reveals his understanding of its religious themes and imagery.

Howard instinctively drew his symbol key in the form of a mandala, beginning with a prominent center and expanding along a vertical axis. Mandalas are found in many religions and in states of psychological conflict and have been observed frequently in the drawings of psychotic patients (Jung, 1969). Jung suggested that they have a therapeutic effect on their creators by helping them to

> compensate for the disorder and confusion of the psychic state—namely, through the construction of a central point to which everything is related, or by a concentric arrangement of the disordered multiplicity and of contradictory and irreconcilable elements. This is an *attempt at self-healing* on the part of Nature. (p. 4)

Howard's rerendering (see Figure 8.2) is far more orderly and geometric and includes important new elements such as the circle within the square. According to Jung (1969), the "squaring of the circle," an image found in many alchemical diagrams, is "one of the most important [archetypal motifs] from the functional point of view. Indeed, it could even be called the archetype of wholeness" (p. 4). Howard's incorporation of the archetype of wholeness in the rerendering of his key reflects the integration of his psychotic episode.

Therapeutic Outcomes

After 2 months, Howard left the hospital and "immediately returned to the same state of consciousness I had been in before the odyssey." He saw that he needed to regain the ability to concentrate and function. "I was totally exhausted—physically, emotionally and mentally. I stopped taking the Thorazine they had been giving me at the hospital and have never taken any similar medication since."

At the end of our work on the case study, Howard wrote a note reflecting on his Mental Odyssey:

> I have gained much from my experience. From my perspective, the odyssey was a success and I do not regret the experience in any way. However, I would not recommend a trip into controlled madness to anyone. The best that one can hope to achieve is a fleeting glimpse through the mists, no matter how transforming. The risks are too great considering that tried and true paths, leading one safely, step-by-step, to a lasting enlightenment and joy are already available.

Howard contacted me once more, 11 years after the publication of the case study. He had graduated with a bachelor's degree in psychology and wanted to discuss graduate school options with me. He had not taken any medication since leaving the hospital and had not been hospitalized. I later learned that he did enroll and obtained a graduate degree in psychology.

Figure 8.2. Howard's pencil drawing of the same "key" 12 years later. From "The Myths in Mental Illness," by D. Lukoff and C. Everest, 1985, *Journal of Transpersonal Psychology, 17*, p. 137. Copyright 2000 by the Association for Transpersonal Psychology. Reprinted with permission.

BRYAN

Client Demographics, Relevant History, and Presenting Concern

After a series of manic psychotic episodes that required four hospitalizations over a 2-month period, Bryan, a 47-year-old army veteran, was discharged to the Veteran's Administration Day Treatment Center and assigned to my (DL) caseload. I had seen Bryan only once during those previous 2 months. As had been the pattern over the past 16 years of his illness, it was Bryan's friends, rather than police or mental health professionals, who took him to the hospital. At the meeting to arrange his hospitalization, Bryan looked totally disheveled. He paid little attention as ashes fell off his cigarette and burned his clothes. Even when the cigarette burned down to his fingers, he seemed unaware of the pain. Bryan appeared to be in another world; neither I nor anyone else could make contact with him.

A brief history notes that Bryan completed his undergraduate degree and a graduate film studies program before being drafted in 1966. The first symptoms of his condition and his first hospitalization occurred within a year after his discharge from the army in 1968. Both he and the doctors at the VA attribute the onset of illness to his military service. Married and divorced twice, Bryan had a close relationship with his 20-year-old daughter who lived nearby. Because Bryan received a full stipend from the VA for his 100% service-connected disability, he had been able to maintain a three-room apartment where he pursued the lifestyle of an independent artist.

When Bryan was functioning well, he was productive—drawing, painting, and occasionally exhibiting his pieces at bars and cafes. He wrote essays, short stories, poetry, and letters to editors, which had been published in newspapers and magazines. In the past, Bryan had made documentary films, and he continued to volunteer 1 day a week at a local film society.

Assessment and Diagnosis

Psychopathology. Bryan met the *DSM–III* diagnostic criteria for bipolar Disorder, Manic With Mood-Congruent Psychotic Features. He had grandiose delusions of inflated worth, power, and knowledge, along with a delusional preoccupation that space aliens were controlling him. His episode also meets the criteria for a religious or spiritual problem because core issues of transcendent meaning were involved (described later).

Transpersonal Diagnosis. Maslow's (1943) hierarchy of needs model guided my assessment and development of a treatment program to maximize Bryan's functioning and well-being.

> There is a hierarchy of five sets of goals or purposes or needs which are set in the following order of prepotency. First, satisfaction or gratification of body needs. . . . Second, the safety needs. . . . Third, love, affection, warmth, acceptance, a place in the group. Fourth, desire for self-esteem, self-respect, self-confidence, for the feeling of strength or adequacy. . . . Fifth, self-actualization, self-fulfillment, self-expression, working out of one's own fundamental personality, the fulfillment of its potentialities, the use of its capacities, the tendency to be the most that one is capable of being. (Maslow, 1943, pp. 85–92)

Bryan's basic physical and safety needs were all being met, thanks to his VA disability stipend. It was the higher level needs that were not being fulfilled.

At our first individual therapy session, Bryan appeared blunted and depressed. He complained that he didn't feel creative and had no interest in art or writing. He believed he was overmedicated and requested that I ask his psychiatrist to lower the dosage. Given his recent string of hospitalizations, I did not think a medication change was indicated. Yet I took very seriously his complaint of being creatively blocked.

Bryan's identity as an artist was essential to his maintaining an active social existence. Bryan's social network consisted mostly of artists and their families and friends. Some persons with bipolar disorder prefer living in a grandiose delusional reality rather than coping with their difficult life situations. This withdrawal into inner fantasy has been termed the "wish to be crazy" (Van Putten, Crumpton, & Yale, 1976). I was concerned that Bryan's creative block could lead to his losing touch with the circle of artists who gave him the motivation to wish not to be crazy. Bryan also fulfilled his belonging and love needs, the third level on Maslow's hierarchy, through his friends in the artistic community.

Treatment Goals, Process, and Intervention Strategies

The therapy focused on rekindling Bryan's creative energies through writing. Kaplan (1964), who edited a revealing collection of first-person accounts of mental illness, noted that in such descriptions, "the patient takes over the role of the psychiatrist and scientist and reflects on the meaning of what he has been experiencing. The act of writing itself implies such reflectiveness and concern" (p. ix). Because psychosis involves substantial alterations in subjective experience, it offers a rich source for vividly expressive writing. Madness has been a recurring theme in great literature, and written accounts of madness have a rich heritage (Sommer & Osmond, 1960; Vonnegut, 1975).

Despite having produced many essays and short stories, Bryan had not previously written about his experiences with manic psychosis. He seemed intrigued at the prospect of expressing the fantastic nature of his psychotic experiences, particularly because this was the first time in his 18 years of hospitalizations that he had encountered space aliens.

He agreed that writing about his recent psychotic experiences was a creative task he could undertake and accomplish. The next week, he came to his therapy session with a five-page essay titled "Being Controlled." Over the next 10 sessions, he wrote five more essays: "One Manic-Depressive's Sense of Time," "Being a Messenger," "Another Hospital," "Big Questions," and "Some Implications of Dinosaurs Having Souls." Bryan called this "creativity therapy."

Neither the essays nor the events described in them were organized chronologically. There was no story with a beginning, middle, and end, just well-described fantastic experiences and events. As an artist, Bryan was concerned with transforming his fantastic nonordinary experiences into artistic creations that would provide aesthetic experiences for himself and enjoyment for others.

With Bryan's assistance, I edited his essays by placing the events in a time sequence. The resulting story surprised me because neither his hospital intake nor discharge notes mentioned that Bryan had undergone an alien abduction experience (AAE).

> Alien abduction experiences are characterized by subjectively real memories of being taken secretly and/or against one's will by apparently nonhuman entities, usually to a location interpreted as an alien spacecraft (i.e., a UFO). (Appelle, Lynn, & Newman, 2000, p. 254)

Bryan reported experiencing the key elements of alien abduction: capture, examination, communication with aliens, otherworldly journey, theophany (receipt of spiritual messages), return to earth.

Many people who have had such experiences report that their lives have been radically altered on a deep spiritual level by their encounters with aliens. Kenneth Ring (1992), one of the world's chief authorities on near-death experiences (NDEs), conducted research comparing people who reported alien abduction experiences with people who had experienced NDEs. He concluded that they are *alternate pathways* to the same type of psychospiritual transformation that expresses itself in greater awareness of the interconnectedness and sacredness of all life. Although AAEs can be spiritually transformative, they can also present as spiritual problems as patients work on integrating their difficult aspects (Grof & Grof, 1989).

In my personal contact with the mental health professionals who were involved in treating Bryan during his manic psychosis, his experiences with space aliens were seen only as symptoms of his bipolar disorder. They had never been given any attention in his treatment. Yet such experiences can be the focus of therapy.

> The risk of providing therapy can be minimized, and positive outcomes best assured, when the focus of treatment deals with educating clients about possible explanations for the AAE, encouraging them to understand the AAE in terms of its meaning in their life, and otherwise working on coping strategies that transcend the inevitable inconclusiveness about the AAE's objective reality. (Appelle et al., 2000, p. 271)

I did not employ a joining strategy by participating in Bryan's delusional world as some therapists have done with psychotic patients (Lindner, 1954). Nor did I see my role as helping Bryan to "reality test" these beliefs. John Mack (1999), who has also worked extensively with alien abduction experiencers, noted that in therapy, "There is no injunction to establish the literal or material actuality of the reported experiences. . . . I do not consider that abduction reports necessarily reflect a literal, physical taking of the human body" (Mack, 1999, pp. 29, 31). Despite taking a neutral stance toward the physical reality of his AAE, I acknowledged to Bryan both the powerfulness and strangeness of his experiences.

Because Bryan insisted his were not "Jungian experiences," I did not impose discussions of myth or AAEs or spirituality in our sessions, which would have brought out Bryan's resistance. Although Bryan would deny that there was anything transpersonal about his experiences, I was aided in conducting therapy with him by my transpersonal context, namely, viewing the AAE as a type of spiritual problem.

As he began writing and drawing again, his depression diminished, and he began to feel more creative. In a letter Bryan wrote to a friend while in the midst of our therapy, he stated:

> I would say part of the cure for so-called "mental illness" is communication between client and a qualified person. Not so much "craft" or "O.T." [occupational therapy] but finding out what makes that individual tick. I

am doing that mostly by writing in that I feel I might otherwise pay good money to learn that it is all in my head.

Therapeutic Outcome

During our weekly "creativity therapy" sessions, Bryan accomplished both of our therapeutic objectives—engaging in artistic creation and reconnecting with his social network. At the beginning of the therapy, Bryan was still preoccupied with space aliens. By the end of the 3 months of creativity therapy, his preoccupation had dissipated. He resumed pursuing an artist's lifestyle, put on an exhibit of his paintings in a neighborhood bar, and reestablished contact with his artist colleagues.

After Bryan showed a filmmaker friend his essay "One Manic-Depressive's Sense of Time," the friend decided to make a movie based on it and cast Bryan in the starring role. I attended its premiere and champagne reception at an art gallery. For Bryan as an artist, the production of a film based on his writings transformed his psychotic episode into a constructive part of his personal mythology (Feinstein & Krippner, 1988).

Jamison (1996) studied artists with bipolar disorder and found that many have periods of psychosis interspersed with periods of creative and productive functioning. Bipolar disorder in particular seems to have a vital connection to the rhythms of artistic creativity. In fact, even the artists in Jamison's sample who had been treated for mood disorder felt that their mood swings were a positive influence.

Bryan's writing and art explicitly concerned space aliens. As a transpersonal therapist, I viewed these beliefs as part of his delusional system but also considered such experiences as glimpses into mystical, visionary, and creative realms. Through therapy, they were transformed into a constructive part of Bryan's spiritual connection with transcendent realities.

After reviewing my case study, Bryan expressed the concern that others might perceive him as "weird" for having had such unusual experiences. I suggested that he write a final statement about what the episode meant to him. Bryan's reflections that follow indicate a positive integration of his psychotic experiences.

Looking Back

Months have passed since writing the stories of my experience. Now, I don't want to fall back on such terms as "psychotic episode" or "delusional." Those are words others use to objectify a unique, complex experience best told by the person going through it. For that time, a benevolent and enlightened entity was with me—a higher intelligence—neither god nor devil, channel nor a vivid imagination. For lack of a better term, I came to call this manifestation a "space alien," as I seemed directed by the unknown.

I urge that more such experiments take place between doctor and patient in a "give and take" relationship (unlike Freud) and scientific (though unlike Skinner). . . . Bipolar disorder, rather than really being a "disorder," may be evolutionary in nature and could be a key to understanding the mind and beyond.

CONCLUSION

As illustrated in these two case examples, the transpersonal approach to integrating psychotic experiences involves three phases:

Phase 1: Telling One's Story
Phase 2: Tracing its Symbolic/Spiritual Heritage
Phase 3: Creating a New Personal Mythology

Perry (1974) has noted that following a psychotic episode, "What remains . . . is an ideal model and a sense of direction which one can use to complete the transformation through his own purposeful methods" (p. 38). Some clinicians have expressed the concern that having patients discuss their delusional experiences could exacerbate their symptoms by reinforcing them. Yet in a study in which patients with psychotic disorders were encouraged to explore their psychotic symptoms, telling their stories did not result in such exacerbation (Lukoff, Wallace, Liberman, & Burke, 1986). Many ex-patients have pointed out that exploring the spiritual dimensions of their psychotic experiences is important in their recovery (Clay, 1987).

Recently the American Psychological Association published an edited book on anomalous experiences (Cardena, Lynn, & Krippner, 2000) defined as a variety of unusual experiences that appear to challenge our understanding of the world but that have often been ignored or ridiculed by mainstream psychology. The authors noted that many anomalous experiences include religious and spiritual content. In fact, the types of anomalous experiences addressed in the book overlap with the types of spiritual emergencies identified by Grof and Grof (1989). Five types (mystical, psi related [paranormal], alien abduction, near-death, and past life) appear in both typologies. The visionary category also overlaps with the hallucinatory type, and shamanic crisis overlaps with anomalous healing experiences.

Anomalous experiences such as mystical, psi-related, and near-death experiences can have been documented to be distressing for some individuals and lead to contact with mental health professionals. Thus, the transpersonal psychotherapeutic approaches described in this chapter for spiritual emergencies and psychotic episodes could also be applied to many types of anomalous experiences.

REFERENCES

American Psychiatric Association. (1952). *Diagnostic and statistical manual of mental disorders*. Washington, DC: Author.

American Psychiatric Association. (1968). *Diagnostic and statistical manual of mental disorders* (2nd ed.). Washington, DC: Author.

American Psychiatric Association. (2000). *Diagnostic and statistical manual of mental disorders* (4th ed., text rev.). Washington, DC: Author.

Appelle, S., Lynn, S., & Newman, L. (2000). Alien abduction experiences. In E. Cardena, S. Lynn, & S. Krippner (Eds.), *Varieties of anomalous experience: Examining the scientific evidence* (pp. 253–282). Washington, DC: American Psychological Association.

Asante, M. (1984). The feminine principle in Tibetan Vajrayana Buddhism: Reflection of a Buddhist feminist. *Journal of Transpersonal Psychology, 16,* 167–178.

Assagioli, R. (2000). *Psychosynthesis: A collection of basic writings*. New York: Synthesis Center.

Benson, H. (1975). *The relaxation response*. New York: Avon.

Boorstein, S. (Ed.). (1996). *Transpersonal psychotherapy* (2nd ed.). Albany: State University of New York Press.

Boorstein, S. (2000). Transpersonal psychotherapy. *American Journal of Psychotherapy, 54,* 408–424.

Buckley, P. (1981). Mystical experience and schizophrenia. *Schizophrenia Bulletin, 7,* 516–521.

Campbell, J. (1972). *Myths to live by*. New York: Viking Press.

Cardena, E., Lynn, S., & Krippner, S. (Eds.). (2000). *Varieties of anomalous experience: Examining the scientific evidence*. Washington, DC: American Psychological Association.

Chinen, A. (1996). The emergence of transpersonal psychiatry. In B. Scotton, A. Chinen, & J. Battista (Eds.), *Textbook of transpersonal psychiatry and psychology*. New York: Basic Books.

Clay, S. (1987). Stigma and spirituality. *Journal of Contemplative Psychotherapy, 4,* 87–94.

Cortright, B. (1997). *Psychotherapy and spirit: Theory and practice in transpersonal psyhotherapy*. Albany: State University of New York Press.

Daniels, M. (2002). The transpersonal self: Comparing seven psychological theories. *Transpersonal Psychology Review, 6*(2), 4–21.

Dass, R. (1970). Baba Ram Dass lecture at The Menninger Foundation. *Journal of Transpersonal Psychology, 2,* 91–140.

Deatherage, O. (1996). Mindfulness meditation as psychotherapy. In S. Boorstein (Ed.), *Transpersonal psychotherapy* (2nd ed., pp. 209–240). Albany: State University of New York Press.

Deikman, A. (1996). Sufism and psychiatry. In S. Boorstein (Ed.), *Transpersonal psychotherapy* (2nd ed., pp. 241–260). Albany: State University of New York Press.

Edwards, D. (1995). *Guidelines for conducting clinical and phenomenological case studies*. Unpublished manuscript, Rhodes, South Africa.

Epstein, M. (1998). *Going to pieces without falling apart*. New York: Broadway Books.

Fagianelli, P. (1995). *The relationship of aikido training and psychotherapy training in licensed mental health professionals who are advanced practitioners of aikido*. Unpublished manuscript, Saybrook Graduate School, San Francisco.

Feinstein, D., & Krippner, S. (1988). *Personal mythology: The psychology of your evolving self*. Los Angeles: Tarcher.

Garfield, C. (1975). Consciousness alteration and fear of death. *Journal of Transpersonal Psychology, 7,* 147–175.

Goleman, D. (1971). Meditation as meta-therapy: Hypotheses toward a proposed fifth state of consciousness. *Journal of Transpersonal Psychology, 3,* 1–26.

Gray, L. (2002). *Shamanic counseling and ecopsychology*. Retrieved April 20, 2003, from http://woodfish.org/

Grof, C. (1993). *The thirst for wholeness: Addiction, attachment, and the spiritual path*. New York: HarperCollins.

Grof, S. (1993). *The holotropic mind: The three levels of human consciousness and how they shape our lives*. San Francisco: HarperCollins.

Grof, S., & Grof, C. (Eds.). (1989). *Spiritual emergency: When personal transformation becomes a crisis*. Los Angeles: Tarcher.

Harner, M. (1990). *The way of the shaman*. San Francisco: HarperCollins.

Heckler, R. (1985). Aikido and children. In R. Heckler (Ed.), *Aikido and the new warrior*. Berkeley, CA: North Atlantic Books.

Hillman, J. (1992). *Revisioning psychology*. New York: HarperCollins.

Hutton, M. (1994). How transpersonal psychotherapists differ from other practitioners: An empirical study. *Journal of Transpersonal Psychology, 26,* 139–174.

Huxley, A. (1944/1990). *The perennial philosophy*. New York: HarperCollins.

James, W. (1958). *The varieties of religious experience*. New York: New American Library of World Literature. (Original work published 1902)

Jamison, K. (1996). *Touched with fire: Manic depressive illness and the artistic temperament*. New York: Touchstone.

Jamison, K., Gerner, R., Hammen, C., & Padesky, C. (1980). Clouds and silver linings: positive experiences associated with primary affective disorders. *American Journal of Psychiatry, 137,* 198–202.

Jung, C. G. (1969). *Mandala symbolism*. Princeton, NJ: Princeton University Press.

Kabit-Zinn, J. (1990). *Full catastrophe living: Using the wisdom of your body and mind to face stress, pain, and illness*. New York: Delta.

Kaplan, B. (Ed.). (1964). *The inner world of mental illness*. New York: HarperCollins.

Koenig, H., McCullough, M., & Larson, D. (2001). *Handbook of religion and health*. New York: Oxford University Press.

Kornfield, J. (1993). *A path with heart: A guide through the perils and promises of spiritual life*. New York: Bantam Doubleday.

Krippner, S. (1990). Beyond the blind and dumb. *Transpersonal Psychology Interest Group Newsletter, 3*, 3.

Laing, R. D. (1972). Metanoia: Some experiences at Kingsley Hall. In H. M. Ruitenbeck (Ed.), *Going crazy*. New York: Bantam.

Leslie, R. (1976). Yoga and the fear of death. *Journal of Transpersonal Psychology, 8*, 128–132.

Lieff, J. (1982). Eight reasons why doctors fear the elderly, chronic illness and death. *Journal of Transpersonal Psychology, 14*, 47–60.

Lindner, R. (1954). The jet-propelled couch. In R. Lindner (Ed.), *The fifty minute-hour*. New York: Holt, Rinehart & Winston.

Lines, D. (2002). Counseling within a new spiritual paradigm. *Journal of Humanistic Psychology, 42*, 102–123.

Lukoff, D. (1985). The diagnosis of mystical experiences with psychotic features. *Journal of Transpersonal Psychology, 17*, 155–181.

Lukoff, D. (1996). Transpersonal psychotherapy with psychotic disorders and spiritual emergencies with psychotic features. In B. Scotton, A. Chinen, & J. Battista (Eds.), *Textbook of transpersonal psychiatry and psychology*. New York: Basic Books.

Lukoff, D. (2003). The importance of spirituality in mental health. In B. Horrigan (Ed.), *Voices of integrative medicine* (pp. 174–184). St. Louis, MO: Elsevier Science.

Lukoff, D., & Everest, H. C. (1985). The myths in mental illness. *Journal of Transpersonal Psychology, 17*, 123–153.

Lukoff, D., Lu, F., & Turner, R. (1992). Toward a more culturally sensitive *DSM–IV*: Psychoreligious and psychospiritual problems. *Journal of Nervous and Mental Disease, 180*(11), 673–682.

Lukoff, D., Lu, F., & Turner, R. (1998). From spiritual emergency to spiritual problem: The transpersonal roots of the new *DSM–IV* Category. *Journal of Humanistic Psychology, 38*, 21–50.

Lukoff, D., Wallace, C. J., Liberman, R. P., & Burke, K. (1986). A holistic health program for chronic schizophrenic patients. *Schizophrenia Bulletin, 12*, 274–282.

Luskin, F. (2001). *Forgive for good: A proven prescription for health and happiness*. San Francisco: Harper.

Mack, J. (1999). *Passport to the cosmos: Human transformation and alien encounters*. New York: Crown.

Maslow, A. (1943). Preface to motivation theory. *Psychosomatic Medicine, 5*, 85–92.

Mayer, M. (1999). Qigong and hypertension: A critique of research. *Journal of Alternative and Complementary Medicine, 5*(4), 371–382.

Miller, W. (1990). Spirituality: The silent dimension in addiction research. *Drug and Alcohol Review, 9*, 259–266.

Perry, J. (1974). *The far side of madness*. Englewood Cliffs, NJ: Prentice Hall.

Perry, J. (1992). *Mental breakdown as a healing process*. Retrieved April 24, 2003, from http://www.global-vision.org/interview/perry.html

Peteet, J. (1993). A closer look at the role of a spiritual approach in addictions treatment. *Journal of Substance Abuse Treatment, 10,* 263–267.

Podvoll, E. (1990). *The seduction of madness: Revolutionary insights into the world of psychosis and a compassionate approach to recovery at home.* New York: HarperCollins.

Richards, W., Grof, S., Goodman, L., & Kurland, A. (1972). LSD-assisted psychotherapy and the human encounter with death. *Journal of Transpersonal Psychology, 4,* 121–150.

Ring, K. (1992). *The Omega Project: Near-death, UFO encounters, and mind at large.* New York: Morris.

Rothberg, D. (1990). Epistemology and the study of mysticism. In R. Forman (Ed.), *The problems of pure consciousness: Mysticism and philosophy* (pp. 163–210). New York: Oxford University Press.

Saposnek, D. (1980). Aikido: A model for brief strategic therapy. In R. Heckler (Ed.), *Aikido and the new warrior* (pp. 178–197). Berkeley, CA: North Atlantic Books.

Scotton, B. (1985). Observations on the teaching and supervision of transpersonal psychotherapy. *Journal of Transpersonal Psychology, 17*(1), 57–76.

Scotton, B. (1996). Introduction and definition of transpersonal psychiatry. In B. Scotton, A. Chinen, & J. Battista (Eds.), *Textbook of transpersonal psychiatry and psychology* (pp. 3–8). New York: Basic Books.

Scotton, B., & Hiatt, J. (1996). The contribution of Hinduism and yoga to transpersonal psychiatry. In B. Scotton, A. Chinen, & J. Battista (Eds.), *Textbook of transpersonal psychiatry and psychology* (pp. 104–113). New York: Basic Books.

Seligman, M. (2001). *Spirituality and depression: A century-long research review.* Retrieved April 24, 2003, from http://www.nihr.org/programs/researchreports/centurylongresearch.cfm

Sethi, S., & Seligman, M. (1993). Optimism and fundamentalism. *Psychological Science, 4,* 256–259.

Sogyal Rinpoche. (1994). *The Tibetan book of living and dying.* San Francisco: HarperCollins.

Sommer, R., & Osmond, H. (1960). Autobiographies of former mental patients. *Journal of Mental Science, 106,* 648–662.

Sperry, L. (2001). *Spirituality in clinical practice.* Philadelphia: Brunner-Routledge.

Sutich, A. (1969). Some considerations regarding transpersonal psychology. *Journal of Transpersonal Psychology, 1,* 11–20.

Sutich, A. (1973). Transpersonal therapy. *Journal of Transpersonal Psychology, 5,* 1–14.

Tart, C. (1992). *Transpersonal psychologies: Perspectives on the mind from seven great spiritual traditions.* New York: HarperCollins.

Taylor, E. (1983). *William James on exceptional mental states: The 1896 Lowell Lectures.* New York: Scribner.

Taylor, E. (1990). *Shadow culture: Psychology and spirituality in America*. Washington, DC: Counterpoint.

Taylor, K. (1995). *The ethics of caring: Honoring the web of life in our professional healing relationships*. Santa Cruz, CA: Hanford Mead.

Taylor, K. (Ed.). (2003). *Exploring holotropic breathwork: Selected articles from a decade of the inner door*. Santa Cruz, CA: Hanford Mead.

Valle, R. (1989). The emergence of transpersonal psychology. In R. Valle & S. Halling (Eds.), *Existential–phenomenological perspectives in psychology* (pp. 257–268). New York: Plenum Press.

Van Nuys, D. (1971). A novel technique for studying attention during meditation. *Journal of Transpersonal Psychology, 3*, 125–134.

Van Putten, T., Crumpton, E., & Yale, C. (1976). Drug refusal in schizophrenia and the wish to be crazy. *Archives of General Psychiatry, 33*, 1443–1446.

Vaughan, F. (1979). Transpersonal psychotherapy: Context, content and process. *Journal of Transpersonal Psychology, 1*, 101–110.

Vaughan, F. (1991). Spiritual issues in psychotherapy. *Journal of Transpersonal Psychology, 23*, 105–120.

Vaughan, F. (1993). Healing and wholeness: Transpersonal psychotherapy. In R. Walsh & F. Vaughan (Eds.), *Paths beyond ego: The transpersonal vision* (pp. 160–164). Los Angeles: Tarcher.

Vonnegut, M. (1975). *The Eden express*. New York: Bantam.

Waldman, M. (1990). Reflections on death and reconciliation. *Journal of Transpersonal Psychology, 21*, 167–174.

Walsh, R. (1999). *Essential spirituality: The 7 central practices to awaken heart and mind*. Hoboken, NJ: Wiley.

Walsh, R., & Vaughan, F. (1996). Comparative models of the person and psychotherapy. In S. Boorstein (Ed.), *Transpersonal psychotherapy* (2nd ed., pp. 15–30). Albany: State University of New York Press.

Wasson, R. G., Hofmann, A., & Ruck, C. (1978). *The road to Eleusis: Unveiling the secret of the mysteries*. New York: Harcourt Brace Jovanovich.

Watts, A. (1957). *The way of Zen*. New York: Penguin.

Watts, A. (1974). Psychotherapy and eastern religion: Metaphysical bases of psychiatry. *Journal of Transpersonal Psychology, 6*, 18–31.

Welwood, J. (2000). *Toward a psychology of awakening: Buddhism, psychotherapy, and the path of personal and spiritual transformation*. Berkeley, CA: Shambhala.

Wilber, K. (1980). *The spectrum of consciousness*. Wheaton, IL: Quest.

Wilber, K. (2000). *Integral psychology: Consciousness, spirit, psychology, therapy*. Boston: Shambhala.

Wing, J., Cooper, J., & Sartorius, N. (1974). *Description and classification of psychiatric symptoms*. Cambridge, England: Cambridge University Press.

Wittine, B. (1989). Basic postulates for a transpersonal psychotherapy. In R. Valle & S. Halling (Eds.), *Existential–phenomenological perspectives in psychology*. New York: Plenum Press.

9

THE EXPERIENTIAL
FOCUSING APPROACH

ELFIE HINTERKOPF

DESCRIPTION OF THE APPROACH

Historical and Theoretical Basis

Eugene Gendlin (1996), a philosopher and psychologist at the University of Chicago, developed the experiential focusing approach. He began his research with Carl Rogers in the 1950s by studying the differences between successful and unsuccessful psychotherapy (Rogers, Gendlin, Kiesler, & Truax, 1967). Coming from the philosophical tradition of Dilthey, Dewey, Merleau-Ponty, and McKeon, Gendlin developed a philosophy of the implicit and applied it to the work of Rogers. Out of this interaction came a further theory of personality change (Gendlin, 1964). He originated the focusing method (1969, 1981) to teach clients to become more successful and then developed the experiential focusing approach or focusing-oriented psychotherapy (1996) as an articulated theoretical orientation to further psychotherapeutic change. Experiential focusing is also a process that can enhance the effectiveness of any theoretical orientation (Gendlin, 1996).

The experiential focusing approach is broader than the use of the focusing method in three respects. The first is that it is an elaboration and extension of the client- or person-centered approach. The second is that it may be used to make any other psychotherapeutic or spiritual approach more powerful. The third is that the experiential focusing process helps a therapist sense the complexity of a therapeutic situation. It can help the therapist choose from a number of orientations, interventions, and innovations. It can guide the therapist in a therapeutic relationship, for example, to state tentatively the possibility of transference and to express congruence, empathy, and positive regard (Gendlin, 1996).

Hinterkopf (1994, 1998) expanded the experiential focusing approach to apply it to spirituality in psychotherapy. The approach may be used to help clients work through religious and spiritual problems, deepen existing spiritual experiences, and bring about new, life-giving connections to spirituality. In this model, the spiritual experience is grounded in the living, self-sentient body, rather than split off from a merely physiological, reductive body.

The philosophy that underlies experiential focusing psychotherapy uses a special kind of concept that puts interaction first. Human beings have bodies that live in situations. They are not isolated in physical space and are different from mathematical units. This philosophy provides a new epistemology for the social and behavioral sciences.

Gendlin and his associates found that success in psychotherapy depended largely on what *clients* were doing and how they verbalized their problems. Whether a client would prove to be successful in therapy could be predicted well above chance on the basis of audiotapes of the first few therapy sessions as measured on the Experiencing Scale (Gendlin, Beebe, Cassens, Klein, & Oberlander, 1968; Gendlin & Tomlinson, 1967; Klein, Mathieu, Gendlin, & Kiesler, 1970). The Experiencing Scale measures the degree to which clients are attending to their experiencing as indicated by their verbal behavior.

Experiencing (EXP; Gendlin, 1962, 1981, 1984) refers to a client's immediately sensed but implicit experience in a situation. Implicit experience is typically sensed as a subtle, bodily feeling that involves vague meanings in a situation. The client feels "something" but does not yet know what it is.

The EXP Scale measures verbal behavior from low to high on a 7-point scale. The scale, which has high interrater reliability, is used by trained raters to rate tape-recorded segments of counseling interviews (Mathieu-Coughlin & Klein, 1984). At a low EXP level, the client narrates events with no reference to present experiencing. At middle EXP levels, the client can identify some emotions and may think about some personal connections to events but does not attend directly to his or her implicit sense of a situation. At high EXP levels, the client refers to his or her experiencing, or a subtle, body sense of a situation.

Gendlin and his associates (Gendlin & Tomlinson, 1967; Klein et al., 1970) found that clients who were at lower levels of experiencing, as measured by the EXP Scale, tended to have unsuccessful outcomes in psychotherapy, whereas those who were above a certain level tended to be successful. This was established in a series of studies for both neurotic patients (Tomlinson & Hart, 1962; Walker, Rablen, & Rogers, 1960) and psychiatric inpatients (Gendlin, 1966; Rogers et al., 1967). Hinterkopf and Brunswick (1981) found similar results with psychiatric inpatients. More recent studies, summarized in Klein, Mathieu-Coughlan, and Kiesler (1986), have also found a correlation between EXP level and outcome.

An important additional finding was that almost all unsuccessful clients, those at low EXP levels, did not increase their EXP level over the course of therapy. This means that they did not learn how to pay attention to subtle, inner, bodily feelings and so were unable to make good use of therapy. To overcome this problem Gendlin developed a method to teach unsuccessful clients to attend inside in this special way and thus become more successful in therapy. He called this method *focusing* (Gendlin, 1969, 1981). Research (Durak, Bernstein, & Gendlin, 1997) has found that training clients in focusing raises the experiencing level in therapy and contributes to therapeutic success.

Thus, the historical and theoretical basis of the experiential focusing approach has deep roots in research. Strong repeated research findings apply to both psychotherapeutic and spiritual growth. Hendricks (2001) summarized and cited the following important research outcomes.

- Twenty-seven studies have shown that higher experiencing correlates with more successful outcomes in therapy. Twenty-three studies show that focusing, measured by instruments other that the EXP Scale, correlates with successful outcome.
- Twelve studies show that focusing or EXP level can be increased through training.
- Several studies have shown that therapist responses deepen or flatten client experiencing. Therapists who focus effectively help their clients do so as well.

The research overwhelmingly supports that training in focusing for both clients and therapists increases success in psychotherapy. This finding holds across cultures, therapeutic orientations, and populations (Hendricks, 2001). Therefore, training in focusing for both therapists and clients is needed.

When using a process approach to psychotherapy, psychotherapeutic growth and spiritual growth are synonymous (Hinterkopf, 1998). Thus, training in focusing is desirable to facilitate spiritual growth. (These ideas and conclusions regarding spirituality are presented in a subsequent section of this chapter.)

Main Theoretical Constructs

A clear definition of *spirituality* can enable psychotherapists to respond more sensitively to their clients. Even though much thought has been given to the topic of spirituality, confusion still exists as to how it should be defined for purposes of psychotherapy. Two misperceptions need to be resolved to arrive at a clear definition of spirituality: the difference between *spirituality* and *religiousness* and the question of *theism* and *nontheism*. These issues can be resolved through Gendlin's (1961, 1964) theory of experiencing.

The first issue relates to the difference between spirituality and religiousness. In this chapter the term *religiousness* is used to mean adherence to the beliefs and practices of an organized church or religious institution (Shafranske & Malony, 1990). *Spirituality* is used to refer to a unique, personally meaningful experience (Shafranske & Gorsuch, 1984). Although spirituality may include various forms of religiousness, it does not necessarily involve religiousness. A clear definition of spirituality helps therapists respond to their clients' spiritual issues whether or not these are associated with a religion.

The second issue relates to theism and nontheism. Most talk about spirituality in Western tradition makes reference to something greater than ourselves, such as God, a higher power, or the divine. On the other hand, people who have divorced themselves from religious organizations sometimes borrow from Eastern traditions and talk about spirituality in terms of "extraordinary" events, such as visions, near-death, past life, and out-of-body experiences. At times they omit mention of God or the divine. Because many people are spiritual but not theistic, a comprehensive definition of spirituality for use in psychotherapy separates spirituality from religious reference to God or the divine. At the same time, a comprehensive definition of spirituality includes the rich expression of religious reference to God or the divine frequently associated with spirituality.

In dealing with spiritual issues, the therapist needs to respond sensitively so that a growth-producing process can occur for the client. If the therapist has a definition of spirituality that excludes some type of content— for example, spirituality is only that which is connected to an organized religion or theism or extraordinary events—then the therapist might respond insensitively to content that does not fit that definition.

The purpose of this section is to present a definition of spirituality that is not restricted by the nature of spiritual content but includes the spirituality of all clients by concentrating on spiritual process. A case example of using the experiential focusing method to facilitate spiritual process is presented, and implications of a process definition of spirituality for the practice of psychotherapy are discussed.

Need for a Process Definition of Spirituality

Gendlin's theory of experiencing (1961, 1964) brings considerable clarity to the confusion found in defining spirituality. Gendlin has made an important distinction between *process* and *content* in psychotherapy. He has described the experiencing *process* as paying attention to vague, implicit, bodily feelings in a special way so that they unfold and bring new explicit meanings that result in physiological relief or release. He has said that *content* involves symbolizations, or what the process is about. Applying this distinction to spirituality, content might involve words such as *God, Christ, Mother Earth, Allah,* and *higher power* and *past-life, near-death,* and *ESP.*

The distinction between process and content is crucial in the practice of psychotherapy in general and for integrating spirituality in psychotherapy in particular. The psychotherapist needs to be able to follow process in therapy to determine whether a response or an intervention has been helpful to a client, that is, has an intervention made a felt difference in a client or merely a mental difference? Content words, such as *God,* have different connotations or meanings for each individual. If a therapist concentrates on spiritual content to the exclusion of process, especially when encountering unfamiliar spiritual content, the therapist may risk becoming judgmental.

My goal in defining spirituality was to propose a definition that would be useful in psychotherapy and would include the spiritual experiences of all clients in therapy (Hinterkopf, 1994, 1995b[1], 1998). This definition would point to the client's experience of spirituality, which would be beneficial to his or her growth.

Therefore, I propose the following definition of spirituality or the spiritual experience: *a subtle, bodily feeling with vague meanings that brings new, clearer meanings involving a transcendent growth process.*

First, the spiritual experience involves a subtle, bodily feeling with vague meanings. The client has a vague, subtle feeling that can be attended to in the body at the present time. Spirituality involves subtle feelings, a bodily sense, and not simply a cognitive belief system. The feelings are not just single emotions such as anger, happiness, or fear. They can be located in the body, for example, in the throat, chest, or stomach. They are more complex, emotional qualities. For example, a client may have a vaguely "good" feeling that involves a large sense of peace and calm in the chest or a vaguely "uncomfortable" feeling that includes a sense of emptiness in the torso area. The feelings are subtle, elusive, hard to describe, and often more than can be put into words. The vague, complex feelings carry implicitly felt meanings or meanings that are only vaguely felt. The exact meaning is not yet known.

Second, this subtle, bodily feeling with vague meanings brings new, clearer meanings. *Bring* implies that people frequently perceive that they do not cause these new, explicit meanings to occur. At first the client senses an unclear feeling that carries only implicit meanings. As the client continues to pay attention to the unclear, subtle feeling in a gentle, caring way, new meanings unfold and become more clear. For example, as a client pays attention to a vague feeling of peace and calm, he or she may receive a new, explicit meaning or understanding of "accepting another person's differences."

---

[1]Available from Focusing Zentumkarlruhe, Schillerstr. 89, 76352 Weingarten, Germany.

Third, a spiritual experience involves a transcendent growth process. *Transcend* means to move beyond one's former frame of reference in a direction of higher or broader scope, a more inclusive perspective. Such transcendence is essential to human growth. A transcendent growth process, found in all human beings, involves moving beyond one's own unhealthy egocentricity, duality, and exclusivity towards more healthy egocentricity, inclusivity, unity, and a capacity to love (Chandler, Holden, & Kolander, 1992). The movement from unhealthy to healthy egocentricity might involve the ability to become more assertive or the increased ability to stand one's ground.

Gendlin (1996) described this growth process in the following way:

> when a person's central core or inward self expands. . . it strengthens and develops, the "I" becomes stronger. The person—I mean that which looks out from behind the eyes—comes more into its own. . . . One develops when the desire to live and do things stirs deep down, when one's own hopes and desires stir, when one's own perceptions and evaluations carry a new sureness, when the capacity to stand one's ground increases, and when one can consider others and their needs. . . . One comes to feel one's separate existence solidly enough to want to be close to others as they really are. It is development when one is drawn to something that is directly interesting, and when one wants to play. It is development when something stirs inside that has long been immobile and silent, cramped and almost dumb, and when life's energy flows in a new way. (pp. 21–22)

Spiritual growth involves bodily felt release, more life energy, feeling more fully present and whole, a sense of feeling larger and being able to accept or reach out to more parts of oneself, to more people, and to more of life (Campbell & McMahon, 1985). For example, a client feeling peace and calm who receives a new understanding of "accepting another person's differences" may have the growth experience of accepting others more as they are, thus reaching out to more people. After a spiritual experience, growth usually occurs in many areas of the client's life.

When I taught focusing in Japan, the importance of a process definition of spirituality for cross-cultural psychotherapy was confirmed by participants in my workshops. In the West, people often think of spirituality as involving more self-transcendence and love for others (content terms). The Japanese are raised with the assumption of oneness and unity with other people and their environment. Their language reflects this assumption. Personal pronouns, such as *I* and *you*, are frequently omitted from sentences. For the Japanese, the process of spiritual growth tends to involve developing more healthy egocentricity, more of a sense of individuality and separation. When Westerners speak of spirituality in terms of unity and self-transcendence (content terms), Japanese people may have the reaction that they don't need spirituality. When I spoke about spirituality in process terms (implicit feelings unfolding into more explicit meanings that bring more easing and life energy), they could see the relevance of spirituality in their own lives.

This definition of spirituality includes what are often referred to as *transpersonal experiences*, events that involve an expansion or extension of consciousness beyond the usual ego boundary and beyond the limitations of time or space (Grof, 1976). Spiritual process may include transpersonal experiences, such as intuitive, psychic, and mystical experiences. When referring to spiritual content, I assume that transpersonal content is included.

The growth involved in spiritual experiences is often essential for personal development. For various reasons, however, the client's experiencing may be "stuck," "structure-bound," or incomplete. When this is the case, the question for therapists is what can be done to help develop and facilitate the spiritual experience. At this point, the experiential focusing method may be applied.

This example demonstrates how I used focusing to help a client experience her spirituality in a way that involved more separation from her father, as well as a sense of becoming more whole. I share highlights of the session that illustrate the client's spiritual experience along with a few of my therapeutic responses. The actual time taken for this part of the session was about 20 minutes.

Mary, a seminary student, said that she wanted to work on the difficulty she had in finding a time to pray. She mentioned that "something seemed to be in the way" of her "taking time just to be with God." It didn't make sense because she now had more free time in her schedule than in previous semesters.

I invited her to take time to pay attention inside to that "something" that seemed to be in the way. I said that she could describe the feeling to me when she had the words. (Words such as *something, sort of,* and *kind of like* frequently indicate unclear feelings with vague meanings. At such times, it is helpful for the therapist to invite the client to take the time to sense into these vague feelings.)

After about 45 seconds, she said that she had "a vague nauseated feeling that felt like gagging along with fear and anxiety in her chest and stomach." She said that she was astonished to have such negative feelings about something that she really wanted to do. I suggested that she stay with the whole feeling in a gentle, caring way and notice what it had to tell her.

After almost a minute, she cried and said that it felt like being alone with her father who had sexually abused her. She realized that she had confused time alone with God with time alone with her father. She reported a feeling of release that corresponded with her realization. In the next session, Mary reported that she had been able to have a daily prayer time.

This example involves a spiritual process, not because it involved God (spiritual content), but because it involved a vague bodily feeling with unclear meanings that, when gently attended to, brought new explicit meanings along with felt release. In Mary's case, the transcendent growth process involved accepting more parts of herself as separate from her father, along with a sense of feeling more whole in her relationship with God.

A transcendent growth process may, but does not necessarily, involve a deity or higher power. Other clients, not referring to a deity or higher power, may report that their spirituality is found in service to others, the environmental movement, or more assertiveness. A transcendent growth process may involve associated qualities, such as faith, love, interconnectedness, living in the flow (the Tao), allowing (rather than trying to control), and nonattachment. A spiritual experience may also involve existential questions, such as questions of meaning and purpose, because such questions frequently lead a person's attention in a direction of higher or broader scope.

The use of such a broad process definition of spirituality can help clients integrate seemingly conflicting parts regarding spiritual issues within them. This definition can help the person rise to a broader view so that he or she can embrace aspects of both parts. For example, one client, who had conflicting parts that she had introjected from her Christian mother and agnostic father, was able to integrate the life-giving parts from both parents. In addition, she was able to reject aspects of both parts that were not life affirming. The result was a reduction of inner conflict and an increased sense of peace within herself.

Although the spiritual experience is usually a dramatic or life-changing moment, it is almost always part of a larger growth process. Before the dramatic moment, there are often many small steps or movements. For example, the client may make a new distinction or connection or give his or her perceptions more recognition than before. Such small steps may be seen as part of the spiritual growth process and need to be affirmed by the psychotherapist.

In psychotherapy, the therapist needs to let the client decide whether a particular experience is spiritual. If a client asks a therapist whether an experience is spiritual, however, I believe it is important that the psychotherapist give at least a brief definition of spirituality to explain his or her response. For example, if a client asks me whether I think his or her experience was spiritual, I might answer, "Yes, if I define spirituality as a special kind of experience in which one reaches out to more parts of oneself, others, and life."

My definition of the spiritual experience assumes that psychological growth and spiritual growth are synonymous (Helminiak, 1987). It must be remembered that this is a process definition, not a content definition. Although the *content* of a spiritual experience, such as God, Christ, or higher power, may be extremely inspiring because it carries such rich, implicit meanings for a particular person, my definition is concerned with the psychospiritual change *process*. To describe the psychospiritual change process in which many growth events occur, the term *psychospiritual experiencing* may be used.

For some purposes, it is useful to make a distinction between spiritual and psychological content. For psychotherapy, however, what is essential is that the same growth process is involved with both. Thus, the therapist treats content of the psychological and spiritual dimensions in much the same manner. Distinctions are not made between the two. The emphasis is placed on the client's process and whether the contents bring relief or more life energy to the client. This means that a psychotherapist who is familiar with psychological issues need not turn away from the client when spiritual issues arise. Rather, the therapist can continue to use the same methods, including focusing, to facilitate psychospiritual growth. Of course, a referral may need to be made when issues arise that are beyond the therapist's expertise.

Any definition of spirituality that depends solely on content will be judgmental because it will exclude some people. Judging whether a client's experience is spiritual, based on content or on the client's words, has the disadvantage that words, such as God, Allah, or Christ, have different meanings or connotations for each person. Instead, this decision can be based on the client's experiencing process. For example, does the client feel more easing and life energy? Is the client able to accept or reach out to more parts of him- or herself, to others, and to more of life?

Gendlin's theory of experiencing can be used to develop a definition of spirituality useful for the practice of psychotherapy. The use of such a process definition has many advantages; most important is that it can include the diverse spiritual experiences of all clients in psychotherapy.

The Felt Sense

The felt sense, the key concept in focusing, is the vague, bodily, holistic sense of a situation. Focusing refers to a quiet, gentle, and powerful way of spending time with a felt sense to allow psychospiritual growth to take place (Hinterkopf, 1983, 1995a, 1998).

The felt sense contains all of the client's inner knowing about a given situation and that which the client does not yet know about him- or herself. A felt sense can lead to the next growth step. It can even sense an answer that has not yet been experienced (Gendlin, 1986). The felt sense is a sense of something before mind, body, and spirit are split apart.

Keeping an open attitude toward that which has not yet been experienced in a felt sense is frequently referred to as being "open to the mystery of life." The felt sense helps a client get in touch with inner wisdom and hear the "still, small voice" within. It helps a client experience the spiritual dimension.

Gendlin used the term *felt* because he meant to describe something actually felt in a person's body. He used *sense* because at first it is just a sense of something unclear and vague, not yet thought out, that has implicit meanings. An example of a felt sense is the vague feeling a person gets when leaving the house and feels that he or she has forgotten something but doesn't know what. Another example of a felt sense is when people meet someone who seems nice on the surface, but for some unknown reason leaves them with a vague, uncomfortable feeling. (In this chapter, the word *feeling* is also used to refer to the felt sense.)

It is important to attend to the vague, implicit felt sense, giving it an attitude of wondering curiosity. Often, staying with the felt sense until one has several words to describe it helps bring new meanings. Whereas successful clients stay with and pay attention to this vague feeling about a problem, unsuccessful clients only repeat that which they already know about an issue.

In the process of focusing, the felt sense unfolds. As a client attends to the felt sense, at least two parts become more clear: (a) body sensations, images, and movements; and (b) emotional qualities. Examples of body sensations are a heaviness in the chest or a pressure in the stomach. An example of a body image is getting a picture of a balloon that corresponds with the pressure in a person's stomach. An example of a body movement is jumping up and down because a person is so excited. Although body sensations are essential in focusing, body images and movements may or may not be present. A felt sense might also involve a sound or a smell.

Examples of emotional qualities are a heavy sadness, a feeling of emptiness, or a ball of anxiety. Emotional qualities are larger than single emotions because they have implicit meanings in them. There are only a limited number of emotions but an infinite number of emotional qualities. While emotions give limited information, emotional qualities can give a vast amount of complex and subtle information about a situation.

After a client has found just the right words to describe the felt sense, the therapist may suggest that he or she ask open-ended "what" questions of the felt sense, such as, "What is it about this whole situation that leaves me feeling this way?" "What is the worst (or best) about this whole situation for me?" and "What does this whole thing need right now?" In the case example that concludes this chapter, the therapist invites the client to wait and *let* new meanings come from the felt sense.

For example, Joe may have a vague sense of uneasiness around his boss. The therapist may invite Joe to stay with the whole vague sense of uneasiness and gently ask the feeling, "What is it about this whole thing that leaves me feeling this way?" After several moments of silence while the client is attending to the feeling, the meaning may emerge: "He reminds me of my father." In this example, the new meaning is a clarification of a situation. At other times, the new meaning can be a solution to a problem or a correction of a mistaken belief.

Words that bring new meanings are different from words that are already known. These words usually come more slowly and involve only a few words at a time. Often these words have an element of surprise. They match the body sense and bring a physical feeling of relief or release with them. Examples of this kind of relief or release are when people remember something forgotten or realize why a seemingly nice person left them with an uncomfortable feeling. It may be painful to realize why an uncomfortable feeling about a person was present, but there is a relief or release in realizing the truth. Gendlin calls this relief or release experience a "felt shift."

When people intellectualize or rationalize, they do not experience a felt shift. When a felt shift occurs, people know that new meanings have come from the felt sense. A release in the uncomfortable feeling indicates that the words authentically express that which is true inside. This means that noticing whether a felt shift has occurred is essential for authentic self-exploration and change in psychotherapy.

A felt shift may be subtle or dramatic. In its subtle form, it might be realizing a new distinction or making a new connection. At times the felt sense can shift without the meaning having been totally clear. In its more dramatic form, the felt shift has also been known as the moment of insight or the "aha!" experience. When a felt shift involves the transcendent dimension, psychospiritual growth takes place. Whether subtle or dramatic, the felt shift needs to be valued. It is important to take time to be with it in order to integrate it.

The following example illustrates how I helped a client identify different parts of a felt sense and suggested an open-ended, "what" question, so that the felt sense could unfold into a felt shift. In this example, the client has a spiritual experience as a result of focusing on a felt sense.

Ms. D.'s daughter had lied to her a number of times in the recent past. Ms. D. said that she had been struggling with this issue for 3 days, and it had left her feeling miserable. She said it left her feeling hopeless, depressed, extremely tense, and, at times, nauseated. (Hopeless and depressed were her emotions.)

To help her access her larger feeling or felt sense, I asked her, "How does this *whole* thing feel in your body?" (Use of the word *whole* in the question and asking Ms. D. to describe exactly how the whole issue felt in her body helped her become aware of her felt sense.) After a long pause, she replied, "It feels tense all over, like something is clamping down on my stomach." (*Tense* was both a body sensation and an emotion. *Like something is clamping down on my stomach* is a body sensation with vague meanings in it.) I reflected her words by saying, "So it feels tense all over, like something is clamping down on your stomach." Then I suggested, "Perhaps you could stay with that feeling and notice whether any other words come to describe the feeling." (I frequently give this suggestion to help a client stay with a felt sense a little longer.) After several moments she said, "It's strange, but it's like steps, mixed up steps, all over my body." I reflected these words by saying, "So it's like steps, mixed-up steps, all over your body."

After about 15 seconds of silence, I suggested, "Perhaps you could ask the feeling, 'What does this whole thing need?' " She waited several moments, paying attention to the feeling. Then taking a deep breath, she said, "It needs giving the whole thing to God. I can now see the face of God, and I'm giving it to God." (This was a new, more explicit meaning.) I asked her how it felt in her body now, and she said that it felt a lot more relaxed and lighter. (This was a felt shift.) At this point, I invited Ms. D. to take time to be with her new feeling. She then said, "It really helped me to have something concrete in my body to give to God. Before it was just swimming around in my head, all mixed up, and I couldn't give it to God, even though I wanted to."

In this example the client's spiritual experience involved vague, subtle, bodily feelings, at first "tense all over, like something clamping down on my stomach" and then, "like mixed-up steps all over my body." As the client paid attention to these feelings, they brought a new meaning: "It needs giving it to God." This new meaning was accompanied by an image, "I can now see the face of God." The transcendent growth process involved a physical release, a deep breath and a more relaxed, lighter feeling in her body. Ms. D. transcended her former frame of reference because she no longer had to solve the problem alone but could give it to God.

Notice the client's use of vague words, such as *like* and *like something*. Such words indicate that the client is paying attention to a vague feeling with unclear meanings or a felt sense. After the client said, "It feels tense all over, like something is clamping down on my stomach," some therapists would make the mistake of reflecting something too definite, possibly followed by a question. For example, they might say, "So you're feeling tense all over. Could it be that . . .?" Instead, it is especially important to reflect all of the client's felt sense words, especially words that indicate lack of clarity, such as *like*, and invite the client to stay with the felt sense even longer (Hendricks, 1986).

Hendricks (2001) gave an example of a therapist who did not recognize the client's felt sense. Hendricks explained that the client may become confused, feel inadequate, defer to the therapist's authority, and disconnect from direct experience.

C1: And yet I feel . . . there's something underneath it all but I don't know what . . . [felt sense] and if I kind of knew what it was . . . I might feel differently, I don't know. But it's vague right now.

T1: Okay. If things could be a little more definite. If you were really able to identify the cause you really think that you'd be able to cope with it then. But right now you can't seem to put your finger on what the real problem is.

C2: Yeah . . . and . . . that . . . like when you say that . . . that makes me mad because I feel . . . you know like I'm . . . intelligent. I can figure things out. And yet . . . right now I don't know what the hell's going on with me. (pp. 238–239)

Hendricks (2001) said,

The therapist is unable to respond to the client's felt sense, which is the rich, intricate, not yet known place from which movement would come. The client has given a clear prescription of what needs to happen next. She literally tells the therapist that if she could just sense more into this unclear place underneath it all, she has a sense that something would move from there. Because the therapist does not know about this level of process, he uses his words in a cognitive, closed, defined way that cannot point to or invite what is not known to open. The client is left self-critical and, probably, rightfully, angry at the therapist. This kind of interaction underscores the need for therapists to develop this sensitivity as part of their training. (p. 239)

Some clients have difficulty identifying emotions. Typically, I help such clients identify several major emotions, such as sadness, anger, fear, and joy, in their bodies. I might suggest that clients remember a sad time in their lives, imagine themselves in that situation, and notice how the sadness feels in their body. For example, when one client remembered when his mother died, I asked him to describe to me his body sensations at the time. He said he felt tears in his eyes, a lump his throat, and a heaviness in his chest. I then had him remember times when he felt anger, fear, and joy.

Some clients may be able to identify emotions mentally but have difficulty locating them in their body. These people may also need help before learning to focus. I explain that the emotions we think we have may be different from the emotions that we actually have in our bodies. As an example, I tell clients that I might think I am disappointed about a loss, but when I check in my body, I might actually be angry about the loss. It is the anger that is actually bothering me and giving my body stress.

The reason for continually identifying bodily feelings by asking, "How does that whole thing feel in your body now?" is that these subtle bodily feelings are a source of wisdom. In focusing, the term *body* means *body, mind, and soul* experienced together. Some religious traditions refer to this as *heart*. Gendlin (1996) explained that the human organism is marvelously complex; it knows far more than we can consciously think at any given time. He says that this is not the body that is reduced to physiology, but rather a body from out of which living happens. It is always implicitly intricate; it includes a whole range of possible experiences that have never happened but could come.

The felt sense is implicitly contextual. It takes other people and the environment into account (Gendlin, 1996). It leads to larger and larger wholes. The felt sense tells a person what is needed in a culture-free way, whether it be more separation from or more unity with others. The felt sense helps a client stay in touch with a pro-life energy that is sometimes called *spirit*. When a client attends to his or her felt sense and it unfolds into a felt shift in which a transcendent growth process occurs, the experience may be considered spiritual.

Keeping a Friendly Focusing Attitude

As part of the focusing method, clients are taught the importance of keeping friendly, accepting, patient, kind, and receptive attitudes while attending to feelings rather than having a self-critical attitude (Hinterkopf,

1983, 1998). A friendly attitude toward feelings brings relief, release, and more life energy. A self-critical attitude brings more tension, constriction, heaviness, and dullness. When clients experience difficulty focusing, it is frequently because they are having difficulty keeping a focusing attitude toward their feelings (felt senses). At such times, the psychotherapist can remind the client to adopt the needed attitude. Remembering to keep this attitude allows feelings to be in process and change. This in turn allows the psychospiritual growth process to take place.

The following example shows how reminding a client to keep a focusing attitude helps bring about a felt shift. Focusing therapy is frequently distinguished by the attitude of being friendly and compassionate toward all bodily experience. When the therapist notices that a client is not being accepting toward some inner bodily experience, the client is invited to try out such an attitude.

Mr. J., a 38-year-old, said that he wanted to focus on his weight problem. I asked him how his weight problem felt in his body. He said that the problem had several feelings including feeling flushed in the face, tense in the neck, bloated in the stomach, and tingling in the hands. He reported that he was sad because he saw himself as a gunny sack bulging with potatoes.

After helping him adopt a kind attitude toward his sadness, I asked him, "How would this whole thing feel if you had a friendly attitude toward it?" He said that it was difficult to imagine a friendly attitude toward the part of himself that wanted to overeat because he felt so ashamed of it. I asked him, "Could you imagine creating one place for your shame and another place for the part of you that wants to overeat?" He said that he could do this. Then I asked him if he could imagine having a friendly, kind attitude toward someone else with the same type of weight problem. After imagining having this attitude toward a friend, he was able to adopt a friendly attitude toward the part of him that wanted to overeat. He then reported feeling more relaxed and having more energy to do something about his weight problem. He said that he realized that he had been trying to exert too much control over this part of himself by keeping it hidden. In a later session he reported, "Remembering to keep a friendly attitude toward my weight problem has made taking action to lose weight almost easy."

This example illustrates how blocks to action (in this case the client's block to losing weight) are frequently released when these parts are carefully listened to in a compassionate Focusing manner. Self-criticism often holds these blocks in place. Adopting an accepting attitude toward the feelings (in this case, both the sadness and the shame) frequently releases the block.

This example is spiritual in nature because the client was able to attend to a subtle, bodily feeling with vague meanings that brought new clearer meanings involving a transcendent growth process. Mr. J.'s subtle, bodily feeling with vague meanings involved an image of a gunny sack bulging with potatoes and his feeling flushed in the face, tense in the neck, bloated in the stomach, tingling in the hands, and sad. A new clearer meaning was his realization that he had been trying to exert too much control over this part of himself by keeping it hidden. The client's experience involved a transcendent growth process because the client was able to have a more compassionate attitude than he previously had for the part of him that wanted to overeat.

Keeping a Certain Distance

Clients often make one of two mistakes when working on a problem. Either they are too close to a problem, usually by being overwhelmed by emotions, or they are too far away from a problem, usually by intellectualizing about it. I have found it important to teach clients to find a certain distance (Hinterkopf, 1983, 1998)—one close enough to feel the problem in their body but far enough away from it to realize that their life is greater than the problem. The appropriate distance from a problem is the distance at which clients can process material and realize change. At this distance, clients experience some relief or release. Clients work through problems most frequently when they are able to keep this distance.

Many clients in therapy are in extreme discomfort, especially when they are overwhelmed by a problem and need more distance. Clients, who have difficulty finding a certain distance, often need suggestions to help them find the appropriate distance. In the next example, I help a client find more distance in T2 and T3. I give the client suggestions for adopting a friendly attitude in T4 and T5.

> Mr. K., a successful public speaker, contacted me because he started having panic attacks while he was giving speeches. He explained that the panic attacks were overwhelming and paralyzing. Until recently he had a self-concept of himself as "superman." He saw himself as a strong, clear, dynamic speaker. When he had a panic attack, it felt as though he was zapped with "kryptonite" that drained him of his energy.

> T1:   So you could say "hello" to that part of you that feels panicked about public speaking. [Silence of 40 seconds] How does this whole thing feel in your body now?

> C2:   I feel a weakness and a jitteriness in my chest, especially in my shoulders, arms, and nerves. They feel like guitar strings that have been strung too tight. I feel a terrifying drain of my energy. I'm paralyzed with fear—frozen. There's a constricted breathing in my chest, like hyperventilating, like death.

> T2:   I wonder if you could imagine putting this whole panic attack out at a distance?

> C3:   That seems too hard to do.

> T3:   Perhaps you could become a neutral observer of yourself, like a reporter, seeing yourself at a distance with the panic attack. You can describe it to me whenever you're ready.

C4: [Silence of 30 seconds] I see myself at a park, walking too close to a fire and getting burned. It's scary. I feel better, but I still feel weak and helpless. [The client said this in a self-critical tone of voice.]

T4: Then it seems especially important that you create a friendly, accepting place for your weak and helpless feelings.

C5: [Silence of 35 seconds] That seems really hard to do. I don't think I've ever accepted that part of myself.

T5: I wonder if you could imagine how you would be toward a friend who had panic attacks while he was speaking publicly.

C6: Yeah, that works. I would be understanding and empathic with a friend who had panic attacks while he was speaking publicly. It feels better now. Now I see myself in a wooded park by a pond and it feels more peaceful and still.

The suggestions in T1, T2, and T3 help the client find more distance and develop an observer self. In C4, he is able to see himself in a park, walking too close to a fire, but feeling somewhat better. Because he seemed self-critical in C4, I give additional suggestions to adopt a friendly, accepting attitude in T4 and T5. This results in the client finding the right distance in C6. His feelings change. He now feels peaceful and still. At a later time, the client reported that his panic attacks had ceased after this session.

Although clients typically need to find the right distance when they are overwhelmed with uncomfortable feelings, it may not be appropriate to help the client find more distance immediately. If clients are expressing emotions, such as crying or expressing anger, it is usually important that the psychotherapist let them express these feelings before trying to help them find the right distance.

The Nature of the Relationship Between Psychology and Spirituality

When using a process approach to psychotherapy, psychotherapeutic growth and spiritual growth are the same. By following process rather than content, the therapist is less likely to interrupt the client's process and more likely to remain nonjudgmental.

The focusing-oriented therapist is aware that the client's connotations or meanings of content words, such as God, Allah, or Vishnu, may be different from the therapist's. The different connotations or meanings may be discussed at some point of the therapy session. During the time that the client is internally sensing, however, it is important that the therapist avoid discussing or asking about such differences or even similarities. Otherwise the therapist may inadvertently interrupt the delicate growth process that may be difficult or impossible for the client to regain at a later time.

The experiential focusing psychotherapist's emphasis is placed on the client's process and whether the content brings relief or more life energy to the client. This means that a psychotherapist need not turn away from the client when unfamiliar spiritual issues arise. Rather, the therapist can continue to use the same methods, including focusing, to facilitate growth.

Therapist's Skills and Attributes

A person may be trained either as a focusing trainer or an experiential focusing–oriented therapist. A focusing trainer teaches people to use the focusing method with individuals or groups. An experiential focusing-oriented therapist uses experiential focusing as a baseline for whatever he or she does in therapy and uses experiential focusing to guide the therapeutic relationship. A focusing therapist is usually able to use a variety of approaches in therapy. Some therapists may learn to use the focusing method only as a skill to be used with other approaches.

A focusing trainer may or may not be a therapist. Those who are not therapists usually come from a helping profession, such as teaching, massage therapy, or hospice work. They are people whose lives join naturally with work in which one attends to an ongoing internal process. A person wishing to be trained as a focusing trainer may locate a certifying focusing coordinator in his or her proximity through the Focusing Institute's Web site (http://www.focusing.org). Certifying coordinators usually have many years of experience using and teaching the focusing method and have made a major contribution to the field. They are certified by the Focusing Institute in New York and are located throughout the United States and around the world.

About 90% of certifying coordinators are focusing-oriented therapists and train other therapists to use experiential psychotherapy in their practice. In universities, focusing-oriented therapy is being taught as part of a course, as a course, and as a major track. Formal training programs in focusing-oriented therapy are located in cities such as New York, Boston, and Chicago and in many countries outside the United States. New university-based training programs are being developed in Washington, California, and abroad. The Focusing Institute does not offer any kind of license to practice psychotherapy. Dr. Hinterkopf offers workshops and training internationally in the focusing method, experiential psychotherapy, The use of experiential focusing for integrating spirituality in counseling, and the use of focusing for dream interpretation.

Experiential focusing therapy may be taught using lectures, group discussion, small group experiential exercises, and supervision. Students are usually required to practice the process in partnerships between training sessions. The training period is usually 2 years, depending on the previous experience of the therapist-in-training. Training is sometimes offered individually. Each certifying coordinator schedules training sessions. The cost of training usually depends on the prevailing charges of such training in each geographical area.

Skills and attributes needed as a baseline for using the experiential focusing approach are congruence, empathy, and positive regard. Psychotherapists need to be trained in focusing to respond to a client's implicit, complex, felt sense material to facilitate process. Focusing does not conflict with any therapeutic method. The therapist who does not recognize the implicit, intricate process in a client may inadvertently discourage the emergent process in the client (Hendricks, 2001). Skills needed by a therapist include giving exact empathic listening and responses to felt sense material, asking open-ended questions, and making focusing suggestions regarding attitude and distance (Hinterkopf, 1998).

Experiential focusing therapists who are effective in using the approach use focusing themselves, often as an orientation toward life. They are spiritually oriented individuals in both their personal and professional lives in that they frequently check their own internal process to sense the complexity of a situation. Professionally, they use their felt sense to choose from a number of orientations, interventions, and innovations. They continually encourage their clients to check their own inner sense of things. In content some focusing-oriented therapists use traditional, spiritual practices, and others do not. For many, focusing is the deepest spiritual practice that they know, even after they have explored many other practices.

Spiritual attributes needed by the focusing-oriented therapist include an ability to have an attitude of openness to the spiritual process in all clients whether they are religious or not. The therapist needs to be able to set aside personal issues temporarily to become present to the client's process. The experiential focusing therapist is able to model and teach a client to respect and value his or her own process and develop a mindful, observer self or witness. Learning to value the focusing process almost always leads to experiences of forgiveness, faith, and hope. Therapists and clients learn to have a sense of meaning and purpose in life and develop a sense of personal strength and autonomy. They learn to make religious and spiritual faith more of an experiential reality. Focusing-oriented therapists are able to rest in not knowing. They know that thin ideas or concepts from a therapist could never be better than a client's own explication. Learning to value the felt shift in a client's process helps clients transcend their former frame of reference and reach out to more parts of themselves, others, and life (Hinterkopf, 1998). This involves the spiritual process.

Strengths and Limitations

Theoretical

The theory behind the focusing-oriented therapy describes the core of the psychospiritual change process. Its strength lies in the fact that it is process oriented. This means that it may be used with any other psychological or spiritual approach to make it more effective. A limitation of focusing-oriented therapy is that it does not teach content. For example, it does not teach what a particular religion or church says about divorce. If a client has questions about the specific content of a religious practice, the therapist may wish to refer the client to a person of his or her own religion. On the other hand, focusing-oriented therapy can help the client sense what is best for his or her own life. Focusing-oriented therapy can also help the therapist sense what content is most helpful to share with the client.

Practical

The experiential focusing approach has been used by a large variety of groupings of psychologists and psychotherapists. These include professionals in agencies and private settings, inpatient and outpatient work, and individual, couple, and family therapy. The focusing approach with spiritual material has been most widely used with individuals in private and agency settings.

A practical limitation is that not all graduate school programs have training in focusing-oriented psychotherapy. The number of graduate school programs having training and research in experiential focusing psychotherapy is steadily growing, however. Two reasons for its late development are the following. The book, *Focusing,* (Gendlin, 1981) was first published by Bantam Books as a self-help method in 1981. Gendlin's book, *Focusing-Oriented Psychotherapy,* was not published until 1996. Thus, focusing-oriented psychotherapy has become widely known only in recent years. Hinterkopf's 1998 book, *Integrating Spirituality in Counseling: A Manual for Using the Experiential Focusing Method,* is used in many graduate school programs that offer a course in spiritual approaches to psychotherapy.

Indications and Contraindications

When using experiential focusing, each therapeutic response is carefully checked to determine whether it brings more easing or more life-forward movement for a client. When a response or suggestion leads a client away from his or her emergent process, for example, when a client experiences more tension or confusion, the response is discontinued. The therapist may suggest that the client disregard a response and return to the last point in the session where there was easing (Hinterkopf, 1998).

Although comfort and ease with imaging are not prerequisites, clients who have difficulty with internal sensing usually have difficulty with focusing. Of course, the focusing process may be initiated by a variety of modalities, such as awareness of feelings, beliefs, behaviors, images, or movement. Even some clients who seem to have difficulty sensing internally may, however, be able to identify their feelings if coached immediately in a gentle manner. For example, a therapist might carefully watch for a felt place, such as tears or other strong feelings, and ask the client, "What are you feeling inside?" If the client asks, "What do you mean?" the therapist might say, "From the tears in your eyes, it looks as if you might be feeling sad, or you might be feeling moved by this whole situation. I wonder if you could sense inside and check your eyes and perhaps your throat and chest to notice what you feel there? For example, if I were feeling sad, I might feel tears in my eyes, tightness in my throat, and heaviness in my chest. You could check how it feels inside for you."

Some clients report that they find it impossible to feel emotions, that is, alexithymia. Such a client may be asked, "What is your experience of feeling nothing?" If a client is able to describe his or her experience, for example, "that everything feels flat like cardboard," the client is already describing a felt sense. Even when clients are unable to respond to focusing-oriented questions or suggestions, the therapist may return to using focusing to sense carefully what is needed.

Cultural and Gender Considerations

The experiential-focusing approach is especially appropriate for use in diverse, multicultural settings because it is process oriented and can be used with any content. It may be used with any religious or spiritual belief or practice. Hinterkopf (1998) presented many examples of using this approach with clients of both genders from diverse cultural settings. Experiential focusing has helped people find a deeply experiential place in groups as diverse as Hindu, Muslim, Buddhist, Jewish, and Christian. People from religions as diverse as Sufi and Quaker have reported that focusing helps them do what their religion asks of them—to find presence and meditate without repressing material from their daily lives (Omidian, 2002; Saunders, 2003). A psychotherapist may even use the approach to support the spirituality of clients who are not religious. The method allows clients of both genders to draw on their own personally and culturally relevant meanings. The beneficial effects of focusing in terms of positive therapy outcome and other variables in research in many countries indicate that the process cuts across gender and cultures (Hendricks, 2001). Anything that is true in a therapy context is also true in a spiritual context from a process-oriented point of view.

Expected Future Developments and Directions

As a need for multicultural approaches to spirituality in psychotherapy becomes more recognized, experiential focusing will become more influential. The Focusing Institute is a not-for-profit organization with purpose of helping to make focusing available to the public and to the international scholarly community through teaching, research, and written materials. The Focusing Institute has trained teachers and therapists around the world who present training programs, workshops, and individual teaching sessions. Its membership is growing. Coordinated research studies in major universities in the United States, Canada, Belgium, Germany, and Japan will continue to be designed and implemented (Hendricks, 2001). In fact, experiential focusing is one of the major schools of psychotherapy in Japan.

CASE EXAMPLE

The following case example is a modified, abbreviated description of earlier case material (Hinterkopf, 1998).[1] It illustrates the focusing-oriented therapy approach. Throughout the session, the therapist used the focusing process to sense what was needed. This included what was needed in the therapeutic relationship and which therapeutic responses would be helpful to further the client's process. In this part of the session, exact listening and focusing questions and responses were used. The part of a session during which the client is paying attention to her felt sense may last from 5 to 40 minutes.

The client in this case example had previously learned focusing, and we had already established a relationship. She was easily able to follow my focusing suggestions. Examples of working with clients who have more difficulty with focusing are presented in *Integrating Spirituality in Counseling* (Hinterkopf, 1998).

The client was experiencing a depressed mood with crying episodes. She had recently undergone two major life stressors: new employment and a new marriage. Notice how keeping a friendly focusing attitude, keeping a certain distance, and asking open-ended focusing questions helped allow new meanings emerge from her feelings.

The client began the session by saying that she felt sad (a single emotion). She then expanded the feeling to find words to describe her larger, vague, holistic feeling (a felt sense), saying that it was an "on-the-verge-of crying sad" in her chest and throat. Becoming aware of and describing this larger feeling allowed more meaning to come from the feeling. I suggested that the client stay with the feeling in a friendly, gentle way (keeping a friendly, focusing attitude). After she acknowledged the feeling, she realized that this was the part of her that just wanted "not to do" and "just wanted to *be* sometimes." She said that this part was in a losing battle against her "always needing to do side." After staying with the client for several moments while she cried, I asked her if it might be helpful for her to set the whole thing out at a little distance (keeping a certain distance). After several moments, the client had an image of two figures on opposite sides of a boxing ring. The two figures represented her two sides. I suggested that she might ask herself the question, "What's the worst of this whole thing for me?" (open-ended focusing question). After some time, the client realized that the worst of it for her

---

[1]Adapted from *Integrating Spirituality in Counseling: A Manual for Using the Experiential Focusing Method* (pp. 89–100), by E. Hinterkopf, 1998, Alexandria, VA: American Counseling Association. Copyright 1998 by the American Counseling Association. Adapted with permission.

was that she always had to choose the "doing side—like there wasn't an option." After a pause I asked her how the whole thing felt in her body now. She said that the part that wanted "to *be*" felt like her stomach was in knots and felt abandoned with sadness in it. The client then chose to ask herself how the whole thing would feel if it were all OK (open-ended focusing question). After almost a minute of waiting in silence, she received a feeling of the two sides being integrated and flowing together in a spiral or circle. She said that she would then no longer need to choose between the two sides. She could then feel peacefulness, serenity, and flowing (felt shift). Because the client had previously told me that her faith in God was important to her, I asked her if it would feel right to ask herself how she experienced God with this experience (open-ended focusing question). In reply to the question that she had asked herself, she said that she could imagine God saying, "Now this is how it is to live in peace." She ended the focusing part of the session by reporting that she felt an opening up to greater joy and to more possibilities. After the focusing part of the session, she reported that the last question had helped her stay with her felt shift longer and allowed it to expand.

In this example, the client experienced a spiritual process because the client directed her attention toward inwardly felt, complex, implicit meanings. She allowed new meanings to emerge and transcended her former frame of reference. During the felt shift, the client experienced a bodily felt release with feelings of peacefulness, serenity, and flowing. The client transcended her former frame of reference in that she was able to integrate a previously ignored part of herself, the part that wanted only to be. In the process of integration, this part, along with the doing part, was transformed into a flowing spiral. The client also attended to spiritual content in that she referred to concepts such as God.

Client Demographics, Relevant History, and Presenting Concern

The client is a 38-year-old, recently married female who is making a career change. She is Catholic in her upbringing and presently attends and is active in both her traditional Christian denomination and in a recently founded, ecumenical denomination. She practices centering prayer and meditation, is devout, and is unorthodox in that she is comfortable in both churches. The client's parents were divorced when she was 5 years old. Her mother is an alcoholic and has attended AA for 10 years. The client neither drinks nor uses drugs. She reports that her present relationship with her mother is good. Her father is deceased. She is in good health except that she has minor back problems. She describes her marriage as being supportive. Her presenting problems include stress and "workaholism" with an inability to take time to relax.

Relationship of the Therapist and Client

In this therapeutic relationship, the therapist practices being a careful listener and helps the client explore and find her own steps of healing especially during the time that she is focusing. At these times the therapist is a companion and guide and is present to the client's experience. The therapeutic interventions are not limited to experiential focusing techniques. At times when the client is not focusing, the therapist might choose to respond using other techniques, such as cognitive or behavioral, although the experiential approach is used as the baseline. The client's experience is carefully checked before and after each intervention to determine whether it brings more relief, release, or life energy in the client.

Assessment: Rationale and Type of Data Collected

In the initial interview, the client was screened for alcoholism and drug abuse with negative results. She reported that her weight was constant, her appetite was good, and she had no suicidal ideas or death wishes. She did not report any problems with her concentration and did not have symptoms of mania. She took interest in her work. She reported, however, that she had felt sad for about 2 months and frequently cried.

I usually begin learning about the client's religious tradition and spiritual orientation in the initial intake interview. Questions I ask include, "Do you have a religious preference or spiritual orientation?" and "What religion was practiced in your home when you were a child?" If a client reports being religious, I might ask, "What is best about your religion for you?" If a client talks about not being religious, but being a spiritual person, I might ask, "How do you experience your spirituality?" What I learn from the client's answers to these questions will help me facilitate her spiritual process in the course of counseling. Also, asking these questions in the intake interview suggests that the subject of spirituality, which includes religion, is an acceptable and relevant dimension of counseling.

I learn the client's vocabulary from the questions I ask in the intake interview and in subsequent counseling sessions. Because words have special meanings or connotations for each person, I am careful to use the same words as the client when working with spiritual issues. It is important for me to be comfortable with using both theistic and nontheistic terms. For example, if the client uses theistic terms such as God, Allah, or Vishnu, it is usually most helpful to use the same words when responding to the client. Nontheistic terms might involve "being related to something greater than myself" or "feeling connected to the whole universe."

Diagnostic and Clinical Case Conceptualization

The *DSM–IV–TR* Axis I diagnosis of Adjustment Disorder With Depressed Mood (American Psychiatric Association, 2000) was given. The client's symptoms started at the time she made a career change. She considered the change a positive one. She nonetheless reported depression with tearfulness. There was no Axis II diagnosis. Because the client had only minor back problems, I did not make an Axis III diagnosis. Her current score on the Global Assessment of Functioning (GAF) Scale was 75. The client reported a positive view of God, saying that her faith gave her comfort during difficult times. This report led me to believe that I could use her religious beliefs to facilitate the therapeutic process. The client's ability to describe her feelings and emotions made her a good candidate for using focusing techniques.

Treatment Goals, Process, and Intervention Strategies

Treatment goals included helping the client reduce depression and stress. The client already had tools available for relaxation. These tools included centering prayer and meditation. She also had received massage treatments for her back. The problem seemed to be in her somewhat unconscious choice of how she used her time. Experiential focusing seemed to be an appropriate approach for exploring this choice. Focusing techniques would probably prove to be useful interventions.

The treatment process that is unique to the experiential focusing approach is that the client is continually encouraged to pay attention to her ongoing, implicit, internal process. If the client has difficulty, she is taught to pay attention to her felt sense. The felt sense is part of the crucial contribution of experiential focusing psychotherapy. The felt sense is more than just emotion or body sensation. As Gendlin wrote in "A Theory of Personality Change" (1964),

> the direct referent is internally complex and an individual feels in touch with himself when he refers to it, while emotions are internally all one quality . . . they are "sheer." They often keep him from sensing that in himself which is the complex ground of the emotion. . . . The emotions of guilt, shame, embarrassment, or feeling that I am "bad" are *about* me or this aspect of my experience and its meaning to me. These emotions are not themselves the experience and its meanings to me. . . . we feel (these emotions) instead of feeling that concerning that which we feel shame, guilt and badness . . . these emotions themselves preclude our feeling what it all is to us . . . because they skip the point at which we might complete, symbolize respond or attend to . . . the incomplete implicit meanings. (pp. 122–123)

Focusing is a powerful process by which a person becomes more intentionally aware. By becoming aware of the body's holistic responses to situations, one often experiences a liberating change in which the issue is experienced. The simple act of giving attention to the body's reactions can allow relaxation of the "grip" the issue holds on a person. The entire issue looks different, and new solutions arise.

Course of Treatment and Frequency and Duration of Sessions

The timeline of the course of treatment was 5 weeks with visits scheduled once per week for 50 to 60 minutes. Some clients continue therapy with me after initial therapeutic goals are met. At such times, my primary role may be that of a companion or guide.

Termination and Relapse Prevention

Termination of treatment occurs when both the client and therapist agree that treatment goals have been met. The experiential focusing approach has in-built forms of relapse prevention in that the client is progressively taught to learn to self-guide her own process.

Focusing may be taught in workshops or in segments during therapy sessions. For example, in one session I might teach a client to pay attention to the larger, implicit felt sense. In another session, I might teach how to keep an accepting, focusing attitude. Once a client has learned to attend to her internal referent on a regular basis, she is able to sense readily the need for therapy at a later time.

Therapeutic Outcomes: Immediate and Long Term

At the end of the session, the client described in the case example reported an absence of sadness. During the next two sessions, she reported a general sense of well-being with almost no sadness. She reported less stress with an ability to take more time to relax. Her GAF was at 85. Her therapy was terminated after five sessions. At 6 and 12 months following termination she reported enjoying her new employment. She said that she was able to use focusing to work through challenges with fellow employees and her husband. Thus, the client continued to have a high level of spiritual and psychological functioning.

REFERENCES

American Psychiatric Association. (2000). *Diagnostic and statistical manual of mental disorders* (4th ed., text rev.). Washington, DC: Author.

Campbell, P., & McMahon, E. (1985). *Bio-spirituality: Focusing as a way to grow.* Chicago: Loyola University Press.

Chandler, C., Holden, J. M., & Kolander, C. (1992). Counseling for spiritual wellness: Theory and practice. *Journal of Counseling and Development, 71,* 168–175.

Durak, G. M., Bernstein, R., & Gendlin, E. T. (1997). Effects of focusing training on therapy process and outcome. *The Folio: A Journal for Focusing and Experiential*

Therapy, 15, 7–14. (Available from the Focusing Institute, 34 East Lane, Spring Valley, NY 10977)

Gendlin, E. T. (1961). Experiencing: A variable in the process of therapeutic change. *American Journal of Psychotherapy, 15,* 233–245.

Gendlin, E. T. (1962). *Experiencing and the creation of meaning.* New York: Macmillan.

Gendlin, E. T. (1964). A theory of personality change. In P. Worchel & D. Byrne (Eds.), *Personality change* (pp. 102–148). New York: Wiley.

Gendlin, E. T. (1966). Research in psychotherapy with schizophrenic patients and the nature of that "illness." *American Journal of Psychotherapy, 20,* 4–16.

Gendlin, E. T. (1969). Focusing. *Psychotherapy: Theory, Research and Practice, 6,* 4–15.

Gendlin, E. T. (1981). *Focusing.* New York: Bantam Books.

Gendlin, E. T. (1984). The client's client. In R. Levant & J. M. Shlien (Eds.), *Client-centered therapy and the person-centered approach.* New York: Praeger.

Gendlin, E. T. (1986). *Let your body interpret your dreams.* Wilmette, IL: Chiron.

Gendlin, E. T. (1996). *Focusing-oriented psychotherapy: A manual of the experiential method.* New York: Guilford Press.

Gendlin, E. T., Beebe J., III, Cassens, J., Klein, M., & Oberlander, M. (1968). Focusing ability in psychotherapy, personality, and creativity. In J. Shlien (Ed.), *Research in psychotherapy III* (pp. 217–241). Washington, DC: American Psychological Association.

Gendlin, E. T., & Tomlinson, T. M. (1967). The process conception and its measurement. In C. R. Rogers, E. T. Gendlin, D. J. Kiesler, & C. B. Truax (Eds.), *The therapeutic relationship and its impact: A study of psychotherapy with schizophrenics* (pp. 109–131). Madison: University of Wisconsin Press.

Grof, S. (1976). *Realms of the human unconscious.* New York: Dutton.

Helminiak, D. (1987). *Spiritual development.* Chicago: Loyola University Press.

Hendricks, M. N. (1986). Experiencing level as a therapeutic variable. *Person-Centered Review, 1,* 141–162.

Hendricks, M. N. (2001). Research basis of focusing-oriented/experiential psychology. In D. Cain & J. Seeman (Eds.), *Humanistic psychotherapies: Handbook of research and practice* (pp. 221–251). Washington, DC: American Psychological Association.

Hinterkopf, E. (1983). Experiential focusing: A three-stage training program. *Journal of Humanistic Psychology, 23,* 113–126.

Hinterkopf, E. (1994). Integrating spiritual experiences in counseling. *Counseling and Values, 38,* 165–175.

Hinterkopf, E. (1995a, April). *Integrating spirituality in counseling.* Paper presented at the meeting of the American Counseling Association, Denver, CO.

Hinterkopf, E. (1995b). *Die Dimension Spiritualitat in Beratung und Therapie.* Unpublished manuscript.

Hinterkopf, E. (1998). *Integrating spirituality in counseling: A manual for using the experiential focusing method.* Alexandria, VA: American Counseling Association.

Hinterkopf, E., & Brunswick, L. K. (1981). Teaching mental patients to use client-centered and experiential therapeutic skills with each other. *Psychotherapy: Theory, Research and Practice, 18,* 394–402.

Klein, M. H., Mathieu, P. I., Gendlin, E. T., & Kiesler, D. J. (1970). *The Experiencing Scale: A research and training manual.* Madison: University of Wisconsin Extension Bureau of Audiovisual Instruction.

Klein, M. H., Mathieu-Coughlan, P. I., & Kiesler, D. J. (1986). The Experiencing Scales. In L. S. Greenberg & W. M. Pinsof (Eds.), *The psychotherapeutic process: A research handbook* (pp. 21–71). New York: Guilford Press.

Mathieu-Coughlan, P. I., & Klein, M. H. (1984). Experiential psychotherapy: Key events in client-therapist interaction. In L. N. Rice & L. S. Greenberg (Eds.), *Patterns of change* (pp. 213–248). New York: Guilford Press.

Omidian, P. (2002). The use of focusing by Afghan aid workers. *Staying in focus: The Focusing Institute newsletter, 2* (2). (Available from the Focusing Institute, 34 East Lane, Spring Valley, NY 10977)

Rogers, C. R., Gendlin, E. T., Kiesler, D. J., & Truax, C. B. (Eds.). (1967). *The therapeutic relationship and its impact: A study of psychotherapy with schizophrenics.* Madison: University of Wisconsin Press.

Saunders, N. (2003). *Focusing on the light: A modest proposal.* Retrieved March 3, 2002, from the Focusing Institute's Web site: http://www.focusing.org/spirituality.html

Shafranske, E. P., & Gorsuch, R. L. (1984). Factors associated with the perception of spirituality in psychotherapy. *Journal of Transpersonal Psychology, 16,* 231–241.

Shafranske, E. P., & Malony, H. N. (1990). Clinical psychologists' religious and spiritual orientations and their practice of psychotherapy. *Psychotherapy, 27,* 72–78.

Tomlinson, T. M., & Hart, J. T. (1962). A validation of the process scale. *Journal of Consulting Psychology, 26,* 74–78.

Walker, A., Rablen, R. A., & Rogers, C. R. (1960). Development of a scale to measure process change in psychotherapy. *Journal of Clinical Psychology, 16,* 79–85.

10

FORGIVENESS-PROMOTING APPROACH: HELPING CLIENTS REACH FORGIVENESS THROUGH USING A LONGER MODEL THAT TEACHES RECONCILIATION

EVERETT L. WORTHINGTON JR., SUZANNE E. MAZZEO, AND DAVID E. CANTER

When most people hear the word *forgiveness*, they automatically think of it as a spiritual, and most of the time, a religious concept. Forgiveness is a central construct of Christianity (Marty, 1998). All major religions value forgiveness (Rye et al., 2000).

Yet many people speak of forgiveness and might experience forgiveness even if they have little connection to any organized religion and do not think of it in particularly spiritual terms. Forgiveness seems to be one of many natural relationship-repair mechanisms. Even more, many psychological wounds have their origins in current or past relationships, and forgiveness can help people

This chapter depends on research supported by the John Templeton Foundation (Grant 239). We gratefully acknowledge that support. Virginia Commonwealth University's General Clinical Research Center also supports the research under Grant NIH 5M01 RR000065.

235

psychologically, even if the relationship is not affected (for example, a middle-aged woman might forgive her deceased father for molesting her as a child and thereby eliminate psychological symptoms and achieve a peace she had not previously known). Forgiveness is thus of interest to individual, couple, family, and group therapies.

Historically, numerous disciplines have written about forgiveness. Philosophers such as Murphy and Hampton (1988) have illustrated philosophy's consideration. Shakespeare, Yeats, and O'Neill tackled forgiveness as a major theme. Religious writers from the major religions have discussed forgiveness (Rye et al., 2000). Interest in forgiving within psychology flourished after publication of *Forgive and Forget: Healing the Hurts We Don't Deserve* (Smedes, 1984). Therapists wrote articles about how forgiveness might be used in psychotherapy (e.g., Fitzgibbons, 1986). Enright studied how children develop reasoning about forgiveness (Enright & the Human Development Study Group, 1994) and soon developed an intervention to promote forgiveness (Hebl & Enright, 1993). Shortly afterward, Worthington, DiBlasio, and McCullough began to study forgiveness (McCullough &Worthington, 1994; Worthington & DiBlasio, 1990). The John Templeton Foundation then put forth a request for proposals in 1997, and research labs studying forgiveness proliferated.

Forgiveness per se is not necessarily part of individual psychotherapy. Forgiveness might find its maximal usefulness in couple, family, or group therapy or in contexts that value community and relationships (e.g., religiously tailored therapy, or therapy in culturally communal groups).

In this chapter, we describe a psychoeducational intervention to promote forgiveness in which one couple meets with a marital "consultant." The approach is directly adaptable for couple therapy, and some of the clinical techniques can be used in individual, group, and family therapies.

DESCRIPTION OF THE APPROACH

Historical and Theoretical Bases

Worthington's intervention was developed at Virginia Commonwealth University (VCU), a secular state university. Whereas Worthington is a Christian who communicates to both secular and Christian communities, not all of his colleagues and graduate students have shared his faith commitment.

In the mid-1980s, Worthington was supervising graduate student Donald Danser. To deal with a couple with intractable marital problems, Worthington and Danser elaborated a 2-session intervention to help this couple deal with issues in forgiveness. The approach centered on confessing each person's transgressions and allowing empathic responses from the partner who heard the confession. Partners took turns making confessions and responding. The couple's relationship was transformed. Colleague Fred DiBlasio and Worthington elaborated the intervention and used it with Christian clients in a Christian counseling agency (see Worthington & DiBlasio, 1990). This has become a cornerstone of DiBlasio's decision-based forgiveness approach (DiBlasio, 1998).

In 1990, Michael McCullough entered graduate school at VCU and he, graduate student Steve Sandage, and Worthington began to collaborate on research studying forgiveness (McCullough et al., 1998; McCullough, Sandage, & Worthington, 1997; McCullough & Worthington, 1994, 1995; McCullough, Worthington, & Rachal, 1997; Sandage, 1997). McCullough, Sandage, and Worthington's (1997) book advanced the thesis that although forgiveness had special significance to Christians, forgiveness was part of common grace. Like love, rationality. and meaning making, forgiveness is a human, not exclusively Christian, activity.

For her dissertation, Jennifer Ripley compared marital enrichment psychoeducational interventions involving Hope-Focused Marriage Enrichment and an early version of Forgiveness and Reconciliation through Experiencing Empathy (FREE; Ripley & Worthington, 2002). That project became an initial pilot study for a larger project—a grant-funded study of early married couples (for a second pilot study, see Burchard et al., 2003). The expanded version of FREE is the focus of this chapter.

Theoretical Forerunners

The theoretical ancestors of the REACH—where REACH is an acrostic in which each letter stands for a step (explained below)—model of forgiveness include emotion-focused couple therapy, integrative behavioral therapy, and structural family therapy overlaid by a focus on hope and a strategy to promote love, faith, and effort in couples. The framework is called hope-focused couple therapy (Worthington, 1999; Worthington et al., 1997). Theologically, the approach has roots in traditional Christianity. Importantly, the framework used in secular work with groups or couples refers little to explicitly religious constructs. Almost no participants have reacted negatively to the approach as being Christian. Because the approach is consistent with Christianity, however, it is easily adapted for use in explicitly Christian contexts (see Worthington, 2003, for a Christian revision of the secular version in Worthington, 2001a).

Unforgiveness

A transgression is a violation of moral boundaries, usually perceived as an offense, or psychological or physical boundaries, usually perceived as a hurt. Offenses result in immediate emotions of anger, whereas hurts usually result in immediate emotions of a combination of anger and fear (i.e., anger is due to the pain–anger connection, and fear usually involves anxiety over being hurt in the future). A transgression typically sets up an "injustice gap" between the expectation that a person has for the eventual outcome, and the current situation within a relationship. The size of the injustice gap is strongly related to, but not 100% correlated with, the amount of unforgiveness a person feels, and it fuels the justice motive (Exline, Worthington, Hill, & McCullogh, 2003). Unforgiveness might develop after rumination of an event, the injustice gap, and its consequences to the victim. Unforgiveness is defined as a complex of negative emotions, including resentment, bitterness, hostility, hatred, anger, and fear, that arise at some delayed time after a transgression and motivate the person to reduce those feelings (Worthington & Wade, 1999).

People Might Grant Forgiveness for Many Reasons

People might grant forgiveness because they (a) are religious and believe forgiveness to be demanded or encouraged by their religion, (b) believe forgiving is morally right in a particular situation, or (c) feel social pressure from the perpetrator, friends, authority figures, or community to grant forgiveness. When one "grants" forgiveness, one decides to forgive. Worthington (2003) defined "decisional forgiveness" as stating a behavioral intention to release others from the interpersonal debt incurred by transgressing, to eschew revenge and avoidance, and to act as if the transgression never happened. One may forgive decisionally yet still feel unforgiving. Decisional forgiveness expresses forgiveness but does not necessarily experience it emotionally.

People Are Motivated to Reduce Felt Unforgiveness

Unforgiveness is an unpleasant negative emotion that people develop by ruminating about hurts or offenses. They generally try to reduce unforgiveness, even if they believe these feelings empower them to do socially positive acts. Most laypeople think of forgiveness as the act one takes to eliminate unforgiveness. Worthington (2001b) identified many ways, however, that people eliminate or reduce unforgiveness. First, people reduce unforgiveness when they see justice done through (a) vigilante effort (i.e., retaliation and revenge); (b) legal justice within the criminal, judicial, or political system; (c) divine justice; or (d) communications and interactions with perpetrators that lower the esteem of the perpetrator or restore material and psychological well-being to the victim (i.e., apology or restitution). Second, people narrow the injustice gap by narrative means such as excusing or justifying the offense. Third, people may accept or forbear a transgression and move on with his or her life. Fourth, people may psychologically defend (e.g., denial or projection) a transgression. Fifth, people may forget relatively benign transgressions. Sixth, people may forgive emotionally.

Forgiveness

Emotional forgiveness—the experience of forgiveness, as distinguished from decisional forgiveness—is defined as the emotional juxtaposition of positive other-oriented emotions such as empathy, sympathy, compassion, altruistic love, or romantic love over the negative emotions of unforgiveness (Worthington & Wade, 1999). As unforgiveness and the positive emotion collide, the intensity of unforgiveness is reduced. If forgiveness is complete, the person might experience, at worst, neutral emotion toward the perpetrator and, at best, residual positive emotion toward the perpetrator. Regardless of how forgiveness is initiated, (e.g., cognitively, behaviorally, decisionally, socially, or spiritually), the process of forgiveness involves neutralization of negative emotions with more positive emotions.

Implications for Therapy

Three immediate implications for promoting forgiveness are important. First, the therapist might permit client catharsis over transgressions but eventually must encourage him or her to modulate negative emotional experience to make emotional replacement easier. Second, any of several positive other-oriented emotions can be juxtaposed against unforgiveness. Third, forgiveness is not the only way that people can deal with transgressions. Because they can legitimately pursue justice, narrative reinterpretation of the offense, or acceptance (Jacobson & Christensen, 1996), they should not be pressured to forgive.

The Pyramid Model to REACH Forgiveness

The five steps to forgiveness within the REACH model consist of one package of essential elements to help people forgive. A more comprehensive model that includes reconciliation (i.e., FREE) serves as the context for the REACH model. FREE uses a 4-session protocol, with the first and last sessions lasting 3 hours each and the middle sessions 2.5 hours each. We try to promote mutual empathy throughout all sessions, so we tend to use a general method of asking one partner to talk about his or her experiences and then inviting the spouse to express understanding and empathy. Then the spouse describes related experiences while the partner expresses empathy. In general, Sessions 1 and 2 deal with transgressions encountered outside of the marriage while partners are learning the REACH model. In Session 3 they learn how to discuss transgressions productively. In Session 4, they actually talk about and try to forgive transgressions within the marriage.

In Session 1, couples and their consultant establish rapport, talk about their marriage and its history, decide on goals for the meetings, and discuss the meanings of unforgiveness and forgiveness. In Session 2, partners learn the crucial elements of the REACH model. They practice empathy and use transgressions outside of their marriage to repeatedly empathize and forgive.

In Session 3, partners learn the remainder of the model. In the last half of the session, they apply the entire model to transgressions the partner has inflicted on them. In Session 4, the REACH model is placed in the context of the third step of a broader 6-step method of reconciliation. Substantial time is spent on Step 2 (talking about transgressions), with less time spent on Step 1 (deciding whether, how, and when to reconcile), Step 4 (repairing damage), Step 5 (dealing with future transgressions), and Step 6 (building more love). Step 3 (forgive through the REACH method) is also emphasized. These are further described in the case study.

The Nature of the Relationship Between Psychology and Spirituality

We have shown in a number of programmatic studies on forgiveness and religion that religious people tend to be more forgiving than nonreligious people (Ripley et al., 2003). We adopt Pargament's (2002) definition of *religion* as the search for the sacred. *Spirituality*, the personal intensity of one's search, has not been investigated (in our research) apart from religion and forgiveness. Christians report being more forgiving as a group than some other religions (McCullough & Worthington, 1999).

Religion and spirituality are moderators that affect whether and to what extent people forgive. We know of no empirical evidence suggesting that if one forgives, one becomes more spiritual or more religious. Clinically, we have seen instances in which a religious person who feels unforgiving toward a transgressor eventually forgives and experiences renewed (or new) religious sensitivity. How often such instances occur has not been empirically determined.

Two studies have recently examined client responses to religiously or spiritually tailored forgiveness interventions. Rye and Pargament (2002) compared a religious forgiveness intervention with a nonreligious intervention among college students who had faced relationship betrayal. They found that the religious matching of values and beliefs was important to people's acceptance of the religious intervention. The secular intervention did not produce as strong an effect for highly religious clients but produced a stronger effect for less religious clients. Hart and Shapiro (2002) compared members in 12-step programs for alcoholism and drug abuse who attended a secular forgiveness intervention modeled on Enright's forgiveness therapy versus a spiritually oriented but typical 12-step group. The spiritually oriented 12-step group had larger effects than the Enright-based secular forgiveness intervention. Hart and Shapiro observed, however, that the forgiveness intervention had positive pre- to postintevention and preintervention to follow-up changes in forgiveness, mediated by client empathy. To date, research is inconclusive concerning religious or spiritual matching for forgiveness interventions.

Therapist's Skills and Attributes

Therapists' individual differences affect their effectiveness at promoting forgiveness. Most of our research has involved psychoeducational groups (of individuals, couples, or parents) or "consultations" with couples, not therapy. At the present, we can discern, through empirical studies, no pattern of therapist characteristics that predicts effective promotion of forgiveness. Across a variety of studies, no consistent link has been found among therapist education, experience, and professional field and outcomes.

On the other hand, some therapists appear to be more effective than others. Thus, the differences must reside in the personal qualities of therapists or ways in which therapists conduct the manualized interventions. Personal attributes of the therapist, such as the ability to form a working alliance, are probably important, although we have not studied this experimentally. Based on theory, we would hypothesize that counselors who demonstrate empathy, sympathy, compassion, and love are likely to help group members forgive because forgiveness is thought to be centrally related to those qualities. The group leader's belief that forgiveness is important probably affects outcomes as well.

None of our empirical studies have yet examined forgiveness interventions in an explicitly religious community, but Worthington has conducted psychoeducational groups and therapy with religious individuals, couples, and families. Worthington believes that the religious conviction of the therapist should match the religious conviction of the client for maximum success. Empirical evidence is not conclusive, however (see Worthington & Sandage, 2001, for a review). Wade and Worthington (2004) studied 212 clients who were attending counseling at explicitly Christian counseling agencies (although not all professed Christianity) and 52 therapists who label themselves as explicitly Christian counselors. In an effectiveness study of seven agencies across the country, Wade and Worthington found evidence of greater client self-reported improvement in dyads of matched religious values than in unmatched dyads. That study provided the strongest evidence to date of the effectiveness of religious matching. At present, the study is under editorial review, and until it passes rigorous peer review, we are hesitant to claim too much.

Strengths and Limitations

Theoretically, the major strength of the REACH and FREE models is the its commonplace acceptance of forgiveness in general culture. This is particularly (but not exclusively) true in cultures that share a Christian heritage. Historian of religion Martin Marty (1998) has argued that indeed forgiveness is the defining value of Christianity and exceeds that practiced in other religions. A limitation, however, is that not everyone, even among committed Christians or people of other faiths, values forgiveness highly. Thus, clinicians must assess a client's values to make sure that the individual wants to forgive. Forgiveness therapy is also likely to appeal only to therapists who embrace forgiveness.

One individual difference might underlie an attraction or repulsion regarding forgiveness interventions. Worthington, Berry, and Parrott (2001) identified two classes of virtues. Warmth-based virtues include forgiveness, gratitude, compassion, sympathy, and the like. Conscientiousness-based virtues include responsibility, accountability, conscientiousness, duty, honesty, and the like. People differ in their likelihood of endorsing warmth-based or conscientious-based virtues. Berry, Worthington, O'Connor, Parrott, and Wade (in press) showed empirical support for such clusters of virtues. Therapists and clients high in warmth-based virtues are likely to want to pursue forgiveness-oriented solution to relational problems. Therapists and clients high in conscientious-based virtues are likely to want to pursue justice-oriented solutions. Thus, a mismatch might frustrate therapists and make clients feel coerced.

Indirect support for warmth- or conscientiousness-based virtues might come from research on psychotherapy. Malcolm and Greenberg (2000) studied the empty chair technique as a way of resolving unfinished business in psychotherapy. Malcolm and Greenberg reported that many clients complete empty-chair dialogues by resolving to be more autonomous and less concerned about the other person and the relationship. Malcolm (2000) noted, however, that other clients spontaneously experienced forgiveness.

A forgiveness-promoting approach will likely appeal to religious counselors, especially to counselors from the Christian tradition. Jewish counselors seem more disposed toward the conscientiousness-based values and are likely not to employ forgiveness therapy as frequently. Dorff (1998), for example, has argued that in Judaism, forgiveness is usually embedded in a broader concept of return (i.e., repentance). Rye et al. (2000) had practitioners of five major religions summarize the position of their religion on forgiveness. Although all stated that their religion valued forgiveness, the experts (except for the Christian religion) agreed that forgiveness was typically not the primary value advocated by their religion. Empirically, in a series of studies on the use of forgiveness by clinical practitioners, DiBlasio (1992, 1993, DiBlasio & Benda, 1991; DiBlasio & Proctor, 1993) and his colleagues found that Christians used forgiveness most often in their therapy, but Jewish therapists and those who professed no religion also used forgiveness interventions to a substantial degree.

A practical weakness of the approach is that it must either be integrated into psychotherapy or used as an adjunct to psychotherapy, both of which limit time spent promoting forgiveness. Research has shown a strong dose-response relationship (Worthington, Kurusu, et al., 2000). Thus, expectations about the degree of forgiveness experienced subsequent to brief intervention must be modest.

Indications and Contraindications

Enright and Fitzgibbons (2000) hypothesized that forgiveness therapy might theoretically be appropriate for several *DSM–IV* diagnoses. Some obvious problems seem appropriate for forgiveness therapy—anger, depression in which rumination is prominent, interpersonal rejection, anxieties over relationship problems, couple issues, and family disruptions. Unfortunately, there are no empirical data to support such recommendations. Personality disorders seem to have a low likelihood of successful response to forgiveness therapy. This is especially true in disorders in which trait empathy is rare, such as narcissistic and borderline personality disorders.

Culture and Gender Considerations

On the surface, forgiveness seems to be something that girls and women might engage in more than their male counterparts, based on Gilligan's (1982) theorizing about women's relational morality orientation—the ethic of care. However, examining efficacy studies in four laboratories, Worthington, Sandage, and Berry (2000) found no differences in men and women in the degree to which each benefited from psychoeducative forgiveness interventions. Male and female participants volunteered for the interventions at different rates. Experimentally, Fincham and his colleagues (Fincham & Beach, 2002; Fincham, Paleari, & Regalia, 2002) also found no difference between partners in married couples. Anecdotally, Luskin (2003), in a conference talk, tells of how Thoresen and he solicited volunteers for a study of forgiveness. Few men responded to the advertisements until the study was portrayed as a grudge-management study.

African Americans have been found to be more religious as a group than have many other ethnic groups (for example, see Thompson & Vardaman, 1997, in families experiencing a homicide). Thus, African Americans might be particularly amenable to forgiveness interventions. This has not been empirically tested.

Expected Future Developments and Directions

In recent years, research on forgiveness has increased dramatically. Many new investigators have been drawn into the field. Inevitably, many of these investigators will create new forgiveness interventions, and we will thus learn more about how to promote forgiveness as these investigators study their interventions.

In our lab, we have systematically modified our approach to promoting forgiveness as empirical studies revealed information. We will continue to use empirical, clinical, theoretical, and theological developments to improve the intervention.

We anticipate making three major shifts in direction. First, we will lengthen the intervention by 4 hours (to 12 or 13 total hours) by providing (a) a module for helping people use other means of dealing with unforgiveness in addition to forgiveness; (b) more attention to sympathy, compassion, and agape love as positive emotions to replace unforgiveness; (c) more emphasis on decreasing rumination; (d) application to becoming a more forgiving person; and (e) more training in how to talk about transgressions. Second, we are adapting the model for use in new contexts—in other cultures, with parents, and with church populations. Third, we will attempt to publish empirical studies on marriage enrichment and divorce prevention. We have just completed a 6-year longitudinal study in which couples early in their marriages receive forgiveness intervention, hope-focused marriage counseling, or neither. The results are currently being analyzed. In the following section, we report a case taken from that psychoeducational intervention with couples. The second author was the consultant. The assessment of the couple was supervised by the third author. We have conceptualized the case as one example of the FREE psychoeducational intervention to promote forgiveness skills in early-married couples.

CASE EXAMPLE

Client Demographics, Relevant History, and Presenting Concern

"Jenny" and "John" were married for 2 months when they were assessed at VCU's Marriage Assessment, Treatment, and Enrichment Center (MATE Center), which conducts funded and unfunded research studies. Neither had been in counseling previously. They had not lived together before marriage. Jenny was a 23-year-old Caucasian college graduate. She was in her first marriage. Raised as a Roman Catholic, she reported attending church activities "a few times a year" and as being "moderately" committed to religion. She had a high-pressure, high-status job as a financial analyst in state government. Her job was stressful and required long hours.

Jenny's husband, John, was a 39-year-old Caucasian college graduate. This was his second marriage. He had divorced 6 years earlier and had one child, a son, Jake, age 6 years. He identified himself as a Methodist who participated in religious activities "about once a month" and was "very much" committed to his religion. John worked as a mortgage broker but lost his job after the initial assessment. The job loss was stressful for the couple.

John and Jenny responded to a newspaper advertisement to participate in a study to promote marital enrichment among couples who had been married 6 months or less. Thus, they did not present with a "problem." They sought the FREE intervention to enhance their marriage by learning methods for promoting intimacy, including strategies to forgive and reconcile to restore intimacy if problems occur.

Relationship of the Therapist and Client

The therapist was a Caucasian female postdoctoral-level psychologist, who used the secular manual to conduct the intervention. The clients did not ask about the therapist's religion, although other, more highly religious couples who completed this intervention did ask.

The therapeutic bond and working alliance were strong, as reported by the couple in assessments carried out as part of the research. Audiotapes of sessions supported their assessment. Interactions were friendly and pleasant yet professional. Humor was used infrequently and initiated by both husband and wife. The consultant was encouraging and complimented accomplishments of both partners.

Assessment: Rationale and Type of Data Collected

Assessment required about 1.5 hours. Couples completed all measures at our lab. They discussed on videotape a decision they needed to make jointly, which will be coded in the future. Salivary cortisol was collected while imagining and a typical couple interaction and will be analyzed in the future (see Berry & Worthington, 2001). Partners then completed self- and spouse-report measures. Couples were assessed five times over 18 months. Only clinically relevant self-report measures are presented here.

Religious Commitment

Highly religious people are typically more inclined to forgive (McCullough & Worthington, 1999) than are moderately or nonreligious people; thus the couple's degree of religious commitment is relevant. The 10-item Religious Commitment Inventory (RCI-10; Worthington et al., 2003; range 10–50) has a mean score of 26 for community adults (SD = 12; range of possible scores 10–50). At initial assessment, John had an RCI-10 score of 31, and Jenny's score was 19.

Personality

Personality was assessed using the 44-item Big Five Inventory (BFI; Benet-Martinez & John, 1998). Jenny and John both scored "high" on extraversion and "average" on agreeableness. On conscientiousness, John scored "average"; Jenny, "high." On neuroticism, Jenny scored "average"; John, "low."

On openness to experience, Jenny scored "high"; John "average." Agreeableness has been found to correlate positively and neuroticism (interpreted as emotional reactivity) as negatively (Berry & Worthington, 2001; Berry, Worthington, Parrott, O'Connor, & Wade, 2001) with forgivingness.

Trait Forgiveness

Trait forgivingness was measured with both the Transgression Narrative Test of Forgivingness (TNTF; Berry et al., 2001) and the Trait Forgivingness Scale (TFS; Berry et al., 2003). On the initial TNTF, John's score was 19, and the Jenny's was 18 (both average). Both Jenny and John obtained TFS scores of 37 (average).

Self-Rated Stress

Stressful life events have become increasingly recognized as important contextual considerations in the course of marriages (Cohan & Bradbury, 1997). Partners estimated the level of stress they felt during the previous week using a 0 to 100 scale, with anchors of 0 = *completely calm and peaceful* and 100 = *the most stressed out you have ever been in your life*. For 516 newly-wed spouses who participated in initial assessment phase, the mean stress was 47 (SD = 27). At initial assessment, both Jenny and John reported stress levels of 80 (high stress).

Psychological Distress

Psychological distress was evaluated using the Brief Symptom Inventory (BSI; Derogatis, 1993), an abbreviated version of the Symptom Checklist–90, Revised (SCL-90-R; Derogatis & Cleary, 1977). The 53-item BSI yields scores for nine primary symptom dimensions (somatization, obsessive–compulsive, interpersonal sensitivity, depression, anxiety, hostility, phobic anxiety, paranoid ideation, and psychoticism) and the three global indices (Global Severity Index [GSI], Positive Symptom Total, and Positive Symptom Distress Index). Raw scores for the dimensions are converted to normed *t* scores (M = 50; SD = 10). A client is considered as a positive clinical case when his or her GSI T-score or at least two dimensions have *t* scores greater than or equal to 63. At initial assessment, John's GSI score was 53, and Jenny's was 56. John's hostility score was 62, and Jenny's was 53.

Unforgiveness and Forgiveness

Jenny and John disclosed the "most serious hurt or offense for which [they had] been unable to completely forgive [their] spouse." John indicated that he was most upset about his wife's lack of involvement with his son before their marriage. This made him feel "angry and sad," and he perceived the offense as *moderately serious*, a score of 3 on a scale that ranged from *not serious* (1) to *very serious* (5). He rated his current forgiveness of this offense as 2 (on a scale ranging from 0 = *no forgiveness* to 4 = *complete forgiveness*).

Jenny indicated that the most serious hurt for which she had had difficulty forgiving John was "lying to me about financial issues. . . . I had to find out and confront him." She reported that she had immediately felt "extremely angry" when she discovered that he had spent money that they had agreed to use jointly for another purpose. She later felt "distrusting and betrayed." Jenny rated this offense as "serious" (a rating of 4 on the 1 to 5 scale). She rated her forgiveness as 3 (on the 0 to 4 scale).

Marital Satisfaction

Marital satisfaction was assessed using the Dyadic Adjustment Scale (DAS; Spanier, 1976). The DAS consists of 32 items (range from 0 to 151). DAS scores of 97 or below indicate clinically significant relationship distress (Heyman, Feldbau-Kohn, Ehrensaft, Langhinrichesen-Rohling, & O'Leary, 2001). At pretreatment, John's score was 107, and Jenny's was 89.

Empathy for the partner for the target transgression was assessed using eight empathy adjectives (Toi & Batson, 1982). Anger was measured with the Trait Anger Scale (Spielberger, Jacobs, Russell, & Crane, 1983). Unforgiveness was assessed via the Transgression-Related Interpersonal Motivations inventory (TRIM; McCullough et al., 1998). The TRIM consists of subscales of revenge and avoidance (see Table 10.1).

Marital Conflict

Being able to deal productively with marital conflict is important for individual spouse and family mental and physical health (Fincham & Beach, 1999). Marital conflict was assessed using Form A of the Conflict Tactics Scale (CTS; Straus, 1979). The CTS comprises three scores: reasoning, verbal aggression, and (physical) violence. It assesses conflict in terms of behavior (e.g., reasoned discussion, verbal aggression, or physical violence) and frequency of behavior (from *never* to *more than once a month*). The range of scores on the reasoning scale (4 items) is 0 to 20, with higher scores indicating more rational processing of conflict (Jenny 13, John 15). The range for the five items of verbal aggression is 0 to 25, with higher scores indicating more verbal aggression (Jenny 8, John 20). For physical aggression (5 items), the range was 0 to 25, with higher scores indicating more physical violence (Jenny 1, John 3). John's verbal aggression score was considerably higher than Jenny's, and he endorsed a higher frequency ("often, but less than once a month") for the violence item of "pushed, grabbed, or shoved the other." Jenny also endorsed this item, but at a frequency of "once that year." John's higher level of aggression noted in his CTS self-rating is consistent with his elevated hostility score on the BSI.

Perception of Intimacy

Jenny and John also rated their perceptions of their emotional, sexual, and spiritual closeness by marking their actual and desired levels for these

TABLE 10.1
Changes in Forgiveness-Related Variables From 2 Through 16 Months
of Marriage (Intervention Occurred During Month 4)

Construct	Range	Median	Wife		Husband	
			Pre	11-Month Follow-up	Pre	11-Month Follow-up
Empathy with specific hurt	8–48	28	27	22	34	36
Anger over specific hurt	15–60	37	22	15	28	17
Unforgiveness of specific hurt	12–60	36	16	15	18	12
Forgiveness of specific hurt	0–4	2	3	3	2	3
Forgiveness of spouse for most serious hurt	0–4	2	2	4	3	4
Forgiveness of spouse for all hurts	0–4	2	3	3	3	4
Forgiven by spouse for most serious offense	0–4	2	1	2	2	3
Forgiven by spouse for all offenses	0–4	2	2	3	2	4

items on 11-point "closeness thermometers." This pencil-and-paper methodology is similar to the scaling technique used in solution-focused therapy. At initial assessment, Jenny's respective desired and actual scores (scaled from 0 to 10) for emotional, sexual, and spiritual closeness were 9 and 3, 8 and 2, and 7 and 6; John's were 10 and 3, 10 and 5, and 10 and 10. Both partners thus indicated a gap between their desired and actual levels of emotional and sexual closeness. They indicated satisfaction with their spiritual closeness.

Diagnostic and Clinical Case Conceptualization

A formal, *DSM–IV* assessment was not conducted, although over the course of the assessment and intervention, a conceptualization of this couple's relationship style was developed. This couple had several strengths. They had a strong commitment to their marriage and shared interests in fitness and outdoor activities. Their personalities seemed complementary. John was much older, but Jenny often acted more responsibly. This was consistent with her leadership role at work and her high scores on conscientiousness on the BFI. John seemed more spontaneous and impulsive. Jenny seemed to feel comfortable with her power as the more driven and responsible partner, yet she enjoyed John's spontaneity. Perhaps with him, she experienced facets of herself other than responsibility. John also seemed to benefit from these differences: Jenny provided structure to his at times disorganized life.

Under stress, as they often were, however, these personality differences may have led to tension. For example, it was difficult for Jenny to forgive John for using money from their savings to purchase personal items without her knowledge. Although Jenny rated her forgiveness as a 3 on a scale of 0 to 4 (discussed earlier), this was likely decisional, not emotional forgiveness. The issue resurfaced during sessions and still seemed to be a source of tension. Jenny might have particular difficulty forgiving this type of offense emotionally because she has difficulty empathizing with it, as it contrasts with her conscientious nature. Given her career as a financial analyst and because she was responsible for managing the family finances, John's transgression seemed serious. Also, given the centrality of career to Jenny's identity, John's erratic work history appeared especially disconcerting.

Other differences in their personalities may also have contributed to marital distress (and satisfaction) at times. John was low on neuroticism (i.e., emotional reactivity), whereas Jenny was average. Jenny became more upset than John over life stressors, including finances. John and Jenny valued commitment marriage, which seemed to derive from spiritual backgrounds. Even though religion is not explicitly dealt with as part of FREE, both John and Jenny commented about religion throughout the intervention.

Treatment Goals, Process, and Intervention Strategies

The primary goal of this intervention was to teach couples a model of forgiveness and reconciliation that they could apply to their marriage. A secondary goal was to teach couples how to build and enhance emotional and physical intimacy. The therapeutic strategy was (a) to facilitate self-discovery or teach (occasionally) and (b) to have couples apply the principles of forgiving and reconciling to specific incidents in their own lives. Initial applications involved working with incidents experienced by each partner separately while the spouse acted as an empathic support. Only after building forgiveness, empathy, and intimacy-restoration skills did partners discuss couple issues.

Session 1

The overall goal of enhancing intimacy was addressed. Partners reflected on what makes them feel intimate with each other, how they could enhance intimacy, and what could threaten intimacy. Forgiveness was characterized as a tool for maintaining and enhancing the couple's marital intimacy and to prevent relational problems (Gottman, 1994). Whereas knowing how to communicate, avoid arguments, and resolve differences are important, we emphasized repairing hurts, forgiving transgressions quickly, and building intimacy and love. Explanations of what is and is not meant by forgiveness (e.g., forgiving is not equivalent to forgetting or overlooking a transgression) were discussed. Each partner discussed a time when he or she was hurt by someone other than the spouse, whom he or she has subsequently forgiven. Partners discussed forbearance, empathy, and reconciliation. For homework, partners thought of a time when they were hurt by someone other than their spouse and forgave the person who had hurt them. This was used in Session 2.

Session 2

In Session 2, the consultant facilitated discussion with the couple about how best to support each other, particularly during stressful times, and introduced the first three steps of the five-step REACH model of forgiveness. The discussion of support was tied to the larger concept of forgiving by encouraging the couple to support one another by (a) quickly forgiving when hurt by one's partner and (b) helping the partner forgive when one of them has been hurt by someone else. The therapist then introduced the REACH model, and partners applied it to their own experience of a hurt. Partners described their feelings about the incident (R = Recall the hurt), why the person may have hurt them, and how the person might have felt or thought. The goal was to increase their understanding of, and compassion for, the offender (E = Empathy) and for each other as they observed each other deal with past hurts. Altruism (the A-step) was defined as an "unselfish regard for another person." Each partner identified how the offender *needed* forgiveness for having harmed the partner. Each partner identified a time when he or she hurt someone else, wanted forgiveness, and was, indeed, forgiven. The consultant elicited their feelings of gratitude upon being forgiven. For homework, partners wrote an account of a time when they were hurt by their spouse. This example was used in subsequent sessions.

Session 3

The last two steps (C = commit to forgiveness; H = hold on to forgiveness during doubts) were discussed. The consultant had John and Jenny discuss whether they had ever doubted that they had truly forgiven. The consultant described the normality of doubting one's feelings of forgiveness, particularly when under stress or when that person hurt you again. Strategies for reminding oneself that the person has forgiven the offender were presented: writing and displaying a certificate of forgiveness; stating aloud that one has forgiven the offender; talking with a friend or spouse, provided he or she is not the offender, about having forgiven; and writing a letter expressing forgiveness to the offender. The importance maintaining forgiveness (H = Hold on) was discussed. Jenny and John were told that forgiving someone is not the same as forgetting the offense, thus it is normal to recall the pain of the offense when the memory of it is triggered. Feeling pain or anger does not mean that one has not forgiven, however. Jenny and John were encouraged to distract themselves when they found that they were ruminating on past hurts. They used the examples from homework to work through each step using a relational hurt. John and Jenny discussed John's betrayal over money in a consultant-facilitated discussion. Each partner's homework assignment was to recall a disagreement with their partner that had been reconciled.

Session 4

In the final session, the consultant focused on strategies for building intimacy and taught a six-step model of reconciliation (see Worthington & Drinkard, 2000). John and Jenny identified behaviors that made them feel closer to the other. John and Jenny provided their own example of a time when they forgave their partner for an offense and subsequently reconciled. Their example was fit to the six-step "Bridge to Reconciliation": deciding to reconcile, creating an atmosphere of softness, forgiving, reversing the negative cascade, dealing with violations of trust, and building love. Most of the work concerned creating a "soft" rather than a "hard" atmosphere and training in how to make a gentle reproach, give a graceful account of their part in the misunderstanding, and decide whether to forgive. Active listening was trained. Jenny and John pledged to demonstrate love over the next month and provide specific examples of how they intended to do so. They discussed the intervention and what they learned from it with the consultant.

Course of Treatment and Frequency and Duration of Sessions

The assessment session was held first. Jenny and John participated in four weekly 2-hour sessions with the consultant. They were followed up for assessment four times. Only the final assessment (11 months after ending the consultation) is reported.

Termination and Relapse Prevention

Termination occurred after four sessions. Because this model is applied early in marriage and because there is a well-documented linear decrease in martial satisfaction over time, relapse prevention (or, more accurately, future problem prevention) was a primary focus throughout all sessions. *Successful* intervention early in marriage might be expected to yield maintenance of initial levels of relational adjustment, conflict severity, and general forgiveness of the spouse. Success would also include prevention of worsening of significant past hurts, such as the target transgressions identified at the outset of the intervention and reevaluated at 11 months postintervention.

Therapeutic Outcomes: Immediate and Long Term

The intervention was considered to be mostly successful (see Table 10.1). At 11 months postintervention, John and Jenny were still together.

Neither spouse's DAS score was in the distressed range. Most ratings of the target transgression were better. The wife's DAS score increased from 89 (a level indicating distress) at the initial assessment to 101 (nondistressed). The husband's DAS score increased from 107 to 112. Changes in forgiveness-relevant variables are given in Table 10.1. Anger and unforgiveness for the target transgression decreased, and forgiveness either increased (John) or stayed the same (Jenny). Forgiving and feeling forgiven increased. Jenny decreased her empathy for John's specific betrayal on the target transgression.

Generally, Jenny did not seem to benefit quite as much as did John from the intervention. There are a number of possible explanations for their difference in responsiveness to the intervention. (a) John was the primary transgressor. This is supported by his higher CTS scores, indicating that he was more verbally and physically aggressive than was Jenny. Thus, John may have repeatedly transgressed, making it difficult for Jenny to forgive completely. (b) Jenny's higher conscientiousness might have made her less able to forgive John than he was able to forgive her. Her conscientiousness may imply a "justice perspective," leading to reduced empathy and forgiving John's transgressions. (c) Jenny's empathy decreased over time. Empathy has been demonstrated to be an important mediator in the forgiveness process (McCullough et al., 1998). Theory suggests that there are additional paths that can lead to forgiveness (Worthington, 2001b): love, affection, sympathy, commitment, and compassion.

Unexpectedly, the couple's spiritual closeness decreased, with the wife's dropping from 6 to 2 and the husband's dropping from 10 to 7. The wife's final stress t score rating was 89, and the husband's was 70, both still quite high. The couple's CTS scores remained similar to what they were at the outset.

Some final, nonquantitative remarks are in order. Several months after the intervention was completed, John contacted the consultant for a referral for anger management. Although it is unknown whether John followed through on this referral, John's contact of the therapist indicated therapeutic benefit (Schumm, Silliman, & Bell, 2000). This might suggest that early-marriage intervention could direct couples to therapy if problems in later marriage became salient.

We discussed a forgiveness intervention, which is appropriate as part of or as an adjunct to couple counseling. In our case study, an early-married couple that had high stress and one partner with a clinically significant DAS score participated in a manual-directed intervention. They completed their critical first year of marriage somewhat improved, whereas the normative first-year response to marriage often results in lower satisfaction and sometimes marital dissolution. Training in forgiveness is a promising but not empirically supported intervention with interpersonal issues.

CONCLUSION

Forgiveness and reconciliation are important for preventing the buildup of problems, which can lead to marital dissolution. By training couples early in their marriages to in ways to forgive and reconcile, we have found that skills in conflict resolution, communication, and the pursuit of intimacy can be strengthened. Couples not only can head off hurt, but can also deal with the transgressions that almost inevitably occur. Our structured psychoeducational intervention with individual couples can be modified to use in marital therapy contexts and even with groups of couples. For couples who value forgiveness and especially those who do so because of their religious beliefs and values, this intervention is a strong adjunct to other treatment and to other efforts to forge a good marriage.

REFERENCES

Benet-Martinez, V., & John, O. P. (1998). Los cinco grandes across cultures and ethnic groups: Multitrait multimethod analyses of the Big Five in Spanish and English. *Journal of Personality and Social Psychology, 75*, 729–750.

Berry, J., & Worthington, E. L., Jr. (2001). Forgiveness, relationship quality, stress while imagining relationship events, and physical and mental health. *Journal of Counseling Psychology, 48*, 447–455.

Berry, J. W., Worthington, E. L., Jr., O'Connor, L. E., Parrott, L., III, & Wade, N. G. (in press). The measurement of trait forgivingness. *Journal of Personality.*

Berry, J. W., Worthington, E. L., Jr., Parrott, L., III, O'Connor, L., & Wade, N. G. (2001). Dispositional forgivingness: Development and construct validity of the Transgression Narrative Test of Forgivingness (TNTF). *Personality and Social Psychology Bulletin, 27*, 1277–1290.

Burchard, G. A., Yarhouse, M. A., Worthington, E. L., Jr., Berry, J. W., Killian, M., & Canter, D. E. (2003). A study of two marital enrichment programs and couples' quality of life. *Journal of Psychology and Theology, 31*, 240–252.

Cohan, C. L., & Bradbury, T. N. (1997). Negative life events, marital interaction, and the longitudinal course of newlywed marriage. *Journal of Personality and Social Psychology, 73*, 114–128.

Derogatis, L. R. (1993). *Brief Symptom Inventory (BSI): Administration, scoring, and procedures manual* (4th ed.). Minneapolis, MN: National Computer Systems.

Derogatis, L. R., & Cleary, P. A. (1977). Confirmation of the dimensional structure of the SCL-90-R: A study in construct validation. *Journal of Clinical Psychology, 33*, 981–989.

DiBlasio, F. A. (1992). Forgiveness in psychotherapy: Comparison of older and younger therapists. *Journal of Psychology and Christianity, 11*, 181–187.

DiBlasio, F. A. (1993). The role of social workers' religious beliefs in helping family members forgive. *Journal of Contemporary Human Services, 74,* 163–170.

DiBlasio, F. A. (1998). The use of decision-based forgiveness intervention within intergenerational family therapy. *Journal of Family Therapy, 20,* 77–94.

DiBlasio, F. A., & Benda, B. B. (1991). Practitioners, religion and the clinical use of forgiveness. *Journal of Psychology and Christianity, 10,* 168–172.

DiBlasio, F. A., & Proctor, J. H. (1993). Therapists and the clinical use of forgiveness. *American Journal of Family Therapy, 21,* 175–184.

Dorff, E. N. (1998). The elements of forgiveness: A Jewish approach. In E. L. Worthington Jr. (Ed.), *Dimensions of forgiveness: Psychological research and theological perspectives* (pp. 29–55). Philadelphia: Templeton Foundation Press.

Enright, R. D. (1998). Comprehensive bibliography on interpersonal forgiveness. In R. D. Enright & J. North (Eds.), *Exploring forgiveness.* Madison: University of Wisconsin Press.

Enright, R. D., & Fitzgibbons, R. P. (2000). *Helping clients forgive: An empirical guide for resolving anger and restoring hope.* Washington, DC: American Psychological Association.

Enright, R. D., & the Human Development Study Group. (1994). Piaget on the moral development of forgiveness: Identity or reciprocity? *Human Development, 37,* 63–80.

Exline, J. J., Worthington, E. L., Jr., Hill, P. C., & McCullough, M. E. (2003). Forgiveness and justice: A research agenda for social and personality psychology. *Personality and Social Psychology Review, 7,* 337–348.

Fincham, F. D., & Beach, S. R. H. (1999). Conflict in marriage: Implications for working with couples. *Annual Review of Psychology, 50,* 47–77.

Fincham, F. D., & Beach, S. R. H. (2002). Forgiveness in marriages: Implications for psychological aggression and constructive communication. *Personal Relationships, 9,* 239–251.

Fincham, F. D., Paleari, F. G., & Regalia, C. (2002). Forgiveness in marriage: The role of relationship quality, attributions, and empathy. *Personal Relationships, 9,* 27–37.

Fitzgibbons, R. P. (1986). The cognitive and emotive uses of forgiveness in the treatment of anger. *Psychotherapy, 23,* 629–633.

Gilligan, C. (1982). *In a different voice: Psychological theory and women's development.* Cambridge, MA: Harvard University Press.

Gottman, J. M. (1994). *What predicts divorce? The relationship between marital processes and marital outcomes.* Hillsdale, NJ: Erlbaum.

Hart, K. E., & Shapiro, D. A. (2002, August). *Secular and spiritual forgiveness interventions for recovering alcoholics harboring grudges.* Paper presented at the annual convention of the American Psychological Association, Chicago.

Hebl, J., & Enright, R. D. (1993). Forgiveness as a psychotherapeutic goal with elderly females. *Psychotherapy, 30,* 658–667.

Heyman, R. E., Feldbau-Kohn, S. R., Ehrensaft, M. K., Langhinrichsen-Rohling, J., & O'Leary, K. D. (2001). Can questionnaire reports correctly classify relationship distress and partner physical abuse? *Journal of Family Psychology, 15*, 334–346.

Jacobson, N. S., & Christensen, A. (1996). *Integrative couple therapy. Promoting acceptance and change*. New York: Norton.

Luskin, F. (2003, October). *Stanford forgiveness projects: Teaching forgiveness*. Talk presented at the Helping People Forgive conference, Atlanta, GA.

Malcolm, W. M. (2000). Relating process to outcome in the resolution of unfinished business in process experiential psychotherapy. *Dissertation Abstracts International, 60*, 4235.

Malcolm, W. M., & Greenberg, L. S. (2000). Forgiveness as a process of change in individual psychotherapy. In M. E. McCullough, K. I. Pargament, & C. E. Thoresen (Eds.), *Forgiveness: Theory, research, and practice* (pp. 179–202). New York: Guildford Press.

Marty, M. E. (1998). The ethos of Christian forgiveness. In E. L. Worthington Jr. (Ed.), *Dimensions of forgiveness: Psychological research and theological perspectives* (pp. 9–28). Philadelphia: Templeton Foundation Press.

McCullough, M. E., Rachal, K. C., Sandage, S. J., Worthington, E. L., Jr., Brown, S. W., & Hight, T. L. (1998). Interpersonal forgiveness in close relationships II: Theoretical elaboration and measurement. *Journal of Personality and Social Psychology, 75*, 1586–1603.

McCullough, M. E., Sandage, S. J., & Worthington, E. L., Jr. (1997). *To forgive is human: How to put your past in the past*. Downers Grove, IL: InterVarsity Press.

McCullough, M. E., & Worthington, E. L., Jr. (1994). Encouraging clients to forgive people who have hurt them: Review, critique, and research prospectus. *Journal of Psychology and Theology, 22*, 3–20.

McCullough, M. E., & Worthington, E. L., Jr. (1995). Promoting forgiveness: A comparison of two psychoeducational group interventions with a waiting-list control. *Counseling and Values, 40*, 55–68.

McCullough, M. E., & Worthington, E. L., Jr. (1999). Religion and the forgiving personality. *Journal of Personality, 67*, 1141–1164.

McCullough, M. E., Worthington, E. L., Jr., & Rachal, K. C. (1997). Interpersonal forgiving in close relationships. *Journal of Personality and Social Psychology, 73*, 321–336.

Murphy, J. G., & Hampton, J. (1988). *Forgiveness and mercy*. Cambridge, England: Cambridge University Press.

Pargament, K. I. (2002). The bitter and the sweat: An evaluation of the costs and benefits of religiousness. *Psychological Inquiry, 13*, 168–188.

Ripley, J. S., & Worthington, E. L., Jr. (2002). Hope-focused and forgiveness-based group interventions to promote marital enrichment. *Journal of Counseling and Development, 80*, 452–463.

Ripley, J. S., Worthington, E. L., Jr., Berry, J. W., Wade, N. G., Gramling, G. S., Canter, D. E., et al. (2003). *Religious commitment and beliefs about big five personality factors as predictors of trait and state forgiving*. Manuscript submitted for publication.

Rye, M. S., & Pargament, K. I. (2002). Evaluation of a secular and religiously integrated forgiveness group therapy program for college students who have been wronged by a romantic partner. *Journal of Clinical Psychology, 58*, 419–441.

Rye, M. S., Pargament, K. I., Ali, M. A., Beck, G. L., Dorff, E. N., Hallisey, C., et al. (2000). Religious perspectives on forgiveness. In M. E. McCullough, K. I. Pargament, & C. E. Thoresen (Eds.), *Forgiveness: Theory, research, and practice* (pp. 17–40). New York: Guilford Press.

Sandage, S. J. (1997). *An ego-humility model of forgiveness: A theory-driven empirical test of group interventions.* Unpublished doctoral dissertation, Virginia Commonwealth University, Richmond.

Schumm, W. R., Silliman, B., & Bell, D. B. (2000). Perceived premarital counseling outcomes among recently married Army personnel. *Journal of Sex & Marital Therapy, 26*, 177–186.

Smedes, L. B. (1984). *Forgive and forget: Healing the hurts we don't deserve.* New York: Harper & Row.

Spanier, G. B. (1976). Measuring dyadic adjustment: New scales for assessing the quality of marriage and similar dyads. *Journal of Marriage and the Family, 38*, 15–28.

Spielberger, C. D., Jacobs, G., Russell, S., & Crane, R. S. (1983). Assessment of anger: The State–Trait Anger Scale. In J. N. Butcher & C. D. Spielberger (Eds.), *Advances in personality assessment* (Vol. 2, pp. 161–189). Hillsdale, NJ: Erlbaum.

Straus, M. A. (1979). Measuring intrafamily conflict and violence: The Conflict Tactics (CT) Scales. *Journal of Marriage and the Family, 41*, 75–88.

Thompson, M. P., & Vardaman, P. J. (1997). The role of religion in coping with loss of a family member in homicide. *Journal for the Scientific Study of Religion, 36*, 44–51.

Toi, M., & Batson, C. D. (1982). More evidence that empathy is a source of altruistic motivation. *Journal of Personality and Social Psychology, 43*, 281–292.

Wade, N. G., & Worthington, E. L., Jr. (2003). Overcoming interpersonal offenses: Is forgiveness the only way to deal with unforgiveness? *Journal of Counseling and Development, 81*, 343–353.

Wade, N. G., & Worthington, E. L., Jr. (2004). *Religions and spiritual interventions in therapy: An effectiveness study of Christian counseling.* Unpublished manuscript.

Worthington, E. L., Jr. (1999). *Hope-focused marriage counseling.* Downers Grove, IL: InterVarsity Press.

Worthington, E. L., Jr. (2001a). *Five steps to forgiveness: The art and science of forgiving.* New York: Crown.

Worthington, E. L., Jr. (2001b). Unforgiveness, forgiveness, and reconciliation in societies. In R. G. Helmick & R. L. Petersen (Eds.), *Forgiveness and reconciliation: Religion, public policy, and conflict transformation* (pp. 161–182). Philadelphia: Templeton Foundation Press.

Worthington, E. L., Jr. (2003). *Forgiving and reconciling.* Downers Grove, IL: InterVarsity Press.

Worthington, E. L., Jr., Berry, J. W., & Parrott, L., III. (2001). Unforgiveness, forgiveness, religion, and health. In T. G. Plante & A. Sherman (Eds.), *Faith and health: Psychological perspectives* (pp. 107–138). New York: Guilford Press.

Worthington, E. L., Jr., & DiBlasio, F. A. (1990). Promoting mutual forgiveness within the fractured relationship. *Psychotherapy, 27*, 219–223.

Worthington, E. L., Jr., & Drinkard, D. T. (2000). Promoting reconciliation through psychoeducational and therapeutic interventions. *Journal of Marital and Family Therapy, 26*, 93–101.

Worthington, E. L., Jr., Hight, T. L., Ripley, J. S., Perrone, K. M., Kurusu, T. A., & Jones, D. R. (1997). Strategic hope-focused relationship-enrichment counseling with individual couples. *Journal of Counseling Psychology, 44*, 381–389.

Worthington, E. L., Jr., Kurusu, T. A., Collins, W. B., Berry, J. W., Ripley, J. S., & Baier, S. N. (2000). Forgiving usually takes time: A lesson learned by studying interventions to promote forgiveness. *Journal of Psychology and Theology, 28*, 3–20.

Worthington, E. L., Jr., & Sandage, S. J. (2001). Religion and spirituality. *Psychotherapy, 38*, 473–478.

Worthington, E. L., Jr., Sandage, S. J., & Berry, J. W. (2000). Group interventions to promote forgiveness: What researchers and clinicians ought to know. In M. E. McCullough, K. I. Pargament, & C. E. Thoresen (Eds.), *Forgiveness: Theory, research and practice* (pp. 228–253). New York: Guilford Press.

Worthington, E. L., Jr., & Wade, N. G. (1999). The social psychology of unforgiveness and forgiveness and implications for clinical practice. *Journal of Social and Clinical Psychology, 18*, 385–418.

Worthington, E. L., Jr., Wade, N. G., Hight, T. L., Ripley, J. S., McCullough, M. E., Berry, J. W., et al. (2003). The Religious Commitment Inventory–10: Development, refinement, and validation of a brief scale for research and counseling. *Journal of Counseling Psychology, 50*, 84–96.

11

THEISTIC INTEGRATIVE PSYCHOTHERAPY

P. SCOTT RICHARDS

The approach to psychotherapy described in this chapter was first described in the book A *Spiritual Strategy for Counseling and Psychotherapy* (Richards & Bergin, 1997). There Allen Bergin and I described a comprehensive psychotherapy strategy that includes a theistic conceptual framework, a body of spiritual therapeutic interventions, and process and ethical guidelines for implementing theistic perspectives and interventions in an effective and appropriate manner. We have decided to call this general psychotherapy strategy or orientation *theistic psychotherapy* (Richards & Bergin, in press).

Figure 11.1 illustrates that our conceptual framework for theistic psychotherapy includes (a) theological premises that are grounded in the theistic worldview, (b) philosophical assumptions that are consistent with the theistic worldview, (c) a theistic personality theory, and (d) a theistic view of psychotherapy. These conceptual foundations provide a rationale concerning why spiritual interventions are needed in psychotherapy, what types of spiritual interventions may be useful, and when such interventions might appropriately be implemented.

A theistic psychotherapy strategy does not, however, tell psychotherapists specifically *how* to implement spiritual interventions in treatment, nor

```
┌─────────────────────────────────────────┐
│         THEISTIC PSYCHOTHERAPY           │
│              APPROACHES                  │
│         THEISTIC INTEGRATIVE             │
│          Theistic–Psychodynamic          │
│           Theistic–Humanistic            │
│            Theistic–Cognitive            │
│          Theistic–Family Systems         │
│          Theistic–Interpersonal          │
└─────────────────────────────────────────┘
```

```
┌─────────────────────────────────────────┐
│            THEISTIC VIEW OF              │
│             PSYCHOTHERAPY                │
│       Ecumenical and Denominational      │
│             Spiritual Goals              │
│           Spiritual Assessment           │
│     Spiritual Practices and Techniques   │
│            Therapeutic Valuing           │
│         Meta-Empathy, Inspiration        │
└─────────────────────────────────────────┘
```

```
┌─────────────────────────────────────────┐
│       THEISTIC PERSONALITY THEORY        │
│   Eternal Spiritual Identity, Spirit of Truth │
│        Agency, Moral Responsibility       │
│     Inspired Integrity, Faithful Intimacy │
│            Benevolent Power              │
│        Marriage, Family and Community     │
└─────────────────────────────────────────┘
```

```
┌─────────────────────────────────────────┐
│    THEISTIC PHILOSOPHICAL FOUNDATIONS    │
│            Scientific Theism             │
│         Moral Absolutes, Agency          │
│       Altruism, Theistic Relationism     │
│      Spiritual Holism, Contextuality     │
└─────────────────────────────────────────┘
```

```
┌─────────────────────────────────────────┐
│     THEISTIC WORLDVIEW OR THEOLOGY       │
│               God exists                 │
│        Humans are creations of God       │
│      Spiritual Communication with God    │
│              Good and Evil               │
│             Life after Death             │
└─────────────────────────────────────────┘
```

Figure 11.1. Theological, philosophical, theoretical, and applied foundations of theistic psychotherapy. Adapted from *A Spiritual Strategy for Counseling and Psychotherapy* (2nd ed.), by P. S. Richards and A. E. Bergin, in press, Washington, DC: American Psychological Association.

does it tell them how to integrate such interventions with mainstream secular perspectives and interventions. Hence, as implied in Figure 11.1, we recognize that our theistic psychotherapy framework and orientation can be applied in practice in numerous ways, as was made clear in our recent *Casebook for a Spiritual Strategy in Counseling and Psychotherapy* (Richards & Bergin, 2004).

In addition to the broad theistic conceptual framework proposed in *A Spiritual Strategy for Counseling and Psychotherapy* (Richards & Bergin, 1997, in press), we also described our own specific theistic approach to psychotherapy, an approach we have decided to call *theistic integrative psychotherapy* to differentiate it from theistic–psychodynamic (e.g., Shafranske, chap. 5), theistic–rational emotive behavior therapy (e.g., Nielsen, 2004), theistic–interpersonal (e.g., Miller, 2004), and other theistic approaches. Our theistic approach is integrative in that we advocate that spiritual interventions should be combined in a treatment-tailoring fashion with a variety of standard mainstream techniques, including psychodynamic, behavioral, humanistic, cognitive, and systemic methods. We do not believe that a theistic approach supercedes the need for such interventions or for medication or hospitalization when necessary. Rather, it should complement these enduring therapeutic traditions and uniquely enrich understanding of human personality and therapeutic change (Bergin, 1988, 1991).

Our theistic integrative psychotherapy approach is also empirical in that it is grounded in current research about psychotherapy and spirituality and will continue to submit its claims to empirical scrutiny. Our approach is also ecumenical and broadly stated so as to make it suitable for therapists and clients from a variety of theistic religious traditions, including many branches within Judaism, Islam, and Christianity. Finally, our approach is denominational in that it leaves room for psychotherapists to tailor it to the fine nuances of specific theistic religious denominations (Richards & Bergin, 1997).

DESCRIPTION OF THE APPROACH

Historical and Theoretical Bases

Although theistic integrative psychotherapy is a relatively new approach, its roots have a long and complex history. The theistic world religions, particularly Judaism, Christianity, and Islam, have significantly influenced Western civilization and intellectual thought during the past few millennia (Hearnshaw, 1987). In contrast, the rise of modern-day psychology and psychiatry occurred during the late 19th and early 20th centuries, a time when modern science was challenging religious authority as the dominant source of truth (Barbour, 1990; Hearnshaw, 1987). To establish psychology and psychiatry as respected sciences, early founders of the behavioral sciences sought to disassociate their theories and clinical work from religious tradition. As a result, naturalistic–atheistic perspectives of personality theory and therapeutic change dominated mainstream psychology and psychotherapy for most of the 20th century (Bergin, 1980; Leahey, 1991).

Despite the longstanding alienation of religious perspectives from the mainstream behavioral sciences, there has been an equally long history of efforts to integrate religion and psychology. It is beyond the scope of this chapter to describe these efforts in detail, but Vande Kemp (1996) has done so. Suffice it to say here that during the 19th and 20th centuries, many articles and books about religion and psychology were written, professional societies dedicated to the integration of religion and psychology were formed, professional journals focusing on religion and psychology were established, and religious hospitals and clinics were opened (Vande Kempe, 1996). Despite all of this, due to the antireligious zeitgeist or "spirit of the times" that prevailed in the behavioral sciences for much of the 20th century, religious perspectives did not gain acceptance or have much influence in mainstream psychological theory or practice (Bergin, 1980). This began to change during the 1980s and 1990s, however, as worldwide cultural and intellectual trends led to the development of a more spiritually open zeitgeist in the mainstream natural and behavioral sciences. Many scholars and practitioners are now contributing to an international, interdisciplinary, ecumenical effort to incorporate theistic spiritual perspectives into mainstream theory, research and practice (Bergin, 1980; Richards & Bergin, 1997, 2000).

Theoretical Basis of Theistic Integrative Psychotherapy

The foundational assumptions of our theistic integrative psychotherapy approach "are that God exists, that human beings are the creations of God, and that there are unseen spiritual processes by which the link between God and humanity is maintained" (Bergin, 1980, p. 99). We also assume that people who have faith in God's power and draw on the spiritual resources in their lives during treatment will have added strength to cope, heal, and grow.

We have grounded our therapeutic approach in the theistic worldview for several reasons. First, we believe in God and in spiritual realities. We think that the naturalistic-atheistic worldview on which all of the traditional mainstream psychotherapy traditions were grounded does not adequately account for the complexities and mysteries of life and of the universe. We agree with many other scholars who have argued that spiritual perspectives are needed to enrich scientific understandings of human beings, of the origins and operations of the universe, and of health and human welfare (Barbour, 1990; Griffin, 2000; Jones, 1994). Although we do not endorse all of the teachings and practices advocated by the theistic world religions, there is much therapeutic potential in these traditions.

Second, we think the theistic worldview provides a more adequate foundation on which to construct theories of human nature, personality, and therapeutic change. A number of scholars have suggested that the secular or naturalistic–atheistic worldview is philosophically and empirically problematic (Bergin, 1980; Griffin, 2000; Slife, 2004; Slife, Hope, & Nebeker, 1999). For example, Griffin (2000) argued that the naturalistic–atheistic worldview not only provides an impoverished view of human nature, but that it is inconsistent with the empirical evidence and with beliefs that are "inevitably presupposed in practice" by both laypersons and scientists (p. 99). We agree with these criticisms of the naturalistic–atheistic worldview.

Third, we prefer the theistic worldview because the majority of people in North America believe in it and derive their values from it. Bergin (1980) argued that mainstream psychological theories and treatment approaches based on naturalistic assumptions "are not sufficient to cover the spectrum of values pertinent to human beings and the frameworks within which they function. Noticeably absent are theistically based values" (p. 98). He further wrote, "Other alternatives are thus needed. . . . The alternative I wish to put forward is a spiritual one. . . . this alternative is necessary for ethical and effective help among religious people" (p. 99). We think that the theistic worldview provides a more culturally and spiritually sensitive conceptual and value framework on which to ground therapeutic approaches and interventions.

Theological and Philosophical Foundations

There are five theistic religions in the world: Judaism, Christianity, Islam, Sihkism, and Zoroastrianism (Smart, 1994). Approximately 60% of the world's population profess adherence to one of these religions (Barrett & Johnson, 2002). Although there is great diversity between and within these five world religions in terms of specific religious beliefs and practices, at a more general level they share a common global worldview. According to the theistic worldview, God exists, human beings are the creations of God, there is a divine purpose to life, human beings can communicate with God through prayer and other spiritual practices, God has revealed moral truths to guide human behavior, and the human spirit or soul continues to exist after mortal death (Richards & Bergin, 1997).

Our theistic integrative psychotherapy approach is also grounded in a number of philosophical assumptions about human nature, ethics, and epistemology that can be harmonized with the theistic worldview. These include the philosophies of *agency, contexuality, theistic holism, theistic relationism, moral objectivism, altruism,* and *scientific theism* (Richards & Bergin, 1997, 2004). These philosophical perspectives are gaining support among contemporary scientists and philosophers of science (e.g., Griffin, 2000; Jones, 1994; Slife, 2004; Slife et al., 1999) and provide a positive and defensible philosophical foundation for our theistic integrative psychotherapy approach.

Theistic View of Personality

We believe that human development and personality is influenced by a variety of systems and processes (e.g., biological, cognitive, social, psychological), but the core essence of identity and personality is spiritual. Consistent with the teachings of most of the theistic world religions, we have theorized that human beings are composed of both a mortal body and an eternal spirit or soul that continues to exist beyond the death of the mortal body. This eternal spirit is of divine creation and worth and constitutes the lasting or eternal identity of the individual. The spirit "interacts with other aspects of the person to produce what is normally referred to as personality and behavior" (Richards & Bergin, 1997, p. 98). Although such a perspective may raise concerns in the minds of some about the problem of mind–body dualism, it is not philosophically irresolvable (e.g., Griffin, 2000). There is also a growing body of empirical evidence consistent with this view (Richards & Bergin, in press).

According to our theistic view of personality development, people who believe in their eternal spiritual identity, follow the influence of God's spirit, and live in harmony with universal moral principles are more likely to develop in a healthy manner socially and psychologically (Richards & Bergin, 1997). Spiritually mature people have the capacity to enjoy loving and affirming relationships with others, have a clear sense of identity and values, and their external behavior is in harmony with their value system (Bergin, 1980). They also feel a sense of closeness and harmony with God and experience a sense of strength, meaning, and fulfillment from their spiritual beliefs. People who neglect their spiritual growth and well-being or who consistently choose to ignore the influence of God's spirit and do evil may be more likely to suffer emotional disturbance and conflicted, unfulfilling interpersonal relationships. Of course, theistic psychotherapists do not act in a blaming, condemning, or judgmental manner toward their clients, regardless of their clients' values, lifestyles, or personal views about spirituality.

Therapeutic change and healing can be facilitated through a variety of means, including physiological, psychological, social, educational, and spiritual interventions. Complete healing and change requires a spiritual process, however. Therapeutic change is facilitated, and is often more profound and lasting, when people heal and grow spiritually through God's inspiration and love. This may occur in a variety of ways, but it often involves an affirmation of clients' sense of spiritual identity. When clients experience a deep affirmation of their eternal, spiritual identity and worth during prayer or other spiritual experiences, it is often a life-transforming event for them. Such experiences help heal clients' sense of shame or feelings of badness and often reorient their values from a secular or materialistic value system to a more spiritually oriented one. These inner changes in self-perceptions and values often lead to outer changes in their lifestyle, which leads to healthier behaviors and reductions in psychological and physical symptoms and problems. Thus, identity affirming spiritual experiences can set people on a path that is conducive to physical and mental health (Richards & Bergin, 1997; Richards, 1999).

Theistic View of Psychotherapy

Table 11.1 summarizes some of the distinctive features of our theistic view of psychotherapy. The sacred writings of all of the major theistic religious traditions affirm God's power to inspire, comfort, and heal. Our orientation assumes that clients who have faith in God's healing power and draw on the spiritual resources in their lives during psychological treatment will receive added strength and power to cope, heal, and grow (Richards & Bergin, 1997). Theistic integrative psychotherapists, therefore, may encourage their clients to explore how their faith in God and personal spirituality may assist them during treatment and recovery.

Another distinctive feature of our viewpoint is that we believe that a theistic moral framework for psychotherapy is possible and desirable. By a moral framework, we mean that there are general moral values and principles that influence healthy human development and functioning and that can be used to guide and evaluate psychotherapy (Bergin, 1980, 1991). Although there is great diversity between and within the theistic religious traditions regarding their beliefs and practices, they agree that human beings can and should transcend hedonistic and selfish tendencies in order to grow spiritually and to promote the welfare of others. There is also general agreement that values and principles such as integrity, honesty, forgiveness, repentance, humility, love, spirituality, religious devoutness, marital commitment, sexual fidelity, family loyalty and kinship, benevolent use of power, and respect for human agency promote spiritual enlightenment and personal and social harmony (Bergin, 1991; Richards & Bergin, 1997).

There is substantial overlap of these theistically based values with health values endorsed by most mental health professionals, ethicists, and moral philosophers (Bergin, 1991). Such values provide theistic integrative psychotherapists with a general framework for evaluating whether their clients' lifestyles are healthy and mature and for deciding which therapeutic goals to endorse. Although therapists must permit clients to make their own choices about what they value and how they will apply these values in their lives, we think it would be irresponsible for therapists not to share what wisdom they can about values when it is relevant to their clients' problems (Bergin, 1991; Richards et al., 1999). This must be done in a tolerant and respectful manner, however, and therapists need to make sure that clients understand they have the right to disagree with the values of their therapist. In other words, we think it can be appropriate for therapists to share values respectfully, but it is not okay for therapists to impose values (Bergin, 1991; Richards, Rector, &Tjeltveit, 1999).

TABLE 11.1
Distinctive Features of Theistic Integrative Psychotherapy

Goals of therapy	Therapist's role in therapy	Role of spiritual techniques	Clients' role in therapy	Nature of the therapy relationship
Spiritual view is part of an eclectic, multisystemic view of humans, and so therapy goals depend on the client's issues. Goals directly relevant to the spiritual dimension include the following: (a) Help clients affirm their eternal spiritual identity and live in harmony with the Spirit of Truth; (b) assess what impact religious and spiritual beliefs have in clients' lives and whether they have unmet spiritual needs; (c) help clients use religious and spiritual resources to help them in their efforts to cope, change, and grow; (d) help clients resolve spiritual concerns and doubts and make choices about role of spirituality in their lives; and (e) help clients examine their spirituality and continue their quest for spiritual growth.	Adopt an ecumenical therapeutic stance and, when appropriate, a denominational stance. Establish a warm, supportive environment in which the client knows it is safe and acceptable to explore his or her religious and spiritual beliefs, doubts, and concerns. Assess whether clients' religious and spiritual beliefs and activities are affecting their mental health and interpersonal relationships. Implement religious and spiritual interventions to help clients more effectively use their religious and spiritual resources in their coping and growth process. Model and endorse healthy spiritual values. Seek spiritual guidance and enlightenment on how best to help clients.	Interventions are viewed as important for helping clients gain more faith in their spiritual identity and worth, understand and work through their religious and spiritual concerns, and draw on the religious and spiritual resources in their lives to assist them in coping, healing, and changing. Examples of major interventions include cognitive restructuring of irrational religious beliefs, transitional figure technique, forgiveness, meditation and prayer, scripture study, blessings, participating in religious services, spiritual imagery, journaling about spiritual feelings, repentance, and using the client's religious support system.	Clients examine how their religious and spiritual beliefs and activities affect their behavior, emotions, and relationships. Make choices about what role religion and spirituality will play in their lives. Set goals and carry out spiritual interventions designed to facilitate their spiritual and emotional growth. Seek to use the religious and spiritual resources in their lives to assist them in their efforts to heal and change. Seek God's guidance and enlightenment about how to better cope, heal, and change.	Unconditional positive regard, warmth, genuineness, and empathy are regarded as an essential foundation for therapy. Therapists also seek to have charity or brotherly and sisterly love for clients and to affirm their eternal spiritual identity and worth. Clients are expected to form a working alliance and share in the work of change. Clients must trust the therapist and believe that it is safe to share their religious and spiritual beliefs and heritage with the therapist. Clients must know that the therapist highly values and respects their autonomy and freedom of choice and that it is safe for them to differ from the therapist in their beliefs and values, even though the therapist may at times disagree with their values and confront them about unhealthy values and lifestyle choices.

Note. Adapted from *A Spiritual Strategy for Counseling and Psychotherapy* (pp. 140–141), by P. S. Richards and A. E. Bergin, 1997, Washington, DC: American Psychological Association. Copyright 1997 by the American Psychological Association.

A third contribution of our theistic viewpoint is that it provides a body of spiritual interventions that psychotherapists can use to intervene in the spiritual dimension of their clients' lives. Spiritual interventions that may be used by theistic integrative psychotherapists include praying for clients, encouraging clients to pray, discussing theological concepts, making reference to scriptures, using spiritual relaxation and imagery techniques, encouraging repentance and forgiveness, helping clients live congruently with their spiritual values, self-disclosing spiritual beliefs or experiences, consulting with religious leaders, and recommending religious bibliotherapy (Richards & Bergin, 1997). Most of these spiritual interventions are actually practices in which religious believers have engaged for centuries. They have endured because they express and respond to the deepest needs, concerns, and problems of human beings (Benson, 1996; Miller, 1999; Richards & Bergin, 1997, 2000).

A fourth element of our viewpoint is that both therapists and clients may seek, and on occasion obtain, spiritual enlightenment to assist in treatment and recovery (Chamberlain, Richards, & Scharman, 1996; Richards & Bergin, 1997). By entering into meditative or prayerful moments, therapists and clients may experience inspired insights. Spiritual impressions can give therapists and clients important insight into problems, as well as ideas for interventions or healing strategies that may be effective.

Nature of the Relationship Between Psychology and Spirituality

Our theistic model postulates that human beings are multisystemic organisms. Biological, social, cognitive, psychological, behavioral, and spiritual systems and processes influence human personality and functioning, but the core of human personality is spiritual. Each person has an eternal, indestructible, personal, spiritual identity that persists through time and eternity. The spiritual is a different realm and cannot be subsumed by other systems, although it is interconnected with them and may be influenced by any of them and vice versa (Richards & Bergin, 1997).

Because spirituality influences and is interconnected with other systems of the human organism, we hypothesize that spiritual growth and wellbeing tend to have a moderate, positive causal influence on psychological growth and well-being. People who enjoy positive spirituality are thus more likely to develop and function in a healthy manner, socially and psychologically. There is now an abundant empirical literature supporting this perspective (e.g., Koenig, McCullough, & Larson, 2001).

We do not believe, however, that the spiritual system completely controls or overrides other systems. Although spiritual healing and growth may have a positive influence on psychological and interpersonal functioning, faith and spirituality is usually not a cure-all. Spiritually mature people may still suffer from physical or psychological disorders, but their spirituality may help them better cope with severe physical, psychological, and interpersonal problems, even though it does not cure them. Furthermore, physical and psychological adversity may actually deepen people's faith and spiritual maturity. Thus, we think it would be incorrect to think that people who struggle emotionally or interpersonally are lacking in their faith or spirituality. We also think that people who are lacking in their spirituality are not necessarily functioning poorly psychologically or interpersonally.

In regard to psychotherapy and healing, we have hypothesized that people who suffer from more severe psychiatric disorders (e.g., schizophrenia, bipolar disorder, dissociative disorders) may need to be treated primarily with medical and standard psychological treatment regimes, such as medication, intensive psychosocial therapies, and hospitalization, and are less likely to benefit from primarily spiritual interventions (Richards & Bergin, 1997). This does not mean that people with severe psychiatric disorders would not benefit if a spiritual component were included in the treatment program, but that the proportion of time spent in treatment would need to lean more heavily toward standard technical resources and interventions. We have also hypothesized that spiritual interventions can be relied on more heavily and will tend to be more beneficial for people with less severe problems.

Therapist's Skills and Attributes

Professional and spiritual preparation is essential for those who wish to be effective theistic integrative psychotherapists. We think there is no substitute for good education and professional training. Theistic integrative psychotherapists must be well trained in mainstream secular psychotherapy traditions so that they can thoughtfully and effectively integrate concepts and interventions from these traditions into their approach. They must also obtain training in multicultural counseling and religious aspects of diversity so that they can adopt an ecumenical therapeutic stance—one that is sensitive and open to diverse spiritual perspectives. The foundations of an ecumenical therapeutic stance are the attitudes and skills of an effective multicultural therapist. Therapists with good ecumenical skills are also aware of their own religious heritage and values and are sensitive to how they could affect their work with clients from different spiritual traditions. They are capable of communicating interest, understanding, and respect to clients who have spiritual beliefs that are different from their own.

Effective theistic integrative psychotherapists also have a number of other attributes, including the capacity to adopt a denominational therapeutic stance when appropriate, establish a spiritually open and safe therapeutic alliance, assess the religious and spiritual dimensions of their clients' lives, implement spiritual interventions in an ethical and effective manner, and help clients access the resources of their spiritual beliefs, practices, and community to assist in the treatment and healing process. We have described these skills and attributes in more detail in other publications (e.g., Richards & Bergin, 1997, 2000).

Theistic integrative psychotherapists must also be psychologically healthy so that they can model healthy psychological and interpersonal behavior for their clients. When necessary, they should seek therapy for themselves. To be effective, theistic integrative psychotherapists must also seek to integrate their secular training and theoretical perspectives with their religious beliefs in a coherent way. This can be a challenge, but it is important for theistic integrative psychotherapists to do this so that their approach is not riddled with theoretical and philosophical inconsistencies (Richards & Bergin, 2004).

We also think theistic integrative psychotherapists need to seek to take care of their own spiritual well-being, so that they are spiritually prepared as they work with their clients. One important aspect of therapists' spiritual preparation is to seek to live congruently with their personal value system. We also encourage theistic integrative psychotherapists to pray and meditate or engage in other spiritual practices that they find help them be more attuned spiritually during their therapy sessions.

Strengths and Limitations

A theoretical strength of this approach is that it is based on a spiritual view of human nature and world that has profound implications for personality theory, psychotherapy, and the processes of healing and change (Bergin, 1991). This perspective contributes uniquely to psychology and psychotherapy by providing a theistic conception of human nature and personality, a moral frame of reference for guiding and evaluating psychotherapy, and a body of spiritual techniques and interventions. It also provides a theistic spiritual view of scientific discovery and the research process (Richards & Bergin, 1997).

A practical strength of this approach is that most psychotherapists are much more likely to encounter clients who approach life with a theistic worldview than other worldviews. In North America, more than 85% of the population professes belief in, adherence to, or affiliation with one of the theistic world religions, and in Europe more than 80% of the population does (Berrett & Johnson, 2002). Thus, from the standpoint of numbers only, there is a need for theistic approaches to psychotherapy—approaches that do not marginalize theistic beliefs and practices.

A theoretical and practical limitation of our theistic integrative approach is that its framework and interventions may not be as applicable and helpful for therapists and clients who are atheistic, agnostic, or who have nontheistic spiritual beliefs. Theistic integrative psychotherapy can be used with such clients, however, although the full potential of the approach may not be realized in such situations. Another limitation of the approach is that it is still an "emerging" approach, as are other theistic psychotherapy approaches. There is a need for more theoretical, applied, and empirical work to be done before *theistic psychotherapy* approaches can take a place of influence and equality among other mainstream psychotherapy traditions.

Indications and Contraindications

Theistic integrative psychotherapy is most clearly indicated for theistic clients, particularly for those who feel that religion and faith in God are important in their lives. It is also indicated for clients who wish to discuss religious and spiritual issues during treatment or who view their spiritual beliefs as relevant to their presenting problems. Theistic integrative psychotherapists can appropriately address a wide variety of religious and spiritual concerns and issues. Role boundaries between therapists and religious leaders need to be respected, however, and it may be appropriate to refer clients to their religious leaders if they have specific doctrinal questions or are seeking spiritual direction that fall outside therapists' expertise or professional role.

In regard to psychiatric or psychological conditions that are most effectively addressed through theistic integrative psychotherapy, more research is needed before definitive guidelines can be given. In general, as mentioned earlier, we have hypothesized that theistic integrative psychotherapy is more efficacious with less severe disorders (e.g., anxiety, depression, guilt, self-esteem and identity problems, marriage and family problems, adjustment disorders). For more severe disorders, many of which may have biological origins, we hypothesize that psychotherapists will need to rely more heavily on more intensive forms of psychological and pharmacological treatments (Richards & Bergin, 1997).

There is growing evidence that theistic treatment approaches that affirm the importance of faith in God or a higher power are effective for treating addictions and eating disorders, particularly for religious people (Miller, 1999; Richards, Hardman, & Berrett, 2001; Ringwald, 2002). There is also evidence that theistic cognitive therapy approaches are effective in the treatment of depression (Propst, Ostrom, Watkins, Dean, & Mashburn, 1992). More research on the efficacy of theistic psychotherapy for other psychological disorders is needed.

Cultural and Gender Considerations

Religion and spirituality are important aspects of diversity and interact with a person's culture, race, gender, sexual orientation, and other characteristics in complex ways (Richards & Bergin, 2000; Richards, Keller, & Smith, 2003; Smith & Richards, in press). It is beyond the scope of this chapter to consider the many ways that religion and spirituality may interact with other aspects of diversity, and so I refer readers to other publications that go into depth about these issues (Fukuyama & Sevig, 1999; Richards & Bergin, 2000, 2004; Smith & Richards, in press).

Given that leaders and members of the theistic world religions have historically contributed much to the oppression and discrimination suffered by minority groups and women, it is imperative that theistic integrative psychotherapists obtain training and seek for competency in multicultural and gender-fair counseling. It can be a challenging and delicate task at times for psychotherapists to show respect for religious authority and tradition while avoiding the perpetuation of racist, sexist, or other stereotypical attitudes and practices that have historically been a part of theistic religions and cultures. It is nevertheless essential for theistic integrative psychotherapists to learn to do this. Thus, in addition to competency in racial, cultural, gender, and lifestyle issues, theistic integrative psychotherapists need to gain expertise in religious and spiritual traditions of the world, including an understanding of how religious traditions have and may continue to promote oppression and discrimination.

Future Developments and Directions

It remains to be seen whether theistic integrative psychotherapy, and other theistic approaches, will gain a place of equality and influence in mainstream psychology and psychotherapy. Much more philosophical, theoretical, and research work is needed if this is to happen. For example, philosophical and empirical work is needed about the following topics: (a) What are the implications of a theistic view for human nature and personality? (b) How effective is theistic psychotherapy for various psychological and interpersonal problems? (c) What is the nature of spirit, spirituality, and spiritual well-being? (d) How does religious and spiritual development occur across the life span? (e) What are the major spiritual needs and issues of human beings? (f) What is the prevalence and role of intuition and inspiration in therapeutic change and scientific discovery? (g) What are the nature, prevalence, effects, and meaning of spiritual experiences (e.g., near-death experiences, afterlife visions, inspirational and revelatory experiences, conversion experiences, healings)? (h) What are the implications and usefulness of epistemological and methodological pluralism?

CASE EXAMPLE

Therapist and Treatment Setting

I received my PhD in counseling psychology in 1988 from the University of Minnesota. I was a faculty member at Central Washington University from 1988 to 1990 and have been a faculty member at Brigham Young University (BYU) since 1990, where I am currently a professor in the Department of Counseling Psychology and Special Education. In addition to my professorial responsibilities at BYU, I am affiliated with the Center for Change in Orem, Utah, where I maintain a small private outpatient practice with adults and older adolescents.

Most of the clients I work with present with issues of depression, anxiety, childhood sexual abuse, eating disorders, legal problems (e.g., theft), marital conflict or other relationship problems, religious concerns, or a combination of these. Typically, I see clients once a week for 60-minute sessions. Length of treatment varies from 2 to 3 months up to 2 years, with an average of about 8 months. In my theistic approach, I feel free to integrate perspectives and interventions from any of the mainstream therapeutic traditions if I believe it will help my clients but only insofar as they do not conflict philosophically or theoretically with my theistic framework and values.

In regard to my personal faith, I am a believing and practicing member of the Church of Jesus Christ of Latter-Day Saints (LDS). I engage frequently in spiritual practices such as private prayer and contemplation, private scripture study, and church and temple attendance. I am a high priest in the church and have served in various lay leadership and teaching positions within my local congregation. I am married to Marcia T. Richards, and we have five children. Our religious faith is an important part of our family life. In addition to attending church services together, we engage in various spiritual practices in our home, such as family prayer, family home evening, and family scripture reading. My personal faith and spirituality serves as the foundation for both my personal and professional life. My belief that all human beings are children of God and of divine worth helps me feel love, concern, and acceptance for my clients, regardless of their religion, race, gender, or lifestyle.

Client Demographics, Relevant History, and Presenting Concern

Janet was a 36-year old, married homemaker and mother of three children. Her responses to several questions on the intake questionnaire revealed that Janet was a devout, orthodox member of the LDS church. Janet had been raised in the Roman Catholic tradition but converted to the LDS faith when she was 12 years old, along with her parents and other siblings. Janet's husband was also a convert to the LDS church and according to Janet remained a devout believer.

Janet presented with issues of (a) unresolved conflict and issues toward her father who had emotionally abused and neglected her throughout her life and (b) difficulty trusting people. On her intake questionnaire, she wrote, "I have a lot of unfelt hurt from childhood. I am overly concerned about the impression I leave on others. My parents still hurt me and it affects me too much. I do not trust people or human nature." She also explained that her father was an alcoholic when she was growing up. Although her father quit drinking when he joined the LDS church, Janet's description of her childhood made it clear that many problems in the family remained even after the drinking had stopped. According to Janet, her father "lived in our home, but wasn't there. He was scary, said mean things, wanted us to be quiet, and have no interests, ideas, feelings, or needs. He is still scary and controlling. He doesn't like to be around me for more than a few minutes. His ideal would be if I visited once a month for a half-hour or less."

Relationship of the Therapist and Client

I think it is essential that the therapeutic relationship be spiritually open and safe. Clients need to know that it is appropriate to talk about their religious and spiritual beliefs and concerns during therapy if they wish. With Janet, I attempted to communicate this in a couple of ways. First, in the initial session, I gave Janet a copy of my written informed consent form, which explicitly gives clients permission to discuss religious and spiritual issues during therapy. Second, when Janet mentioned religious and spiritual issues during the first few sessions, I attempted to communicate interest, understanding, and acceptance. Despite my efforts to make it clear that I was open to discussions about spirituality, a couple of months into therapy during a session where religious and spiritual concerns were at the forefront, Janet still felt the need to pause and ask for reassurance from me that it was okay for her to focus so much on spiritual concerns. I reassured her that it was, and she expressed her gratitude for this. She said that for some reason she had been under the impression before beginning treatment herself that it was not okay to talk about religious and spiritual issues during psychotherapy.

According to my theistic perspective, to be optimally healing, the therapeutic relationship must also include the biblical quality of charity, or brotherly and sisterly love (Fromm, 1956). I seek to care about my clients in an appropriate manner. I also believe that the therapeutic relationship should be spiritually affirming. I seek to affirm in culturally sensitive ways that my clients are creations of God who have eternal, divine potential and worth. In my work with Janet, these qualities of our therapeutic relationship were an important part of her healing and growth. In a letter Janet wrote to me 2 months after she terminated therapy, she expressed the following about the importance of our therapeutic relationship:

> I was completely unprepared for what I found in your office that first visit. You were caring and you connected to what I was sharing with you. You were compassionate about my fears. The thing I remember most is that the room felt like a safe haven. There was a very special spirit in your office. It was peaceful and you were accepting. I left feeling as though my spirit had been soothed and that for the first time in my life I could

let my guard down at least a little. I recognized on that very first visit that I could be real in your office. I was glad that you were kind, but I did not expect you to care about me. Soon I learned that I mattered to you in a real way. Little did I know then just how important that caring would be for my healing.

When I care deeply about my clients' emotional and spiritual welfare and growth, and affirm my faith in their inherent divine worth, I believe I am able to provide a therapeutic relationship that is emotionally and spiritually healing. I also believe that such a relationship makes possible for the Spirit of Truth and love of God to be present during therapy. When clients feel the love and concern of their therapist, it can help open them up to experiencing God's love. Feeling loved is often what helps connect clients with their sense of spiritual identity and divine worth (Richards & Bergin, 1997). Charity, or love, has great healing power.

Assessment: Rationale and Type of Data Collected

I believe that a religious–spiritual assessment should be imbedded in a multisystemic assessment strategy (Richards & Bergin, 1997). During the first two or three sessions with Janet, I globally assessed how she seemed to be functioning physically, socially, behaviorally, intellectually, educationally, psychologically, and spiritually. I relied on Janet's verbal self-descriptions, written responses to my intake questionnaire, and my own clinical impressions about how she was functioning in each of these dimensions. Although with some clients I also administer standardized assessment measures to assist in my assessment and diagnosis (e.g., the Minnesota Multiphasic Personality Inventory—2 [Butcher, 1990], Eating Attitudes Test, Outcome Questionnaire, Religious Orientation Scale, Spiritual Well-Being Scale), I did not feel the need to do so with Janet.

Diagnostic and Clinical Case Conceptualization

I concluded that Janet was physically healthy and free of most somatic symptoms, with the exception of frequent stress-related headaches. She was socially skilled and competent, although she admitted that her difficulty in trusting others prevented her from letting herself get too emotionally close to her friends. She had no behavioral problems. It was obvious that she was very intelligent. Although she had postponed her college education to bear and raise her children, she had recently begun taking university classes part time once all of her children were in school. She was finding this satisfying and enjoying much success.

Janet was basically a psychologically healthy person, but she was suffering from a number of symptoms and issues that were detracting from the quality of her life and relationships. Janet reported some symptoms of moderate depression and anxiety, symptoms that were most often triggered by conflicts in her family relationships. Janet also suffered from deep-seated doubts about her worth and goodness—doubts that had been sown in the abusive and neglectful experiences she had gone through as a child and adolescent. Janet also acknowledged that she and her husband had some "difficulties with physical intimacy." In regard to her spirituality, although it was clear that Janet was a devout believer and that overall her religious involvement was a positive influence in her life, I concluded that she had some perfectionistic tendencies and was overly concerned about religious rules and appearances, perhaps because of her underlying feelings of deficiency and badness. Finally, although I generally resist assigning diagnostic labels to my clients, to comply with insurance company requirements, I gave Janet a diagnosis of depression (not otherwise specified) and generalized anxiety. I deferred making an Axis II diagnosis.

Treatment Goals, Process, and Intervention Strategies

The overall purpose of psychotherapy is to help clients cope with and resolve their presenting problems and concerns and to promote their healing, growth, and long-term well-being. With some, but not all, clients, it is important to focus on religious and spiritual issues during treatment to achieve this overall purpose. Thus, I often pursue spiritual treatment goals with clients, but only after tailoring them to fit each client's unique background and needs (Richards & Bergin, 1997).

In my treatment notes after the first session with Janet, I recorded that we had agreed that "our major goals for therapy would be to (a) help Janet emotionally heal from the pain she still feels about the neglect and emotional abuse she experienced as a child, and (b) help Janet learn to deal effectively in her current life with her mother and father who now live in close proximity." In addition, as treatment progressed, I decided—and Janet agreed—that her faith and spirituality might be important resources in her efforts to heal and grow.

Perhaps the most important spiritual goal I began to pursue early in treatment was that I sought to help Janet affirm and believe more deeply in her eternal spiritual identity and divine worth as a creation of God. According to my theistic perspective of psychotherapy, achieving this goal is essential if lasting therapeutic change and healing is to occur (Richards & Bergin, 1997). I also sought to support and affirm the importance of Janet's desire to live in harmony with her moral values and her understanding of God's will and purpose for her life. This is another important spiritual goal of theistic psychotherapy.

I also made efforts throughout the course of therapy to help Janet examine and better understand what impact her religious and spiritual beliefs might be having on her problems and concerns (e.g., her sense of identity, her relationships with family members, her perfectionism). Finally, I encouraged Janet to identify and use the spiritual resources in her life (e.g., prayer, faith, sacred writings) as a means to assist her efforts to cope, heal, and change. Both of these are spiritual treatment goals that theistic integrative psychotherapists may also pursue with clients when it seems appropriate (Richards & Bergin, 1997).

Janet's psychotherapy lasted for 10 months. During the beginning phase of therapy (approximately months 1–4), Janet and I devoted a lot of the time to exploring her past relationships, particularly with her father, mother, husband, and siblings. During the middle phase of therapy (months 4–7), Janet and I started spending relatively more time examining and working on her current relationships and how she wanted them to be different. These included her relationships with her father, mother, husband, children, and siblings. During the later phase of therapy (months 8–10), Janet and I spent considerable time discussing how her current relationships were changing. We also found it necessary and helpful to spend relatively more time processing the dynamics of our own relationship. Throughout the course of therapy, but particularly during the later phase, Janet and I also spent considerable time talking about how she perceived and felt about her relationship with God.

Beginning Phase of Therapy

In terms of therapeutic content, during the beginning phase of therapy, Janet and I focused primarily on helping her gain insight into how her painful experiences in childhood and adolescence had affected her at the time and how they were continuing to influence her life. Much of the discussion about Janet's past relationships focused on helping her explore and understand how these relationships affected her sense of identity and worth and how she perceived and related to other people.

During this phase of therapy, Janet felt a lot of pain, anger, and grief. Much of her pain and anger focused on her abusive father. She also got in touch with similar feelings about her mother, whom Janet realized had emotionally neglected her children because she had spent so much of her time and energy trying to placate and please her husband. Janet also worked through the pain and shame she felt about being sexually abused as a young teenager. As Janet explored her feelings and memories about her childhood and adolescence, she became more aware of the many negative and hurtful messages that she had internalized regarding her own insignificance and badness.

Gradually, Janet began to question the validity of these internalized messages, recognizing that they did not tell the truth about her true worth and identity. As she began to replace the negative messages with more affirming, truthful beliefs about her capability and lovability, Janet's relationships with her husband, children, siblings, and friends began to change. She began to relate to her husband, children, and siblings in new, more healthy and loving ways.

Following are selected quotes from my case notes that further illustrate some of the issues and concerns Janet and I worked on during the beginning phase of therapy.

Case Notes From May 17. Janet said that she has experienced many emotions this week regarding her childhood issues. She has shared some of her feelings with her husband, and he has been supportive. . . . In a gathering with her mother and siblings with a religious leader that her father had failed to show up for, Janet said she initiated a family disclosure to her religious leader that not everything is okay in her family of origin and that her father has problems. Janet said the rest of the family was with her in acknowledging the family problems to their religious leader. Janet and I explored many other issues related to her feelings about her father and her childhood and what it was like living in an abusive alcoholic system.

Case Notes From June 7. Janet told me that on one occasion this week as she was experiencing feelings about her childhood and sharing them with her husband, Bill, she had an image of her father pouring "black poison" into her. As she discussed this with me, Janet realized that the black poison symbolized the poisonous messages her father sent that she was bad, undeserving of his love, and that she didn't deserve to exist.

Case Notes From June 21. Janet shared some of her feelings and experiences about sexuality today. She said that as a little girl and young woman she was aware that her father was sexually "perverted" (he had affairs, read pornography, and communicated perverted views about sexuality to her and her sisters). She came to feel that sex and men were bad. Janet also disclosed that when she was a teenager an older man sexually abused her on one occasion. She experienced a great deal of pain and feelings of shame as she talked about this experience. Because of these experiences, Janet feels bad about her own sexuality and goodness as a woman.

Case Notes From July 18. Janet shared with me that her mother has decided to divorce her father. After nearly 30 years of enduring emotional and sexual abuse, Janet's mother has finally decided enough is enough. Janet explored her feelings about her mother's decision—feelings of relief primarily, but also some pain from acknowledging again that things really were and are that bad in her parent's relationship.

Case Notes From July 25. Today we looked at some pictures of Janet from her childhood. Before sharing them with me, Janet expressed her fear that I could reject the "real her" if she shared these childhood pictures with me. I told her I would like to "see" the little girl that never felt like she had been "seen" and that I wanted to affirm that she existed and mattered.

Case Notes From August 2. We talked about Janet's sexual relationship with her husband today and the importance of her being in charge of her body and knowing that she has the right to say "no" to sex when she feels like it. This is still a tough issue for Janet—she feels obligation and guilt if she says no. I shared my view that if she knows she has the right to be in charge of her body and say "no" if she wishes, then sex can be a gift and act of love that she shares freely with Bill when she feels like it.

Middle Phase of Therapy

During the middle phase of therapy, we spent more time examining Janet's feelings about her current relationships, including those with her parents, husband, children, siblings, and friends. Janet began to try out new ways of relating and behaving in her current relationships. As she abandoned her previous internalized beliefs that she was bad and deficient and began relating to others out of the conviction and feeling that she was lovable, good, and capable, her relationships began to change for the better.

With her father, Janet no longer tolerated his abusive and invalidated ways. She confronted him appropriately on a number of occasions and succeeded at redefining their relationship in a manner that left her feeling more empowered and honest—although she had to face the painful fact that her father was unwilling, or perhaps incapable, of having a genuine, loving relationship with her.

With her mother and siblings, Janet resigned from her "caretaker role," which meant she quit assuming too much responsibility for fixing everyone else emotionally. Instead, she started relating to her mother and siblings as a daughter and sister. She established clearer boundaries and began enjoying these relationships more, although at times she bumped up against some anger and disappointment from those who wanted her to continue being the family caretaker or "fixer upper."

Janet reported that her relationship with her husband also began to change and improve. She forgave him for past mistakes he had made in their relationship. She began opening her heart to him and his love, rather than pushing him away emotionally. Their communication and trust improved, and they became much more happy with their sexual relationship. With her children, Janet became less demanding and concerned about them behaving "properly" and more able to enjoy having fun and being playful with them. As Janet became more self-accepting, the playful, creative part of her personality began to emerge much to the delight of her children and her husband.

Following are some selected quotes from my case notes that further illustrate some of the issues and concerns Janet and I worked on during the middle phase of therapy.

Case Notes From August 28. Janet shared with me a letter she wrote to her father this week. She did not give him the letter but did share some of her hurt and anger with him directly when he came to her home. She is redefining herself in relation to him and refusing to let him make her feel like she is bad and insignificant.

Case Notes From September 8. Today Janet talked more about her relationship (lack of) with her father. Janet has decided she wants to let him know that although she is willing to see him and allow her children to see him, not everything is okay. She still has a lot of hurt and anger toward him and wants him to know this.

Case Notes From September 22. This week Janet recognized more clearly her role in her family of origin as the "family caretaker" and as her mother's "counselor." I encouraged Janet to begin the process of resigning or retiring from these unhealthy roles.

Case Notes From October 12. Janet set some limits and boundaries to take care of herself emotionally this week. She told her husband she did not want a young adult from another state to come live with them for a month. She was assertive and appropriate in letting Bill know this, and he was supportive once he understood her feelings.

Case Notes From October 19. Today Janet and I talked more about her feelings regarding her sexuality. She now recognizes that the sexual abuse she experienced as a teenager was not her fault. She has experienced much anger at her abuser during the past few weeks and seems to be moving emotionally to a place where she is viewing herself and her sexuality in a more positive, accepting manner.

Case Notes From October 26. Janet is growing in emotional awareness and insight into how her childhood affected her and continues to affect her. She and her husband are communicating effectively and working on their issues. Janet also talked about her imaginary childhood friend, "Janet Smarty-Pants," a dimension of her childhood personality that was sassy, tomboyish, and rebellious—a part that her parents made so unacceptable to Janet that she denied it was part of her. She also explored her fear about letting this part of her personality come forth again.

Case Notes From November 6. Janet said today that she and her husband have been enjoying getting acquainted with the "Janet Smarty-Pants" part of her personality.

Case Notes From November 20. Janet's feelings of self-worth and self-esteem are blossoming, and her relationship with her husband is continuing to improve. They are communicating more than they ever have. Janet is affirming her lovability and goodness. Janet asked me today whether I care about my clients or whether this is "just a job to me." I expressed my caring and respect for her and told her that she does "exist" and "matter" in my heart and mind. Janet shared a sacred spiritual experience she had this past week in which she felt God's love and His affirmation of her goodness.

Final Phase of Therapy

Although Janet and I spent some time during the beginning and middle phases of therapy talking about her relationship with God, we focused on this topic relatively more during the final phase of therapy. During the middle phase of therapy, Janet's relationship with God began to change for the better. She had once viewed God as a distant, judgmental, and unloving being, not too much different from her view of her father. Because of her feelings of deficiency, Janet had never prayed for herself, but only for others. Because of therapy and her own spiritual experiences, Janet had, by the final phase of therapy, gained much faith and confidence that God loved and accepted her. Her faith that God valued her and viewed her as real and important grew strong. She began to pray to God not only for others but also for herself. Her prayers became expressions of love, gratitude, and faith.

During the later phase of therapy, Janet and my therapeutic relationship also began to figure more prominently in her healing. Throughout the course of therapy, Janet had found it difficult to trust that I cared about her and viewed her as important and good, and she frequently tested me to see if this was true. During the middle phase of therapy, her fears that I would soon reject and emotionally abandon her frequently surfaced. Because she trusted me enough to be honest with me, she chose to stay in therapy and share her fears about rejection rather than withdrawing emotionally and dropping out of therapy. We spent a considerable amount of time discussing her fears of rejection and examining how the messages she had internalized in her childhood and youth influenced her expectations and perceptions of me. As her trust in me and in my caring grew, Janet's self-confidence and self-acceptance began to blossom.

During the later stage of therapy, Janet tested out many of the other things that she had learned during therapy in the context of our relationship. It became important for her to know what I really felt concerning a variety of issues—for example, would I accept her if she was honest and assertive with me? Would I enjoy her if she was spontaneous and playful? Would I, like other men she had known, only care about her as a sexual object, or would I value her as a multidimensional woman and child of God? Would I, like her father, conclude that Janet was stupid and not worth listening to? Would I believe she was worthwhile, good, and important?

As therapy progressed toward its completion, Janet grew in her realization and confidence that her experience with me was not the same as the abusive and neglectful relationships she had experienced in her past. In this sense, our relationship served as a corrective emotional experience for her. Our relationship challenged and modified many of the internalized beliefs that Janet had formed about herself and her relationships. In the later stage of therapy, our relationship was characterized by deep feelings of caring and appreciation for each other. My love and affirmation of Janet's goodness and worth helped challenge her deeply rooted belief that she was unlovable, bad, and incapable.

Following are selected quotes from my case notes to illustrate further some of the issues and concerns that Janet and I worked on during the final phase of therapy.

Case Notes From December 4. Janet has some special emotional and spiritual experiences this week that were very healing for her and helped her to forgive herself for mistakes she feels she has made in her life. Janet radi-ated joy and peace as she shared these experiences with me. I believe she truly felt of the healing influence of God's love this week. Janet's relation-ship with Bill, her husband, continues to grow. Their communication is open and affirming, and Janet said their sexual relationship is better than it has ever been.

Case Notes From December 18. Today Janet and I spent most of the session talking about our relationship. Although it has been a difficult and slow process, Janet explained that she has grown to trust that I really do believe she is good, capable, and lovable. She shared that early in therapy she had not believed I would care about or value her. Then for several months she had feared that the caring I had developed for her would be based on her value as a sexual object. Now she trusts that I care about her and value her for her intelligence, her goodness, her personality, and her worth as a daughter of God. She expressed her love and appreciation for me, and I reaffirmed mine for her.

One-Year Follow-Up

Approximately 1 year after the termination of her therapy, I contacted Janet to see how she was doing and to ask for her permission to write about her case for this book chapter. Janet informed me that she is doing well, both personally and in her marriage, family, and spiritual life. Janet said that she continues to feel good about her own lovability, capability, and goodness. She also continues to feel loved and accepted by God.

Janet also said her marriage is better than it has ever been. She and Bill are still communicating well and enjoying each other. Janet also said that she is more relaxed as a mother and enjoys her children much more (and they her).

Janet said that her father is still "a jerk" but that she feels good about the boundaries she has established in her relationship with him. He no longer has the ability to hurt her so frequently as he did in the past, and so she can be around him without feeling bad about herself. Janet said her relationship with her mother is better than it was, although again she feels that her mother is not capable of a genuinely loving and close relationship.

Because Janet's children are now all in school, she made the decision to return to university as a full-time student. She is enjoying much success and is planning to go to graduate school when she receives her degree later this year. In a letter Janet sent me, she shared the following additional percep-tions about how she had been helped by therapy:

> The "me" that was in your office one year ago did not need changing but emergence. Therapy freed me to be who I really am and come to love

and trust that beautiful person. I had a lot of pain and hundreds of hurt-ful messages stored inside of me. You replaced them with truth and love. Because of therapy, it was much easier to learn of the kind of love Heav-enly Father has for me.

When I learned that God loves me, trusted me, and saw me as a wor-thy daughter, I was freed to enjoy my life. I used to think that I was likely to "ruin" those I loved because I was made of "bad stuff." I approached my relationships with fear. When I recognized my goodness, I did not look for my loved ones to fail as a result of my "badness," but could ap-preciate their goodness and enjoy loving them. Because of therapy, I have learned to love my family in more joyful and accepting ways.

I now consider my womanhood a dynamically divine bestowal that is part of the gift of me. Sexual relations with my husband have become a way of experiencing and showing love. It is a reaffirmation of my good nature, not a distortion of it.

I now believe that when I pray I am praying to a Father who loves me and is delighted to hear from and be a part of my life. He loves me be-cause he knows me to my very core. He sees the good in me and so do I. From this sense of goodness, I find the desire and courage to share myself with others and grow in their love.

Summary of Intervention Strategies

In regard to intervention strategies, I employed a variety of treatment methods. Consistent with Carl Rogers's (1961) person-centered approach, I did much empathic listening and responding to facilitate Janet's exploration and emotional experiencing and insight. As Janet's internalized maladaptive beliefs and perceptions were identified, I frequently employed my own ver-sion of cognitive therapy to help her recognize and challenge them. In en-couraging Janet to behave more assertively toward to father, mother, and siblings, I drew on behavior therapy literature in assertiveness training. The amount of time I spent focusing on Janet's past and present maladaptive rela-tionship patterns were influenced by Strupp and Binder's (1984) time-lim-ited psychodynamic perspective. My willingness to allow my relationship with Janet to become part of the "grist for the mill" of therapy was also influ-enced by this psychodynamic perspective, as well as by the existentialist per-spective that therapeutic healing best occurs in the context of a genuine "I–Thou" relationship.

But the core of my work with Janet was influenced by my conviction that she is a creation of God, a daughter of God, with divine potential, lovability, and worth. As I worked with her, I sought to communicate that message to her again and again in the words I used and in the way I treated her. Because of that perspective and conviction, I also employed a number of spiritual interventions that I believed would help reinforce her true identity, including frequent discussions about religious and spiritual concepts, privately praying for Janet outside of our therapy sessions, encouraging Janet to pray, meditate, and read sacred writings on her own outside of our therapy sessions, and sharing my own faith in God and in the reality of God's love on a number of occasions during our therapy sessions. I believe that these theistic perspectives and interventions were central to Janet's healing and growth.

REFERENCES

Barbour, I. G. (1990). *Religion in an age of science: The Gifford lectures 1989–1991* (Vol. 1). San Francisco: HarperCollins.

Benson, H. (1996). *Timeless healing: The power and biology of belief.* New York: Scribner.

Bergin, A. E. (1980). Psychotherapy and religious values. *Journal of Consulting and Clinical Psychology, 48,* 75–105.

Bergin, A. E. (1988). Three contributions of a spiritual perspective to counseling, psychotherapy, and behavior change. *Counseling and Values, 32,* 21–31.

Bergin, A. E. (1991). Values and religious issues in psychotherapy and mental health. *American Psychologist, 46,* 394–403.

Berrett, D. B., & Johnson, T. M. (2002). Religion. In *Britannica book of the year* (p. 303). Chicago: Encyclopedia Britannica.

Butcher, J. N. (1990). *MMPI–2 in psychological treatment.* New York: Oxford University Press.

Chamberlain, R. B., Richards, P. S., & Scharman, J. S. (1996). Spiritual perspectives and interventions in psychotherapy: A qualitative study of experienced AMCAP therapists. *AMCAP Journal, 22,* 29–74.

Fromm, E. (1956). *The art of loving.* New York: Harper & Row.

Fukuyama, M., & Sevig, T. (1999). *Integrating spirituality into multicultural counseling.* Thousand Oaks, CA: Sage.

Griffin, D. R. (2000). *Religion and naturalism: Overcoming the conflicts.* Albany: State University of New York Press.

Hearnshaw, L. S. (1987). *The shaping of modern psychology.* New York: Routledge & Kegan Paul.

Jones, S. L. (1994). A constructive relationship for religion with the science and profession of psychology: Perhaps the boldest model yet. *American Psychologist, 49,* 184–199.

Koenig, H. G., McCullough, M. E., & Larson, D. B. (2001). *Handbook of religion and health.* New York: Oxford University Press.

Leahey, T. H. (1991). *A history of modern psychology.* Englewood Cliffs, NJ: Prentice Hall.

Miller, L. (2004). A spiritual formulation of interpersonal psychotherapy for depression in pregnant girls. In P. S. Richards & A. E. Bergin (Eds.), *Casebook for a spiritual strategy in counseling and psychotherapy* (pp. 75–86). Washington, DC: American Psychological Association.

Miller, W. R. (1999). *Integrating spirituality into treatment: Resources for practitioners.* Washington, DC: American Psychological Association.

Nielsen, S. L. (2004). A Mormon rational emotive behavior therapist attempts Qur'anic rational emotive behavior therapy. In P. S. Richards & A. E. Bergin (Eds.), *Casebook for a spiritual strategy in counseling in psychotherapy* (pp. 213–230). Washington, DC: American Psychological Association.

Propst, L. R., Ostrom, R., Watkins, P., Dean, T., & Mashburn, D. (1992). Comparative efficacy of religious and nonreligious cognitive–behavioral therapy for the treatment of clinical depression in religious individuals. *Journal of Consulting and Clinical Psychology, 60,* 94–103.

Richards, P. S. (1999). *Spiritual influences in healing and psychotherapy.* Presented at the 107th Annual Convention of the American Psychological Association, William C. Bier Award Invited Address to Division 36 (Psychology of Religion), Boston.

Richards, P. S., & Bergin, A. E. (1997). *A spiritual strategy for counseling and psychotherapy.* Washington, DC: American Psychological Association.

Richards, P. S., & Bergin, A. E. (Eds.). (2000). *Handbook of psychotherapy and religious diversity.* Washington, DC: American Psychological Association.

Richards, P. S., & Bergin, A. E. (2004). *Casebook for a spiritual strategy in counseling and psychotherapy.* Washington, DC: American Psychological Association.

Richards, P. S., & Bergin, A. E. (in press). *A spiritual strategy for counseling and psychotherapy* (2nd ed.). Washington, DC: American Psychological Association.

Richards, P. S., Hardman, R. K., & Berrett, M. E. (2001, August). *Evaluating the efficacy of spiritual interventions in the treatment of eating disorder patients: An outcome study.* Paper presented at the 109th Annual Convention of the American Psychological Association, San Francisco.

Richards, P. S., Keller, R., & Smith, T. B. (2003). Religious and spiritual diversity in the practice of psychotherapy (pp. 269–286). In T. B. Smith (Ed.), *Practicing multiculturalism: Affirming diversity in counseling and psychology.* Boston: Allyn & Bacon.

Richards, P. S., & Rector, J. R., & Tjeltveit, A. C. (1999). Values, spirituality, and psychotherapy (pp. 133–160). In William R. Miller (Ed.), *Integrating spirituality in treatment: Resources for practitioners.* Washington, DC: American Psychological Association

Ringwald, C. D. (2002). *The soul of recovery: Uncovering the spiritual dimensions in the treatment of addictions.* New York: Oxford University Press.

Rogers, C. R. (1961). *On becoming a person.* Boston: Houghton Mifflin.

Shafranske, E. P. (2004). A psychodynamic case study. In P. S. Richards & A. E. Bergins (Eds.), *Casebook for a spiritual strategy in counseling and psychotherapy* (pp. 153–170). Washington, DC: American Psychological Association.

Slife, B. D. (2004). Theoretical challenges to therapy practice and research: The constraint of naturalism. In M. J. Lambert (Ed.), *Bergin and Garfield's handbook of psychotherapy and behavior change* (5th ed., pp. 44–83). New York: Wiley.

Slife, B. D., Hope, C., & Nebeker, R. S. (1999). Examining the relationship between religious spirituality and psychological science. *Journal of Humanistic Psychology, 39*, 51–85.

Smart, N. (1994). *Religions of the west.* Englewood Cliffs, NJ: Prentice Hall.

Smith, T. B., & Richards, P. S. (in press). Toward the integration of spiritual and religious issues in racial–cultural counseling and psychology. In R. Carter (Ed.), *Handbook of racial–cultural psychology.* Thousand Oaks, CA: Sage.

Strupp, H. H., & Binder, J. L. (1984). *Psychotherapy in a new key: A guide to time-limited psychodynamic therapy.* New York: Basic Books.

Vande Kemp, H. (1996). Historical perspective: Religion and clinical psychology in America. In E. P. Shafranske (Ed.), *Religion and the clinical practice of psychology* (pp. 71–112). Washington, DC: American Psychological Association.

12

INTENSIVE SOUL CARE: INTEGRATING PSYCHOTHERAPY AND SPIRITUAL DIRECTION

DAVID G. BENNER

This chapter presents an intensive retreat-based combination of psychotherapy and spiritual direction. Rooted in psychoanalytic psychotherapy, intensive soul care (ISC) incorporates elements of analytical and existential psychotherapy as well as select techniques from other psychotherapeutic approaches into daily (or twice-daily) sessions. It also draws on understandings and practices of Christian spiritual formation and direction, particularly those associated with the Ignatian spiritual exercises. The relationship between psychology and spirituality that is imbedded within the approach is presented in terms that demonstrate the distinction between spirit and soul, as well as their inextricable interconnection. The approach is then illustrated by means of an extended case study.

Anyone who dares to put ideas in print must be prepared for the experience of enforced humility that comes when one changes publicly presented positions. In *Psychotherapy and the Spiritual Quest* (Benner, 1988), I argued that psychotherapy and spiritual direction were different enough in focus and goals that practitioners should not attempt to integrate them. In the 10 years between that book and *Care of Souls* (Benner, 1998), I became convinced that it was both possible and, in some circumstances, desirable to integrate these two forms of soul care. In this chapter, I present the theoretical foundation for this conviction and illustrate the way in which some of my practice does just this.

DESCRIPTION OF THE APPROACH

Historical and Theoretical Basis of Approach

The historical roots of my efforts to integrate psychotherapy and spiritual direction lie in my life story. The heritage of my childhood was a strong personal spirituality that was not well integrated within the rest of the fabric of my being. It oriented me toward the experience of the transcendent and the pursuit of both psychological and spiritual wholeness, but it left my spirituality dangerously dissociated from my psychological and physical aspects of self. I was attracted to psychology as part of my quest to better understand the place within persons where the psychological and spiritual converged. Somehow I never doubted that such a place existed, although—apart from my encounter with Jung—little in my undergraduate work in psychology and religious studies offered much encouragement for this conviction. Graduate clinical training within the scientist–practitioner model of clinical psychology was of even less help in seeing how psychology and spirituality were interconnected.

Postdoctoral training in psychoanalytic psychotherapy began to suggest possibilities of understanding and addressing the dynamics of the inner life that interested me. Fairbairn's (1952) understanding of the human relational hunger for a perfect other hinted at what I could understand to be spiritual dynamics. Winnicott's (1971) notion of the transitional space also pointed to the place where the spiritual might reside within the psyche. Arieti's (1976) discussion of the synthesis of primary and secondary process thinking that lies beneath creativity also created important space for the spiritual, as did Kohut's (1971) discussion of the role of experiences of transcendence in the journey from primary narcissism to the Grandiose Self. McDargh (1983) and Meissner (1984) were even more helpful. Then I rediscovered Jung (1933, 1961). His vision of the nature of the psyche situates the spiritual right at the very heart of personhood. Clearly the spiritual and psychological were not mutually exclusive domains.

Throughout this period, I sought to make my psychotherapy spiritually sensitive by inviting inclusion of anything that the patient experienced as spiritual if this was felt to be relevant to our work together. I also routinely took a brief spiritual and religious history. What I discovered was that few patients objected to being asked about their spiritual or religious background, and most identified aspects of either that background or their present religious or spiritual experience that they wished to make part of our work together. I listened and worked with whatever material was shared with no agenda beyond nurturing spiritual awareness and response. My belief was that it was better to be in touch with one's spirituality than not, and increasingly I became convinced that allowing for the inclusion of spiritual material in therapy facilitated rather than compromised the process.

My first efforts to explore ways of broadening this framework came in 1984 when I was approached by someone who asked if I was willing to work with him in daily sessions for 3 weeks while he moved from his home into a hotel in order to clear space in his life and work intensively on his problems. I told him I was intrigued with the request but did not feel in a position to offer what he wanted. His request did set me in search of a way of doing so, however.

This came at the point of my discovery of spiritual direction and the retreat tradition of Roman Catholicism. Neither had been a part of the Protestant world in which I had grown up but both suggested possibilities for broadening the psychotherapeutic frame.

Spiritual direction, I discovered, lacked the problem or pathology focus of psychotherapy but shared many other important features. The spiritual director—or guide on the inner journey, as such people are often called—accompanies those who seek spiritual growth as they explore their awareness of and response to the divine. Often this accompaniment is offered within the context of a retreat where conversation with the director forms only a small part of each day, the rest of the time spent in journaling, prayer, and other forms of soul work conducted in solitude. I immediately began to explore ways of offering psychotherapy within the context of a retreat and began to search for ways of making better use of the spiritual material that emerged during sessions.

The theoretical basis of the approach that was beginning to emerge likewise had its roots in psychoanalytic psychotherapy, particularly the British object relations tradition associated with the writings of Winnicott (1971) and Fairbairn (1952). Although I have never considered myself a purist, my overall framework has been psychodynamic theory.

In a somewhat eclectic fashion, I wove into this framework techniques and understandings from analytical and archetypal psychology. My clinical dream work became increasingly Jungian, drawing from not only Jung but also such Christian analysts as Kelsey (1978) and Sanford (1978), and my therapeutic process became increasingly attentive to the presence of *numinous* experiences. Corbett's (1996) understanding of the ways of dealing with these experiences in psychotherapy was influential in this, as was that of Moore (1992). Hillman (1975) gave me a vision of both a psychology and psychotherapy of the soul.

The third theoretical stream of influence has been existential psychology. Yalom (1980), Frankl (1963), Tournier (1957), and van Kaam (1972) have all made important contributions to my view of persons and therapeutic process.

The final major set of influences on my model have come from Christian spiritual formation and direction, particularly the Ignatian spiritual exercises.[1] Beyond this, I have also been greatly influenced by the writings of Pennington (1982) and Keating (1992) on centering prayer, particularly their understanding of the way in which silent prayer contributes to transformation of the inner self (Keating, 1998). No spiritual writer, however. has more influenced my understanding of the dynamics of the soul than Thomas Merton. His discussions of the false self (Merton, 1961a), the role of solitude in spiritual growth (Merton, 1993), and the nature of spiritual freedom (Merton, 1961b) have all had a profound influence on me and my work.

Tyrrell's (1982) model of Christotherapy is a final noteworthy influence. Taking much of its form from the Ignatian spiritual exercises, Tyrrell integrated insights and techniques from psychotherapeutic practice in an effort to facilitate both psychological and spiritual growth. My own approach shares this goal but takes more of its form from psychotherapy.

Overview of Approach

ISC is a synthesis of psychotherapy and spiritual direction that is offered within the context of a residential retreat and designed to help those who seek treatment for psychological problems and support for spiritual growth. Ideally suited for those who are living out their spiritual journey within the Christian tradition, the approach can be modified in ways that make it of benefit to those on any spiritual journey as long as they enter the experience with informed consent. Depending on the individual and the stage of the work together, ISC can look and function much like psychotherapy, spiritual direction, or any balance of the two.

Referrals for ISC result from either acquaintance with someone who has gone through the process or encounter with things I have written. Participants usually come from a distance, typically making their first contact by e-mail. Because retreats are booked at least a year in advance, the first stage is an extended period of e-mail interaction designed to identify the central spiritual and psychological issues that will structure the work together and determine suitability of the retreat portion of ISC. Almost all participants have had previous psychotherapy or spiritual direction, and at least one of these typically continues throughout this preparatory period. This first phase also includes guided work on an autobiographical essay, regular journal writing, dream reporting, and the completion of a number of psychological tests. These materials are all submitted and processed before the decision to proceed to the retreat.

---

[1]A good accessible introduction to these exercises can be found in Barry (1991), and the psychological sophistication of this process is admirably described by Meissner (1999).

The face-to-face portion of the work usually lasts 2 or 3 weeks, the specific length negotiated before the start of the retreat and very infrequently changed during its course. This is typically followed by further e-mail interaction and frequently with subsequent shorter retreats. The participant stays in either a retreat center or a hotel and meets with the therapist once or twice a day for sessions of an hour and a half each time. Participants spend the rest of the day in mutually agreed-on activities, typically giving emphasis to solitude, journaling, contemplative activities (i.e., walking, painting, etc.), and other forms of soul work. During this time, participants are encouraged to abstain from drugs, alcohol, sex, television, and social interaction and to minimize phone calls and set aside other responsibilities of daily life. Weekends are free for the individual to do whatever is desired.

Typical participants in ISC are in their late 30s or 40s, with some degree of identification with Christianity, seeking help with their spiritual journey and sensing that some psychological problems are getting in the road of that journey. The most common psychological problems of participants are related to DSM–IV Axis I diagnoses of mood or anxiety disorders, although several people with Axis II diagnoses of narcissistic or schizoid personality disorders have participated with significant benefit.

The Relationship Between Psychology and Spirituality

Rereading things I have written on the relationship of psychology and spirituality over the past three decades, I am struck by how much my understanding has been in continuous flux. Perhaps this is the sign of not understanding the matter correctly, but perhaps it also reflects something of the amorphous nature of spirituality.

By "spirituality" I mean any awareness of and response to the divine (whatever is perceived to be ultimate) that moves one toward transcendent connectedness and surrender. I understand the capacity for such awareness to be fundamental to human personhood. I also understand the human longing for transcendent connectedness and surrender to be the most basic longing of the human spirit. I am convinced, however, that this longing is associated with great ambivalence.

Although we seek meaning and a coherence to existence that will help us find our place, we also quickly become defensive when our autonomy and egocentricity are threatened. Transcendent connectedness and surrender may hold the possibility of leading us to the home for which we long but they also unquestionably hold the promise of disturbing the transitional places we have adopted as home. Drawing on the Ignatian understanding of disordered attachments (Silf, 1999), I understand addictions and compulsions as, in part, distractions from our deepest spiritual hunger—shutting down awareness and deadening longings. Other forms of psychopathology function in similar ways.

The etymological roots of the English words *spirituality* and *psychology* lead us, of course, back to the concepts of spirit and soul. Unfortunately, however, the association of both these words with religion has resulted in most psychologists assuming that neither concept has any place in psychology. With Hillman (1975), I, however, am convinced that psychology needs to be repositioned from the perspective of the soul. Doing so will reconnect it to the spirit, for, properly understood, spirit and soul are inextricably interconnected.

Hillman noted that the soul calls one "down and in" while the spirit calls one "up and out" (Hillman, 1975, p. 26). Spirit is about height, and soul is about depth. Karasu (1999) suggested that the journey of the soul is into the valleys and dark places of experience, whereas the journey of the spirit is toward self transcendence through a relationship between self and other. Soul and spirit are nevertheless intimately linked, and the journeys of both are, I believe, essential for the development of full personhood. The journey toward transcendence must be a journey that is grounded in the self, and adequate grounding of the self always takes us beyond self to other.

In my opinion, the psychological and spiritual form the two faces of the coin of the inner self. Although growth in one is not absolutely dependent on growth in the other, growth in either provides opportunities for growth in the other. No one seeking psychotherapy ever presents with a problem that could be described as purely psychological. Psychopathology can be understood as representing some combination of soul suffering and spirit longing. The therapist who seeks to be sensitive to both psychological and spiritual aspects of functioning will be attentive to both of these. He or she will listen for the spiritual implication of the apparently psychological problem and the psychological implications of the apparently spiritual longing. Pathology will be understood in broader terms than presented by current diagnostic classifications (American Psychiatric Association, 1994) and will always include such things as the human experience of isolation, alienation, sense of meaningless, existential guilt, and the forfeit of one's potential (Karasu, 1999, p. 155). Psychopathology, as Maslow (1970) reminded us, is human diminution, not merely symptoms. As I have come to understand the matter, human well-being and pathology always involve both spiritual and psychological dimensions.

Therapist's Skills and Attributes

Therapists seeking to provide intensive soul care should

- possess a solid grounding in psychodynamic theory and practice;
- be familiar with existential, analytical, transpersonal, or other road maps of the soul that make room for the spiritual within the psychological;

- be committed to their personal journey toward psychological and spiritual well-being; and
- have personal experience in spiritual direction, including the completion of a guided experience of the Ignatian spiritual exercises.

Strengths and Limitations; Indications and Contraindications

The major advantage of ISC is the potential its intensity affords for deep and significant work on both psychological and spiritual issues. The year of preparation for the retreat allows the 30 to 40 hours of face-to-face contact within a typical retreat to be highly focused. When this is combined with the opportunities to spend much of the rest of the time during the retreat in related soul work, the intensity of the total experiences allows an unique opportunity for deep encounter with both self and the divine.

ISC requires that the one seeking help be able to clear his or her schedule for several weeks and that he or she possess the motivation to engage in extremely intense soul work. When this is combined with the need to travel, it is also quite expensive. The central role of solitude also requires sufficient ego strength to support productive introspection and a tremendously honest encounter with one's depths. The intensity of the retreat often leads to the development of strong transference reactions that cannot always be resolved within available time. It is therefore inappropriate for those with borderline, or lower level narcissistic character pathology as well as those with a psychotic level of functioning. It is also not well suited for children or adolescents.

On the other hand, it is ideal for those relatively healthy individuals wishing help in dealing with both psychological problems and spiritual longings. Those facing midlife readjustment or reappraisal appear to be ideal candidates, although some in their late 20s and early 30s have been able to make excellent use of the process.

Cultural and Gender Considerations

ISC is equally applicable for men and women across cultural groups.

Future Developments and Directions

The next stage of ISC involves training more practitioners and outcome research.

CASE STUDY

Client Demographics, Relevant History, and Presenting Concern

Angie is a 40-year-old woman who contacted me by e-mail after reading one of my books. She identified herself as a lesbian and stated that her present spiritual path was neo-pagan Wicca. She pursued this path by periodic involvement in workshops and retreats, and it shaped her occasional attempts at meditation. She also reported that she had been in twice-a-week psychoanalytic psychotherapy for the past several years. During the 14 months between when she first contacted me and when she came for a retreat, we were in weekly e-mail contact, and she continued to work with her psychotherapist.

Raised in a fundamentalist Christian church, Angie had one sibling, an older sister. She described her family as highly dysfunctional; her mother was a closet alcoholic, her father was repeatedly unfaithful to her mother, there was a climate of constant family fights, and all of this was hidden within an extremely legalistic and moralistic church that knew nothing of the reality of their family life. She felt ignored by her father and emotionally abused by her mother, who seemed to pick on her and showed sadistic and often cruel features in her dealings with Angie.

At age 10, Angie was sent to a private Christian school because of a learning disability and her need for remedial programming. She described this escape from home as the best thing that ever happened to her. At this school, she also experienced the first thing she was prepared to describe as spiritual. She reported that she loved the liturgy of the daily chapel services, and during her years in this school, she developed the habit of spending quiet times in the chapel. She said that she often had a sense of divine presence at these times. A few years later, however, she declared herself an atheist and refused to attend chapel services. Nevertheless, she continued making intermittent visits to the chapel and reported drawing peace from doing so.

Angie had few friends during school years and said she was unhappy much of the time. She was referred to a psychologist at age 16 because of suicide attempt but refused to return after the first session. College years were somewhat happier for her; she moved to a distant part of the country and began to feel that she was far enough from her family to be able to establish her own identity and life. Although she never went to church services, she continued the habit of regular visits to a campus chapel, and the few friends she had during these years were people she met there. Once while drunk at a party with several of these friends, one of them raped her. Crying in the chapel one day after this, a chaplain approached her and offered solace. After coming to trust him enough to share some of her experiences, he also raped her. This ended her habit of meditating in chapels.

Shortly after graduation, Angie declared herself a lesbian. Her parents expressed shock and disgust, and within a few months her father left her mother. All the family's secrets became public knowledge within their church. Angie felt personally responsible for the shame that was subsequently heaped on the family, as well as for its breakup. As part of a resolution to cut all ties with her family and her past, she moved to England to pursue graduate studies, taking permanent residence there after completing an MBA. At the point of contacting me, she was working as an advertising executive in England. She told me that she had not had any contact with any member of her family for 14 years.

Angie experienced chronic depression for most of these years. She was on various antidepressants for most of this time and was in psychotherapy when she first contacted me. She stated that although her therapy had alleviated her depression, she didn't think that her therapist understood her spiritual longings. She said her primary goal was to get her spiritual life back on track, but she also wanted to deal with the psychological problems that were getting in the road of doing this.

In response to being asked how she felt about the prospect of working with a Christian when her current path was neo-pagan Wicca, Angie reported that she thought that this would be helpful because she knew she needed to deal with her own Christian past before being able to move forward. She also stated that in the past several years, she had begun to associate with a church. Although she did not attend services, she had developed a friendship with a priest in this congregation and had returned to her childhood habit of occasionally meditating in the church. Slowly she felt herself being drawn back into a Christian world, although her fears about doing so were enormous. I told her that I knew virtually nothing about neo-pagan Wicca and asked if there were some things she would recommend that I read. She replied that she would tell me what I needed to know about this when we met.

Relationship of the Therapist and Client

I understand my role in ISC as that of a soul curate. The English phrase "care of souls" comes from the Latin *cura animarum*, with *cura* referring to actions designed to bring about both cure and care. A soul curate is, therefore, someone who seeks to provide both care and cure of the soul, the "soul" being a metaphor for the place of convergence of the psychological and spiritual dimensions of the inner self.

I bring somewhat more of my self to the ISC encounter than I do to a typical psychotherapy relationship. I invite those seeking my help to call me by my first name if they wish, and I approach them as a fellow traveler on a journey, not simply as a person in need of my specialized competencies. This does not mean, however, that the relationship is one of mutuality. I accept responsibility to direct the process of our work together and acknowledge that I bring both specialized competencies and a familiarity with maps of the terrain covered in the journey. I am also clearly there for the other; she or he is not there for me. The relationship is a professional one, even though it is often somewhat more personal than might be typical in traditional psychoanalytic psychotherapy.

A third party to this relationship, from my point of view, is God. As in a relationship of spiritual direction, I seek to be personally attentive to the presence and leading of the Spirit of God, and I encourage the person seeking my help to share this attentiveness to whatever her or she understands to be the divine.

Assessment: Rationale and Type of Data Collected

As already indicated, during the first phase of e-mail interaction, I collect information about the person from four major sources: a detailed autobiography, his or her journal (including dream reports), the Minnesota Multiphasic Personality Inventory—2 (MMPI–2; Butcher, Dahlstrom, Graham, Tellegen, & Kaemmer, 1989), and our ongoing e-mail interchanges.

I ask that the autobiography give equal attention to each of the three thirds of the client's life lived to the point of our contact. I suggest that it focus on experience rather than events and ask that it include information about religious or spiritual background, experiences and concerns. I suggest that most people need something like 15 to 30 double-spaced pages to accomplish this and ask that it be completed over a period of weeks or months, not days. Like others, Angie reported that completing the is autobiography was extremely helpful.

I also encourage participants to begin regular journaling if they are not already doing so. I suggest that this need not be daily but should not be less frequent than weekly. I encourage using this as a container for reflection on current experience and as an aid to attentiveness to one's inner life. If the person has a sense of relationship with the divine, I also encourage consideration of using one's journal as a place of dialogue with the divine. I provide a suggested framework for dream work (Benner, 1998, pp. 157–183) as well and encourage sharing portions of the journal with me that contain a sequence of remembered dreams and the record of any work done on them.

Angie's journal initially took the form of dialogue with me. I encouraged her to make it dialogue with herself, and this made it more productive. Her journal gave me a good sense of the strength of her present spiritual longings, her frustration and inadequacies in interpersonal relationships, the significant level of depression that she continued to experience, the presence of a high degree of obsessionality and hostility, and the extremely dark nature of her dreams.

Her dreams terrified her. They were filled with monsters, goblins, chaos, bottomless pits, and ever-present danger. She reported that she had dreams like the ones she shared with me almost every night, frequently waking in the morning with an enormous sense of relief that night had ended. She was unable to do any productive work on these dreams, and we agreed that she do nothing further with them until we were together.

I include an MMPI–2 as a means of gaining an overall picture of the person's level of mental health and the nature of their psychopathology. The Welsh code for Angie's profile was 42'7+80-631/5:9# F+-LK/, suggesting a high degree of psychopathology, including depression, antisocial tendencies, impulsivity, immaturity, limited self-knowledge or capacity for productive introspection, social introversion, low self-esteem and feelings of personal inadequacy, hypersensitivity to negative evaluations, and mistrustfulness. It also suggested the presence of both a mood disorder and personality disorder.

Our e-mail interactions also provided a good deal of information about Angie. She was both open to trying to learn to trust me and highly suspicious of me. I was surprised and impressed with how honest she was in her self-reflection. She was also strongly reactive to anything that she could construe as weakness or fallibility on my part—responding to this with rage and disappointment.

Several misunderstandings threatened to end our relationship. In one of these, reading something I had written, she discovered a discussion of the role of surrender in spirituality. Although the passage in question spoke of the danger of surrender to anything other than Perfect Love, she immediately wrote me an angry e-mail, telling me how irresponsible it was for me, as a psychologist, to recommend surrender to anyone or anything. She then accused me of being "a typical male" in my "uncritical acceptance of the way power is abused in relationships." Other misunderstandings also temporarily destabilized our relationship, each causing her pulling back to reconsider whether she wished to continue work with me. In each case, she decided to continue, and over time our alliance became more solid. Likewise, my doubts about her suitability for the retreat decreased, and my hopefulness about such work increased.

One final source of information was an initial diagnostic assessment and a treatment progress note from her psychotherapist, who described her as having a major depressive symptom disorder and character pathology with mixed depressive and borderline features. She indicated that although Angie developed strong transference reactions, she had been consistently able to examine productively and then subsequently diffuse these. She also reported that Angie was cutoff from her emotions and that little productive work had yet been done on her traumatic experiences. In overall terms, however, she stated that in spite of an at times volatile therapeutic course, Angie had made good progress and was an excellent candidate for intensive psychotherapy.

Diagnostic and Clinical Case Conceptualization

Diagnostically, I judged that Angie probably warranted an Axis I diagnosis of major depressive disorder and an Axis II diagnosis of avoidant personality disorder.

My formulation placed unresolved trauma central to her psychological and spiritual sense of stuckness. An emotionally abusive and sadistic relationship with her mother, the cool indifference of her father, and the two experiences of rape all made understandable her mistrust of authority figures—males in particular—and religious institutions. Unresolved trauma was also probably related to her deep-seated hostility, suspiciousness, and chronic alcohol abuse. Beneath the residue of trauma, however, an avoidant and depressive personality structure seemed to be associated with a predisposition to introjection, guilt, and withdrawal. Her transference patterns suggested the presence of splitting, as did her reported difficulty in accessing feelings. Her object relations development was consistent with this picture, suggesting that her social discomfort was not simply based on interpersonal skill deficits but also reflected developmental immaturity that was probably rooted in an attachment disorder. The volatility of her emotions and her tendency to impulsivity and acting out also suggested impairment of affect regulation.

In terms of her strengths, the biggest surprise was the presence and persistence of her spiritual longings. One might have expected her toxic religious background and experiences to permanently eliminate spiritual awareness. I took the presence of her spiritual hunger to be a favorable prognostic sign, as was her current experience in psychotherapy. The degree of trust and the strength of her engagement with me at the end of the e-mail phase of our work were also good signs. Together, they suggested the presence of a higher level of ego strength that was revealed in the MMPI–2.

Treatment Goals, Process, and Intervention Strategies

Following 40 hours of e-mail interaction over 14 months, the retreat portion of our work together was structured as a two 90-minute sessions each day for 15 days spread over 3 weeks. Sessions were set for first thing each morning and late each afternoon.

Most people coming for ISC choose to stay at a retreat center and see me either there or in my nearby clinical office. Angie preferred to stay in a downtown hotel, stating that pastoral settings made her as anxious as religious ones, whereas cities were a source of comfort.

Week 1

I began our first session by asking Angie to restate what she hoped she hoped to achieve from the retreat phase of our work together. "I am not sure if God exists," she said. "If she does, I don't know if it is reasonable to hope that she is available for personal contact, and if she is, I don't know why she seems so elusive. What I want is help in dealing with whatever is blocking me from getting answers to these questions."

Although I had learned a good deal about her religious background from her autobiography, I had not obtained much information about her spiritual experience. I suggested that we use the first session to explore this, asking her to tell me more about her experiences of God's presence or absence. She told me of the combination of awe and comfort she felt as a school girl in chapel services. She said she had occasional experiences of this since then, mostly during meditation. She also said that she had recently begun to feel peace when in a church as long as there was no service underway. She said that her best guess was that there was a personal deity and that this deity was unavailable to her because something in her was fundamentally defective.

Asking about her neo-pagan Wicca spiritual journey, she told me that this had begun when she first moved to England. She said that she simply could not ignore her spiritual longings and had started attending Wiccan workshops in an attempt to find an alternative to Christianity. The results had been mixed. Although she continued to practice periodically the meditation techniques learned in this group, she found they often led her to frightening places within herself. The most positive aspect of her meditation was that it occasionally involved a sense of divine presence. On two occasions, she reported an inner encounter with a woman who seemed to either be a messenger of the deity or the deity herself.

At the end of the first session, we discussed how she wished to use the time before our session later that day. She stated that she wanted to journal on some of the things our conversation had brought to mind and that then she wanted to meditate. I asked her to describe briefly her meditative technique. She told me that she would typically begin by closing her eyes and grounding herself by visualizing roots going down to the earth beneath her. She then simply sat in quietness and openness and receive whatever came to her. I asked her if she would be offended if I were to offer private prayer for her during the interval between sessions, and she said that what I did on my own was my business. She instructed me not to pray for her out loud when we were together unless she requested it and not to read the Bible to her. She told me she was turned off by scriptures from her fundamentalist days when the Bible was used as a weapon. I assured her of my easy agreement to her requests.

I was struck by a difference in demeanor when Angie came to the second session. She seemed more calm and less mistrusting. In response to my question about how her afternoon had gone, she told me of her meditative experience. She began with her usual routine but quickly found herself in the presence of the woman whom she had met several times over the course of the previous years. This time, the woman drove up toward her in a school bus. Angie described her as "calm and glowing with inner light." Their interaction was brief, with the woman smiling at her and saying, "the journey will be OK." Angie then opened her eyes and spent the afternoon journaling.

When I asked her how she felt about this encounter, Angie stated that she felt wonderful when she was in it but couldn't describe her present feelings. She said that she used to feel things intensely before being raped but felt virtually nothing since then. She also told me of her frustration when her therapist would ask her what she was feeling and urged me not to do so. We spent the rest of this session exploring this loss of contact with her feelings and discussing the structure for the rest of the retreat.

Angie began the next session by telling me that before being raped, she had loved to draw and paint. She said her specialty was trees and that had been able to reproduce their texture so realistically, people often said looking at her paintings was like touching the trees. She gave up painting after being raped because she could no longer reproduce what she saw. This had frustrated her immensely, and she had not experienced any interest in painting until recently. She said she was wondering about buying pencils and a sketch pad. I encouraged her to do so.

The next session, she told me that she had bought sketching materials but was again frustrated by her inability to draw. She had sat in her room looking at a tree outside her hotel window but felt absolutely incapable of drawing what she saw. Exploring the connection between the trauma of the rape, her repression of her feelings, and her subsequent inability to draw, I suggested that she might have shut down all body awareness as a way of dealing with her pain and that this loss of kinesthetic sensitivity might be behind her lost capacity to see and reproduce texture in her art. This intrigued her, and we spent much of the rest of this session exploring the implications of this possibility. We also discussed her experience between sessions, and she reported that her efforts at meditation had been unproductive but that she was finding journaling to be a helpful way of processing her experiences in our sessions.

In the next session, I described a multisensory hypnotherapeutic approach (Mills & Crowley, 1986) that I wished to try if she were agreeable. Based on Ericksonian indirect hypnotherapy (Erickson & Rossi, 1981), it involves the telling of stories that interweave kinesthetic, visual, and auditory sensory elements to facilitate access to out-of-awareness sensory modalities (in Angie's case, the kinesthetic). After asking her willingness to have me tell a story that might not make much sense, would certainly be quite boring, and to which she need not even listen or keep her eyes open, she expressed skepticism but consent. I then recounted a rambling story about a little girl who was unusually attuned to the world around her—engaging it with all her senses. I described the way in which, without having to try, this little girl could see warmth, smell colors, and feel sounds. She was also particularly gifted in being able to draw things she experienced by means of any of her senses. I then told her that over time this little girl seemed to forgot how to connect these sensory channels. Her drawings became flat and insipid, and she became so frustrated that she eventually gave up drawing. But, I told her, one day the little girl suddenly again began to see, feel, and hear everything around and within her and was once again able to use her art to express everything she experienced.

When finished the telling of this story, I asked Angie about the experience. She told me I was the worst storyteller she had met and that she hoped I wasn't dependent on telling stories to earn my living. She also said she had stopped listening to my stupid story shortly after it began. She estimated the time involved as 5 minutes while it had, in fact, been 30. This, and her behavior, suggested the presence of a significant trance experience.

Angie entered the next session with a fist full of drawings she had done since the previous session. She was also more animated, telling me how excited she was to find that she could again draw things she could see. She also told me of a dream in which the woman she encountered during the meditation experience approached her again in her school bus and asked her to come with her for a ride. The woman took her to her family home and together they looked at it from a distance as the bus seemed to fly slowly over it. She was able to observe herself and her family on the day when she told them of her homosexuality, but said that she didn't feel anything. The woman told her that when she was ready to feel the things she needed to feel, she would be able to do so. She then woke up with a sense of well-being.

Asking if she was ready to talk about what happened at home and allow the feelings to be a part of this, she said she was. Her feelings were, in fact, quite present in this and the sessions that followed. The primary focus for the remaining sessions in the first week was the exploration of her childhood experiences within her family. Her feelings were often strong, and she expressed them directly during this work. They included rage, disappointment, profound loneliness, fear and deep-seated shame. None of these feelings were, however, so overwhelming that she showed any decompensation or dissociation.

Each session also included exploration of her use of the times of solitude between sessions. Angie used most of this for drawing and journaling, bringing much of what she produced to sessions. Her art was, by this point, richly adjunctive and usually closely related to her therapeutic work within sessions. Her efforts at meditation during the week were much less productive. She stated, however, that she wanted to set that aside for the moment because she was finding the work on her childhood helpful and thought that she could get back to more of a focus on her spirituality after doing so. I concurred with this judgment.

Week 2

Angie began Week 2 by telling me that she had decided to go to church on the weekend. This was the first time she had attended a church service in more than a decade, and it did not go well. Upset when the priest read the Bible, she stormed out in the middle of the service.

Reviewing the experience of the first week, Angie stated that she felt she had made a significant breakthrough in being able to deal with her past. She said that this had been possible in large part because she had mysteriously found herself again in contact with her feelings. She said she was profoundly skeptical that this could have anything to do with my "stupid story" but wondered if I had any more stories I wanted to tell. She also said that she wished now to shift the focus back to her spiritual experience. She then told me of her meditation after leaving church.

Once again, the woman bus driver appeared, drove her to a church, and then invited her to follow her inside. Although this made her apprehensive, she did as she was asked. Entering the church, she immediately recognized the interior as the chapel from her private school. She took her usual place in the chapel and immediately began to feel a deep sense of peace. She said that for the first time in many years, she also had a sense that God was present. After a while the bus driver came and told her it was time to go back. After following her outside the church, she found herself back in her room in regular consciousness.

This experience left Angie with a surprising but welcome sense of well-being. She said she guessed it was like the feeling of being loved, although she couldn't say this with any confidence because she had never known that feeling herself. I asked if she was open to modifying her meditative technique and to taking a simple phrase that I would provide as a focus of a meditation. She seemed eager to do so. I suggested that she allow herself to meditate on the phrase "Angie is deeply loved" and tell me where this led her in our next session.

Angie entered the next session with a smile, telling me that her meditation had been quite remarkable. She said that she began in her usual way, but after repeating "Angie is deeply loved" several times, she found herself inside the school chapel once again. Once again she reported feeling both peace and a sense of God's presence. But this time she said she also had a keen sense of being loved. When I asked her by whom she was loved, she said, without hesitation, "by God." She then talked about how different such a God would be from the God she had met in her home and childhood church, and we explored the implications for her spiritual journey that would ensue if God was, indeed, characterized by love. Noting that the God she was encountering seemed—apart from the usual gender designation—to be the Christian God, she wondered how she might be able to get to know this God with her fear of church and antagonism to the Bible. She asked if I had any ideas.

I asked if since she had found it helpful to meditate on a phrase I had generated, might she be open to meditating on a phrase from the Bible. She agreed, laughingly suggesting that perhaps this would help desensitize her to the Bible. I suggested that before the next session, she meditate on the phrase "For God so loved Angie," this being an adaptation of a fragment of a biblical phrase with which she said she was familiar ("For God so loved the world"). Returning to the next session, she said that her meditation had been quite different in that it had not involved any visual component. She said she was initially suffused with a sense of peace and well-being. Quickly, however, feelings of deep shame and self-loathing began to contaminate this. Not being able to get beyond this in meditation, she had turned to journaling, composing a letter to her mother in which she expressed both her rage as well as her unwillingness to continue to believe the lies she learned from her mother about her lack of worth. Our discussion of her feelings of shame led to her to the rape experiences. which became the focus of the remainder of this session. She ended this session by stating that she wished to use the same phrase for her next meditation.

The next several days continued this focus on her profound sense of shame and longing to deeply believe her belovedness by God. This included some productive trauma work on her experiences of rape. Reporting that she had thought she had finished this work in her previous therapy, she discovered that knowing she was loved by God now helped her face her shame more directly and fully. Doing so also seemed to make it more believable that she was, in fact, deeply loved.

The quality of both her art and dreams began to change as this second week progressed. She reported the first nights in many years in which she did not have nightmares, instead telling me about dreams that included both signs of continuing anxiety or pain but also indications of emerging hope and peace. The emotional tone and colors used in her paintings also began to shift, something she noted when one day she commented on the "maudlin pastel palate" she feared she was developing.

She also made good use of journaling during this second week. On her own initiative, she began a journal-based discourse with God. which she shared with me each day. Over the course of the week, she moved from questions and expressions of anger to increasing indications of openness to know and experience divine love and presence. She also informed God that she wasn't sure how Jesus fit into the picture because she had trouble relating to him as a man. She said that if Jesus was to be made a part of her spiritual practice and beliefs, he would have to be willing to be—at least in her mind—a woman. She also confessed that this was how she had come to be comfortable with me, this leading us to several sessions of exploration of not only the her positive transference to me but also her relationship with other men.

Week 3

Angie began the first session of the third and final week by asking if I could help her take her meditation a step further. She reported that she had continued to use the phrase "For God so loved Angie" as a base of meditation over the weekend and that it was leading her nowhere new or productive. She said she now had a strong, persistent feeling that God did love her but that she wanted to figure out where, if at all, Jesus fit into the picture. She said this was important because she needed to know if her spiritual path was to be Christian.

I asked her if she might find my telling a story of Jesus to be a useful way to get to know him or her. She quickly agreed, and I launched into an Ericksonian (Erickson & Rossi, 1981) rendering of the encounter between Jesus and his disciples around the children whom she invited to come to her. Describing this group of children who were being chased away by adults who thought they were bothering Jesus, I built the story around Jesus' invitation that they come and climb up on her knee. Deeply engaged with this story as I told it, at the end she commented on how different this Jesus was from the one she had been introduced to in church as a child. Asking if this really was what Jesus was like, she went on to say that if she could be sure that she really was this loving and gentle, she longed to get to know her better.

Sessions for the remainder of this week were similarly built around the hypnotic telling of either an incident in the life of Jesus or a story told by him. These included such things as his encounter with the woman at the well, his description of himself as a good shepherd, and his story about the feast for those who were most broken and disenfranchised. In each case, Angie subsequently made each story the basis of her meditation between sessions. She also continued a journal-based dialogue with God and used our sessions largely to talk about her anxieties and hopes about her emerging encounter with Jesus. Near the end of this week, she visited a nearby church and reported at the next session that she found herself sitting in front of a crucifix deeply experiencing Jesus' love for her. She said that as she looked at this, she saw Jesus as a woman but could understand how others might related better to her as a man.

Therapeutic Outcomes: Immediate and Long Term

Ending the retreat, Angie spoke of a significant reduction in depression and the presence of a new sense of well-being. She stated that she continued to feel a deep sense of peace and felt assured of God's love for her. She indicated that she did not wish to return to psychotherapy because she felt she had gained all she could from this. I urged her to continue her work with her therapist, or, at the very least, to return to her for a chance to process the experience with me.

I next heard from her 4 months later. She said that she had not returned to her therapist and had discontinued her medication. She reported being less depressed than she had been for at least 10 years and that her self-esteem and relationships with men were both also dramatically improved. Although she said still felt safest with gay men, she had come to feel safe enough with one straight male colleague that she was cautiously developing a friendship with him. She indicated that she had continued to paint and had several pieces showing in a small gallery. She also reported a continuing deep sense of peace and well-being, as well as a deep and relatively stable sense of God's presence and love for her. She also said she was surprised to discover a beginning devotion to Jesus, who remained mostly female with some male qualities. Finally, she also indicated periodic attendance at and involvement in a church and that she was finding this helpful.

No single case can, of course, adequately represent either the types of people or typical process or outcome of any treatment approach. In one important way, Angie was atypical of ISC recipients. Her spiritual path was not—at least at the beginning of our work together—clearly or self-consciously Christian. Most recipients of ISC are committed to the Christian spiritual path, often well advanced on it. Some, however, like Angie, are either much closer to the beginning or unclear about the nature of the path they are on. One advantage of selecting a case such as hers is that it illustrates the way in which ISC, an approach explicitly grounded in a Christian understanding of psychospiritual formation, can be usefully adapted to work with people who do not clearly identify with either Christian faith or spirituality. The disadvantage is that it fails to illustrate much of the way in which the Ignatian vision of spiritual formation informs the model, other than the way in which the route is understood to begin with a grounding in God's love.

In many other ways, however, Angie's experience in ISC is typical. It illustrates the way in which ISC always involves some combination of psychotherapy and spiritual direction. It also illustrates the way in which the focus of the work tends to swing between the spiritual and psychological aspects of functioning as well as the way in which recipients typically report gains in both.

REFERENCES

American Psychiatric Association. (1994). *Diagnostic and statistical manual of mental disorders* (4th ed.). Washington, DC: Author.

Arieti, S. (1976). *Creativity: The magic synthesis*. New York: Basic Books.

Barry, W. A. (1991). *Finding God in all things: A companion to the spiritual exercises of St. Ignatius*. Notre Dame, IN: Ave Marie Press.

Benner, D. G. (1988) *Psychotherapy and the spiritual quest*. Grand Rapids, MI: Baker.

Benner, D. G. (1998). *Care of souls: Revisioning Christian nurture and counsel*. Grand Rapids, MI: Baker.

Butcher, J. N., Dahlstrom, W. G., Graham, J. R., Tellegen, A., & Kaemmer, B. (1989). *Minnesota Multiphasic Personality Inventory—2*. Minneapolis, MN: University of Minnesota Press.

Corbett, L. (1996). *The Religious function of the psyche*. London: Routledge.

Erickson, M. H., & Rossi, E. L. (1981). *Experiencing hypnosis*. New York: Irvington.

Fairbairn, W. R. D. (1952). *An object relations theory of personality*. New York: Basic Books.

Frankl, V. (1963). *Man's search for meaning*. New York: Knopf.

Hillman, J. (1975). *Revisioning psychology*. New York: Harper & Row.

Jung, C. G. (1933). *Modern man in search of a soul*. New York: Harcourt Brace & World.

Jung, C. G. (1961). *Memories, dreams, and reflections*. New York: Pantheon.

Karasu, B. (1999). Spiritual psychotherapy. *American Journal of Psychotherapy, 53*, 143–162.

Keating, T. (1992). *Open mind, open heart*. New York: Continuum.

Keating, T. (1998). *Invitation to love: The way of Christian contemplation*. New York: Continuum.

Kelsey, M. (1978). *Dreams: A way to listen to God*. New York: Paulist Press.

Kohut, H. (1971). *The analysis of the self*. Madison, CT: International Universities Press.

Maslow, A. (1970). Neurosis as a failure of human growth. In W. S. Sahakian (Ed.), *Psychopathology today: Experimentation, theory and research*. (pp. 122–130). Itasca, IL, Peacock.

McDargh, J. (1983). *Psychoanalytic object relation theory and the study of religion*. Lanham, MD: University Press of America.

Meissner, W. W. (1999). *To the greater glory: A psychological study of Ignatian spirituality*. Milwaukee, WI: Marquette University Press.

Meissner, W. W. (1984). *Psychoanalysis and religious experience*. New Haven, CT: Yale University Press.

Merton, T. (1961a). *New seeds of contemplation*. New York: New Directions/Penguin.

Merton, T. (1961b). *The new man*. New York: Bantam Books.

Merton, T. (1993). *Thoughts in solitude*. Boston: Shambhala.

Mills, J. & Crowley, R. (1986). *Therapeutic metaphors for children and the child within*. New York: Brunner/Mazel.

Moore, T. (1992). *Care of the soul: A guide for cultivating depth and sacredness in everyday life*. New York: HarperCollins.

Pennington, M. B. (1982). *Centering prayer*. New York: Image Books/Doubleday.

Sanford, J. (1978). *Dreams and healing: A succinct and lively interpretation of dreams*. New York: Paulist Press.

Silf, M. (1999). Inner compass: An invitation to Ignatian spirituality. Chicago: Loyola Press.

Tournier, P. (1957). *The meaning of persons*. London: SCM Press.

Tyrrell, B. J. (1982). *Christotherapy II*. New York: Paulist Press.

van Kaam, A. (1972). *The art of existential counseling*. Denville, NJ: Dimension Books.

Winnicott, D. W. (1971). *Playing and reality*: New York: Basic Books.

Yalom, I. (1980). *Existential psychotherapy*. New York: Basic Books.

13

INTEGRATIVE SPIRITUALLY
ORIENTED PSYCHOTHERAPY

LEN SPERRY

In this psychotherapeutic approach, the clinician functions as both psychotherapist and spiritual guide. The psychological and spiritual dimensions of human experience are considered to be related with the spiritual having primacy because spirituality is understood to be our response to our most basic longing and desire. As an integrative approach, it is based on a composite developmental and pathology model of health and well-being; it views growth in a holistic fashion including the biological, psychological, social, and spiritual dimensions; and it blends a number of concepts and methods derived from other approaches. Special attention is directed to a comprehensive assessment of the client's overall health status, psychological strengths and defenses, and moral and spiritual development considerations. Spiritual considerations include relationship with God, God-image or God-representation, core psychospiritual schemas, and spiritual practices including involvement in a spiritually supportive community. In this approach, the clinician listens for both psychological and spiritual meaning. Goals of this approach are to promote the processes of both cure (i.e., symptom relief, improved functioning, or even major personality change) and healing (i.e., self and social transformation). Various psychotherapeutic and spiritual modalities are utilized to achieve this goal.

DESCRIPTION OF THE APPROACH

Historical and Theoretical Basis

Spiritually oriented approaches to psychotherapy arise out of specific theoretical and contextual circumstances. Accordingly, integrative spiritually oriented psychotherapy is rooted in a blend of theoretical approaches and constructs (i.e., the biopsychosocial and biopsychosociospiritual models, biopsychosocial therapy, spiritual direction and developments in virtue and attachment theory) and in unique contextual circumstances (i.e., my training and experience with complex and often difficult-to-treat patients and clients in an academic medical center). Four historical roots and four theoretical assumptions inform this approach and are briefly described in this section.

Historical Roots

1. Biopsychosociospiritual Model. Before my clinical experience as an attending physician and professor of psychiatry and behavioral medicine at an academic medical center, I had successfully practiced a single modality-oriented psychotherapy with relatively high-functioning individuals in a private-practice setting. Unfortunately, the success I had experienced with this approach did not translate well to the difficult-to-treat individuals who were routinely referred to our tertiary care treatment clinic by frustrated single-modality-oriented clinicians in the community. It did not take long before I became acquainted with and embraced the biopsychosocial model. As described by Engel (1977), the biopsychosocial model is a holistic perspective for understanding and explaining the interfacing biological, psychological, and social forces that influence health, illness, and well-being. More specifically, an adequate understanding and explanation of an individual's situation is possible only when the clinician considers the biological, psychological, and social dimensions affecting the individual because a holistic and multidimensional explanation is more powerful and complete than simply a psychological or a biological or a social explanation. The obvious corollary was that a biopsychosocial and multidimensional understandings should be followed by biopsychosocial, multidimensional, and multimodal treatment interventions. Thereafter, I evaluated all clients from a biopsychosocial perspective. Although I continued to utilize a single modality approach with psychotherapy clients whose issues were primarily psychological, I sought to plan and implement multidimensional, multimodal interventions with those clients whose issues were broader. I came to call this approach biopsychosocial therapy (Sperry, 1988, 1999a, 2000a, 2000b, 2001a, 2001b). Biopsychosocial therapy is not so much a uniquely new treatment approach as it is an articulation and systematization of a way of conceptualizing and implementing treatment based on biopsychosocial principles.

About this same time, I was receiving referrals of individuals for whom religious and spiritual issues were reflected in their psychiatric presentation. Although the biopsychosocial model was helpful in these cases, it seemed somewhat reductionist because of its omission of the spiritual dimension. The recognition of a more comprehensive and integrative perspective that included the spiritual dimension evolved in my research and writing as the *biopsychosociospiritual* perspective (Sperry, 1986, 2000a). I began to conceive of biopsychosocial therapy that was sensitive to the spiritual dimension as integrative spiritually oriented psychotherapy (Sperry, 1998, 2003a, 2003b).

2. *Spiritual Direction.* In many ways my approach to spiritually oriented psychotherapy, as well as that of other practitioners (May, 1982; Tyrell, 1982), is somewhat similar to the practice of spiritual direction. Psychotherapy approaches that are receptive and effective in dealing with a client's spiritual concerns, such as transpersonal psychotherapy, incorporate some or many of the functions of spiritual direction (Sperry, 2003a) and involve both therapeutic and spiritual listening. The various transpersonal psychotherapies consider the therapeutic relationship to be the ideal context for dealing with both the spiritual and psychological dimensions (Cortright, 1997). It is notable that the use of meditation and other spiritual practices in psychotherapy has been normative for most transpersonal approaches. Although many of these approaches are not overtly Christian in their orientation, these approaches appear to have successfully and effectively combined many or all of the spiritual direction functions along with the psychotherapy functions within the role of the spiritually oriented psychotherapist. Their clients may also be involved with a meditation teacher or group, but many, if not all, of the spiritual direction functions are performed by their psychotherapists. There are several spiritual direction functions, and they appear to be remarkably similar to psychotherapy functions (Sperry, 2003a). Nine such functions have been described and are briefly summarized in Exhibit 13.1.

3. *Attachment Theory and God-Image.* God-images—that is, an individual's internal representations of God—have been the subject of clinical research and practice for some time (Rizzuto, 1981, 1991). Attachment theory contends that individuals' emotional relationships with others are significantly influenced by early attachment with their parents (Ainsworth, Behar, Waters, & Wall, 1978). Neurobiological research suggests that although early attachments influence brain structure, effective psychotherapy of other life-changing experiences can change these neural networks (Siegel, 1999). Recent research on attachment and God-images indicates that God evinces all of the defining characteristics of an attachment figure to whom individuals turn to for a safe haven and secure base. Such attachment to God, even when parental attachment has been insecure, appears to confer the kinds of psychological benefits associated with secure interpersonal attachments (Kirkpatrick, 1999).

EXHIBIT 13.1
Similarity of Functions in Psychotherapy (P) and Spiritual Direction (SD)

Therapeutic Listening Versus Spiritual Listening. Listening therapeutically in P, which fosters resolution, personality change, or cure, is similar but different from listening for spiritual meaning, which fosters transformation, spiritual wholeness, or healing (SD). *Initial Evaluation: Spiritual Assessment.* Whereas the initial evaluation in P elicits presenting problem, social and developmental history, and so on, the assessment in SD elicits the client's religious upbringing, image of God, basic values and beliefs, and involvement in a spiritual community, prayer, and other spiritual practices.

Differential Diagnosis: Differentiating Spiritual Experiences From Psychopathology. Akin to the function of differential diagnosis in P, a similar SD function is differentiating spiritual experiences, issues, and emergencies from psychopathology. Individuals, who may have no obvious personal vulnerability or family history of mental illness can have unusual or troubling spiritual experiences on their spiritual journey (e.g., mystical experiences such as visions can present similar to psychosis; "dark night of the soul" experiences are similar to depressive disorders).

Symptom Reduction and Improved Functioning: Transformation. Transformation is perhaps the central issue and goal of SD. Transformation is the process of undergoing a radical change of mind and heart, a dying to the false self and a continually assenting to one's true self that reflects the image and likeness of God. Transformation is a lifelong process and reflects *healing.* This contrasts with *cure*, that is, symptom resolution, increased functioning, or major personality change, which is the ultimate goal of psychotherapy.

Therapeutic Alliance Versus Therapist–Client–God Relationship. SD is a powerful means of developing one's relationship with God because SD involves a relationship among God, the client, and the director. Although there are some obvious similarities between the establishment of a therapeutic alliance between client and psychotherapists in P and fostering the relationship in SD direction, there is also an obvious difference.

Clinical Intervention Versus Spiritual Advisement. To foster its goal of transformation, SD focuses on advising the client about prayer, meditation, and the use of spiritual practices. The closest analogue to this advisement in P are clinical interventions such as interpretation, cognitive restructuring, "homework," and, of course, giving advice.

Mutual Collaboration Versus Discernment. In P, mutual collaboration in making decisions about treatment fosters the client's commitment to the therapeutic process. In SD, the process of discernment involves the director listening with the client to discern God's will for the client, asking probing questions, offering suggestions, and providing a supportive, prayerful presence for deep listening.

Psychological Resistance Versus Spiritual Resistance. Resistance occurs in both P and SD, although the director may not possess the therapist's skill and experience to recognize and deal with it.

Transference and Counter-Transference. Transference and counter-transference are issues in both P and SD, although the director may not possess the therapist's skill and experience to recognize and deal with it.

I typically elicit a client's God-images at the onset of treatment and monitor it at selective points over the course of treatment. Just as a client's early recollections tend to change in a positive direction as therapy progresses, it has been my observation that God-images similarly change as positive therapeutic change occurs. A recent clinical outcomes study found that clients' images of God positively changed over the course of outpatient therapy (Cheston, Piedmont, Eanes, & Lavin, 2003).

4. *Positive Psychology and Strength–Virtue Research*. Good character consists of the practice of various virtues. Fostering virtue is central in spiritual formation and spiritual direction and is an integral feature of integrative spiritually oriented psychotherapy. Unlike psychological constructs such as personality and self that focus primarily on the individual, character is a construct in moral philosophy and theology that focuses on the individual's relationship and responsibility to the community. Thus, character and virtue are principally social rather than personal constructs.

In the past, when there was considerable overlap between psychology and moral philosophy, virtue and character were important elements in both experimental and applied psychology. As psychology strove to become a scientific and value-free discipline, virtue and character moved out of favor in the early part of the 20th century (Allport, 1937). Recently, virtue and character have been retrieved in the field of scientific psychology (McCullough & Snyder, 2000), and the ascendancy of the positive psychology movement—an effort to redress the negative, pathological, and clinical focus of the field—has made virtues and human strength one of its thee pillars (Seligman & Csikszentmihalyi, 2000). A key tenet of positive psychology is that strengths and virtues function to build character and buffer against misfortune and the expression of psychopathology and appear to be the key to developing psychological resilience (Seligman & Peterson, 2003). Clinically relevant research is underway on such virtues as self-control, love, hope, humility, patience, wisdom, courage, gratitude, and forgiveness.

Theoretical Assumptions

Four basic theoretical assumptions of integrative spiritually oriented psychotherapy are briefly articulated here.

1. *Primacy of the Spiritual Dimension*. Integrative spiritually oriented psychotherapy assumes that all dimensions of human experience—biological, psychological, social, and spiritual—are considered in the treatment process. Of these the spiritual dimension has primacy over the other three because it involves ultimate concerns and gives meaning and direction to life. As noted earlier, integrative spiritually oriented psychotherapy is derived from the *biopsychosociospiritual* model and biopsychosocial therapy; with its emphasis on character and virtue, it extends beyond the individual's needs and concerns to the larger community. Other basic assumptions include that God exists, that spirituality provides a moral framework for therapy, and that faith and spiritual experiences are important for healing and well-being. Although therapeutic listening may be operative in spiritual direction, spiritual listening is its sine qua non.

2. *Developmental–Growth Perspective*. From the 1960s until the third edition of the *Diagnostic and Statistical Manual* appeared, self-actualization

was a reimbursable treatment goal, and the developmental model was the heart and soul of psychotherapy, particularly for the growth-oriented approaches. With *DSM–III* and managed care, the pathology model effectively displaced the developmental model (Sperry, 2002a). A revival of a developmental focus in psychotherapy is underway, however (Sperry, 2002a). A developmentally focused psychotherapy conceptualizes a client's needs and concerns on a continuum, or developmental line, ranging from pathological states to growth states. Thus, therapy goals can be specified as "problem-focused" or "growth focused" as therapy progresses and the client moves along his or her developmental line. Three distinct ranges on this developmental line can be specified: the disordered, the adequate, and the optimal ranges. Accordingly, the goal of traditional psychotherapy for clients with personality disorders often focuses on moving clients from the disordered range to somewhere within the adequate range of functioning. When that point is reached, therapy is assumed to have been successful. From a spiritual perspective, however, such a goal for change or growth can be limiting. Instead, I contend that the goal of spiritually oriented psychotherapy can extend as far into the optimal range of functioning as is possible. Integrative spiritually oriented psychotherapy is based on this developmental model (Sperry, 2002a).

3. *Transformation as the Goal.* Across the major religious and spiritual traditions, transformation is considered the end point or outcome of the spiritual journey. Spiritual transformation is a process of change into a mature relationship with God that has repercussions for human relationships and human actions. As such, it is a journey of growth and development that includes experiences of self-transcendence, that is, the capacity to view life from a larger, more objective perspective. Transformation is also referred to as *conversion experience* (Rambo, 1993) and *quantum change* (Miller & C'de Baca, 2001) wherein spiritually transforming experiences, whether sudden or gradual, often result in significant life changes, such as identity and life meaning, both self-defining personality functions (Paloutzian, Richardson, & Rambo, 1999).

In the Christian tradition, transformation implies both self-transformation and social transformation of the community and world under the reign of God (Sperry, 2002b). Although integrative spiritually oriented psychotherapy may include the traditional therapeutic goals of symptom alleviation and return-to-baseline functioning, it is primarily focused on transformation. Clinically, six markers of transformation are assessed and evaluated over the course of treatment: biological, affective, moral, intellectual, sociopolitical, and spiritual (Gelpi, 1998; Sperry, 2002b).

4. *Integrative and Tailored Treatment.* An integrative approach to spiritually oriented psychotherapy is by definition comprehensive or holistic instead of being narrow and reductionist. It provides a critical correlation and synthesis of various psychological and spiritual constructs and address all the

dimensions of human experience—biological, psychological, social, and spiritual—rather than just one or two. Furthermore, it emphasizes the process or journey of transformation and the dimensions of transformation. Such an approach differs from spiritually oriented approaches that are primarily psychologically focused, reductionist, and single-modality treatments.

Integrative spiritually oriented psychotherapy as described here is a comprehensive approach based on a *biopsychosociospiritual* perspective. It fosters the integration of theory and tailored treatment modalities and interventions. Tailored treatment refers to specific ways of customizing treatment modalities and therapeutic approaches to "fit" the client's unique needs, cognitive, emotional, and personality styles, and treatment expectations (Sperry, 1995).

The treatment process evolves in phases—engagement, assessment, intervention, maintenance–termination—and tailoring is essential at each phase (Sperry, 1999a, 2002b). In the engagement phase, the therapist endeavors to establish a working therapeutic relationship and maximize the client's readiness and motivation to change and develop. In the assessment phase, an evaluation is made of the client's symptomatic distress and impairment, as well as maladaptive and patterns of affects, thoughts, and behavior. Such schemas, particularly, psychospiritual schemas, can involve spiritual themes that reflect unhealthy religious beliefs and practices (Cecero, 2002). In addition, a spiritual assessment is undertaken that includes virtues spiritual practices and markers of transformation (Sperry, 2002b). In the intervention phase, effort is focused on modification of maladaptive patterns or transformation (or both). In the maintenance–termination phase, the focus is on maintaining the change and, when appropriate, reducing the client's reliance on the treatment relationship.

Based on a comprehensive biopsychosociospiritual evaluation, treatment is planned and tailored to the client's needs, personality style, and expectations. Various psychotherapeutic, psychospiritual, spiritual, and biological or somatic interventions and strategies are used in this plan (Sperry, 2001c).

Psychotherapeutic interventions include cognitive restructuring of dysfunctional religious beliefs and related strategies to modify maladaptive schemas. They also include psychodynamic interpretation, fostering a corrective emotional experience, social-skills training when indicated, and specific intersession assignments (i.e., homework).

Psychospiritual interventions include spiritual discussions, mindfulness, the practice of virtue, spiritual journaling, and experiential approaches (i.e., focusing). When indicated, referral or collaboration with the client's minister or spiritual guide may occur (Sperry, 2001c).

Spiritual practices may be encouraged, such as prayer, fasting, almsgiving, meditation, reading spiritual or inspirational texts, participation in a religious or spiritual community, stewardship of natural resources, or civic involvement (Sperry, 2001c, 2002b).

Biological interventions include medication or referral for medication evaluation or management, diet and nutritional supplementation or referral for a nutritional evaluation and prescription, exercise prescription, referral for such evaluations and prescriptions, and other stress management strategies as indicated (Sperry, 1999b).

The Relationship Between Psychotherapy and Spirituality

Spirituality is understood to be about our deepest desire, which everyone experiences but which can never be fully satisfied because it is always stronger than any satisfaction. In addition, it involves our ultimate concerns and gives meaning and direction to life. Accordingly, spirituality is neither a marginal activity nor an option that only a few pursue or want to discuss in psychotherapy. More specifically, spirituality is what we do with that desire, how we channel our energy and the disciplines and habits we choose to live by that lead either to a greater integration or to disintegration within ourselves and in our relationships with others, including God (Rolheiser, 1999).

Spiritual growth is understood to parallel psychological growth. There is some interdependence between the psychological and the spiritual, as well as between the biological and social dimensions of human experience and growth. Although growth in one dimension tends to foster growth in the other, however, growth is one is not absolutely dependent on the other. A basic implication is that psychological and spiritual issues can be discussed and therapeutically processed in the same session, and growth in one areas tends to foster or at least set the stage for growth in the other. For many clients, both spiritual disciplines and psychotherapeutic work are necessary to achieve wholeness.

Therapist's Skills and Attributes

Requisite Knowledge and Skills

Providing integrative spiritually oriented psychotherapy in a competent manner assumes that the therapist has a working knowledge of the psychodynamic theory involving object relations theory and God-images (Kirkpatrick, 1999; Rizzuto, 1981), attachment theory (Ainsworth et al., 1978), and an understanding of core schemas originating from the work of Adler (1956) and further developed by cognitive therapists such as Beck and colleagues (1990) and Young (1999; Young, Klosko, & Weishaar, 2003). It requires that the therapist listen for both therapeutic and spiritual meaning, that is, the sacred in human experience and circumstances. It also requires solid grounding in some integrative psychotherapeutic approach, such as biopsychosocial therapy, in which the spiritual dimension has been incorporated into the case conceptualization and treatment plan. Furthermore, the effective use of this approach requires a reasonable degree of competence in planning and implementing tailored, biopsychosocial interventions along with psychospiritual interventions, spiritual practices, and somatic interventions, as noted earlier.

Training and Experience

At a minimum, this approach requires that the therapist have some personal experience as a client in spiritual direction or spiritually oriented psychotherapy. Ideally, the therapist should be involved in ongoing spiritual formation. In addition, those using this approach should have some experience, preferably supervised, with integrating spiritual interventions in psychotherapeutic treatment.

Personal and Spiritual Attributes

First and foremost, this approach assumes that the therapist will be sensitive and respectful of clients' spiritual practices and religious and denominational beliefs and will refrain from proselytizing or similar behaviors. At the present time, this approach has been developed and practiced within a Christian spiritual framework. As such, the approach would seem more likely to be accessible to therapists who have made an abiding commitment to ongoing personal and spiritual development, living out that commitment within a broadly conceived Christian or other theistic approach to spiritual formation. Involvement in a supportive spiritual community is also assumed.

Strengths and Limitations

Theoretical Strengths and Weaknesses

The main advantages of integrative spiritually oriented psychotherapy are its comprehensive and holistic focus and its capacity to be effective with a wide range of presentations involving both high-functioning individuals as well as complex and more severely impaired individuals with spiritual and psychological issues. With regard to theoretical weakness, it may be that as it attempts to integrate constructs from divergent theoretical approaches, there is the tendency, as there is in all integrative approaches, to view various constructs as more theoretically and clinically compatible than is possible or realistic.

Practical Strengths and Weaknesses

Perhaps the main strength of this approach is that because it is a tailored approach to treatment, it is applicable to a broad range of client needs and styles. Ironically, this is perhaps the approach's main weakness; integrative spiritually oriented psychotherapy requires or demands extensive knowledge and experience in effectively utilizing a wide variety of interventions, and the willingness of the therapist or clinician to accommodate and tailor treatment to client need and style. It also assumes that therapists have made a personal commitment to their own ongoing spiritual formation, which some therapists may perceive as a deterrent or weakness.

Integrative spiritually oriented psychotherapy is of particular interest to those who appreciate that multiple factors affect and influence spiritual issues, who value the integrative perspective, and who believe that tailored treatment optimizes outcomes.

Indications and Contraindications

Because this approach is comprehensive and holistic in scope, it is indicated in a wide variety of presentations ranging from severe psychiatric disorders with spiritual issues to high-functioning individuals with various spiritual and religious concerns. There are no obvious contraindications to this approach.

Cultural and Gender Considerations

Because this approach emphasizes a collaborative working relationship in which therapist and client and mutually engage in the process, a high degree of cultural sensitivity and competence is required of the therapist. The approach is equally applicable to both male and female clients.

Expected Future Developments and Directions

Societal and Cultural Trends

It is anticipated that as increasing numbers of adults seek out spiritual and psychological care, especially baby boomers, individuals with more complex biopsychological conditions will need a treatment that is geared to their biopsychosocial needs. Integrative spiritually oriented psychotherapy and similar holistic and integrative approaches have the potential to be effective treatment modalities to the extent that they are tailored to client needs and styles.

Theoretical and Research Developments

It is anticipated that future theoretical developments and empirical research in attachment theory and in the neurosciences will further validate the theoretical basis for this approach and expand its clinical applicability. At the present time, no controlled research on this approach is underway.

CASE EXAMPLE[1]

Client Demographics, Relevant History, and Presenting Concern

Presenting Problem

Gwen, a 42-year-old, married, Euro-American female, was referred by her family physician for evaluation and treatment of "chronic depression" of

---

[1]Adapted from *Casebook for a Spiritual Strategy in Counseling and Psychotherapy* (pp. 142–152), by P. S. Richards and A. E. Bergin, 2004, Washington, DC: American Psychological Association. Copyright 2004 by the American Psychological Association.

approximately 5 years' duration. He had prescribed her a trial of Prozac, which had numerous side effects but "didn't work."

Before starting the medication, she had consulted with two psychotherapists for two and three sessions respectively before terminating treatment. She claimed that neither therapist had understood her and "they probably couldn't help me anyway." When asked what the likelihood was that I could understand her any more than the other therapists she had seen, she said she had read a newspaper article in which I was quoted about spiritual issues in psychotherapy and thought that I might have something to offer her.

Treatment History

Six years before the onset of the treatment, Gwen had been hospitalized for an eating disorder, presumably bulimia. She had used exercise, self-induced vomiting, and laxatives as "control" measures. The hospitalization was precipitated by marital conflict and increasing suspiciousness about her husband Jason's presumed infidelity. She left the inpatient program after 4 days, against medical advice. Hospital records indicated that she had been suspicious about the motives of the treatment team. When I first evaluated her, Gwen showed prominent obsessive and perfectionistic traits as well as some narcissistic and paranoid features. She denied any family history of psychological or substance abuse treatment. She noted, however, that some relatives believed that a relative's untimely death may have been due to suicide. Apparently, the relative, her father's second cousin, had considerable mood lability.

Situation at Time of Initial Consultation

Gwen had been married to Jason for 23 years. There were two children, a 22-year-old son, Alex, and a 21-year-old daughter, Nancy. Gwen was a guidance counselor in a local private high school, and Jason was a senior vice president at a local bank. She had been a lifelong member of the Episcopal Church. She attended parochial elementary and high schools and after graduation immediately went on to the state university to major in English literature. She met Jason during her sophomore year at the university and married him soon after they graduated.

Developmental History

Gwen was the older of two siblings. Her younger sister, age 38, graduated from college and worked as a insurance underwriter. She never married and had little, if any, "religious sentiment," according to Gwen. Both of Gwen's parents were alive and had lived in the same house for 39 years. Although they were relatively healthy, Gwen's father was recently diagnosed with early-stage prostate cancer and had been treated for high blood pressure for more than 20 years. Her parents were reportedly active in their church for several years. Her father had served as the chair of church's finance committee for about 30 years, and her mother was a religious education teacher in the church's Sunday school program for several years.

Relationship of the Therapist and Client

The therapeutic relationship is central in integrative spiritually oriented psychotherapy. Because therapeutic outcomes are largely dependent on the client's engagement in an empathic therapeutic process, it was important to elicit Gwen's explanation of the nature of her concerns and her expectations for treatment, as well as in negotiating treatment goals and the plan of treatment. Because of her perception that past therapies and therapists had not really understood or helped her, it was incumbent on me to demonstrate understanding and caring. Thus, in the initial sessions, I endeavored to come to a meeting of hearts and minds with her. As noted later, this meant increasing her level of confidence and trust in me and the treatment process. Because symptom relief was so important to her at the first sessions, it was essential to deal with her sensitivity to medication side effects as well as her suspiciousness and wariness.

Assessment: Rationale and Type of Data Collected

A detailed initial intake evaluation, including a full spiritual assessment, was completed. Previous records were reviewed, and psychological testing, which consisted of the Millon Clinical Multiaxial Inventory (MCMI–III) and the Beck Depression Inventory (BDI) were administered. The MCMI–III suggested the diagnosis of dysthymic disorder and somatoform disorder NOS (not otherwise described) as well as obsessive–compulsive personality disorder with paranoid, narcissistic, and histrionic features. The BDI score was 17, suggestive of a moderate degree of depression.

Records for her only psychiatric hospitalization were reviewed. Results of the Minnesota Multiphasic Personality Inventory administered during her inpatient hospitalization revealed a 9–4 pattern. On projective testing consisting of the Thematic Apperception Test (TAT) and Rorschach, considerable anger directed at her patents was elicited. TAT themes included fathers as demanding individuals whose expectations were impossible to meet as well as daughters not noticed by fathers. There were also themes of mothers who were ungiving, incompetent, and wanting to be taken care of by daughters. The report concludes that she "deals with her anger by being resistive in a childlike way rather than constructively by taking control of situations."

Spiritual Assessment

Gwen's formal practice of her religion had diminished considerably since her son had graduated from high school. She indicated that she only kept up church attendance and traditional spiritual practice "to set a good example for my children." For the past several years, her spiritual practices had included daily formula prayer, occasional scripture reading, and Sunday worship services. She had once tried to meditate but had given up after about a week or so "because I was just too distracted and flooded with worrisome thoughts." At the outset of treatment, she described her image of God as " judge and taskmaster." On further inquiry, she described God as an elderly male who "made hard demands, who checked up on you and wasn't easily pleased." To her, he was also emotionally withholding, unsupportive, and critical. Not surprisingly, but unrecognized by Gwen at the outset of therapy, her image of God was a composite description of both her parents.

For Gwen, faith had meant believing there was a God, and that achieving salvation was up to her. She had to work hard and be perfect, or she would be viewed as worthless in the sight of God and in the sight of those in her parish. It's not surprising that she felt "uncomfortable" in her church community when her world was falling apart before and after she was hospitalized. Unfortunately, her perfectionistic beliefs that she was "never good enough" were ego-syntonic with her religious beliefs, that is, "God helps those . . ." and "God is always watching and seeing your sins." It shouldn't be surprising that her image of God was that of judge and taskmaster. Fortunately, as treatment continued, these beliefs that supported her self-view began to moderate, as did her image of God.

Gwen indicated that she had not been active in her church congregation for nearly 6 years. She explained that she "didn't feel comfortable around those people anymore." When asked what she meant, she noted that after her son had graduated and moved away her desire to serve on church committees with the friends of his parents had greatly diminished. Later, it would come to light that she felt "unworthy" around these same individuals "after I messed up my life" at the time of her inpatient hospitalization. This attitude toward her church congregation persisted until it was processed during the course of therapy.

Diagnostic and Clinical Case Conceptualization

Gwen met criteria for the following DSM–IV diagnoses:

Axis I: Mood disorder, NOS (296.50); eating disorder NOS (307.50) by history
Axis II: Obsessive–compulsive personality disorder (301.4) with narcissistic, histrionic and paranoid features
Axis III: None
Axis IV: Marital distress
Axis V: GAF 54 (68 highest in the previous 12 months)

Although there may have been some genetic loading for Gwen's mood disorder, it is more probable that psychodynamic factors, such as perfectionism and her high need for control, were related to her eating disorder. Her avoidant–anxious attachment style appeared to reflect both her involvement with both parents, that is, a self-preoccupied and emotionally withholding mother and a strict, demanding, and abusive father. It also reflected her self-view of being of driven and fearful of displeasing others and her worldview that life and others are cruel, demanding, and uncaring. It is not surprising that she imagined God as demanding, critical, and withholding, nor that she reacted to others with anger and suspiciousness when distressed. Her discomfort and limited contact with community support, particularly her church, seemed related to feelings of unworthiness and perceived nonacceptance from others. The spiritual practices she described (i.e., limited to formula prayer and church attendance) were consistent with her religious tradition and limited to being based on fear and duty. It is interesting to note that her religious beliefs about "earning" salvation appear to reinforce her own perfectionistic beliefs and strivings. Finally, three areas of strength that may have potential therapeutic value can be noted. First, she reported that she had refrained from laxative use and purging for nearly a year before this course of therapy. Second, she had previously exhibited perseverance in maintaining church attendance and spiritual practices to set a positive example for her son. Third, she has maintained a long-term relationship with her husband despite conflicts.

Treatment Goals, Process, and Intervention Strategies

Gwen initially wanted medication and "some therapy until things get better" but indicated that making a commitment to remain in ongoing treatment would be difficult for her. I agreed to prescribe and monitor medications carefully and to involve her in all treatment decisions.

Short-Term Goals of Therapy

It was mutually decided that the initial focus of psychotherapy would be on reducing the stressors related to her depression and eating disorder. I carefully avoided the kind of transference "traps" that might result in prematurely termination. Although she had essentially eliminated purging behaviors in the past year, she did admit to exercising vigorously every day. In other words, she had replaced one compulsive behavior (purging) for another (excessive exercising). In time she agreed to continue to refrain from any purging behaviors and to adopt a relatively moderate exercise plan, an agreement she would keep throughout the course of treatment.

As treatment progressed, consisting of psychotherapy and medication, therapy became more directed toward the spiritual aspects of her drivenness and perfectionism as they related to her parents and her God-image. She described her father as strict, demanding and verbally and emotionally abusive and her mother as self-preoccupied and emotionally withholding. As noted earlier, her image of God was demanding, critical and withholding. In addition there was some unfinished business involving her estranged son. As these issues were processed and resolved she eventually reconciled with him.

Long-Term Goals of Therapy

The long-term goal of therapy was first to modify her obsessive–compulsive style from the disordered to the adequate range and then, by mutual agreement, from the adequate to a more optimal level. Specifically, this meant attempting to transform her basic perfectionistic pattern so that she might become more comfortable with affects, less reliant on her thinking function, and thereby more spontaneous and playful. Her core beliefs or schemas about being hardworking, good, and avoiding mistakes to feel accepted and worthwhile were examined and processed as was her need to be in control and overly responsible. Interpretation and cognitive restructuring were the main therapeutic strategies employed to modify the affective, cognitive, and relational aspects of her obsessive style. The specific goal was to increase her capacity for emotional involvement. This is represented as "average" level of functioning on the obsessive developmental line.

One point of difference between a traditional psychotherapeutic perspective and the integrative spiritually oriented perspective that I practice involves different treatment goals, particularly with regard to individuals with personality disorders. Whereas the goal of traditional psychotherapy with these individuals is typically symptom remission and return to baseline functioning, the goal of integrative spiritually oriented psychotherapy is personal and spiritual growth and well-being. More specifically, the goal is psychological and spiritual transformation.

What Gwen brought to treatment were her brokenness and cravings, as well as her intelligence, tenacity, and related strengths. Viewing therapy from the perspective of developmental lines, treatment was focused on reconfiguring her obsessive–compulsive personality style and building on her gifts and strengths. Not the least of these was her religious tradition.

From the perspective of her religious background, her sense of brokenness and cravings served as the basis for spiritual transformation. It was my role to support her efforts toward spiritual growth, particularly when she became discouraged. It also became my role to refocus and reframe her cravings as motivators or prompters of spiritual and psychological growth, rather than as simply triggers of binging and purging. Because her religious tradition also held that a community of believers—that is, parishes, retreats, and so on—can be an instrument of healing and growth, it was important that we found ways to incorporate this community dimension, and particularly spiritual resources within the community, into the therapy process. Consequently, I supported her desire to participate in quarterly experiential focusing retreats.

Similarly, I encouraged her efforts to bring the focusing method and journaling "home" with her. Initially, she began practicing focusing with her husband on Sunday evenings. In time, they invited some friends to join them. Later, I supported her as she transitioned back in to her parish community.

Therapeutic Strategy

The general therapeutic strategy for fostering Gwen's movement from the adequate to the optimal range involved both reconstructive strategies and developmental strategies. With regard to reconstructive strategies, an initial treatment focus is to help clients specify the limited number of situations in which it is reasonable or necessary to be especially goal directed and conscientious. For Gwen, this meant 8:00 a.m. to 3:00 p.m., Monday through Friday, 9 months a year, for her job, and perhaps another 10 hours a week on household duties and volunteer activities in her church. It would also mean that she would be prompted to practice becoming more spontaneous and less rigid in important and meaningful relationships in which she felt reasonably safe, such as with her husband, her boss, and her pastor.

With regard to obsessive–compulsive personality style, three ranges of functioning can be described, as noted earlier. In the disordered range, individuals are characterized by perfectionism and feeling avoidance, which interfere with task completion and relationships. Individuals' thinking and attitudes are overly rigid, and they tend to be pessimistic and to avoid feeling. In the adequate range of functioning, individuals are less perfectionistic, and the rigidity in tasks and relationships is moderated by some degree of emotional involvement and responsivity. In the optimal range, individuals are conscientious but not driven, and are more spontaneous. They are individuals who display a balance of personal integrity with generosity, hopefulness, and kindness.

Psychological Transformation

A number of specific strategies were used in working toward this goal of psychological transformation. These included attending to the theme of perfectionism in a fine-grained and focused manner. For example, Gwen's self-view or self-schema was "I am responsible if something goes wrong," whereas her underlying view of the world was "Life is always unpredictable and expects too much. So I must always work hard, be in control, and not make mistakes." Characteristic of the disordered range is Gwen's absolute conviction that she must be responsible in all situations, that life is always unpredictable and demanding, and that she must do her best in all situations. At the average range, however, her schemas would be less absolute, which means that there are a limited number of circumstances and situations in which she could let down her guard with regard to conscientiousness, rigidity, and feeling avoidance. The rest of the time, she was likely to be on her guard. In the optimal range, these conviction are still operative but are highly situation specific, meaning that Gwen could be more spontaneous and playful in many situations.

Another useful strategy was to help Gwen master some of her subtle and persistent perfectionistic patterns, that is, those trigger events or thoughts that initiate a sequence of perfectionistic thinking—including self-righteousness—and behaviors and related responses. Three of Gwen's more subtle perfectionistic patterns involved safeguarding her money, being overly focused on time, and dealing with mild cravings.

With regard to money, her husband affectionately referred to her as "my little tightwad" because she shopped for bargains, used coupons, and looked for discounts. The transformation of this attitude of stinginess is generosity.

With regard to focus on time and deadlines, she reported setting her watch and clocks in her home and car 20 minutes ahead so that she would be "on time," which was interesting because she was 5 to 10 minutes late for some of our sessions. Her packed schedule allowed no time for traffic delays, which were not supposed to happen in a perfect world. Needless to say, Gwen was extremely conscientious of time and resented it when others wasted it. The transformation of this attitude of time conscientiousness is becoming more spontaneous and playful.

A third concern involved the way she dealt with cravings. When stressed and tired, emotionally deprived, or having a queasy stomach, she would reached for caffeine, particularly chocolate, colas, and coffee, or she would seek out situations that were stimulating, such as high adventure movies and television programs. The resulting "adrenaline buzz" as she called it, temporarily appeased her cravings. She would immediately feel better but would soon felt like a worthless failure. Although small doses of caffeine was preferable to full-scale binging and purging, the end result was the same: she felt she had failed and resolved to try harder to be perfect. Reframing her cravings as growth motivators and establishing a relapse prevention strategy allowed her to short circuit this vicious cycle.

Similarly, being fun loving and carefree was difficult for Gwen. A common underlying maxim for her was, "I must do it and do it exceedingly well." The transformation of this attitude of duty-conscientiousness would involve achieving a degree of balance in her life among conscientiousness, spontaneity, and integrity. In addition, she tended to live in the future rather than the present. Accordingly, the transformation of this pattern involves the prescription to live in the present moment.

Not surprisingly, experiential focusing exercises were initially difficult for Gwen given her ruminative cognitive style. She was constantly processing new and old concerns, so much so that she became overwhelmed by this mental chatter and background noise, which made it all but impossible to focus on the present. Because both centering meditation and focusing require a quieting or derailing of this ruminative style, she learned to use a simple prayer word—some would call it a mantra—to derail this mental chatter; the word was "Jesus."

Characteristically, Gwen was demanding of herself and others. She constantly monitored others' actions against social norms and against her own personal norms. Not surprisingly, few people matched up to her standards, and she would judge others as being irresponsible. The actions of others triggered her moral indignation. Needless to say, she came across as judgmental and sometimes moralistic. For Gwen, transformation of this overall attitude would be hopefulness and kindness. Although these perfectionistic strivings are somewhat subtle and not only acceptable but also reinforced in our culture of achievement and success, Gwen began to recognize that they were inhibiting her personal and spiritual development and that changing them would be challenging.

Such a therapeutic direction with Gwen was effective to the extent that it focused on these fine-grained dimensions of perfectionism with the goal of becoming a conscientious but spontaneous person who could balance personal integrity with generosity, hopefulness, and kindness. In other words, instead of being compulsively perfectionistic in all matters, she might intentionally strive for a high level of excellence in a few selected areas of her life but not in others.

For Gwen, modifying the triggers for her perfectionistic pattern were essential in transforming this dynamic. On closer examination, we found that self-righteous thoughts such as "That's not right" or "That's sloppy work" inevitably triggered her perfectionistic pattern. Subsequently, we worked together to find ways of neutralizing such triggers and replacing then with a nonrighteous thought: "This moment is as perfect as it can be." Such a neutralizing thought became like a mantra that Gwen repeated whenever she was in "high-risk" situations that might trigger her perfectionistic pattern. With a little experimenting, Gwen also found that if she hummed to herself while going into high-risk situations, she could also derail the perfectionistic pattern.

Spiritual Transformation

As noted earlier, a number of spiritual disciplines were incorporated into the treatment process. These included prayer, particularly centering prayer and meditation, spiritual journaling, and participation in a healthy religious community. This participation provided her social support as well as a corrective emotional experience regarding some of her harsh and perfectionistic religious beliefs and attitudes. Spiritual discussion of her life situation and stressors in light of their spiritual meaning was a part of the therapeutic process. Furthermore, cognitive restructuring of dysfunctional religious beliefs appeared to influence a shift in her image of God.

Developing virtue and building on strengths was another focus of therapy. For Gwen, efforts to further develop the virtues of patience and serenity facilitated movement to optimal range of functioning. Gwen was receptive to focusing on these two virtues. Interestingly, she came across a few research articles on positive psychology about the virtue of patience, which served to reinforce and validate her efforts in this area.

Course of Treatment and Frequency and Duration of Sessions

Initially treatment was mutually agreed to be scheduled weekly in 50-minute sessions unless situations warranted meeting more often. Because of her wariness of being "controlled," she did not want to commit to ongoing therapy and reserved the right to stop treatment at anytime. She did agree to discuss the matter before doing so, however. As it turned out, treatment lasted for 3 years.

First Year of Treatment

After 6 months of weekly sessions, Gwen was sufficiently stable and confident to consider "going on with life" as she put it. For some time, she had entertained the thought of going back to school to become a high school guidance counselor or possibly an addictions counselor working with patients with eating disorder. Before her marriage, she had taught for 2 years and had enjoyed the challenge of working with kids in a junior high school setting. She believed that staying at home alone only fostered her depressed thinking and ruminations and wanted to "get out and do something with my life." She had been accepted in a master's-level counseling program, and although she could attend full time, she opted for a part-time program of study, fearing that she could not be as good a student as needed to be if she took more than two courses at a time. She also wanted to reduce session frequency from weekly to monthly sessions. Reluctantly, I agreed to this request.

Second Year of Treatment

Approximately 1 year later, when she was nearly half way through her graduate program, she mentioned attending a weekend spirituality workshop at a Catholic retreat center. It was a retreat based on experiential focusing, the approach developed by Gendlin (1981; see also chap. 9, this volume). Something about this experience touched her deeply, but she had difficulty describing this experience and the feelings it triggered. She also indicated that she had read an article on spirituality I had recently published and wondered whether our sessions could include the religious and spiritual dimension. She said the prospects of starting a counseling practicum in a nearby high school was disconcerting to her, and she was ready to resume weekly sessions. She entertained the thought of participating in additional spirituality retreats in the coming year.

Third Year of Treatment

Over the next year, Gwen became somewhat less self-critical and driven and more centered and at peace with herself. She attributed much of this centeredness and peacefulness to the regular practice of the focusing strategy she had learned during her various retreats. Her moodiness, which now appeared more like a dysthymic disorder than major depression, seemed to have moderated considerably. As a result, we endeavored to wean off the antidepressant and to monitor her without medications for the next few months. It appeared that she no longer needed the medication.

Termination and Treatment Outcomes

Three years after beginning this process, we mutually agreed to terminate ongoing treatment. Gwen felt good about her progress and confident about the future. Our mutually agreed-on relapse plan was to follow up with a session at 3 months and then to have phone contact at 3-month intervals for the first year. It was understood that, if indicated, an emergency session could be arranged. As therapy was winding down, her Global Assessment of Functioning score was in the low 90s.

Therapeutic Outcomes: Immediate and Long Term

Within 2 months of beginning treatment, Gwen was nearly asymptomatic. The slow titration of medications permitted a therapeutic effect without any of the side effects she had experienced previously. Her increasing trust in the treatment process facilitated her willingness to continue in ongoing therapy with a focus on growth and transformation.

As we prepared for termination, Gwen was much more centered, less driven, experienced few cravings, and felt much better about herself. In reviewing our work together, we agreed that she had achieved her stated treatment goals. We then discussed two options: moving into a maintenance mode preparatory to termination or shifting the treatment focus to "growth" goals in therapy, that is, moving toward the optimal range of functioning. With little hesitation, she chose to focus on growth goals. At the time, I recall making the predictive interpretation that she might find it difficult to discern the difference between true growth and more subtle perfectionistic strivings. I indicated, however, that one of my roles on this journey would be to help her discern these differences.

Gwen and her husband became more actively involved in their church community, with both involved in leading a youth group. Just after Thanksgiving, she experienced a brief relapse with her eating disorder. The next spring, her husband opted for early retirement and announced that it was time for her "to be the breadwinner." The prospect of taking such responsibility initially overwhelmed her because she feared making a mistake and not being the perfect wife and guidance counselor. These concerns were processed from both a psychological and a spiritual perspective. In time, she made sufficient progress so that sessions were reduced first to monthly and then quarterly. At the time of this writing 3 years later, she remains off medication.

REFERENCES

Adler, A. (1956). *The individual psychology of Alfred Adler* (H. Ansbacher & R. Ansbacher, Eds.). New York: Harper & Row.

Ainsworth, M., Behar, M., Waters, E., & Wall, S. (1978). *Patterns of attachment.* Hillsdale, NJ: Erlbaum.

Allport, G. (1937). *Personality: A psychological interpretation.* New York: Holt.

Beck, A., Freeman, A., Davis, D., & Associates. (1990). *Cognitive therapy of personality disorders.* New York: Guilford Press.

Cecero, J. (2002). *Praying through our lifetraps: A psychospiritual path to freedom.* Totowa, NJ: Resurrection Press.

Cheston, S., Piedmont, R., Eanes, B., & Lavin, L. (2003). Changes in client's image of god over the course of outpatient therapy. *Counseling and Values, 47,* 96–108.

Cortright, B. (1997). *Psychotherapy and spirit: Theory and practice in transpersonal psychotherapy.* Albany: State University of New York Press.

Engel, C. (1977). The need for a new medical model: A challenge to biomedical medicine. *Science, 196,* 129–136.

Gelpi, D. (1998). *The conversion experience: A reflective guide for RCIA participants and others.* New York: Paulist Press.

Gendlin, E. (1981). *Focusing.* New York: Bantam Books.

Kirkpatrick, L. (1999). Attachment and religious representations and behavior. In J. Cassidy & P. Shaver (Eds.), *Handbook of attachment: Theory, research and clinical applications* (pp. 803–822). New York: Guilford Press.

May, G. (1982). *Care of mind, care of soul: A psychiatrist explores spiritual direction.* San Francisco: HarperCollins.

McCullough, M., & Snyder, C. (2000). Classical sources of human strength: Revisiting an old house and building a new one. *Journal of Social and Clinical Psychology, 19,* 1–10.

Miller, W., & C'de Baca, J. (2001). *Quantum change: When epiphanies and sudden insights transform ordinary lives.* New York: Guilford Press.

Paloutzian, R., Richardson, J., & Rambo, L. (1999). Religious conversion and personality change. *Journal of Personality, 67,* 1047–1080.

Rambo, L. (1993). *Understanding religious conversion.* New Haven, CT: Yale University Press.

Richards, P. S., & Bergin, A. E. (Eds.). (2004). *Casebook for a spiritual strategy in counseling and psychotherapy*. Washington, DC: American Psychological Association.

Rizzuto, A. (1981). *The birth of the living God: A psychoanalytic study*. Chicago: University of Chicago Press.

Rizzuto, A. (1991). Religious development: A psychoanalytic point of view. In F. Oser & W. Scarlett (Eds.), *Religious Development in Childhood and Adolescence* [Special Issue]. *New Directions for Child Development, 52*, 47–60

Rolheiser, R. (1999). *The holy longing: The search for a Christian spirituality*. New York: Doubleday.

Seligman, M., & Csikszentmihalyi, M. (2000). Positive psychology: An introduction. *American Psychologist, 55*, 1, 5–14.

Seligman, M., & Peterson, C. (2003). Positive clinical psychology. In L. Aspinwall & U. Staudinger (Eds.), *A psychology of human strengths* (pp. 305–318). Washington, DC: American Psychological Association.

Siegel, D. (1999). *The developing mind*. New York: Guilford Press.

Sperry, L. (1986). Care of body, care of spirit: Medical dimensions of spiritual well-being. *Journal of Christian Healing, 8*, 27–31.

Sperry, L. (1988) Biopsychosocial therapy: An integrative approach for tailoring treatment. *Individual Psychology, 44*, 225–235.

Sperry, L. (1995). *Handbook of diagnosis and treatment of DSM–IV personality disorders*. New York: Brunner/Mazel.

Sperry, L. (1998). Spiritual counseling and the process of conversion. *Journal of Christian Healing, 20*, 37–54.

Sperry, L. (1999a). Biopsychosocial therapy. *Journal of Individual Psychology, 55*, 233–247.

Sperry, L. (1999b). The somatic dimension in healing prayer and the conversion process. *Journal of Christian Healing, 21*, 47–62.

Sperry, L. (2000a). Spirituality and psychiatry: Incorporating the spiritual dimension into clinical practice. *Psychiatric Annals, 30*, 518–524.

Sperry, L. (2000b). Biopsychosocial therapy: Essential strategies and tactics. In J. Carlson & L. Sperry (Eds.), *Brief therapy with individuals and couples*. Phoenix, AZ: Zeig, Tucker & Theisen.

Sperry, L. (2001a). The biological dimension in biopsychosocial therapy: Theory and clinical applications with couples. *Journal of Individual Psychology, 57*, 310–317.

Sperry, L. (2001b). Biopsychosocial therapy with individuals and couples: Integrative theory and interventions. In L. Sperry (Ed.), *Integrative and biopsychosocial therapy: Maximizing treatment outcomes with individuals and couples* (pp. 67–99). Alexandria, VA: ACA Books.

Sperry, L. (2001c). *Spirituality in clinical practice: Incorporating the spiritual dimension in psychotherapy and counseling*. New York: Brunner/Routledge.

Sperry, L. (2002a). From psychopathology to transformation: Retrieving the developmental focus in psychotherapy. *Journal of Individual Psychology, 58*, 398–421.

Sperry, L. (2002b). *Transforming self and community: Revisioning pastoral counseling and spiritual direction.* Collegeville, MN: Liturgical Press.

Sperry, L. (2003a). Integrating spiritual direction functions in the practice of psychotherapy. *Journal of Psychology and Theology, 31,* 3–13.

Sperry, L. (2003b). Integrative spiritually-oriented psychotherapy: A case study of spiritual and psychological transformation. In P. Richards. & A. Bergin (Eds.), *Casebook for a spiritual strategy in counseling and psychotherapy.* Washington, DC: American Psychological Association.

Tyrell, B. (1982). *Christotherapy II: A new horizon for counselors, spiritual directors and seekers of healing in growth in Christ.* New York: Paulist Press.

Young, J. (1999). *Cognitive therapy for personality disorders: A schema-focused approach* (rev. ed.). Sarasota, FL: Professional Resources Press.

Young, J., Klosko, J., & Weishaar, M. (2003). *Schema therapy: A practitioner's guide.* New York: Guilford Press.

III

COMMENTARY AND CRITICAL ANALYSIS

14

APPROACHES TO SPIRITUALLY ORIENTED PSYCHOTHERAPY: A COMPARATIVE ANALYSIS

LEN SPERRY AND EDWARD P. SHAFRANSKE

Ten contemporary approaches have now been described and clinically illustrated in chapters 4 through 13. Many new concepts and novel applications that typically are not covered in standard psychotherapy texts were presented in those chapters. This chapter is intended to provide the reader with a cognitive map to aid his or her understanding and critical reflection on the concepts and clinical applications of these 10 approaches. The map consists of the underlying premises and perspectives that infuse and energize these approaches, as well as a comparative chart that permits a side-by-side analysis of these 10 approaches. First, we discuss the underlying models of the relationship of psychotherapy and spirituality, then we provide a side-by-side comparison chart or matrix followed by a narrative analysis.

MODELS OF THE RELATIONSHIP OF PSYCHOTHERAPY AND SPIRITUALITY

As spiritually oriented psychotherapy develops as a specialized field, it will, of necessity, need to specify its basic philosophical premises and perspectives. For theoretical and clinical developments to occur, the basic relationship between the psychological and spiritual dimensions of life must be articulated, and such an articulation will have two primary considerations: whether the two dimensions are to be viewed as similar or different and whether the psychological or the spiritual dimension has primacy. Thus, there are four possibilities: similarity of dimensions with primacy of the psychological; similarity of dimensions with primacy of the spiritual; difference of dimensions with primacy of the psychological; and difference of dimensions with primacy of the spiritual. In addition to these four, there appears to be a fifth premise that reflects a *holistic* view, wherein the dimensions differ in some respects, yet there is no primacy.

From each of these premises about the relationship of the psychological and spiritual dimensions arises a unique perspective on the relationship of psychotherapy and spirituality. The following five characterizations and perspectives represent models of the relationship of spirituality and psychotherapy (Sperry & Mansager, 2003).

1. *The psychological and spiritual dimensions of human experience and development are essentially the same, with the psychological dimension having primacy.* Spirituality and psychotherapy are essentially the same. The implication is that spiritual growth is a facet of psychological growth, as is social and interpersonal aptness. By doing effective psychotherapeutic work with a client, the client becomes more whole and thereby more spiritual as well. There is little or no need for spiritual disciplines, unless the client finds them useful.

2. *The psychological and spiritual dimensions of human experience and development are essentially the same with the spiritual having primacy.* Like Relationship 1, the psychological and spiritual dimensions are considered similar, however in Relationship 2, the spiritual dimension has primacy. This perspective represents a theoretical possibility with limited probability. Aside from the traditional Jungian approach and a few traditional approaches to spiritual direction and pastoral counseling, this perspective is seldom found in contemporary approaches to psychotherapy that are sensitive to the spiritual dimension.

3. *The psychological and spiritual dimensions of human experience and development are different, although at times overlapping, with the psychological having primacy.* Spirituality is distinct from, but may parallel, psychological growth. While the spiritual and psychological can intermingle and be synergistic (i.e., growth in one area can be reflected in the other), it is not inevitable. Psychological growth therefore does not necessarily involve nor lead to growth in spirituality. Spirituality is

also distinct from psychotherapy and in some approaches associated with this perspective, psychological growth precedes spiritual growth. If deeper or subtler psychological conflicts arise while doing spiritual work, the focus "returns" to process psychological issues before resuming a focus on spiritual issues.

4. *The psychological and spiritual dimensions of human experience and development are different, although at times overlapping, with the spiritual dimension having primacy.* Spirituality is distinct from, but may parallel, psychological growth. Still, spiritual growth does not necessarily require psychological growth or vice versa. Although the spiritual and psychological can intermingle and can be synergistic, that is, growth in one area can be reflected in the other, this is not inevitable. The implication is that both spiritual disciplines and psychological and psychotherapeutic work are necessary.

5. *The psychological and spiritual dimensions of human experience and development are different yet neither has primacy (nor is reducible to the other).* Spirituality and psychology and psychotherapy are understood as contiguous, goal-oriented processes that strive toward different ends. When the client's immediate concern involves symptom relief or problem resolution, psychotherapeutically oriented strategies and methods are appropriate. When the client's concern involves seeking, searching, striving for transcendence and transformation, more spiritually oriented strategies and methods may be applied. Such a holistic orientation moves comfortably between psychological therapy and spirituality or spiritual direction addressing either short- and long-range goals or transcendent ones as they arise.

A COMPARATIVE ANALYSIS OF THE 10 APPROACHES

This section provides a side-by-side comparative and a narrative analysis of the 10 approaches based on a number of considerations. These include the following: historical and theoretical bases, the nature of the relationship between psychology and spirituality, therapist's skills and attributes, indications and contraindications, culture and gender considerations, strengths and limitations, and expected future developments and directions. Table 14.1 provides a side-by-side comparison of these considerations. The narrative analysis occasionally indicates points of convergence with the psychoanalytic and Jungian foundations noted in chapters 2 and 3.

TABLE 14.1
Comparative Analysis of 10 Spirituality Oriented Psychotherapy Approaches

Approach	Historical and theoretical bases	Relationship between spirituality and psychotherapy	Therapist's skills and attributes	Therapeutic indications and contraindications; culture and gender considerations	Strengths and weaknesses; future trends
Spiritually oriented cognitive–behavioral therapy (SO-CBT) (Tan & Johnson)	*Historical roots:* Roots in CT, BT, REBT and dominance of CBT in psychotherapy today; biblical support of CBT and the rise of SO-CBT *Theoretical premises:* SO-CBT's belief-orientation, teaching emphasis, and therapeutic focus on modifying beliefs is compatible with religious clients; theistic realism; research and outcomes based; interventions include	SO-CBT involves an explicit, rather than implicit, integration of spirituality and therapy because it is a structured, directive, and explicit approach; spirituality parallels psychological growth, but it does not depend on it; primacy of the spiritual is emphasized (Model 4)	*Professional:* capacity for a collaborative relationship, to conceptualize the case, and to select and apply appropriate CBT technique *Therapist attributes:* interpersonal warmth, lack of personal psychopathology, tolerance of negative client affective states, abstract conceptual abilities, respect religious beliefs and experiences; theistic realism	*Indications:* applicable and effective for most disorders except for some psychoses; spiritual disciplines useful for many clients *Culture:* SO-CBT has been used with Christian, Hindu, Muslim, Jewish, and Buddhist clients; religious Asian Americans may have a preference for SO-CBT *Gender:* guidelines available for	*Strengths:* strong research support for efficacy of CBT and SO-CBT; high appeal among clients and therapists *Limitations:* few empirical studies; few training and supervision opportunities *Trends:* more research on the efficacy of SO-CBT with specific clinical disorders and religious groups; integration of *spiritual direction* in SO-

continues

Spiritually oriented psychoanalysis (Shafranske)	*Historical roots:* Freud's critique of religious experience; God-representations expressing internal objects derived from human interaction and fantasy; self psychology; Spero's critique; current focus is on the relational perspective	scriptural disputation, use of religious imagery	*Personal:* therapist's personal faith perspective can influence the effectiveness of SO-CBT	effective use of CBT with female clients	CBT; use of CBT/SO-CBT for chronic health problems
	Theoretical premises: Alterations in psychological state can serve a transcendent purpose in spiritual practices; religion provides culturally given motifs for representing self-experience in relationship to the	Psychological and spiritual growth is divergent, parallel, and ultimately integrative; development occurs within each domain and may lead to an emergent reorganization of one's psychology and spirituality in a hierarchical fashion, resulting in increased complexity	*Professional:* technical skills from analytic training; attitude of respect and commitment; be nonjudgmental, open-minded, and open-ended; affirm the collaborative nature of the psychoanalytic process	*Indications:* client must possess sufficient ego strength and psychological mindedness	*Strengths:* allows for a comprehensive analysis of unconscious processes and unfolding of awareness
		(Model 3)	*Personal:* an openness to the nuances of religious experience and its impact on the totality of psychic life is more readily accomplished by therapists for whom spirituality is a meaningful dimension	*Contraindications:* impulse disorders, psychopathic character structures, or severe borderline personality organizations	*Limitations:* commitment of time and resources; may be less relevant to those seeking solution-focused direction and advice
				Culture: the focus on individual psychodynamics; delimits the role of culture	*Trends:* continuing research on intersubjectivity; attachment; relationship of brain–unconscious processes; psychological processes involved in spirituality
				Gender: the relational approach is sensitive to the feminist perspective	

continues

TABLE 14.1
(Continued)

Approach	Historical and theoretical bases	Relationship between spirituality and psychotherapy	Therapist's skills and attributes	Therapeutic indications and contraindications; culture and gender considerations	Strengths and weaknesses; future trends
	sacred; spirituality encourages a transcendent relationality				*Strengths*: applicable to most clients interested in developing their spiritual lives
Existential–humanistic (Elkins)	*Historical roots*: Kierkegaard, Maslow, May, Allport, Rogers, Jung, as well as James, Tillich, Otto, Frankl, Buber, and Hillman; tension of humanistic vs. transpersonal advocates *Theoretical premises*: key constructs: soul, sacred and spirituality; when the soul is nourished through regular contact with the sacred dimension	Psychology encompasses the spiritual dimensions; psychotherapy should be conceived of in sufficiently broad terms to include the soul, the sacred, and the spiritual dimensions; the psychological has primacy, however (Model 3)	*Professional*: need basic therapeutic skills and appreciation of the psychospiritual realm *Personal*: without a developed spiritual life, therapists tend to deal with soul-level issues on an I–It vs. I–Thou basis; the deeper therapists have gone on their own spiritual journey, the greater the chance of engaging clients on a soul-to-	*Indications*: useful to most with well-developed capacity for self-reflection *Contraindications*: psychotic, defensive, or fundamentalistic; not for those with limited self-reflective capacity; not for those who have been deeply wounded by spiritual systems *Culture*: widely applicable but may need to adapt clinical ap-	*Limitations*: theoretical difficulty of defining the constructs of *spirituality, soul,* and *sacred* *Trends*: continue fostering spirituality in the practice of psychotherapy; incorporate Eastern and other spiritual systems into human-

continues

	the result is spiritual growth or spirituality; the client suffers at the level of the soul, and psychotherapy is the process by which the soul is nurtured and healed		soul basis and helping them	proach to those with non-Western values *Gender:* equally applicable	*ism;* strive to broaden the view of science and research methods to better value subjectivity and phenomenological realities
Interpersonal psychotherapy (IPT) (Miller)	*Historical roots:* developed by Klerman as treatment of depression with the goal of symptom reduction and better social functioning; spiritually oriented ITP (ITP-S) was articulated by Miller *Theoretical premises:* Interpersonal Relationships are: (a) divine; (b) vehicles for spiritual evolution; and (c) transform us	Spiritual growth underlines psychological health; primacy of the spiritual; basic conviction that suffering serves spiritual growth; beliefs in the primacy of spiritual growth and the spiritual significance of all interpersonal relationships propels therapy forward (Model 4)	*Professional:* beyond proficiency with techniques of IPT, the therapist must be comfortable with the belief in a purposeful loving universe, which guides individuals through relationships *Personal:* ideally, therapists personally subscribe to underlying IPT-S beliefs about spiritual growth, suffering, and the spiritual significance of all IPRs	*Indications:* most appropriate for clients who operate a priori from within a spiritual perspective; useful for most Axis I and II presentations *Contraindications:* may not be useful for clients having a crisis of faith or with a nontheistic or agnostic stance on the universe *Culture:* sensitivity to differing cultural views of clients *Gender:* equally applicable	*Strengths:* IPT-S is a spiritually structured, concrete therapy that can meet the needs of nontraditional therapy clients *Limitations:* clients having a crisis of faith or who are agnostic or atheistic *Trends:* increasing need among nontraditional clients for structured, concretely focused therapies such aslike IPT-S; no formal training programs or research project planned

continues

TABLE 14.1
(Continued)

Approach	Historical and theoretical bases	Relationship between spirituality and psychotherapy	Therapist's skills and attributes	Therapeutic indications and contraindications; culture and gender considerations	Strengths and weaknesses; future trends
Transpersonal (TP)–integrative (Lukoff & Lu)	*Historical roots:* founded by Maslow and Sutich; expanded by Grof, Wilbur and Vaughan because other approaches omitted the spiritual or transpersonal (T) dimension, consciousness (C); evolving transpersonal psychotherapy (TP); *DSM-IV* Religious Spiritual Issues category	Individuals are spiritual and psychological beings, with spiritual primacy; spiritual beliefs and experiences are explored from a psychological perspective in TP (Model 4)	*Professional:* openness to T and ability to assess it; foster T context for therapy while using techniques from other approaches	*Indications:* spiritual crises, psychotic disorders, substance abuse issues, death and grief issues, help in differential diagnosis of depression and OCD	*Strengths:* provides for genuine dialogue with traditional healers
			Personal: TP therapists are expected to work on their own development and to develop qualities of attention, clarity, compassion, nonattachment; should have firsthand experience of transpersonal states and engage in spiritual practices	*Contraindications:* meditation not for acute psychotic or dissociative states	*Limitations:* no consensus on T self or how T self-identity is achieved; not a complete approach in itself
	Theoretical premises: key constructs: C is infinite; "T Context" for therapy (attitude regarding healing suffering, growth); aim is to expand C; spiritual emergencies; integrative approach			*Culture:* TP facilitates collaboration with traditional healers of non-Western traditions	*Trends:* contribute to interreligious dialogue regarding political conflict; TP clinical approaches will expand without using TP constructs; research on spiritual healing in complementary and alternative medicine
				Gender: accepting of feminine values	

continues

Approach		Historical roots / Theoretical premises	Training	Indications / Contraindications / Culture / Gender	Strengths / Limitations / Trends
Experiential-focusing (EF) (Hinterkopf)	Distinguishes process and content; although content (spiritual and psychological) are distinct, process is not (Model 5)	*Historical roots:* Gendlin's EF approach; expanded by Hinterkopf to spirituality issues; research validates its role in increasing positive outcomes in psychotherapy. *Theoretical premises:* basic constructs: felt sense, felt shift, spiritual experience; focusing is a gentle, powerful way of spending time with a felt sense to foster psychological and spiritual growth; a felt shift signals growth	*Professional:* requires specific training in EF as it applies to therapy; ability to provide exact, empathic listening responses to felt sense material; congruence, empathy and positive regard. *Personal:* effective EF therapists are spiritually oriented and practice the EF method themselves; EF may be the deepest spiritual practice they use	*Indications:* useful in all settings to facilitate process in talk therapies; continue using method with client ease. *Contraindications:* discontinue with client tension or discomfort. *Culture:* appropriate in diverse multicultural settings because focus is process oriented. *Gender:* equally applicable	*Strengths:* wide applicability; useful adjunct to any therapy approach. *Limitations:* A content-less method; limited training. *Trends:* continued, coordinated clinical outcomes research throughout the world; international focus on training therapists, scholarly research, and public dissemination
Forgiveness in psychotherapy (Worthington, Mazzeo, & Canter)	Religion and spirituality are moderators of forgiveness (Model 1)	*Historical roots:* focus on forgiveness in couples counseling leads to empirical research and development of the REACH model	*Professional:* formal training in manualized forgiveness groups; although not as yet empirically verified, therapist's agreeableness, empathy, sympathy, compas-	*Indications:* anxiety, anger, and depression rooted in relationship problems; use as an adjunct or as part of therapy. *Contraindications:* personality disorders	*Strengths:* appeals is greater for Christian therapists who value their Christianity. *Limitations:* less appeal for therapists for whom forgive-

continues

TABLE 14.1
(Continued)

Approach	Historical and theoretical bases	Relationship between spirituality and psychotherapy	Therapist's skills and attributes	Therapeutic indications and contraindications; culture and gender considerations	Strengths and weaknesses; future trends
	Theoretical premises: operationally defined core constructs: unforgiveness, forgiveness, and "injustice gap"; forgiveness can be an effective intervention when consistent with client's values, religious beliefs and when forgiveness is desired		sion, and love are likely to have a positive impact on those in forgiveness groups *Personal*: the therapist's religious conviction should match those of the client for maximum success of the approach	with empathic deficit, (e.g., narcissism) *Culture*: African Americans seem amenable to approach *Gender*: female clients appear more willing to engage in forgiveness groups	ness is not highly valued; this intervention must be integrated in ongoing therapy *Trends*: model is being lengthened and empirically tested in new contexts (e.g., parenting, Christian, and international settings)
Theistic psychotherapy (Richards)	*Historical roots*: a wide variety of theistic sources that coalesced *Theoretical premises*: God exists;	Primacy of the spiritual is posited; although change and healing are facilitated through many dimensions, healing and change is pri-	*Professional*: capacity to adopt a multicultural and denominational stance, assess spiritual dimension, ethically implement spiritual	*Indications*: theistic clients with less severe disorders who wish to discuss or have concomitant spiritual issues	*Trends*: further philosophical and empirical development, including clinical outcomes research

continues

	spiritual processes link us to God; those with faith can draw on spiritual resources in therapy; the approach is integrative, empirical, ecumenical (multicultural), and denominational, with regard to tailoring treatment to specific religious denominations marily a spiritual process (Model 4)	interventions. and help clients access useful spiritual resources *Personal:* foster personal spiritual well-being; seek to live congruently with one's personal value system; use spiritual practices to increase spiritual attunement with clients	*Contraindications:* severe psychological disorders *Culture:* sensitive to multicultural and ecumenical concerns *Gender:* equally applicable	Americans have theistic beliefs, the approach has wide applicability *Limitations:* May not be as applicable for those with nontheistic beliefs *Trends:* further philosophical and empirical development, including clinical outcomes research
Intensive soul care (ICS) (Benner)	*Historical roots:* personal experience; psychoanalytic, theory, analytical, archetypal and existential psychology; Christian spiritual direction and Ignatian spiritual *Theoretical premise:* the soul and spirit are intimately linked, and journeys of both are essential for full growth;	The psychological and spiritual form two faces of the coin of the inner self; no real distinction between soul (psyche) and spirit; both are intimately linked, and the journeys of both are essential for full growth (Model 5)	*Professional:* expertise in psychodynamics theory and practice; working knowledge of existential, analytic, and transpersonal approaches to spirituality *Personal:* commitment to personal psychospiritual well-being within a Christian perspective; involvement	*Indications:* healthy individuals with high ego strength, honesty, and psychospiritual issues *Contraindications:* not for adolescents, children, psychotics, borderline clients or lower functioning narcissistic clients; requires availability to spend 2–3 weeks in intensive treatment	*Strengths:* the intensity of the approach can lead to significant change in a short time *Limitations:* suitable for only a small percent of therapists and clients *Trends:* increased training of practitioners; research focused on clinical outcomes

continues

TABLE 14.1
(Continued)

Approach	Historical and theoretical bases	Relationship between spirituality and psychotherapy	Therapist's skills and attributes	Therapeutic indications and contraindications; culture and gender considerations	Strengths and weaknesses; future trends
	psychopathology always represents some combination of soul suffering and spiritual longing; ICS is an intensive experience of psychotherapy and spiritual direction in a retreat context to foster focused growth	client in spiritual directional and Ignatian exercises		*Culture:* applicable across compatible cultural and religious groups *Gender:* equally applicable	
Integrative spiritually oriented psychotherapy (Sperry)	*Historical roots:* bio-psychosocio-spiritual model and biopsychosocial therapy; spiritual direction; attachment theory–God image; positive psychology and virtue and strengths research	The psychological and spiritual dimensions differ yet are interdependent; spiritual aspect has primacy; spirituality is distinct from, but may parallel, psychological growth, yet both spiritual disciplines	*Professional:* able to conceptualize and provide tailored, integrative therapy with a spiritual component; skilled in interpretation and schema change *Personal:* experience	*Indications:* wide ranging, from severe disorders to high functioning clients with spiritual issues *Culture:* high cultural competency required because therapist–client mu-	*Strengths:* applicable to most presentations; holistic and comprehensive *Limitations:* requires extensive knowledge, experience, and high personal commitment

continues

Theoretical premises: primacy of spiritual dimension; developmental-growth perspective; goal is transformation; integrative, outcomes based, and tailored treatment

and psychotherapeutic work are necessary to achieve wholeness (Model 4)

in spiritual direction and with spiritual disciplines; commitment to ongoing spiritual development

tuality is a key factor

Gender: equally applicable

Trends: approach will develop and expand with research findings and client expectations of holistic approach

BT = behavioral therapy; CBT = cognitive–behavioral therapy; CT = cognitive therapy; IPR = interpersonal relationship; REBT = rational emotive behavior therapy.

Historical Bases

Not surprisingly, psychological theories and theorists were a dominant influence on most of these spiritually oriented approaches. Other influences included the awareness of the spiritual dimension in therapeutic experiences such as spiritual emergencies in the transpersonal–integrative approach or issues of forgiveness in couples counseling for forgiveness in psychotherapy. Issues of personal growth and spiritual experiences of therapists, such as spiritual direction, were influential for others such as intensive soul care. Virtue and the biopsychosocial model were important for integrative spiritually oriented psychotherapy. Similarly, spiritual resources was influential in several approaches including the theistic, transpersonal–integrative, and spiritually oriented cognitive–behavioral. Philosophical and religious constructs, for example, the *numinous*, were important in the Intensive Soul Care approach. Image of God or God-representations were important influences in both the psychoanalytic approach and in integrative spiritually oriented psychotherapy. Finally, archetypes are a dimension of intensive soul care, as well as the Jungian foundation.

Theoretical Bases

Underlying theoretical premises are rather broad among these approaches and range from soul (intensive soul care) and cultural influences (spiritually oriented psychoanalytic), to God's existence (theistic) and biblically focused cognitive disputation (spiritually oriented cognitive–behavioral). For example, religion provides culturally given motifs for representing self-experience in relationship to the sacred. This is a premise of the spiritually oriented psychoanalytic approach wherein spirituality encourages a transcendent relationality. The intrapsychic premise that the psyche is the medium of the experience of the sacred in the Jungian foundation contrasts with the social–relational premise that interpersonal relationships are theaters through which the spiritual evolves of the interpersonal psychotherapy approach. In terms of outcomes, the aim of transpersonal–integrative is to expand consciousness, whereas the goal of integrative spiritually oriented psychotherapy is personal and spiritual transformation. Spiritually oriented cognitive–behavioral, theistic psychotherapy, and forgiveness in psychotherapy are more directive and avowedly research and outcomes based. On the other hand, the experiential focusing and existential–humanistic approaches, like the Jungian foundation, are more experiential and internally focused.

The Relationship Between Psychology and Spirituality

When we first asked the authors to specify their respective views of the relationship between the psychological and the spiritual dimensions and of psychotherapy and spirituality, we received rather profound statements—some offered in operational terms quite and others in philosophical or even poetic language. To compare these views, it became clear that a common language and a common set of constructs were necessary. Accordingly, we sent all authors a copy of the five perspectives described earlier (Sperry & Mansager, 2003) and asked each to indicate which model was closest to and best represented their basic premises and perspectives on the relationship of the psychological and spiritual dimensions and on psychology–psychotherapy and spirituality.

The 10 approaches spanned the spectrum of the five models. The forgiveness approach appears to be closest to Model 1 in which the psychological and spiritual dimensions are similar, although the psychological dimension has primacy. The spiritually oriented psychoanalytic and the existential–humanistic approach appears to be closest to Model 3 in which the psychological and spiritual dimensions differ, although the psychological dimension has primacy. Five of the approaches (theistic, integrative spiritually oriented, spiritually oriented cognitive–behavioral, interpersonal, and transpersonal–integrative) seem closest to Model 4 in which the psychological and spiritual dimensions are seen as different, although at times overlapping, with the spiritual dimension having primacy. Only two approaches, intensive soul care and experiential focusing, come close to Model 5, the holistic perspective. In that model, the psychological and spiritual dimensions of human experience and development are viewed as different, although at times overlapping, with the spiritual dimension having primacy.

Initially, we had thought that many of the approaches would espouse the holistic perspective (Model 5), but that was clearly not the case. It may well be that because of the significant influence of psychological reductionism that dominates most psychological theories and most training programs, it is almost unconceivable for an approach to espouse the holistic view that neither the psychological dimension nor the spiritual dimension has primacy.

Therapist's Skills and Attributes

It was not surprising that the authors specified either the technical skills or requisite training that a therapist would need to practice that approach effectively. For example, specific training in focusing as it applies to therapy is essential for those using the experiential focusing approach, just as the capacity to adopt an ecumenical stance, assess the spiritual dimension, ethically implement spiritual interventions, and assist clients to access useful spiritual resources is required in the theistic approach. As implied in the Jungian foundations chapter, therapists should have a working knowledge of archetypes, mythology, and world religions to use that approach effectively.

What was surprising is that a majority of the authors did not specifically note personal attributes expected of therapists using the approaches. The exceptions were intensive soul care (e.g., involvement as client in spiritual direction and Ignatian spiritual exercises), integrative spiritually oriented psychotherapy (e.g., experience in spiritual direction and with spiritual disciplines; commitment to ongoing spiritual development), and transpersonal–integrative (e.g., therapists are expected to engage in spiritual practices, such as meditation).

Cultural and Gender Considerations

Many of the authors stated or implied that cultural sensitivity was essential to the effective practice of their approach but gave few specifics on this topic, although some authors did expand on this. For example, Tan and Johnson indicated that spiritually oriented cognitive–behavioral therapy has been effectively used with Christian, Hindu, Muslim, Jewish, and Buddhist clients. Furthermore, these authors noted that religious Asian Americans (particularly if they are Christian) often have a clear preference for a spiritual approach to cognitive–behavioral therapy. Worthington, Mazzeo, and Canter's chapter on forgiveness indicates that African Americans, a group that has been found to be more religious than others, may be particularly amenable to that intervention, although this has not been empirically tested.

All authors essentially indicated that their approaches are equally applicable to male and female clients. Regarding the forgiveness approach, anecdotal evidence suggests that women may be more willing to engage in forgiveness groups. The chapter on the transpersonal–integrative approach indicate that it is accepting of feminine values, and Shafranske noted that the psychoanalytic approach is sensitive to the feminist perspective. Furthermore, Tan and Johnson indicated that guidelines have been developed for the effective use of the spiritually oriented cognitive–behavioral approach with female clients.

Strengths and Limitations

Virtually all the authors identified clinical or therapeutic strengths of their approach—for example, approaches offered significant psychospiritual change in a short time (intensive soul care), wide applicability (integrative spiritually oriented psychotherapy), a useful adjunct to any therapy approach (experiential focusing), or a spiritually structured, concrete therapy that meets the needs of nontraditional therapy clients (interpersonal psychotherapy). On the other hand, Corbett and Stein noted that the Jungian approach is independent of traditional dogma and was thus of particular interest to therapists who practice with sensitivity to the spiritual. Only two authors indicated any theoretical or research-based strengths. These include increasing empirical support for theistic psychotherapy approach, and strong research support for efficacy of both cognitive–behavioral approach and the spiritually oriented cognitive–behavioral approach.

What is noteworthy, but not particularly surprising, is that few authors noted the limitations of their approach. An exception was Sperry's chapter on integrative spiritually oriented psychotherapy, which noted that requirements for therapists who practice this approach are high: It requires extensive knowledge and experience in providing integrative therapy and tailoring treatment to the spiritual needs of clients, as well as a high personal commitment to one's own spiritual development. Similarly, Benner noted that the intensive soul care approach is suitable for only a small percentage of therapists and clients who are able to schedule the intensive time frame required. The chapter on the theistic approach noted that it may not be as applicable to clients or therapists with nontheistic beliefs. Finally, the forgiveness and experiential focusing approaches were noted to be therapeutic adjuncts that can be incorporated into other full-scale approaches or systems. Some readers may be surprised to learn that the transpersonal–integrative approach is not a complete approach itself and is typically used with a psychodynamic or existential–humanistic orientation to therapy.

Expected Future Developments and Directions

When asked to speculate on future developments and directions, authors typically anticipated increasing need and recognition for their approaches. Interestingly, Lukoff and Lu predicted that spiritually oriented transpersonal–integrative clinical approaches will greatly expand and evolve without using transpersonal psychology constructs. Proponents of some approaches anticipated that education and certification of therapists will be a priority. For instance, Hinterkopf anticipated an expanded international focus on training therapists in experiential focusing, as did Benner with regard to the intensive soul care approach.

Proponents of a few approaches pointed to anticipated theoretical or research developments. For example, Corbett and Stein anticipated that, for the Jungian approach, future breakthroughs in quantum physics may further clarify processes such as synchronicity. With regard to psychoanalysis, Shafranske suggested that there will be continuing research on intersubjectivity, attachment theory, as well as in the relationship of brain–unconscious processes and psychological processes involved in spirituality. Tan and Johnson were the most specific in predicting future research progress anticipating more research on the efficacy of spiritually oriented cognitive–behavioral therapy focusing on specific clinical disorders and religious groups. They also suggested it will be extended to chronic health problems. Finally, Hinterkopf expected that there well be continued, coordinated clinical outcomes research on experiential focusing, including research protocols in other countries.

CONCLUDING COMMENT

The increasing interest in the spiritual dimension of human experience and the concurrent development of several traditional, contemporary, and emerging spiritually oriented approaches is remarkable given psychology's longstanding endeavors to remain a value-free science and eschew religious and spiritual concerns. This chapter has attempted a comparative analysis of the 10 approaches described and illustrated in previous chapters.

A side-by-side comparison of these approaches reveals some commonalities, but also considerable differences. Common to all approaches is a sensitivity and awareness of the importance of the spiritual dimensions in the lives of clients, as well as therapists. Differences among these approaches abound—not only in terms of basic premises, but also in conceptualizing and assessing spiritual issues and planning and implementing interventions. Table 14.1 provides a summary of these approaches, and the chapter narrative has analyzed and discussed similarities and differences between them. Of utmost importance for the continued growth of this specialty area in psychology and psychotherapy is the need for ongoing theory development. An essential part of theory development is the articulation of basic philosophical premises useful in operationalizing concepts and researchable hypotheses that can foster research initiatives and facilitate clinical developments. Our contribution to theory development has been the generation of the five basic premises and perspectives described earlier in this chapter. The next chapter continues a discussion of anticipated future developments in theory, research, and the professional practice of spiritually oriented psychotherapy.

REFERENCE

Sperry, L., & Mansager, E. (2003). *Spirituality and psychotherapy: Five conceptual models.* Unpublished manuscript.

15

FUTURE DIRECTIONS: OPPORTUNITIES AND CHALLENGES

EDWARD P. SHAFRANSKE AND LEN SPERRY

A human being is part of the whole called by us universe, a part limited in time and space. He experiences himself, his thoughts and feelings as something separated from the rest, a kind of optical delusion of his consciousness. This delusion is a kind of prison for us. . . . Our task must be to free ourselves from this prison by widening our circle of compassion to embrace all living creatures and the whole of nature in its beauty.

—*Albert Einstein*

Spiritually oriented psychotherapy aims to address psychological conflicts and suffering in a manner that offers the widest possible aperture for the apprehension of human meaning and the offer of compassion. Such an approach, although built on a scientific foundation, is not limited by empiricism, but incorporates openness to the transcendent realities related to the sacred. Such a posture avers that humanity is situated within a larger universe of meaning and relationship. Such a universe is beyond that which can be observed and understood within the narrow parameters of empirical science. A spiritual approach does not impose a spiritual worldview on patients; rather we suggest that spiritually oriented psychotherapy offers an approach that is more responsive to patients as whole persons. Such an approach respects and responds to most patients' expressed desire to have spiritual issues addressed in their care, as reported by Puchalski, Larson, and Lu (2000, p. 544) and in a Gallup survey in which 70% of adults said it was very or somewhat important to have a doctor who is spiritually attuned to them (Gallup, 2002).

We do not believe that spiritually oriented psychotherapy will nor should supplant other forms of treatment. It is not a panacea, nor is it appropriate for every clinical situation; rather, it is intended to complement other forms of psychological and psychiatric treatment for situations in which spirituality or religiosity plays a significant role in a patient's orienting system. As we have seen in preceding chapters, the inclusion of spirituality as a clinical focus originates in the patient's life and is presented to be relevant to the clinical situation. Furthermore, attention to spirituality is part of an integrated, holistic effort to assist patients in achieving resolution of conflict and improved health, as well as to apply meaning to challenges and adversities they face in life.

OPPORTUNITIES AND CHALLENGES

There are a number of opportunities and challenges to be faced in the further development of spiritually oriented psychotherapy. We enumerate a number of these challenges in this closing discussion in the hope of encouraging and directing systematic scholarship and science-derived efforts toward the consideration of issues we consider particularly relevant in addressing spirituality in clinical practice. We suggest that three overarching, interrelated values inform such an enterprise: (a) respect for the integrity of individual spiritual beliefs and the varieties of religious experience, (b) science-informed practice, and (c) ethical practice. The first value affirms the uniqueness of individuals' experiences of the sacred and counters potential devaluation through reductionism to purely psychological categories. Furthermore, this value encourages appreciation for the wide spectrum of spiritual expression. We believe that science-informed practice provides the best opportunity for the systematic development of knowledge and clinical applications, which enhance professional practice and protect the public welfare. We are mindful of the challenges involved; however, the evolving literature in religious coping and in positive psychology points to the feasibility of such efforts. Research programs require an understanding of science, which is appropriate to the subject, and involve qualitative as well as quantitative methods to understand fully the psychological aspects of spirituality. Although stated last, ethics must inform every step of scholarship and clinical application. There are a number of ethical issues involved in offering spiritually oriented psychotherapy—in particular, establishing criteria to assess competence to practice and guidelines addressing dual roles and inappropriate influence require timely consideration. We highlight a number of issues, stated as questions, organized under knowledge, practice, and education and training, that require further consideration.

Knowledge

- What are the constituents of the constructs of religion and spirituality, and how are they differentiated from each other and other systems of human meaning?

- What is the relationship between psychology and spirituality? As noted in chapter 14, there are a number of approaches to this relationship, which have implications for the development of theory and practice.
- What are the effects of spiritual beliefs, affiliations, and practices on emotional and physical health and subjective well-being?
- What are the effects of spiritually derived virtues and ultimate purposes on emotional and physical health and subjective well-being?
- Is there an identifiable developmental trajectory in spirituality, and how is this related to psychological development?
- What is the relationship between spirituality and other aspects of cultural diversity?

Practice

- What are the implicit ontic commitments within existing models of psychotherapy? What are the effects of these commitments? What are the ontic commitments within spiritually oriented psychotherapy?
- What approaches and procedures may be used to assess spirituality as differentiated from religiosness?
- What are the similarities and differences between psychotherapy, religious counseling, and spiritual direction? What are the unique features of spiritually oriented psychotherapy?
- Should the integration of spiritual resources into psychotherapy be conducted by psychotherapists or by a religious professional through collaboration? What guidelines should be established regarding boundary violations with respect to displacing or usurping religious or spiritual authority?
- What guidelines and ethics should inform efforts to modify spiritual beliefs and practices that have been demonstrated to compromise directly the emotional or physical health of the patient?
- What is the impact of the spiritual commitment of the psychotherapist on the provision of spiritually oriented psychotherapy?
- What competencies are required to ensure the ethical practice of spiritually oriented psychotherapy? What procedures should be undertaken to obtain informed consent, to avoid dual roles, and to establish minimum competence to practice? Should spiritually oriented psychotherapy be considered a specialty or a proficiency?

Education and Training

- What are the domains of knowledge and practice in spirituality that should be minimally addressed in the training of a mental health professional? What are the core competencies, and how are they to be developed and assessed?
- What are the core components in curriculum and in clinical training?
- Should spiritually oriented psychotherapy be considered a specialty or a proficiency? At what stage of education, training, and professional development should such training take place?
- What guidelines should be established in education and training to establish competency? What are the requirements for supervisor competency?

These questions point to the complex interrelationships among the domains of knowledge, qua science, practice, and education and training to ensure the ethical practice of spiritually oriented psychotherapy. It is fortunate that many of the existing models of psychotherapy can readily incorporate a spiritually attuned approach, as illustrated in the preceding chapters, and may be seen as extensions of existing practice. It is also encouraging that the development of spiritually oriented psychotherapy parallels or complements other important developments in the field of psychology. For example, positive psychology is investigating the role of virtues and values in the enhancement of health and in psychological strengths and is establishing a research agenda, which broadly considers spirituality and religiousness to be important variables.

CONCLUSION

We began with the observation that we are entering a renaissance in psychological healing. This book has aimed to contribute to such a renewal through the development of clinical approaches that take seriously the role of spirituality in a holistic approach to mental health. Spiritually oriented psychotherapy provides a means by which spirituality, which plays such an important role in the lives of most clients, may be addressed in the therapeutic discourse as clients seek increased meaning in life, face spiritual crises and doubt, and heal their suffering.

REFERENCES

Gallup, G., Jr. (2002, May 28). *Religion may do a body good*. Retrieved November 1, 2003, from the Gallup Organization Web site: http://www.gallup.com/poll/tb/religvalue/20020528.asp

Puchalski, C. M., Larson, D. B., & Lu, F. G. (2000). Spirituality courses in psychiatry residency programs. *Psychiatric Annals, 30,* 543–548.

INDEX

Borderline personality disorders, 70, 113
Borges, Jorge Luis, 62, 66
Boston School of Psychotherapy, 179
Bouyer, Louis, 33
Brief Symptom Inventory (BSI), 246
Brigham Young University (BYU), 272
Brunswick, L. K., 209
"Bryan" case example, 195–200
BSI (Brief Symptom Inventory), 246
Buber, Martin, 134, 136, 141–142
Bucke, R. M., 59
Buddha, 81
Buddhism, 52, 80, 182, 186
Buddhists, 16, 71, 81–82
Burning bush, 55
BYU (Brigham Young University), 272

California Institute of Asian Studies, 179
California Institute of Integral Studies, 179
Canada, 16
Catholicism, 119, 164
CBT. *See* Cognitive–behavioral therapy
Center for Change, 272
Central Washington University, 271–272
Change
    and CBT, 80
    facilitation of, 264–265
    as universal vehicle of spiritual growth,
       161–162
Children
    beliefs of, 37, 39–41
    child–parent relationship, 69
Chomsky, N., 52n.1
Christian approach to CBT, 82–83, 88–89
Christianity
    and forgiveness, 235, 237, 242
    and integrative psychotherapy, 312
    and interpersonal psychotherapy, 156
    and Jungian approach, 55–56
    and theistic psychotherapy, 261, 263
Christians
    and CBT, 81, 85, 86, 89, 95
    and forgiveness, 237, 240
    and integrative psychotherapy, 315
    and Jungian approach, 71
    and religious affiliation, 16
    spirituality among, 77
    as therapists, 70
Christotherapy, 290
Christou, E., 54
Church of Jesus Christ of Latter-Day Saints
    (LDS), 272, 273

Civilization and Its Discontents (S. Freud), 64
"Claire" case example, 157–158
Clinical intervention, 310
Closeness thermometers, 248
"Cloud of unknowing," 12
Cognitive–behavioral therapy (CBT), 68,
    77–99
    activities of, 79
    assessment in, 91–93
    Belief orientation of, 80–81
    case example of, 89–99
    cultural/gender considerations for, 88–
      89
    diagnostic/clinical conceptualization in,
      93
    efficiency of, 86
    future of, 89
    historical/theoretical bases of, 78–79
    implicit vs. explicit integration of, 82–
      84
    indications/contraindications for, 87–
      88
    and spirituality–psychology relation-
      ship, 82–84
    spiritually oriented, 80–82
    strengths/limitations of, 85–87
    termination/relapse prevention in, 97–
      98
    therapeutic outcomes with, 98–99
    therapeutic relationship in, 90–91
    therapist's skills/attributes for, 84–85
    treatment/intervention in, 94–97
Cognitive disputation, 81
Cognitive events, 78
Cognitive Therapy, 79, 85
Collected Works (Carl Jung), 53
Collective unconscious, 179
Commitment, 161
Communism, 34
Comparative analysis, 335–349
Compassion, 139
Complexes, 53
Confession, 236–237
Conflict Tactics Scale (CTS), 247, 252
Conscientiousness-based virtues, 242
Conscious representations, 39
Content, process vs., 210–211, 214–215
Context, 181–182, 219
Conversion experience, 312
Corbett, L., 289
Cosmic reality, 41
Counterculture, 133–134, 179

ABOUT THE EDITORS

Len Sperry, MD, PhD, is professor and coordinator of the doctoral program in counseling at Florida Atlantic University and is clinical professor of psychiatry at the Medical College of Wisconsin. A fellow of the American Psychological Association, he is also a distinguished fellow of the American Psychiatric Association and a fellow of the American College of Preventive Medicine. In addition to being a diplomate in clinical psychology of the American Board of Professional Psychology, he is certified by the American Board of Psychiatry and Neurology and the American Board of Preventive Medicine. Among his over 300 publications are 47 professional books, including *Spirituality in Clinical Practice: Incorporating the Spiritual Dimension in Psychotherapy and Counseling; Sex, Priestly Ministry and the Church; Transforming Self and Community: Revisioning Pastoral Counseling and Spiritual Direction;* and *Ministry and Community: Recognizing, Healing and Predicting Ministry Impairment.* He is listed in *Who's Who in America, Best Doctors in America,* and *Guide to America's Top Physicians* and is a recipient of two lifetime achievement awards, including the Harry Levinson Award from the American Psychological Association. He has served on several editorial boards, including *Counseling and Values,* the *Journal of Family Psychology, The Family Journal,* the *American Journal of Family Therapy,* the *Journal of Individual Psychology, Depression and Stress,* the *Journal of Child Psychiatry and Human Development,* and the *Journal of Pastoral Counseling.*

Edward P. Shafranske, PhD, ABPP, is professor of psychology and director of the doctoral program in clinical psychology at Pepperdine University. A fellow of the American Pyschological Association (APA), Dr. Shafranske has been the president of APA's Division 36 (Psychology of Religion), a member of the APA Council of Representatives, chair of the California Psychological Association Division of Education and Training, and cochair of the Committee on Graduate Education of the American Psychoanalytic Association. His publications include *Religion and the Clinical Practice of Psychology* (APA, 1996) and *Clinical Supervision: A Competency-Based Approach* (APA, 2004; with Carol A. Falender). He served as associate editor of the *Encyclopedia of Psychology* (APA, 2000), is a member of the editorial board of the *International Journal for the Psychology of Religion*, and was awarded the William Bier Award and the Distinguished Service Award by APA Division 36. In addition to academic and research activities, Dr. Shafranske maintains a private practice in clinical psychology and psychoanalysis in Irvine, California.